LEARNING ELECTRONICS

THEORY AND EXPERIMENTS WITH COMPUTER-AIDED INSTRUCTION FOR THE APPLE

R. Jesse Phagan and Bill Spaulding

TAB BOOKS Inc.
Blue Ridge Summit, PA

Dedicated to Our Children:
Bettina and Barrett Phagan
and to
Daniel Spaulding

FIRST EDITION
FIRST PRINTING

Copyright © 1988 by TAB BOOKS Inc.
Printed in the United States of America

Library of Congress Cataloging-in-Publication Data

Phagan, R. Jesse.
Learning electronics : theory and experiments with computer-aided
instruction for the Apple / by R. Jesse Phagan and Bill Spaulding.
p. cm.
Includes index.
ISBN 0-8306-0182-1   ISBN 0-8306-2982-3 (pbk.)
1. Electronics. 2. Electronics—Computer—assisted instruction-
-Computer programs. 3. Apple computer. I. Spaulding, William.
II. Title.
TK7816.P43 1988
621.381—dc19   88-17067
                                                            CIP

TAB BOOKS Inc. offers software for
sale. For information and a catalog,
please contact TAB Software Department,
Blue Ridge Summit, PA 17294-0850.

Questions regarding the content of this book
should be addressed to:

Reader Inquiry Branch
TAB BOOKS Inc.
Blue Ridge Summit, PA 17294-0214

Contents

Preface

When learning a technical subject such as electronics, there are three important approaches to the learning process that must be followed: theory, math, and hands-on experience. Each of these should be tied directly together in order to achieve maximum learning efficiency.

As an electronics teacher, it has been my responsibility to order the books for students and to make recommendations on which books would be good for them to buy on their own. I have never been able to find a book that covers all three of the important learning approaches.

By using the theory to explain how things work, the math to perform the necessary calculations, and the hands-on practice to make everything fit together, this book does all three. To top it all off, there are computer programs to assist in the learning process.

Teachers everywhere recognize that the computer can be a great help in the learning process because the computer requires student involvement in the process. The more aspects of the subject that the student is involved with, the more information he will retain.

Students using this book will be involved through the use of practice problems, hands-on exercises, and computer-assisted instruction.

Introduction

Student-managed learning is the main emphasis of this book. The key is involvement by the student in the learning process. The major learning units contain completed sample problems, followed by practice problems. There are hands-on practice exercises designed to help with the learning of meters and oscilloscopes. At the end of the chapters, there are tests that have been used in an actual classroom. Also, two main examinations are provided. The student learns with practice.

A major highlight to provide student involvement is the computer program. Each chapter, starting with Chapter 3, has computer programs designed to quiz the student in the important concepts of electronics theory, math, and the use of test equipment. Also, some programs provide practice and experience with ohmmeters, voltmeters, ammeters, and the oscilloscope.

The field of electronics technology is constantly changing. Although the basics of dc and ac remain the same, the methods of learning have changed. The effort placed on the various basic subjects needs to reflect the applications of the advanced electronics. The math areas studied in the basics help with a complete understanding and are used to predict circuit behavior. To study electronics in the last part of the 20th century requires student involvement and a book that puts the emphasis where it belongs, to provide a sound foundation in the building blocks.

USING THE PROGRAMS WITH THE APPLE

The DOS has not been included as part of the disk. The instructions on how to use and load the disk are included with the disk.

When the program is run, the main menu will appear. The student then selects the desired program.

At the ends of Chapters 3 to 15 are descriptions of the programs for each chapter, and instructions on how to use them. In the appendix is a print-out of all of the programs that are written in BASIC.

Each program is a quiz. Grades can be displayed

any time by typing "E", which will also allow access to the main menu:

PROGRAM NAMES (MAIN MENU):

A) Introduction	I) Dc Analysis
B) Shop Math	J) Oscilloscope ac
C) Eng. Notation	K) Phase Angle
D) Color Code	L) Time Constants
E) Ohmmeter	M) Magnetism
F) V&A Meter	N) Transformers
G) Ohmmeter	O Reactance
H Oscilloscope dc	P) Resonance

HANDS-ON EXPERIENCES

The hands-on experiences throughout this book have been designed to use a minimum of equipment and parts. They have also been designed so that the actual component values are not crucial.

Equipment

- ☐ Multimeter.
- ☐ Variable dc power supply (6-volt battery may be substituted).
- ☐ Oscilloscope.
- ☐ Audio function generator (sine waves and square waves).

Parts

- ☐ 10 different values resistors including 10 kilohm.
- ☐ 2 different variable resistors.
- ☐ Switch.
- ☐ Transformer.
- ☐ .001 microfarad capacitor.

Chapter 1

Introductory Topics

Chapter Objective: To become familiar with common technical words used in the electronics trade, types of jobs available, and safety practices. Also included in this chapter is an explanation of what "computer assisted instruction" is and how to make use of it.

Chapter Outline:
- ☐ Electronics Terms
- ☐ Job Market
- ☐ Electrical Safety
- ☐ Computer Assisted Instruction (CAI)
- ☐ Using the Programs in this Book
- ☐ Student Projects
- ☐ Safety Test

INTRODUCTION

Electronics are used throughout any modern household. It is overwhelming to think how much people in the late 20th century depend on electricity and electronics. Try to imagine how badly your own house would function without electricity for just a week.

The study of electronics begins with the study of electricity. The student should make every effort to understand the principles of electricity that are presented.

ELECTRONICS TERMS

In every field there are words that are used to describe things that are unique to that field. This is especially true when dealing with technical subject areas. A student needs to adopt the technical words of his/her field as part of the normal thought process. In this section a few words will be mentioned. Throughout the remainder of the book other words will be introduced and applied. The purpose of this section is to introduce some of the words with which the student may have already come in contact.

Electronics is a very broad term used to describe devices that use electricity in more advanced ways than just for light, heat or motors. Examples are: radio, TV, computers, calculators, quartz clocks, robots, etc.

Electricity is the flow of electrons through a conductor. Electricity is generally used to produce heat, give off light (as in the case of a light bulb), operate motors, and operate electronic devices. Examples of devices using electricity: refrigerators, toasters, electric stoves, clothes dryers, etc.

Conductor is the medium through which electricity flows. A good conductor is copper wire. A poor conductor is usually called an *insulator*. An example of an insulator is plastic.

Resistance is a term used to describe opposition to the flow of electricity. Resistance is the property of a conductor that causes heat when electricity flows.

Voltage is the term used to describe an electrical force. Voltage is a potential to perform work. *Work*, in electrical terms, has examples such as: heat, motors, operation of a radio, etc. In the United States, household voltage is 120 volts (also referred to as 110 or 117 depending on the local tradition). Most cars use a 12 volt battery. Although these examples are of quite different forms of electrical energy, the size of the numbers describes the amount of potential electrical energy.

Current is the term used to describe the amount of electrical energy (electrons) flowing through the wire. The unit for current is ampere. It can be measured and a number can be assigned to show its relative size for comparison to other measurements of current. As an example: the circuit breaker or fuse for an average household circuit is 15 or 20 amps. The current of a 120 watt light bulb is approximately 1 amp.

Power is a term used to describe the amount of electrical work performed. The unit of measure is the *watt*. The best example is the wattage rating of a light bulb. A higher wattage gives a brighter light and gives off more heat. A higher powered bulb also uses more current than a smaller wattage bulb.

Other terms also used in both electricity and electronics will be introduced with the appropriate subject matter. The purpose of this discussion is only to mention some of the common words a new electronics student may not be familiar with.

JOB MARKET

The job market in the electronics field varies considerably depending upon the geographical location. Since the location is unknown and therefore can not be discussed in this book, we will discuss, instead, the level of jobs and their relationship to education.

There is no question that the opportunities in electronics related fields will continue as more products are developed and require servicing.

Bachelor's Degree

A four-year degree or higher opens up a vast number of opportunities. Generally speaking, a higher education means considerably more money. The type of work acquired with a B.S. degree is usually considered "engineering" in some form. It could be developing new products, updating older products, and sometimes more advanced levels of servicing. Computer related jobs usually require a four-year degree or higher, especially programming.

Associate Degree

The associate degree is a two-year degree intended for a junior engineer or a technician. The associate degree will provide the student with a well rounded education, including English skills, and good technical skills. Many companies prefer the AS degree for their technicians because they also have some engineering training.

Post-Secondary Technical Schools

Technical schools, after high school, are an excellent way to receive the necessary skills to be a technician. This type of education somewhat limits the advancements of a technician only because many companies prefer an AS degree and it is also difficult to receive college transfer credits if a further education is ever desired. However, if an individual knows that being a technician is what he/she wants, the technical schools usually do a much better job of developing the necessary technical skills.

Technical High School

Technical high schools are an excellent way to get a "starting" education in order to enter the field of electronics. Most technical high schools will prepare the student with many of the same types of skills as a post-secondary school. Usually the big difference between them is the depth of study and understanding.

Technician vs Engineer

Engineering is usually thought of as a "desk" job. This isn't necessarily true, though engineers usually are responsible for more paperwork than a technician. The engineer is considered to have a more in-depth understanding of how the circuits operate, because their education level is higher.

A technician usually performs the "hands-on" jobs. A technician's job includes operation of test equipment, repair and maintenance of equipment, and assisting engineers. Technicians are often involved in design work, but the majority of technician duties will involve repair and maintenance. Usually the jobs with the title of "field engineer" are filled by skilled technicians.

It is possible for self-taught individuals to find a place in the field of electronics because the repair of equipment is a talent that may be self-taught. Often, self-taught technicians find it necessary to either work at their own business, or for a small company that hires depending upon ability rather than upon education.

ELECTRICAL SAFETY

Safety needs to be considered in every aspect of a person's life. Generally speaking, safety is a matter of knowing the dangers, being trained in dealing with them, and using common sense.

A technician deals with many of the common dangers such as ladders, falls, cuts, etc. Tools present a special problem because a technician's job depends on the skillful and constant use of both hand and power tools. The items that are discussed in the following sections have been selected because they address the most common issues.

Also, keep in mind that safety glasses are often recommended when using many tools or being in the vicinity of flying particles. Use your safety glasses!

Hand Tools

Many of the hand tools that are in use by technicians perform very specific functions, some of which are cutting, pinching, twisting, heating, etc. Tools of this nature can cause very serious injury to a person's skin. Not only is the tool's normal working edge dangerous, but the handle itself can cause injury, especially where the two handles come together.

Another cause of injury with seemingly harmless tools, such as a screwdriver, is when the tool is being used improperly. If a screwdriver slips from the screw and strikes a person's hand, a very serious cut can result.

The reason for mentioning this type of danger with hand tools is to try to impress the idea on the student that proper training and common sense are both required to maintain safety on the job.

Power Tools

Power tools, such as an electric drill or electric saw, present dangers and safety problems from both the tool itself and from the electricity to operate it.

All power tools are intended to operate in a specified manner. Do not try to force the tool to perform a function that it is not intended to perform. For example, a drill is designed to have pressure in the direction of the drill bit, NOT sideways on the bit. When some people find a hole is slightly too small, they try to enlarge the hole by placing pressure on the side of the drill bit. This practice is extremely dangerous.

One major problem with any device that uses electricity is the fact that the outside can become electrically "hot." This happens for a variety of reasons. If the outside portion is metal, a person touching it can receive a shock that is fatal.

All new power tools are either "double insulated" or they have a three prong plug. If the tool is double insulated it will have a two prong plug and all of the outside of the tool will be made of heavy plastic. All tools with a metal outside must have a three prong plug. If the tool becomes defective and a wire from the inside touches the outside, the ground prong (ground wire) will cause the circuit breaker to trip and prevent shock. It is, therefore, extremely important for the round prong to be connected to electrical ground. If a three prong electrical outlet is not available, an adapter plug can be used provided the adapter plug's ground wire is connected to the outlet box screw. Under no circumstances is it safe to use a two-wire extension cord with a tool with three prongs.

Electrical Shock

The amount of electrical shock necessary to kill a human being is surprisingly low. It is the electrical current flowing through the person's body and the path it takes that determines the severity of the shock. It is not the voltage, as most people think, that kills. Whenever a person comes in contact with a voltage source, current will flow through the person's body and the amount of current will depend on two variables: voltage and body resistance.

A person's body resistance depends upon many factors. For example, examine the skin of your hand. There are places where the skin is dry and tough, which offers high resistance, and there are places where the skin is moist and soft, such as between the fingers, which offers low resistance. If the skin is broken then the resistance of blood and inside tissue is very low. When a piece of wire is snipped with cutting pliers, it usually has a sharp edge. If that sharp edge contacts the skin in such a manner as to cut it and the wire has voltage, a fatal shock is likely.

A person's body resistance is also affected by environmental conditions, such as moisture in the air, or standing in water. Any time the skin is moist, it will have a much lower resistance than normal. A lower body resistance requires a much lower voltage to cause serious shock.

If the path of current flow is through the heart, such as passing from one hand, through the arm and chest, and out the other arm and hand, then the danger is much more severe than just through the hand. Given the right circumstances, a voltage as small as 40 volts can cause a fatal shock to a normal, healthy person. Voltages as high as the household voltage of 120 volts are certainly enough to kill a person.

Some people feel that a household voltage of 120 volts isn't dangerous because they have had shocks and not been killed. A shock is an accidental injury, and like any accident, it should be avoided whenever possible . . . it only takes one fatal accident.

Most electrical shocks will cause the victim to suddenly jump clear of the voltage source. However, a shock that could lead to a dangerous situation happens when the person cannot release on his own.

If you observe a person receiving an electrical shock, you must protect yourself from shock and remove the person from the electrical supply. The best way to do this is to use an insulated object such as a piece of dry wood to push the person off the electrical source. Keep in mind, fatal shocks happen when the person becomes paralyzed from the electricity flowing through the body.

Safety Rules

1. Wear safety glasses whenever there is danger of flying particles or liquids.
2. Never use a tool for a job that it was not intended to perform.
3. Be certain power tools are properly grounded or double insulated.
4. Do not rely on electrical safety devices, because they often fail.
5. Do not assume an electrical circuit is dead because a wire is not connected.
6. Avoid wet or moist conditions when working around electricity.
7. Avoid wearing jewelry when near electricity.
8. Never defeat a safety or interlock device.
9. Use a CO_2 fire extinguisher, rather than water on electrical fires.
10. When observing another person receiving a shock, push him/her from the electrical source with something insulated, or disconnect the electricity at its source.
11. Always act with common sense and never take unnecessary chances.
12. Do not work near electricity or operate power tools when taking medicine or alcoholic beverages.

13. Always follow the instructions provided by the manufacturer.

COMPUTER ASSISTED INSTRUCTION (CAI)

The personal home computer has made great changes in teaching and learning techniques. When we consider that school systems all over the country have computers in classrooms, and a vast number of people have computers of their own at home, it only makes sense that the computer could be put to work in teaching.

In a Classroom

The computer has made it possible to introduce a concept called "student managed learning." This has not replaced the teacher, but instead allows the teacher to concentrate more on one-to-one teaching. This method of teaching in a classroom atmosphere is still in the beginning stages. It also allows for another approach called "competency based learning," which is based on the fact that most people learn the best when they teach themselves at their own pace and use the classroom teacher to answer questions and solve problems.

Learning at Home

Many people have found that they can teach themselves, with the use of computers and books, almost any subject they want to know about. Programs are written for every level of learning and there are new programs coming out all the time.

There are many advantages to teaching oneself at home. For example; it is a relatively inexpensive way to learn a new subject and find out exactly how much interest one has in the subject. If a student is taught at school and at home, the learning process is much easier and the student retains much more and does better in school.

Some colleges are now willing to recognize self-taught individuals and give them a chance to take bypass examinations to receive college credits. This is especially true of the basic subject areas.

What CAI is Not

Computer Assisted Instruction is not a way of replacing books or good study habits. It will not replace the memorization of formulas, or definitions.

Computers, like books, are programmed or written by someone who makes every effort to answer all the questions that could be thought of by a student. This obviously is an impossible task. The student must learn to interpret the information that the computer is offering. When a student is reading a book, if there is something not understood fully, he or she needs to read it again or ask someone else. This is also the case with using computer programs.

What CAI Is

Computer Assisted Instruction is an alternate method of learning. Books by themselves are hard to learn from and to retain information from. The programs selected for the computer are intended to get the student involved in the teaching/learning process.

The key phrase is student involvement. Most people feel they "learn the hard way." What is "the hard way?" When someone says that, they usually mean that they must "do it themselves" in order to retain the information.

CAI allows the student to participate. The programs will offer some instructional material, some question/answer practice, some tests. If the student reads through the necessary material in the book first, then goes to the computer and allows the computer to reinforce what the book says, there will be a winning combination.

This Book and CAI

For each chapter, from Chapter 3 to 15, there will be at least one computer program. The listings are in Appendix E. The material selected for the program has been taken from the text material and is intended to challenge the student in the learning process.

All of the programs are intended to have the student read the text first, then try the programs. It may be necessary to re-read the text in order to get a full understanding.

The end of each chapter has a list of the programs available for that chapter and a brief discussion of what they are and how they will help the student.

All of the student projects, practice exercises, and tests try to cover every angle of the material. When the student finishes a chapter, he or she should feel competent in that subject area.

USING THE PROGRAMS IN THIS BOOK

The programs included in this book are written in BASIC and, if the student desires, he/she can copy the program from the book directly into the computer.

Many of the programs include graphics to help the student to better see the more complicated concepts.

Read the Book First

It is very important for the student to read the entire chapter before starting on the programs. In this way, the student has a good idea of what is expected in the chapter and has some practice before starting the programs.

Load the program for the particular chapter and try to perform the tasks the computer asks for. It will probably be necessary for the student to return to the proper section of the book to assist with understanding the programs.

Programs and Book Go Together

Studying a technical subject, such as electronics, is a very difficult task. It is not the same thing as reading a novel. With a novel, if the reader does not understand a certain point, it usually doesn't matter. With a technical subject, every point is important and must be understood fully.

Therefore, allow the book and the programs to work together to teach the subject matter. It will be very easy for the student to want to only use the programs since many of them will be "fun." Do not allow yourself to get caught in the trap of only depending on one source of the teaching/learning experience.

STUDENT PROJECTS

The projects for this chapter are intended to help the student to be better introduced to the subject of electronics technology.

1. Make a list of electrical/electronic terms that you can remember hearing at some time. Make a brief definition and give an example of any words that you are familiar with.
2. Using the newspaper from your area, or preferably a big city, look in the help wanted section to find out what jobs are available and the education level required.
3. Visit a high school guidance counselor to obtain information on what types of jobs are available in the electronics field and what education level is required.
4. Check in your own home for safety hazards. Make a list of the hazards and have them fixed as soon as possible.
5. Do some research on the subject of electrical shock: what it is, how to avoid it, how to perform first aid on a victim.
6. Make a list of the common sources of electrical shock and how to avoid them.
7. Make a list of safety rules to include many of the common safety problems.
8. Make a safety poster with the top 10 or more safety rules.

SAFETY TEST

The following safety test is to highlight some of the safety points. **Remember: Safety Requires Common Sense.**

Select the one best answer for each of the following multiple choice questions.

1. When using an electric drill:
   a. never plug the three conductor drill cord into a two conductor extension cord.
   b. side pressure on the drill bit is acceptable at slow speeds.
   c. never allow the drill to be grounded.
   d. safety glasses are not required.

2. When an electric wire is disconnected:
   a. it is safe to handle the wire.
   b. voltage may still be present.
   c. there is no danger of shock.
   d. the circuit breaker will trip.

3. In case of a fire in or near electrical equipment:
   a. use water to extinguish.
   b. use CO_2 (carbon dioxide) to extinguish.
   c. turn off the power and allow the fire to burn itself out.
   d. trip the circuit breaker by hand and the fire will go out.

4. A double insulated tool:
   a. has a three prong plug.
   b. has a two prong plug.
   c. cannot give electrical shock.
   d. has a metal handle.

5. When observing a victim receiving an electrical shock:
   a. wait until the victim falls clear before turning off power.
   b. do not move the victim.
   c. immediately give artificial respiration.
   d. first remove the source of electrical power or move the victim.

6. When using electrical equipment, be sure you're standing on a dry floor. Water and electricity cause:
   a. electrical shock
   b. gas
   c. explosion
   d. rust

7. If there's an emergency you may have to use a fire extinguisher. It's important to know where the fire extinguishers are located and to:
   a. test them
   b. read the instructions posted on them
   c. keep one near you at all times
   d. store flammables under them

8. Always protect your eyes when you're working with power equipment, an air hose or soldering. To prevent eye injury or blindness, wear:
   a. safety glasses or face shield
   b. a cap with a visor
   c. sun glasses
   d. waterproof clothes

9. Serious muscle and back injuries can result from lifting something incorrectly. The right way to lift something from the floor is:
   a. with your back
   b. slowly
   c. with your leg muscles
   d. with your arm muscles

10. It's dangerous to leave tools or materials sticking out over the edge of the work bench or table because:
    a. the tools could be damaged
    b. they could damage the table surface
    c. someone could bump into them
    d. it looks messy

11. When handling electrical equipment, be sure:
    a. that you're grounded
    b. the wires are exposed for inspection
    c. your hands are dry and you're standing on a dry floor
    d. the polarity is positive

12. If you need to use an extension cord, always check to see that the cord is:
    a. in good condition
    b. the right color
    c. well worn with frayed ends
    d. light weight

13. Another important safety rule for power cords is:
    a. put in the middle of the floor where it can be seen
    b. keep them out of the way of traffic
    c. hide them under a carpet

d. none of these

14. The best way to hold a drill is:
    a. firmly and comfortably, away from your face
    b. with a very tight grip
    c. without bending your elbows
    d. with one hand on the cord

15. As you begin to work with any electronic equipment, if you are not sure if the wiring is "hot" or not, always:
    a. assume that it's dead
    b. smell the wire for heat
    c. turn off the power at its source first
    d. feel the wire

16. The only *right* way to test wiring is:
    a. with a metal object
    b. with an insulated object
    c. with your fingers
    d. with proper testing equipment

17. All connections must be completed:
    a. before the power is turned on
    b. before you examine the wiring
    c. only by a qualified technician
    d. after the power is turned on

18. To pass a hot soldering iron to someone else:
    a. lay it down so the other person can pick it up
    b. hand it tip first so he/she can see it's hot
    c. hold it by the tip so he/she can take the handle
    d. pass it holding the cord

19. A good way to test if a soldering iron is hot is:
    a. on a piece of paper
    b. on a piece of solder
    c. on a wet sponge
    d. touch with a wet finger

20. It is important that the area you are soldering in is:
    a. wet so it won't burn
    b. clean and dry
    c. near a water source
    d. kept dark to help see any sparks

Chapter 2
Tools of the Trade

Chapter Objectives: To identify some tools of the electronics trade and know their common uses. To learn basic soldering techniques.

Chapter Outline:

- ☐ Basic Hand Tools
- ☐ Soldering

INTRODUCTION

The list of tools available to the technician is endless. Some are general purpose and used by everyone, and others are specialty tools that are only used in certain applications.

This chapter will present some of the very basic general purpose tools that would be used by technicians. The emphasis here will be clearly on an introduction, knowing that as the student technician develops knowledge of the electronics subject, skill with tools will also develop.

BASIC HAND TOOLS

Hand tools are used by skilled technicians to make it possible to repair circuits and all types of machinery. The tools discussed here are a sample of the more common tools available.

Cutting Pliers

A pair of diagonal cutters, nicknamed "dykes," is especially useful for cutting wire. The cutters are available in many different sizes and it is often necessary to keep a small and large pair to cut the wide range of wires that are encountered.

The wire is placed in the diagonally shaped cutting jaws for the purpose of cutting the wire. This tool is intended to cut through the wire and should not be used for the purpose of removing only the insulation.

Safety practices must be observed in the vicinity of the cutting edge. Extreme caution should also be observed if cutting near other wires that are not intended to be cut.

Long-Nose Pliers

Long-nose pliers are used for a wide range of operations. However, the primary purpose is to hold, bend, pull and push a piece of wire.

The shape of the nose ranges from long and skinny to short and not-so-skinny. The size and shape is usually a matter of personal preference, and a matter of the size of the wire being worked with. Some long-nose pliers also have cutters built in. It is usually best, however, not to use "combo" tools because it will result in a compromise that may be unfavorable.

Caution when using long-nose pliers is usually a matter of not squeezing the insulation on the wire. Squeeze only the wire itself.

Wire Strippers

The primary purpose of wire strippers is to remove the insulation from the wire. The type shown in the drawing can be adjusted to the exact size of the wire with an adjusting screw. By adjusting to the exact size of the wire, the handles can be closed all the way to the adjusted stop and it will not damage the wire.

Caution must be exercised, especially when using stranded wire, not to cut any of the strands and with solid wire not to nick it with the cutting edge.

Slip-Joint Pliers

Slip-joint pliers fall into the category of general-purpose pliers, which are available in a wide range of sizes and shapes. The main purpose of these pliers is to hold or squeeze objects.

Pliers are often used to hold nuts on bolts. If the nut is too tight on the bolt, damage to the nut can result.

Caution must also be exercised when holding objects. Many things are made of plastic, which can easily be damaged by the metal teeth of the pliers. It is often helpful to place a heavy piece of cloth under the teeth to prevent damage.

Crescent Wrench

A crescent wrench often comes as part of a set. Some have different size crescents at each end and some have the round at one end the same size as the crescent at the other. The fixed crescent wrench is the ideal tool to use to hold a nut. If the crescent is exactly the same size as the nut, there will be little or no damage to a nut that is very tight on the bolt.

Adjustable Crescent

An adjustable crescent wrench is used when the correct size of fixed crescent is not available. A thumb screw is used to adjust the wrench to the size of the nut. When used to hold nuts that are not too tight, one adjustable crescent can be used to replace a complete set of fixed crescent wrenches.

The problem with the adjustable type of crescent wrench is that it may not hold tight enough on a very tight nut and will result in damage to the nut.

SOLDERING

Soldering is a technique used to hold two metal objects together. A metal solder is melted and forms a bond between the two pieces of metal to be joined.

Soldering Tools

In addition to the basic hand tools required for cutting, stripping and holding the wire, soldering requires solder and something to melt the solder.

There are two general groups of tools for melting solder: soldering irons and soldering guns. Both require electricity and use a heating element to heat the tip for the purpose of melting the solder.

The soldering *iron* is usually fairly small and will produce a lower heat than the soldering *gun*, which is usually large, with a larger heating element.

Wattage Ratings

Soldering tools have a wattage rating which indicates the amount of heat that will be produced by the tip. A lower wattage rating produces less heat.

Soldering irons have wattage ratings that range from 15 watts to 60 watts. Some electronic components are easily damaged by heat and need to be installed with very low wattage irons. An iron with a wattage rating of 25 watts is usually low enough to be used with electronic components. The problem with low wattage irons is that they do not melt the solder very fast, and when used with heavy wire may not produce enough heat.

Soldering guns have wattage ratings that range from 40 watts to 500 watts, or higher. High wattage guns are useful for soldering wires or pieces of metal, not for electronic components.

Solder

Solder is a metal alloy that melts very easily and is used as the "glue" for metal. There are two general types of solder: the kind for plumbing and the kind for wires.

Plumbing solder is solid and it is necessary to use a separate flux. The *flux* is used for cleaning the two surfaces to be bonded. In plumbing, an acid flux is used which is very effective in cleaning the copper pipes.

Electrical solder is hollow, with the flux inside the core. The flux is a paste and as the solder melts, the flux runs out and cleans the surfaces. The flux used for electrical connections is a rosin and is not corrosive. Acid flux is corrosive and must not be used for electrical connections.

The best all-around solder to use for electronics work is a very thin solder (rosin core with a 60/40 alloy) because it melts fast.

Solder Connections

A solder connection must possess one impor-tant standard—there must be a good electrical connection. Connections are made between two wires: a wire to a terminal; wire to a component; component to a circuit board; wire to a circuit board; etc. All are metal to metal, usually copper, and all connections must be good electrically (they must pass electricity).

During the process of soldering, the two metals to be joined are *both* heated to a point where they *both* can melt the solder. The solder is then touched to the metal and the solder melts. As the solder melts, the flux runs out of the core and cleans away small deposits of dirt and corrosion. The molecules from the solder bond themselves to the molecules of the metal. The solder bond holds the two metals together and provides a good electrical path. The bonded solder also stops any corrosion from taking place and disturbing the bond.

Bad Solder Joints

A bad solder joint, often called a cold or frac-tured joint, is one where there is not a good electri-cal connection.

There are three things that cause a bad solder joint: 1) the metals were not *both* hot enough to melt the solder; 2) the joint was moved while the solder cooled causing the joint to crack and the metals to no longer form a good electrical contact; 3) corro-sion on the metal was not removed by the rosin flux.

Chapter 3
Shop Math

Chapter Objective: To review the rules of basic math and to demonstrate proficiency in its use prior to the study of electronics. Some students will be able to skip this chapter due to satisfactory training in school. If a grade of 80% correct or better is not received on the pretest, the student should go through the practice exercises to obtain basic math competency.

Chapter Outline:

SHOP MATH PRETEST

A calculator *may not* be used when taking this test. Solve each of the problems as indicated by the instructions for each section.

Part 1. Evaluation of Fractions

Arrange the following sets of numbers in descending order, starting with the largest.

(1) $\dfrac{1}{4}$ $\dfrac{2}{5}$ $\dfrac{3}{10}$ $\dfrac{1}{8}$

(2) $\dfrac{3}{4}$ $\dfrac{9}{16}$ $\dfrac{7}{8}$ $\dfrac{17}{32}$

Part 2. Arithmetic with Fractions

Perform the indicated operations, reduce to lowest terms.

(3) $3\dfrac{5}{6} - 1\dfrac{1}{3} =$

(4) $6\frac{2}{5} + 9\frac{1}{3} =$

(5) $5\frac{2}{3} \times 4\frac{1}{6} =$

(6) $3\frac{1}{2} \div 4\frac{4}{6} =$

(7) $4\frac{1}{6} - 2\frac{2}{3} =$

(8) $5\frac{3}{4} + 6\frac{1}{3} =$

(9) $1\frac{24}{12} \times 2\frac{39}{13} =$

(10) $3\frac{4}{5} \div 3\frac{8}{10} =$

(11) If the numerator of a fraction is made larger, does the value of the fraction increase or decrease?

(12) If the denominator of a fraction is made larger, does the value of the fraction increase or decrease?

Part 3. Arithmetic with Fractions

Perform the indicated operations with each of the following decimal numbers.

(13) $53.46 + 3.5 + 2.901 =$
(14) $12.2 \times 8 =$
(15) $0.0012 + 5.409 + 9.2 =$
(16) $49 \div 7 =$
(17) $56.05 - 23.9 =$
(18) $25.25 \times 25.5 =$
(19) $100.0 + 10.001 + 3.059 =$
(20) $5.6 \div 8 =$
(21) $0.0035 - 0.0009 =$
(22) $10 + 100 - .01 + .001 - 01.01 =$
(23) $7.2 \div 12 =$
(24) $87.5 \div 0.6 =$
(25) $12.5 \times 8.752 =$

Part 4. Converting Fractions to Decimals

Change the following fractions to decimals. Round to three decimal places.

(26) $\frac{2}{5} =$

(27) $\frac{7}{8} =$

(28) $3\frac{6}{7} =$

(29) $5\frac{4}{5} =$

(30) $\frac{9}{6} =$

(31) $\frac{7}{2} =$

Part 5. Converting Decimals to Fractions

Change the following decimals to fractions. Reduce the answer to lowest terms.

(32) $0.333 =$
(33) $0.6 =$
(34) $0.625 =$
(35) $3.3 =$
(36) $6.25 =$
(37) $8.400 =$
(38) $4.03 =$
(39) $7.75 =$

Part 6. Arithmetic with Positive and Negative Numbers

Perform the indicated operations with each of the following numbers.

(40) $-5 + 3 =$
(41) $(-2)(-3) =$
(42) $7 - 4 =$
(43) $(-3)(4) =$
(44) $2 - 9 =$
(45) $-5(3) =$

(46) $0.5 - 0.7 =$

(47) $6 \times -3 =$

(48) $-1.5 - -3.6 =$

(49) $-32 \div 8 =$

(50) $-\dfrac{3}{4} - \dfrac{5}{8} =$

(51) $\dfrac{-4 \times 3}{6} =$

(52) $-\dfrac{3}{5} + \dfrac{13}{15} =$

(53) $\dfrac{-3 \times -5}{-5 \times 3} =$

(54) $22 + -33 =$

(55) $\dfrac{(7)\,(-2)\,(-2)}{(-3)\,(-7)\,(4)} =$

Part 7. Raising Numbers to a Power

Perform the following indicated operations.

(56) 2^2

(57) -3^2

(58) -2^3

(59) 3^3

Part 8. Square Root

Take the square root of each of the following numbers. If the numbers given are not perfect squares, approximate to one decimal place.

(60) $25 =$

(61) $81 =$

(62) $8 =$

(63) $0.04 =$

Part 9. Values of Numbers

With each of the following, use the given value to find the two unknown values.

(64) $\dfrac{1}{4}$	decimal value?	percent value?
(65) $.5$	fraction value?	percent value?
(66) $33\dfrac{1}{3}\%$	fraction value?	decimal value?
(67) $.125$	fraction value?	percent value?
(68) $\dfrac{3}{8}$	decimal value?	percent value
(69) $.1\%$	fraction value?	decimal value?
(70) $.4$	fraction value?	percent value?

Part 10. Percent tolerance

With each of the following tolerance problems, determine the minimum and maximum allowable values based on the percent tolerance given.

(71) $100 \quad \pm \quad 5\%$

(72) $270 \quad \pm \quad 5\%$

(73) $330 \quad \pm \quad 10\%$

(74) $470 \quad \pm \quad 20\%$

(75) $1000 \quad \pm \quad 1\%$

(76) $2200 \quad \pm \quad 5\%$

(77) $3500 \quad \pm \quad 10\%$

(78) $4900 \quad \pm \quad 15\%$

(79) $8700 \quad \pm \quad 2\%$

(80) $10,000 \quad \pm \quad 10\%$

Part 11. Solving Equations

Solve each of the following equations.

(81) $x + 4 = 9$

(82) $y + 6 = -4$

(83) $a - 5 = 0$

(84) $2a + 3a = 10$

(85) $4y = 3y + 2$

(86) $-100 = -5y$

(87) $7(5x - 2) = 6(6x - 1)$

(88) $8(2x + 1) = 4(7x + 8)$

(89) $0(x + 3) = 2x$

(90) $x = \dfrac{4}{x}$

Part 12. Solving Formulas

With each of the formulas below, substitute the given quantities and solve the formula for the remaining unknown. Note: π stands for the Greek letter which has the value of 3.14.

(91) $A = W \cdot P$ [Given: $W = 1500$, $P = .05$]

(92) $F = \dfrac{9}{5} C + 32$ [Given: $C = 20$]

(93) $F = \dfrac{9}{5} C + 32$ [Given: $F = 40$]

(94) $d = r \cdot t$ [Given: $r = 50$, $t = 2.5$]

(95) $A = \frac{1}{2} b \cdot h$ [Given: $A = 32$, $b = 4$]

(96) $P = 2L + 2W$ [Given: $P = 200$, $W = 40$]

(97) $E = I \cdot R$ [Given: $I = 2$, $E = 120$]

(98) $X_c = \dfrac{1}{2 \pi f C}$

Given: $f = 60$, $C = .002$
Note: all terms are multiplied.

(99) $\dfrac{1}{R_T} = \dfrac{1}{R1} + \dfrac{1}{R2} + \dfrac{1}{R3}$

Given: $R1 = 40$, $R2 = 60$, $R3 = 80$

(100) $X_L = 2 \cdot \pi \cdot f \cdot L$

Given: $f = 50$, $L = .1$

INTRODUCTION

The purpose of this chapter, in general, is to ensure that the student is properly prepared in the areas of basic mathematics prior to the study of electronics.

This section deals with a classification called basic math. The objective here will be to provide the rules and show some sample problems in the areas of fractions, decimals, percentages. Keep in mind, the emphasis will be on review of the rules. It is assumed here that the student has already learned basics at some point and needs only to have the rules refreshed.

FRACTIONS

Fractions will be dealt with in two groups: (1) definitions, improper fractions and mixed numbers, reducing and equivalent fractions; (2) arithmetic with fractions. The groups have been selected so the rules of each group are similar. There are practice exercises at the end of each group.

Definitions

Fraction. Part of a whole. The fraction in mathematics is written as one number over another, which actually means the top number is divided by the bottom number. For example: ⅗ means 3 divided by 5.

Numerator. The top number of a fraction. The numerator tells how many parts of the whole. A larger numerator represents a fraction with a larger value. For example; ¾ is larger than ¼.

Denominator. The bottom number of a fraction. The denominator tells how many parts the whole was divided into. If the denominator is increased, the whole was divided into more parts. If the size of the numerator remains the same, the fraction is smaller with a larger denominator. An example is the slicing of a pie. If the pie is sliced into 8 pieces, each piece is smaller than if it were only sliced into 4 pieces.

Whole Number. A number that does not contain a fractional part. An example is the counting numbers: 1, 2, 3, 4, etc.

Mixed Number. A number that contains both a whole number and a fraction. For example; 2⅔.

Improper Fraction. The numerator is larger than the denominator. This means the value of the fraction is larger than 1. A proper fraction is always less than 1. Therefore, the improper fraction should be changed to a mixed number as a final answer. For example; 3/2 is equal to 1½. Note: an improper fraction is used when performing certain mathematical operations.

Reducing Fractions. To lower the size of both numerator and denominator, without changing the value of the fraction. Example: ⅘ = ¾ = ½. Reducing to the lowest terms is best.

Equivalent Fractions. To raise (or lower) the size of both numerator and denominator, without changing the value of the fraction. This is necessary to find common denominators or to compare the values of several fractions.

Common Denominator. Fractions are changed to have the same denominator, while still retaining their original value. This is necessary with addition and subtraction. Example; ½ = ⁵/₁₀, ⅖ = ⁴/₁₀.

Improper Fractions, Mixed Numbers, Reducing and Equivalent Fractions

Addition and subtraction allow the use of mixed numbers or improper fractions. Multiplication and division do not allow mixed numbers, and they must be performed with fractions only. Regardless of which mathematical operation is performed, the final answer should be presented in the form of a proper fraction or mixed number, with the fractions reduced to lowest terms.

☐ To change a mixed number to an improper fraction, multiply the whole number times the denominator and add the numerator to this product. Write that result over the original denominator.

Examples: Mixed Numbers to Improper Fractions

$$3\frac{2}{3} = \frac{17}{5} \qquad 3 \times 5 = 15 + 2 = \frac{17}{5}$$

$$2\frac{1}{3} = \frac{7}{3} \qquad 2 \times 3 = 6 + 1 = \frac{7}{3}$$

$$4\frac{2}{5} = \frac{22}{5} \qquad 4 \times 5 = 20 + 2 = \frac{22}{5}$$

$$7\frac{1}{2} = \frac{15}{2} \qquad 7 \times 2 = 14 + 1 = \frac{15}{2}$$

$$8\frac{3}{4} = \frac{35}{4} \qquad 8 \times 4 = 32 + 3 = \frac{35}{4}$$

☐ To change an improper fraction to a mixed number, divide the numerator by the denominator. This division will produce a

whole number or a whole number and a remainder. The remainder placed over the original denominator will be the fractional part.

Examples: Improper Fractions to Mixed Numbers

$$\frac{22}{11} = 2 \qquad\qquad 22 \text{ (divided by) } 11 = 2$$

$$\frac{25}{11} = 2\frac{3}{11} \qquad 25 \div 11 = 2 \text{ r } \frac{3}{11}$$

$$\frac{17}{2} = 8\frac{1}{2} \qquad 17 \div 2 = 8 \text{ r } \frac{1}{2}$$

$$\frac{23}{3} = 7\frac{2}{3} \qquad 23 \div 3 = 7 \text{ r } \frac{2}{3}$$

$$\frac{8}{5} = 1\frac{3}{5} \qquad 8 \div 5 = 1 \text{ r } \frac{3}{5}$$

☐ To reduce a fraction to lower terms, divide both numerator and denominator by the same number. To find an equivalent fraction, multiply numerator and denominator by the same number.

Examples: Reducing Fractions

$$\frac{4}{8} = \frac{1}{2} \qquad \text{Divided both by } 4$$

$$\frac{3}{9} = \frac{1}{3} \qquad \text{Divided both by } 3$$

$$\frac{5}{25} = \frac{1}{5} \qquad \text{Divided both by } 5$$

$$\frac{16}{18} = \frac{8}{9} \qquad \text{Divided both by } 2$$

$$\frac{27}{45} = \frac{3}{5} \qquad \text{Divided both by } 9$$

Examples: Equivalent Fractions

Change the fraction on the left to an equivalent fraction with the denominator shown on the right.

$$\frac{7}{8} = \frac{?}{16} \quad \text{Multiply by } 2 = \frac{14}{16}$$

$$\frac{2}{5} = \frac{?}{45} \quad \text{Multiply by } 9 = \frac{18}{45}$$

$$\frac{3}{4} = \frac{?}{12} \quad \text{Multiply by } 3 = \frac{9}{12}$$

$$\frac{1}{9} = \frac{?}{63} \quad \text{Multiply by } 7 = \frac{7}{63}$$

$$\frac{5}{8} = \frac{?}{32} \quad \text{Multiply by } 4 = \frac{20}{32}$$

Practice Problems: Fractions

A. Change the following mixed numbers to improper fractions:

(1) $3 \frac{2}{3} =$

(2) $13 \frac{3}{7} =$

(3) $4 \frac{1}{20} =$

(4) $1 \frac{2}{3} =$

(5) $5 \frac{5}{6} =$

(6) $3 \frac{7}{8} =$

(7) $2 \frac{3}{5} =$

(8) $4 \frac{3}{10} =$

(9) $7 \frac{5}{9} =$

(10) $2 \frac{3}{4} =$

B. Change the following improper fractions to mixed numbers. Reduce answer to lowest terms.

(11) $\frac{19}{4} =$

(12) $\frac{37}{6} =$

(13) $\frac{28}{3} =$

(14) $\frac{37}{8} =$

(15) $\frac{28}{7} =$

(16) $\frac{34}{25} =$

(17) $\frac{47}{9} =$

(18) $\frac{11}{4} =$

(19) $\frac{18}{2} =$

(20) $\frac{40}{10} =$

C. Arrange the following sets of numbers in ascending order, from smallest to largest.

(21) $\frac{5}{8} \quad \frac{3}{4} \quad \frac{7}{16} \quad \frac{1}{2}$

(22) $\frac{3}{32} \quad \frac{3}{16} \quad \frac{1}{8} \quad \frac{5}{64}$

(23) $\frac{4}{10} \quad \frac{51}{100} \quad \frac{12}{25} \quad \frac{1}{2}$

(24) $\frac{15}{16} \quad \frac{33}{32} \quad 1 \quad 1\frac{1}{64}$

(25) $5\frac{1}{4} \quad 5\frac{3}{64} \quad 5\frac{1}{3} \quad 5\frac{4}{9}$

ARITHMETIC WITH FRACTIONS

The rules for arithmetic with fractions are separated into two sections: multiplication/division and addition/subtraction. When it is thought of in this way, there are only two sets of rules that need to be learned. There are practice exercises at the end of this section.

Multiplication/Division

☐ Mixed numbers must first be changed to improper fractions prior to multiplication or division.

☐ Multiply the numerators, then multiply the denominators. Answer must be reduced to lowest terms.

☐ With division problems, invert the divisor (the number following the division sign) and multiply.

Sample Problems: Multiplication/Division

SP#3-1 Multiply: $2\dfrac{3}{4} \times \dfrac{2}{5} =$

Step 1: Change mixed numbers to improper fractions:

$$2\frac{3}{4} = \frac{11}{4}$$

Step 2: Multiply numerators, then multiply denominators:

$$\frac{11 \times 2}{4 \times 5} = \frac{22}{20}$$

Step 3: Reduce to lowest terms:

$$\frac{22}{20} = 1\frac{2}{20} = 1\frac{1}{10}$$

SP#3-2 Divide: $4\dfrac{2}{3} \div 3\dfrac{1}{2} =$

Step 1: Change mixed numbers to improper fractions:

$$4\frac{2}{3} = \frac{14}{3}$$

$$3\frac{1}{2} = \frac{7}{2}$$

Step 2: Re-write the problem to show improper fractions:

$$\frac{14}{3} \div \frac{7}{2}$$

Step 3: Invert the divisor then multiply:

$$\frac{14}{3} \times \frac{2}{7} = \frac{28}{21}$$

Step 4: Reduce to lowest terms:

$$\frac{28}{21} = 1\frac{7}{21} = 1\frac{1}{3}$$

Addition/Subtraction

☐ It is not necessary to change mixed numbers to improper fractions, although it is often easier, especially with subtraction.

☐ A common denominator is required to add or subtract fractions. A common denominator is a denominator that is the same number for two or more fractions.

☐ The common denominator is found by determining which number it is that all denominators of the fractions can divide into evenly.

☐ To add or subtract the numerators, keeping the common denominator, always reduce the answer to lowest terms.

Sample Problems: Addition/Subtraction

SP#3-3 Add: $\dfrac{1}{2} + \dfrac{2}{3} =$

Step 1: The common denominator is 6. Change the fractions to their equivalent with this denominator:

$$\frac{1}{2} = \frac{3}{6}$$

$$\frac{2}{3} = \frac{4}{6}$$

Step 2: Re-write the problem using the common denominator:

$$\frac{3}{6} + \frac{4}{6} =$$

Step 3: Add the numerators, keeping the common denominator:

$$\frac{3 + 4}{6} = \frac{7}{6}$$

Step 4: Reduce to lowest terms:

$$\frac{7}{6} = 1\frac{1}{6}$$

SP#3-4 Add: $2\frac{3}{4} + 3\frac{2}{5} =$

Step 1: Find common denominator and change to equivalent. Note: this problem can be done in mixed numbers or with improper fractions. CD = 20

$$2\frac{3}{4} = 2\frac{15}{20}$$
$$3\frac{2}{5} = 3\frac{8}{20}$$

Step 2: Re-write the problem with the common denominator:

$$2\frac{15}{20} + 3\frac{8}{20} =$$

Step 3: Add the whole numbers, then add the fractions:

$$2 + 3 = 5$$

$$\frac{15}{20} + \frac{8}{20} = \frac{23}{20}$$

Step 4: Combine the whole number with the fraction and reduce to lowest terms:

$$5\frac{23}{20} = 6\frac{3}{20}$$

SP#3-5 Subtract: $7\frac{2}{5} - 3\frac{1}{2} =$

Step 1: It is usually best with subtraction to first change to improper fractions:

$$\frac{37}{5} - \frac{7}{2} =$$

Step 2: Common denominator is 10. Change to equivalent:

$$\frac{37}{5} = \frac{74}{10}$$

$$\frac{7}{2} = \frac{35}{10}$$

Step 3: Subtract numerators keeping common denominator. Reduce to lowest terms.

$$\frac{74}{10} - \frac{35}{10} = \frac{39}{10}$$

$$\frac{39}{10} = 3\frac{9}{10}$$

Practice Exercises: Arithmetic with Fractions

Perform the indicated operations. Reduce all answers to lowest terms.

(1) $\frac{1}{2} \times \frac{1}{4}$

(2) $\frac{1}{2} \div \frac{1}{4}$

19

$$(3) \quad \frac{1}{2} + \frac{1}{4}$$

$$(4) \quad \frac{1}{2} - \frac{1}{4}$$

$$(5) \quad \frac{2}{3} \times \frac{3}{5}$$

$$(6) \quad \frac{3}{4} \div \frac{4}{7}$$

$$(7) \quad \frac{5}{6} + \frac{2}{5}$$

$$(8) \quad \frac{6}{7} - \frac{1}{3}$$

$$(9) \quad 6 \times \frac{2}{3}$$

$$(10) \quad \frac{6}{7} \div 3$$

$$(11) \quad 2\frac{2}{6} + 0\frac{3}{9}$$

$$(12) \quad 6\frac{3}{4} - 5$$

$$(13) \quad 2\frac{1}{7} \times 3\frac{4}{3}$$

$$(14) \quad 1\frac{1}{2} \div 4\frac{2}{4}$$

$$(15) \quad 3\frac{3}{10} + 2\frac{2}{15}$$

$$(16) \quad 8 - 2\frac{3}{7}$$

$$(17) \quad \frac{4}{5} \times \frac{6}{7} \div \frac{8}{9}$$

$$(18) \quad \frac{1}{2} \times \frac{3}{4} \times \frac{5}{6}$$

$$(19) \quad \frac{3}{4} + \frac{1}{3} + \frac{5}{8} - \frac{2}{6}$$

$$(20) \quad \frac{1}{2} + \frac{5}{6} - \frac{1}{3} - \frac{1}{4}$$

DECIMALS

Arithmetic with decimals is very similar to using whole numbers. Therefore, most people find it fairly easy to work with decimals. Also decimals are more familiar to most people because money is handled in decimal form.

This section on decimals is primarily to review the rules and demonstrate some sample problems in case the student needs the review. Practice problems are available at the end of the section.

Addition/Subtraction with Decimals

☐ When adding or subtracting decimals, it is necessary to operate on numbers with the same place value. This is best done by aligning the decimal points in a column.

Sample Problems: Addition/Subtraction

SP#3-6 Add: 2.3 + 3.65 + 10.321 =

Align the decimal points in a column. If desired, zeros may be added to make an equal number of decimal places for each number. Add the numbers in the same place value columns.

$$\begin{array}{r} 2.3 \\ 3.65 \\ + \ 10.321 \\ \hline 16.271 \end{array}$$

SP#3-7 Subtract: 4.2 − 1.863 =

Align the decimal points and place zeros to have equal columns for borrowing during subtraction.

$$\begin{array}{r} 4.200 \\ - \ 1.863 \\ \hline 2.337 \end{array}$$

Multiplication with Decimals

☐ When multiplying numbers with decimals, proceed as if using whole numbers—ignoring the decimal.

□ To determine the decimal place of the answer, count from the right a number of decimal places equal to the *total* decimal places of the numbers multiplied.

Sample Problem: Multiplication

SP#3-8 Multiply: $3.245 \times 2.3 =$

Multiply ignoring the decimals, then count the total number of decimal places. The total number of places is 4—3 in the top number and 1 in the bottom number. Count from the right, the total number of places.

$$\begin{array}{r} 3.245 \\ \times\ \ 2.3 \\ \hline 7.4635 \end{array}$$

Division with Decimals

□ If the number outside of the division bracket has a decimal point, it is necessary to move the decimal to the right enough places to be at the bracket. Move the decimal of the number inside the bracket enough places to equal the move outside.

□ Perform the division placing the answer above the proper place, and place the decimal point directly over the corrected decimal inside the bracket.

Sample Problem: Division

SP#3-9 Divide: $36.3 \div .08$

Step 1. Write the problem using the division bracket. Notice (.08) needs to have the decimal point moved to place it at the right of the number, next to the bracket.

$$.08\overline{)36.3}$$

Step 2. Move the decimal in both (.08) and (36.3) two places to the right. Add zeros to the inside number (36.3) to complete the move.

$$08\overline{)3630.}$$

Step 3. Divide, placing the answer and the decimal in their correct places.

$$8\overline{)3630.00}^{453.75}$$

Changing Fractions to Decimals and Decimals to Fractions

□ To change a fraction to a decimal—divide the numerator by the denominator.

Sample Problem: Fraction to Decimal

SP#3-10 Change $\dfrac{5}{8}$ to a decimal.

$$5 \div 8 = 0.625$$

□ To change a decimal to a fraction—remove the decimal point and write the number over the equivalent place value and reduce to lowest terms. The place value is a multiple of 10 with the same number of zeros as the original decimal number.

Sample Problem: Decimal to Fraction

SP#3-11 Change .75 to a fraction.

$$.75 = \frac{75}{100} = \frac{3}{4}$$

Practice Problems: Decimals

Perform the indicated operations on each of the following.

(1) $2.8 + 12.19$
(2) $0.8 - 0.5$
(3) $.4 \times 3$
(4) $9.63 \div 3$
(5) $6.3 + 1.07 + 3$

(6) 0.28 – .19

(7) 0.5 × 0.043

(8) .372 ÷ .06

(9) 2.8 + 1.90 + 51.012

(10) 6.9 – 2.47

(11) 0.2 × 0.03

(12) 1.04 ÷ 2

(13) 49 + .07 + 3.5 – 12.608

(14) 100 + .001 – 10.01 + 1.10

(15) 16.32 ÷ 0.008

(16) 0.002 × .0003 × 1.01

(17) $\dfrac{1}{2 \times 3.14 \times 100 \times .002}$

(18) $\dfrac{1}{2 \times \pi \times 50 \times .0000001}$

(19) $\dfrac{1}{6.28 \times 10000 \times 0.00000005}$

(20) $\dfrac{.159}{100{,}000 \times .000000150}$

Change the following fractions to decimals.

(21) $\dfrac{3}{8}$

(22) $\dfrac{2}{5}$

(23) $\dfrac{3}{16}$

(24) $2\dfrac{3}{9}$

(25) $5\dfrac{1}{8}$

Change the following decimals to fractions. Reduce to lowest terms.

(26) 1.3

(27) .667

(28) .009

(29) .4

(30) .3125

PERCENT TOLERANCE

There are many different types of percentage problems. Of these, there is really only one type that is used on a regular basis in the field of electronics. That type of percentage problem is "tolerance."

All electronic components, instruments, measurements, calculations and the operation of equipment have a tolerance that is considered acceptable. It is very important for the student of electronics to understand that, with all the fancy calculations made, there is a range that is considered acceptable.

Most tolerances relating to electronics are stated as a ± percentage of the ideal. (± means "plus or minus".) A tolerance of ± 10% means the measurement can be high or low by 10% of the ideal and still be within an acceptable range.

Changing Percents to
Decimals and Decimals to Percents

In order to deal with a percentage mathematically, it is necessary to change the percentage to a decimal. Then the mathematical operation can be performed using the decimals.

☐ To change a percentage to its decimal form—remove the percent sign and move the decimal to the left two (2) places.

☐ To change a decimal to a percent—move the decimal to the right two (2) places and attach the percent sign.

Examples: Percents and Decimals

10%	= .10	1.5%	= .015
15%	= .15	2.5%	= .025
20%	= .20	7.5%	= .075
100%	= 1.00	.15%	= .0015
235%	= 2.35	.25%	= .0025
500%	= 5.00	.5%	= .005
1%	= .01	12.5%	= .125
2%	= .02	15.75%	= .1575
5%	= .05	20.375%	= .20375

Percent Tolerance

☐ Tolerance is a percentage of the nominal (ideal) value to allow a calculation of the maximum and minimum acceptable values.
☐ Max and min values are calculated by taking the percentage of the nominal value and adding or subtracting from the nominal value.

Sample Problems: Percent Tolerance

In each of the following problems, use the percent tolerance given, and the nominal value, to find the maximum and minimum acceptable values.

SP#3-12 200 +/−10%

Step 1. Change percent to decimal.

$$10\% = .1$$

Step 2. Multiply the decimal times the nominal value to find the tolerance.

$$200 \times .1 = 20$$

Step 3. Find the maximum value by ADDING the tolerance to the nominal value.

$$200 + 20 = 220$$

Step 4. Find the minimum value by SUBTRACTING the tolerance from nominal value.

$$200 - 20 = 180$$

SP#3-13 33,000 +/−15%

Step 1. Change the percentage to its decimal equivalent.

$$15\% = .15$$

Step 2. Multiply the decimal times the nominal value to find the tolerance.

$$33,000 \times .15 = 4950$$

Step 3. Find the maximum value by ADDING the tolerance to the nominal value.

$$33,000 + 4950 = 37,950$$

Step 4. Find the minimum value by SUBTRACTING the tolerance from the nominal value.

$$33,000 - 4950 = 28,050$$

Practice Problems: Percent Tolerance

With each of the following, determine the maximum and minimum allowable values.

(1) 100 +/−5%
(2) 470 +/−10%
(3) 860 +/−20%
(4) 1000 +/−10%
(5) 1500 +/−15%
(6) 2200 +/−1%
(7) 3300 +/−2%
(8) 4700 +/−5%
(9) 6800 +/−10%
(10) 10,000 +/−10%

POSITIVE AND NEGATIVE NUMBERS

Both positive and negative numbers are of importance when dealing with subject areas in the electronics field.

Negative numbers have essentially two definitions: (1) numbers with a value less than zero also called minus numbers. An example is—a thermometer; (2) opposite positive, often used in terms of direction—an example is—going backwards.

Positive and negative numbers are often called "signed numbers" for simplicity. All numbers, except zero, have either a positive or negative sign. If no sign is written, then the sign is positive. Zero is neither positive nor negative—zero has no sign.

Addition and Subtraction of Signed Numbers

☐ When adding: if the signs of the two numbers are the same, then add the numbers and keep the same sign.

□ When adding: if the signs of the two numbers are different, then subtract the numbers and take the sign of the larger number.

□ When subtracting: change the sign of the number being subtracted and change the subtraction sign to an addition sign. Follow the rules for addition.

Examples: Addition/Subtraction

Addition with same signs:

$$6 + 5 = 11$$
$$-3 + -4 = -7$$

Addition with opposite signs:

$$-7 + 3 = -4$$
$$-1 + 9 = 8$$
$$8 + -4 = 4$$
$$2 + -6 = -4$$

Subtraction:

$$5 - 3 = 5 + -3 = 2$$
$$6 - -2 = 6 + +2 = 8$$
$$-3 - 1 = -3 + -1 = -4$$
$$-4 - -9 = -4 + +9 = 5$$

Multiplication and Division with Signed Numbers

□ The operations of multiplication or division are performed without regard to the signs. The positive or negative sign is placed on the final answer (product or quotient).

□ Same signs produce a positive answer. Opposite signs produce a negative answer.

Examples: Multiplication/Division

Multiplication/division with same signs:

$$2 \times 5 = 10$$
$$-3 \times -6 = 18$$
$$6 \div 2 = 3$$
$$-8 \div -4 = 2$$

Multiplication/division with opposite signs:

$$3 \times -2 = -6$$
$$-1 \times 4 = -4$$
$$9 \div -3 = -3$$
$$-12 \div 6 = -2$$

Fractions with Signs

□ When dealing with fractions, there are three signs to consider: (1) the sign in front or the addition/subtraction sign; (2) the sign of the numerator; (3) the sign of the denominator.

□ A fraction is positive if all three signs are positive or if two of the three signs are negative.

□ A fraction is negative if all three signs are negative or if one of the three signs is negative.

Examples: Positive and Negative Fractions

Positive fractions:

$$+ \frac{3}{5} = + \frac{-3}{-5} = - \frac{-3}{5} - \frac{3}{-5}$$

Negative fractions:

$$- \frac{5}{6} = - \frac{-5}{-6} = + \frac{-5}{6} = + \frac{5}{-6}$$

Practice Problems: Positive and Negative Numbers

Perform the indicated operations on the following signed numbers.

(1) $15 + 12$
(2) $-7 + 0$
(3) $2 + -4$
(4) $-5 + -7$
(5) $6 - 5$
(6) $2 - 8$
(7) $-5 - 3$
(8) $-2 - 7$
(9) $8 - -1$

(10) $5 - -15$
(11) $-9 - -6$
(12) $-3 - -7$
(13) 2×4
(14) 5×-2
(15) -6×7
(16). -5×-8
(17) -1×0
(18) $9 \div -1$
(19) $-8 \div 2$
(20) $-12 \div -6$

Determine if the following fractions are positive or negative.

(21) $+ \dfrac{1}{3}$

(22) $\dfrac{3}{4}$

(23) $\dfrac{-3}{-7}$

(24) $- \dfrac{2}{-3}$

(25) $- \dfrac{4}{7}$

(26) $- \dfrac{-5}{-6}$

(27) $+ \dfrac{-2}{9}$

(28) $+ \dfrac{3}{-7}$

(29) $- \dfrac{-4}{5}$

(30) $\dfrac{-2}{5}$

SOLVING EQUATIONS

The study of electronics, and most scientific subjects, involves the use of many formulas. The proper use of formulas requires using basic algebra to manipulate the equation and solve for the unknown. This section will concentrate on the skills needed to solve equations.

Variables, Coefficients, and Constants

A variable is a letter used in an algebraic expression to represent an unknown numerical value. Most formulas contain several variables. In order to solve the formula, a numerical value must be known for all of the variables but one. The one remaining variable will be found by using algebra.

A *coefficient* is a number that is written beside (usually in front of) a variable. It is a constant, because it does not change, and its purpose is to be a multiplier for the variable.

A *constant* is a number that is part of the equation. It remains the same value regardless of how the variables are changed.

Solving Equations

☐ When solving equations, the final goal is to have the unknown by itself on one side of the equation, equal to the number on the other side. The equation at this stage does not indicate any arithmetic to be performed. Example: x = 5
☐ Terms are "transposed" (mathematically moved) from one side of the equation, to the other, by performing arithmetic that is opposite to the operation indicated by the equation. Operations of transposition must be performed equally on both sides of the equation.
☐ Only "like terms" can be added or subtracted. *Like terms* are ones that either do not have a variable or the variables are identical. The coefficients do not have an effect if the variables are identical.

Examples of like terms:

☐ Any Number by Itself; 1, 2, 3, etc.
☐ Identical variables; x, 2x, 3x, etc.

Examples of unlike terms:

☐ Nonidentical Variables; x, y, a

Sample Problems: Solving Equations

SP#3-14 Addition: transpose by subtraction.

Step 1. Starting equation:

$$x + 3 = 7$$

Step 2. Notice the indicated addition on the left side. Remove this addition by subtracting 3 from both sides.

$$x + 3 - 3 = 7 - 3$$

Step 3. Perform the subtractions as indicated. Notice the left side has only the x remaining and the right side has only a number. This equation is now solved.

$$x = 4$$

Step 4. Check the results by substituting the answer into the original equation in place of the variable. ( ) shows the substitution.

$$(4) + 3 = 7$$

SP#3-15 Subtraction: transpose by addition.

Step 1. Starting equation:

$$y - 8 = 4$$

Step 2. The left side of the equation indicates subtraction. Remove this by adding to both sides.

$$y - 8 + 8 = 4 + 8$$

Step 3. Perform the arithmetic and the equation will be solved.

$$y = 12$$

Step 4. Substitute into the original equation to check the answer.

$$(12) - 8 = 4$$

SP#3-16 Multiplication: transpose by division.

Step 1. Starting equation:

$$4a = 20$$

Step 2. Multiplication is indicated by writing a number alongside the variable. This is called a coefficient. Remove it by dividing both sides.

$$\frac{4a}{4} = \frac{20}{4}$$

Step 3. Perform the arithmetic and the equation will be solved.

$$a = 5$$

Step 4. Substitute into the original equation to check the answer. Note: parentheses ( ) next to a number or variable, without an addition or subtraction sign, indicate multiplication.

$$4(5) = 20$$

SP#3-17 Division: transpose by multiplying.

Step 1. Starting equation:

$$\frac{x}{5} = -2$$

Step 2. The division is removed by multiplying both sides.

$$\frac{x(5)}{5} = -2(5)$$

Step 3. Perform the arithmetic and the equation will be solved.

$$x = -10$$

Step 4. Substitute into the original equation to check answer.

$$\frac{(-10)}{5} = -2$$

SP#3-18 Solving a complex sample equation.

Step 1. Original equation:

$$2x + 7 = 19 - 4x$$

Step 2. First remove addition and/or subtraction. Subtract 7 in one step and then 4x in another step. Do not combine steps because it gets very confusing.

$$2x + 7 - 7 = 19 - 4x - 7$$

Step 3. Simplify by performing the arithmetic shown in step 2.

$$2x = 12 - 4x$$

Step 4. To remove the 4x from the right side, add.

$$2x + 4x = 12 - 4x + 4x$$

Step 5. Simplify by performing the arithmetic shown in step 4.

$$6x = 12$$

Step 6. Solve the equation by dividing by 6.

$$x = 2$$

Step 7. Substitute into the original equation to check answer.

$$2(2) + 7 = 19 - 4(2)$$
$$4 + 7 = 19 - 8$$
$$11 = 11 \text{ (checks)}$$

Practice Problems: Solving Equations

With each of the following equations: solve for the unknown.

(1) $x + 4 = 9$
(2) $x + 3 = 7$
(3) $4 = -6 - y$
(4) $y + 3 = -1$
(5) $a - 5 = 0$
(6) $7 - a = 6$
(7) $2a + 3a = 10$
(8) $x + 5 + 3x = 6$
(9) $4y = 3y + 2$
(10) $81 = 9x$
(11) $-100 = -5y$
(12) $5 + y = 6y - 7 + 5y$
(13) $100 = 50 + x + 25$
(14) $(x)(x) = 4$
(15) $3 - y - 2y = 6 - 6y - 6y$

SOLVING FORMULAS

Formulas and equations are essentially the same thing, as far as the mathematics is concerned. The difference is that a formula contains several different unknowns, where the equation contains one unknown. To solve the formula, all of the unknowns will have values given, except one. The formula then becomes an equation, with one unknown. Solving this equation is actually solving the formula for that particular unknown.

Sometimes it is necessary to re-arrange the formula to make it easier to solve for a particular unknown. When this is done, the indicated arithmetic will be transposed from one side of the equation to the other.

☐ When formulas are transposed, they solve for a different variable on the other side of the equals sign.

Sample Problems: Transposing Formulas

SP#3-19 Solve for C:

$$F = \frac{9}{5} C + 32$$

(This is the formula used to find Fahrenheit degrees when Centigrade is given. Transposing will allow finding Centigrade when Fahrenheit is given.)

Step 1. Subtract 32 from each side.

$$F - 32 \; \frac{9}{5} = C$$

Step 2. Multiply both sides by ⅝. This is the same as dividing by ⅘.

$$(F - 32) \; \frac{5}{9} = C$$

Note: it is necessary to enclose the left side in ( ) because every term of that side must be multiplied. When using numbers, it is best to solve inside the ( ) first.

Step 3. The formula can be turned around to have the C on the left side since this is more standard. It is not necessary. The formula is finished the way it is.

$$C = \frac{5}{9} \; (F - 32)$$

SP#3-20 Solve for L:

$$P = 2L + 2W$$

(This is the formula to find perimeter of a rectangle when length and width are known. Transposing will allow solving for length when perimeter and width are given.)

Step 1. Subtract 2W from both sides.

$$P - 2W = 2L$$

Step 2. Divide both sides by 2.

$$\frac{P - 2W}{2} = L$$

☐ When using formulas, usually all of the values will be given except one. When this is the case, simply substitute the given values in place of their respective variables. It is not necessary to transpose the equations prior to substituting values.

Sample Problems: Substituting Values

SP#3-21 Find the value of C for F = 68

$$F = \frac{9}{5} \; C + 32$$

Step 1. Substitute the given value.

$$(68) = \frac{9}{5} \; C + 32$$

Step 2. Subtract 32 from both sides.

$$36 = \frac{9}{5} \; C$$

Step 3. Multiply both sides by ⅝.

$$C = 20$$

SP#3-22 Find L for P = 200 and W = 40

$$P = 2L + 2W$$

Step 1. Substitute the given values.

$$(200) = 2L + 2(40)$$

Step 2. Simplify by performing indicated arithmetic.

$$200 = 2L + 80$$

Step 3. Subtract 80 from both sides.

$$120 = 2L$$

Step 4. Divide both sides by 2.

$$L = 60$$

Practice Problems: Formulas

With each of the following formulas, substitute the given values and solve for the remaining unknown.

(1) $I = \dfrac{V}{R}$ 　　Find: I
　　　　　　　Given: V = 100
　　　　　　　　　　R = 25

(This formula is Ohm's law to solve for current, I, with voltage, V, and resistance, R.)

(2) $I = \dfrac{V}{R}$ 　　Find: R
　　　　　　　Given: V = 50
　　　　　　　　　　I = 10

(3) W= Pt 　　　Find: P
　　　　　　Given: W = 2500
　　　　　　　　　t = 5

(This formula is used to find work, W, with power, P, and time, t.)

(4) W = Pt 　　　Find: W
　　　　　　Given: P = 250
　　　　　　　　　t = 10

(5) $P = I^2R$ 　　Find: R
　　　　　　Given: P = 160
　　　　　　　　　I = 2

(This formula is used to find power, P, with current, I, and resistance, R.)

(6) $P = I^2R$ 　　Find: I
　　　　　　Given: P = 25
　　　　　　　　　R = 1

(Note: to solve for I, it will be necessary to take the square root.)

(7) $R_T = R_1 + R_2$ 　　Find: R_T
　　　　　　　　Given: R_1 = 10
　　　　　　　　　　　R_2 = 25

(This formula is used to find total resistance,

R_T, in a series circuit with two resistors, R1 and R2.)

(8) $R_T = R_1 + R_2$ 　　Find: R_1
　　　　　　　　Given: R_2 = 100
　　　　　　　　　　　R_T = 350

(9) $\dfrac{1}{R_T} = \dfrac{1}{R_1} + \dfrac{1}{R_2}$ 　　Find: R_T
　　　　　　　　　　　Given: R_1 = 10
　　　　　　　　　　　　　　R_2 = 25

(This formula is used to find total resistance, R_T, in a parallel circuit with two resistors, R1 and R2.) Note: it is easiest to use decimals.

(10) $\dfrac{1}{R_T} = \dfrac{1}{R_1} + \dfrac{1}{R_2}$ 　　Find: R_2
　　　　　　　　　　　Given: R_T = 10
　　　　　　　　　　　　　　R_1 = 15

(11) $R_T = \dfrac{(R_1)\,(R_2)}{R_1 + R_2}$ 　　Find: R_T
　　　　　　　　　　Given: R_1 = 30
　　　　　　　　　　　　　R_2 = 60

(This is called the "short-cut" formula for finding the total resistance of two resistors in parallel.)

(12) $R_T = \dfrac{(R_1)\,(R_2)}{R_1 + R_2}$ 　　Find: R_1
　　　　　　　　　　Given: R_T = 100
　　　　　　　　　　　　　R_2 = 200

(13) $X_L = 2\,(\pi)\,f\,L$ 　　Find: X_L
　　　　　　　　　Given: (π) = 3.14
　　　　　　　　　　　　f = 100
　　　　　　　　　　　　L = .2

(This formula is to find inductive reactance, X_L, when given frequency, f, and inductance, L. (π) is a constant in the formula and is always equal to 3.14. Note: all terms are multiplied.)

(14) $X_L = 2\,(\pi)\,f\,L$ 　　Find: f
　　　　　　　　　Given: L = .1
　　　　　　　　　　　　X_L = 37.68

$$(15)\ X_c = \frac{1}{2\,(\pi)\,f\,C}$$

Find: X_c
Given: $f = 1590$
$\quad\quad C = .0000001$

(This formula is to find capacitive reactance, X_c, when given frequency f, and capacitance C.

PROGRAMS FOR THIS CHAPTER

The programs for this chapter are designed for the student to review and practice the rules of shop math. The programs are a good way for the student to quickly find out if he or she remembers the rules and can perform the problems.

It is very important to make an honest attempt at solving the problem, rather than just guessing and allowing the computer to tell you the correct answer.

Each program has "help hints" to review the rules, whenever there is a wrong answer.

Upon completion of each quiz, or whenever desired, press N for your score and return to the SHOP MATH menu.

Figure 3-1 shows the shop math program menu and a sample to preview.

SHOP MATH COMPETENCY TEST

A calculator may not be used when taking this test. Solve each of the problems as indicated by the instructions for each section.

Part 1. Evaluation of Fractions

Arrange the following sets of numbers in ascending order, starting with the smallest.

$$(1)\ \frac{3}{5}\quad\frac{7}{10}\quad\frac{11}{20}\quad\frac{12}{15}$$

$$(2)\ \frac{5}{6}\quad\frac{2}{3}\quad\frac{11}{12}\quad\frac{23}{24}$$

Part 2. Arithmetic with Fractions

Perform the indicated operations, reduce to lowest terms.

$$(3)\quad 5\frac{5}{6} - 2\frac{2}{3}$$

$$(4)\quad 4\frac{3}{4} + 2\frac{5}{8}$$

$$(5)\quad 3\frac{15}{16} - 2\frac{31}{32}$$

$$(6)\quad 2\frac{1}{8} \div \frac{68}{16}$$

$$(7)\quad 6\frac{2}{9} \times 5\frac{3}{3}$$

$$(8)\quad 4\frac{5}{8} - 2\frac{1}{4}$$

$$(9)\quad 8\frac{2}{5} \times 8\frac{1}{3}$$

$$(10)\quad 5\frac{3}{7}\qquad 4\frac{2}{3}$$

(11) If the numerator of a fraction is made smaller, does the value of the fraction increase or decrease?

(12) If the denominator of a fraction is made smaller, does the value of the fraction increase or decrease?

Part 3. Arithmetic with Decimals

Perform the indicated operations with each of the following decimal numbers.

(13) $35.64 + 5.3 + 9.201$
(14) 13.3×9
(15) $0.0023 + 5.408 + 10.5$
(16) $64 \div 8$
(17) $65.03 - 23.8$
(18) 1.25×60.5
(19) $50.0 + 500.005 + 5.550$
(20) $8.1 \div 9$
(21) $0.0067 - 0.0038$
(22) $10 + 10 - .01 + .001 - 01.01$
(23) $8.8 \div 11$
(24) $9.31 \div 0.5$
(25) 10.5×8.075

```
              SHOP  MATH  MENU


      1  FRACTION  TO  DECIMAL

      2  DECIMAL  TO  FRACTION

      3  MIXED  TO  IMPROPER

      4  IMPROPER  TO  PROPER

      5  EVALUATION

      6  OPERATIONS

      7  PERCENT

      8  +  AND  -  NUMBERS

      9  RETURN  TO  MAIN  MENU


WHAT  IS  THE  NUMBER  OF  YOUR  SELECTION  ?




              PROGRAM  SAMPLE:



1.  WHAT  IS  THE  DECIMAL  EQUIVALENT  OF
    THIS  FRACTION

              1/2=?  .5



              CORRECT




    SPACE  BAR  =  NEXT,  E  =  EXIT
```

Fig. 3-1. Shop math program menu and program sample.

Part 4. Converting Fractions to Decimals

Change the following fractions to decimals. Round to three decimal places.

(26) $\dfrac{3}{5}$

(27) $\dfrac{5}{8}$

(28) $3\dfrac{5}{7}$

(29) $4\dfrac{1}{6}$

(30) $\dfrac{8}{6}$

(31) $\dfrac{7}{3}$

Part 5. Converting Decimals to Fractions

Change the following decimals to fractions. Reduce to lowest terms.

(32) 0.666
(33) 0.3
(34) 0.625
(35) 5.6
(36) 6.75
(37) 6.5
(38) 4.05
(39) 5.25

Part 6. Arithmetic with Positive and Negative Numbers

Perform the indicated operations.

(40) $-6 + 2$
(41) $(-4)(-5)$
(42) $9 - 5$
(43) $(-2)(9)$
(44) $1 - 8$
(45) $(6)(-7)$
(46) $0.5 - 0.7$
(47) 9×-8

(48) $-2.5 - -4.7$
(49) $-45 \div 9$

(50) $-\dfrac{5}{6} - \dfrac{2}{3}$

(51) $\dfrac{-5 \times 3}{-6 \times -5}$

(52) $-\dfrac{2}{5} + \dfrac{11}{15}$

(53) $\dfrac{-6}{-8 \times 3}$

(54) $11 + -22$

(55) $\dfrac{(10)\ (9)\ (-7)\ (-6)}{(-5)\ (-4)\ (3)\ (1)}$

(56) $\dfrac{-1 \times -3}{-18}$

(57) $\dfrac{0 \times -1 \times 3}{4 \times -2}$

(58) $\dfrac{-3 \times -2 \times -1}{1 \times 2 \times 3}$

(59) $\dfrac{2 \times 5 \times 8 \times -1}{-1 \times -1 \times -1}$

Part 7. Evaluation of Numbers

With each of the following, use the given value to find the two unknown values.

(60)	$\dfrac{3}{4}$	decimal value?	percent value?
(61)	.25	fraction value?	percent value?
(62)	$66\dfrac{2}{3}\ \%$	fraction value?	decimal value?
(63)	.125	fraction value?	percent value?
(64)	$\dfrac{3}{8}$	decimal value?	percent value?
(65)	.1%	fraction value?	decimal value?

32

(66) .6	fraction value?	percent value?
(67) .5%	fraction value?	decimal value?
(68) .2	fraction value?	fraction value?
(69) 7.5%	fraction value?	decimal value?
(70) 10.5%	fraction value?	decimal value?

Part 8. Percent Tolerance

With each of the following tolerance problems, determine the minimum and maximum allowable values based on the percent tolerance given.

(71) 100 +/− 1%
(72) 270 +/− 2%
(73) 330 +/− 5%
(74) 470 +/− 10%
(75) 680 +/− 20%
(76) 1000 +/− 10%
(77) 5500 +/− 15%
(78) 8200 +/− 5%
(79) 10,000 +/− 15%
(80) 10 +/− 1%

Part 9. Solving Equations

Solve each of the following equations.

(81) $x + 5 = 9$
(82) $7 + y = -10$
(83) $a - 8 = 0$

(84) $2a + 16 = 4a$
(85) $12 - 5x = 3x - 12$
(86) $-x = 16 + 3x$
(87) $-250 = -25y$
(88) $125 = -5a$
(89) $7(5x - 2) = 6(6x - 1)$
(90) $8(2x + 1) = 4(7x + 8)$

Part 10. Solving Formulas

With each of the formulas below, substitute the given quantities and solve the formula for the remaining unknown. Note: $\pi = 3.14$

(91) $A = W\,P$ (Given: W = 1200, P = .06)

(92) $F = \dfrac{9}{5}\,C + 32$ (Given: C = −40)

(93) $F = \dfrac{9}{5}\,C + 32$ (Given: F = 32)

(94) $d = r\,t$ (Given: r = 55, t = 2)
(95) $A = \tfrac{1}{2}\,b\,h$ (Given: A = 64, b = 8)
(96) $P = 2L + 2W$ (Given: P = 100, W = 20)

(97) $R_T = \dfrac{(R_1)\,(R_2)}{R_1 + R_2}$ (Given: R_1 = 10, R_2 = 30)

(98) $\dfrac{1}{R_T} = \dfrac{1}{R_1} + \dfrac{1}{R_2} + \dfrac{1}{R_3}$
(Given: R_1 = 10, R_2 = 25, R_3 = 10)

(99) $X_c = \dfrac{1}{2\,\pi\,f\,C}$ (Given: f = 50, C = .005)

(100) $X_L = 2\,\pi\,f\,L$ (Given: f = 100, L = .1)

Chapter 4

Engineering Notation

Chapter Objectives: To perform mathematical operations on numbers that are both very large and very small by using powers of 10. Also, to use multiplier names to replace the powers of 10. Exponential notation will also be introduced to simplify the use of an electronic calculator.

This chapter also provides an ideal opportunity for the student to master use of the electronic calculator.

Chapter Outline:

- ☐ Introduction
- ☐ Significant figures/rounding numbers
- ☐ Scientific notation
- ☐ Engineering notation
- ☐ Arithmetic operations with powers of 10
- ☐ Programs for this chapter
- ☐ Engineering notation competency test

INTRODUCTION

Engineering notation, scientific notation and exponential notation are methods of dealing with numbers that are either very large or very small. In electronics, as in most scientific fields, numbers at both extremes are quite common.

In this chapter, the task of determining the significant figures of a number and rounding will be discussed. The electronic calculator, the most widely used tool, makes use of exponential notation when accepting keyboard inputs and displaying the answer.

SIGNIFICANT FIGURES/ROUNDING NUMBERS

With all the calculations that an electronics student makes, it is sometimes believed that all those calculations are accurate. Even though mathematics is very precise, with decimal places carried out to extremes, the accuracy of the calculations really depends on the numbers being used.

Numbers have two sources: measured and theoretical. When calculating circuits with either theoretical or measured values, it is important to keep in mind the fact that the components used in the circuit all have tolerances and the instruments used to measure the circuits have tolerances. All of these tolerances lead to a considerable amount of inaccuracies. There is no sense in having numbers carried to several decimal places if the accuracy is in question. Usually, calculations are made to have three significant figures.

Significant Figures

The significant figures, or digits, of a number are the figures considered reliable. There are two guidelines to follow to determine the significant figures of a number:

1. All nonzero numbers (digits 1 - 9) are significant figures.
2. A zero used as a place holder between two nonzero numbers is significant.

Examples of Significant Figures:

1234 has four significant figures
1230 has three significant figures
1200 has two significant figures
.00123 has three significant figures
0.123 has three significant figures
25.5 has three significant figures

Rounding Numbers

Numbers are rounded to make them easier to work with, especially when arithmetic is involved. For example, if a person is counting money stacked in groups of $1000, an extra $2 might be considered insignificant. Therefore, $1002 would be rounded off to $1000.

Procedure for Rounding Numbers:

1. Determine how many significant figures will appear in the final number. The next digit to the right will determine the outcome of rounding.
2. If the number to the right is 5 or more, add 1 to the last significant figure and drop all the digits to the right.
3. If the number to the right is less than 5, do not adjust the last figure, simply drop all digits to the right.

4. Replace dropped digits with zeros, as place holders, to maintain place values of the significant figures.

Examples of Rounding Numbers

The following are rounded to three significant figures.

806,956 = 807,000
875.5 = 876
80.78 = 80.8
98 = 100

Practice Problems: Rounding Numbers

Round each of the following numbers to three significant figures.

(1) 6408
(2) 4715
(3) 5352
(4) 9880
(5) 102,589
(6) 340,301
(7) 119,815
(8) 209,280
(9) 327.09
(10) 452.11
(11) 999.99
(12) 223.51
(13) 56.257
(14) 69.5002
(15) 10.619
(16) 25.882
(17) 1.0578
(18) 3.5266
(19) 5.9929
(20) 8.9148
(21) 0.003599
(22) 0.002677
(23) 0.005555
(24) 0.006666
(25) 0.003333
(26) 0.009999

(27) 0.900356
(28) 0.870009
(29) 0.505050
(30) 0.959595

SCIENTIFIC NOTATION

Scientific notation is a shorthand method of writing numbers that are extremely large or extremely small. The numbers are written as a number between 1 and 10 times a power of 10.

Place Values

The "everyday" system of numbers that we use is based on powers of 10. Each place value is a multiple of 10. Starting at the decimal point, the first place value is the ones column, which is 10^0 (10 to the zero power; any number raised to the zero power is 1). The next place value is the tens column, which is 10^1 (10 to the 1st power). The next place value is the hundreds column, which is 10^2 (10 to the 2nd power or 10 times 10).

Each place value is the next higher power of 10. Numbers below one, on the right side of the decimal point, have a negative power of 10. The 1st decimal place is 10^{-1} and each place to the right is the appropriate negative power of 10. Table 4-1 shows the power of 10 for each place value. Notice how the powers increase in the positive and negative directions.

Scientific notation takes advantage of the place values each having their own power of 10. The most significant digit, the one furthest to the left, even if it is a decimal number, is always a nonzero number (between 1 and 10). When the number is written in scientific notation, the most significant digit will be a number between 1 and 10, the other digits are written as decimals and the number is shown as multiplied by the power of 10 of the most significant digit. In this way, arithmetic is easier to perform because the majority of place holder zeros have been removed and the powers of 10 can be handled separately.

Exponential Notation

In order to further simplify the writing of numbers in scientific notation, an exponential notation is used. This method replaces the indicated multiplication of 10 to a power with "E" followed by the power of 10. For example, if the desired power of 10 is 10^2, then the exponential form would be E2.

Writing Numbers in
Scientific and Exponential Notation

Numbers larger than 1: are expressed in scientific notation by moving the decimal point to the **left** enough places to write the number between 1 and 10. The number of places the decimal point is moved is the **positive** power of 10.

Table 4-1. Place Values.

Power of 10	"E" Notation	As a Number	Expressed Verbally
10^6	E6	1,000,000	ten to the SIXTH power
10^5	E5	100,000	ten to the FIFTH power
10^4	E4	10,000	ten to the FOURTH power
10^3	E3	1,000	ten to the THIRD power
10^2	E2	100	ten to the SECOND power
10^1	E1	10	ten to the FIRST power
10^0	E0	1	ten to the ZERO power
10^{-1}	E−1	.1	ten to the NEGATIVE FIRST power
10^{-2}	E−2	.01	ten to the NEGATIVE SECOND power
10^{-3}	E−3	.001	ten to the NEGATIVE THIRD power
10^{-4}	E−4	.0001	ten to the NEGATIVE FOURTH power
10^{-5}	E−5	.00001	ten to the NEGATIVE FIFTH power
10^{-6}	E−6	.000001	ten to the NEGATIVE SIXTH power

Examples of Numbers Larger than 1:

$$68,500 = 6.85 \times 10^4 = 6.85E4$$
$$563,000,000 = 5.63 \times 10^8 = 5.63E8$$
$$230 = 2.30 \times 10^2 = 2.30E2$$
$$7,602 = 7.602 \times 10^3 = 7.602E3$$
$$7.3 = 7.3 \times 10^0 = 7.3E0$$

Numbers Less Than 1: are expressed in scientific notation by moving the decimal point to the **right** enough places to write the number between 1 and 10. The number of places the decimal point is moved is the **negative** power of 10.

Examples of Numbers Less Than 1:

$$.1 = 1.0 \times 10^{-1} = 1.0E\text{-}1$$
$$0.023 = 2.3 \times 10^{-2} = 2.3E\text{-}2$$
$$0.000356 = 3.56 \times 10^{-4} = 3.56E\text{-}4$$
$$0.0000003 = 3.0 \times 10^{-7} = 3.0E\text{-}7$$

Adjusting Numbers with Powers of 10

Quite often, numbers are already written as a number times a power of 10, or, with the calculator, as a number times 10 to the exponent of a number. These numbers often do not have the power of 10 in the most proper form (a good analogy is when dealing with fractions that need to be reduced). This is usually a result of having performed arithmetic. Knowing how to adjust properly is very important, especially when using engineering notation and the electronic calculator.

- ☐ The decimal point moved to the **left** is **Postive**; **Right** is **Negative**.
- ☐ Use the rules of signed numbers to add/subtract powers of 10.
- ☐ Examples of adjusting powers of 10:

$$840,000,000E3 = 8.4E11$$
$$0.00035E7 = 3.5E3$$
$$0.0075E3 = 7.5E0 = 7.5$$
$$0.000062E\text{-}3 = 6.2E\text{-}8$$

Removing the Power of 10

Sometimes it is necessary to remove the power of 10. This is especially useful when making changes in engineering notation and interpreting answers produced with a calculator.

To remove a **positive** power of 10: move the decimal to the RIGHT the same number of places as the power of 10.

Examples of Removing Positive Powers:

$$6.7E6 = 6,700,000$$
$$7.5E4 = 75,000$$
$$80E2 = 8000$$

To remove a NEGATIVE power of 10: move the decimal to the **left** the same number of places as the power of 10.

Examples of Removing Negative Powers:

$$8.1E-6 = 0.0000081$$
$$2.9E-3 = 0.0029$$
$$500E-2 = 5.0$$

Practice Problems:
Writing in Scientific Notation

Part A. Writing in Notation Form. Write the following numbers in scientific notation (as a number between 1 and 10 times the proper power of 10. Example: $57,000 = 5.7 \times 10^4$). Also, write each in "E" notation (as a number between 1 and 10 followed by E and the power of 10. Examples: $57,000 = 5.7E4$)

(1) 876,000
(2) 1,030,000,000
(3) 43,000
(4) 25
(5) 6.9
(6) .003
(7) .0000032
(8) 0.0000450
(9) .00000000159
(10) .500
(11) 12,000E5
(12) 5320E3

(13) .000035E3
(14) .045E0
(15) .000000067E9
(16) $25,000 \times 10^{-3}$
(17) 35E-6
(18) .02E-5
(19) $.000056 \times 10^{-3}$
(20) $.950 \times 10^1$

Part B. Removing the Power of 10. Remove the power of 10 from the following numbers.

(21) 4.8E5
(22) 850E3
(23) .003E6
(24) .000025E1
(25) 250E0
(26) 100E-4
(27) 55E-3
(28) 68000E3
(29) $.000025 \times 10^{-6}$
(30) 1×10^1

ENGINEERING NOTATION

Engineering notation is a modification of scientific notation. Scientific notation is used so frequently that names have been given to the various powers of 10. In electronics, and most scientific fields, the names are used only with the powers of 10 that are multiples of 3.

Multiplier Names

The names given to the power of 10 are called multiplier names. Table 4-2 shows the powers of 10, their respective multiplier names and E notation.

Each of the names are also given symbols which are used to further simplify the writing of numbers. The table shows the multiplier names (and symbols) but does not specify any specific unit. For example, the unit for power is the watt, which can be written with the name kilo to represent 1000 watts or milliwatts to represent 1/1000th watt.

The names are all prefixes, which means that each of the names must be written in front of (and attached to) the unit name. This combination of prefix and unit forms a new word, which means the unit is multiplied by the prefix.

The student needs to memorize the various multiplier names and their multiplication values, or powers of 10. Then, as the individual units are introduced, the multiplier names can be attached to the units for the desired results.

Table 4-2. Multiplier Names.

Multiplier Name	Symbol	Multiply By	Power of 10	"E" Notation
tera	T	1,000,000,000,000 (one trillion)	10^{12}	E12
giga	G	1,000,000,000 (one billion)	10^9	E9
mega (meg)	M	1,000,000 (one million)	10^6	E6
kilo	k	1,000 (one thousand)	10^3	E3
Basic unit (no multiplier)			10^0	E0
milli	m	0.001 (one one-thousandth)	10^{-3}	E−3
micro	μ (Greek letter mu)	0.000 001 (one one-millionth)	10^{-6}	E−6
nano	n	0.000 000 001 (one one-billionth)	10^{-9}	E−9
pico	p	0.000 000 000 001 (one one-trillionth)	10^{-12}	E−12

Writing Numbers Using Engineering Notation

☐ To write a number using engineering notation, the number should first be written in scientific notation. There is one modification, however; the power of 10 must be a multiple of 3. The power of 10 is then replaced with the multiplier name.

Table 4-3 shows examples of numbers that have been written in engineering notation and in exponential notation. Keep in mind that exponential notation is a way of expressing 10 raised to a power.

The multiplier names can also be replaced by their respective symbols with the symbol for the unit. For example, kilowatts can be written kW and millivolts can be mV. Notice that the symbols of multipliers larger than 1 are capital letters, except kilo, and that the symbols smaller than 1 are small letters. The unit symbols are usually capital letters.

Converting within Engineering Notation

Sometimes a number will be written with its multiplier and units but it is not written in the most convenient form. When this happens, it is possible, through the use of scientific notation, to convert the multiplier names to a better form. For example; 3,000 kilovolts would be better written as 3 megavolts and 0.025 millivolts would be better as 25 microvolts.

☐ When converting from one multiplier to another, the *actual value* of the number does not change.

☐ Steps to convert within engineering notation:

(1) Replace the multiplier name with its power of 10.
(2) To simplify the conversion, remove the power of 10 by replacing the zeros and returning to a number with no multiplier (return to basic units).
(3) Convert to scientific notation with the desired power of 10.
(4) Replace the power of 10 with its correct engineering notation multiplier name.

Sample Problems of Converting Engineering Notation

SP#4-1 Convert 475 kilovolts to megavolts.

(1) 475 kV = 475E3 V
(2) 475,000 V
(3) .475E6 V
(4) .475 MV (megavolts)

SP#4-2 Convert .000255 milliamps to microamps.

(1) .000255 mA = .000255E-3 amps
(2) .000 000 255 amps
(3) .255E-6 amps
(4) .255 μA (microamps)

Table 4-3. Engineering Notation.

Number with Unit	Written in "E" Notation	Written in Engineering Notation
86,000,000,000,000 hertz	86E12 hertz	86 terahertz
2,000,000,000 hertz	2E9 hertz	2 gigahertz
15,000,000 watts	15E6 watts	15 megawatts
368,000 ohms	368E3 ohms	368 kilohms
20 amps	20E0 amps	20 amps (no change)
0.065 henry	65E-3 henry	65 millihenry
0.000 125 volts	125E-6 volts	125 microvolts
0.000 000 034 seconds	34E-9 seconds	34 nanoseconds
0.000 000 000 005 farads	5E-12 farads	5 picofarads

SP#4-3 Convert .000 004 microfarads to picofarads.

(1) .000 004 μF = .000 004E-6 farads
(2) .000 000 000 004 farads
(3) 4E-12
(4) 4 pF (picofarads)

SP#4-4 Convert 2.5 kilohms to ohms

(1) 2.5 kΩ = 2.5E3 Ω
(2) 2,500 Ω (ohms)

The following set of practice problems will provide the student with practice in converting numbers within engineering notation.

Practice Problems:
Converting Engineering Notation

Convert each of the given numbers to the units shown.

(1)	5,600,000 ohms		kΩ		MΩ
(2)	273,000 hertz		kHz		MHz
(3)	2,900 watts		mW		kW
(4)	15 amps		mA		kA
(5)	.0035 volts		mV		μV
(6)	.125 henry		mH		μH
(7)	.000 000 05 farads		μF		nF
(8)	.000 0087 seconds		μs		ms
(9)	250 milliwatts		W		kW
(10)	1500 millivolts		kV		V
(11)	.055 milliamps		μA		A
(12)	.000 001 milliseconds		s		μs
(13)	630 kilohertz		Hz		MHz
(14)	250,000 kilowatts		MW		W
(15)	.000 75 kiloamps		A		mA
(16)	.005 kilovolts		mV		V
(17)	25 microvolts		mV		nV
(18)	.75 microamps		nA		A
(19)	50 nanofarads		μF		pF
(20)	.05 nanoseconds		s		μs
(21)	150 picofarads		nF		μF
(22)	75 megohms		kΩ		GΩ
(23)	.003 megahertz		Hz		kHz
(24)	1200 gigawatts		MW		W
(25)	.005 terahertz		MHz		GHz

ARITHMETIC OPERATIONS WITH POWERS OF 10

One of the advantages of using scientific and engineering notations is the ease in dealing with arithmetic operations.

There are two sets of rules for handling the decimal point: addition/subtraction and multiplication/division.

Addition/Subtraction

The rule for addition and subtraction with decimal numbers is to align decimal points in a column. By doing this, the addition/subtraction operation is performed with numbers that have the same place value. For example, the ones column, the tens column, etc.

☐ To add or subtract numbers containing powers of 10 (scientific notation or engineering notation); the powers of 10 **must** be the same and the operation will be performed as with any decimal numbers.

Sample Problems of Addition/Subtraction

SP#4-5 Add: 25.3 kilohms + 4.68 kilohms =

(1) The powers of 10 need no change because they are the same.
(2) Perform the addition as with any decimal numbers.

$$
\begin{array}{r}
25.3 \ \text{kilohms} \\
+ \ \ 4.68 \ \text{kilohms} \\
\hline
29.98 \ \text{kilohms}
\end{array}
$$

SP#4-6 Add: 1.5 megawatts + 250 kilowatts =

(1) The powers of 10 are different. Change megawatts to kilowatts.
(2) Add the numbers in kilowatts.

$$
\begin{array}{rr}
1.5 \ \text{MW} = & 1500 \ \text{kW} \\
+ & 250 \ \text{kW} \\
\hline
& 1750 \ \text{kW}
\end{array}
$$

SP#4-7 Add: 15 amps + 3 milliamps =

(1) The powers of 10 are different. Change milliamps to amps.
(2) Add the numbers in amps.

$$
\begin{array}{rr}
3 \ \text{mA} = & 0.003 \ \ \text{A} \\
+ & 15 \ \ \ \ \ \ \text{A} \\
\hline
& 15.003 \ \ \text{A}
\end{array}
$$

SP#4-8 Subtract: .150 kilovolts − 80 volts =

(1) The powers of 10 are different. Change kilovolts to volts.
(2) Subtract the numbers in volts.

$$
\begin{array}{rr}
0.150 \ \text{kV} = & 150 \ \ \text{V} \\
- & 80 \ \ \text{V} \\
\hline
& 70 \ \ \text{V}
\end{array}
$$

Multiplication/Division

It is not necessary to align the decimal points, as it is with addition or subtraction. Instead, the arithmetic operation is performed and the decimal point is adjusted. If the operations of multiplication and division of decimal numbers is examined, two very simple rules can be formed to deal with the powers of 10.

When performing multiplication with decimal numbers, the multiplication is performed and the decimal places are added together. When performing division with decimal numbers, the division is performed and the decimal point is adjusted to the right (in the negative direction).

☐ Perform the arithmetic operation as with any decimal numbers. Adjust the decimal point as follows: to multiply numbers, add the powers of 10; to divide numbers, subtract the powers of 10 (numerator minus denominator).

Sample Problems of Multiplication/Division

SP#4-9 Multiply: 2 milliamps × 25 megohms =

(1) Convert from engineering notation to powers of 10 (E notation) with the basic units.
(2) Perform the multiplication.
(3) Add the powers of 10.
(4) Re-combine the results of the multiplication with the power of 10, then write the final answer in engineering notation.

$$2 \ \text{mA} \times 25 \ \text{M}\Omega = 2E-3 \ \text{A} \times 25E6 \ \Omega$$
$$2 \times 25 = 50$$
$$E-3 + E6 = E3$$
$$50E3 = 50 \ \text{kilovolts}$$

SP#4-10 Multiply: 15 milliamps × 10 volts =

(1) Peform the multiplication.
(2) Add the powers of 10.

$$15 \ \text{mA} \times 100 \ \text{V} = 15E-3 \ \text{A} \times 100E0 \ \text{V}$$
$$15 \times 100 = 1500$$

E−3 + EO = E−3
1500 × E−3 = 1500 milliwatts
1500 mW = 1.5 W

SP#4-11 Multiply: 6.28 × 10 kilohertz × .5 millihenry =

(1) Perform the multiplication.
(2) Add the powers of 10.

6.28 × 10 kHz × .5 mH =
6.28 × 10E3 Hz × .5E−3 H
6.28 × 10 × .5 = 31.4
E3 + E−3 = EO
31.4E0 = 31.4 ohms

SP#4-12 Divide: 100 volts / 25 milliamps =

(1) Perform the division.
(2) Subtract the powers of 10. (numerator minus denominator)

100 V / 25 mA = 100E0 V / 25E−3 A
100 ÷ 25 = 4
E0 − E−3 = E3
4E3 = 4 kilohms

SP#4-13 Divide: 12 milliwatts / 60 volts =

(1) Perform the division.
(2) Subtract the powers of 10. (numerator minus denominator)

12 mW / 60 V = 12E−3 W / 60E0 V
12 ÷ 60 = .2
E−3 − EO = E−3
.2E−3 = .2 milliamps

SP#4-14 Divide: 6 milliwatts / 3 milliamps =

(1) Perform the division.
(2) Subtract the powers of 10. (Use caution when subtracting signs.)

6 mW / 3 mA = 6E−3 W / 3E−3 A
6 divided by 3 = 2

E−3 − E−3 = EO
2E0 = 2 volts

SP#4-15 Multiply: 5 milliamps × 10 kilohms =

(1) Perform the multiplication.
(2) Add the powers of 10.

5 mA × 10 kΩ = 5E−3 A × 10E3 Ω
5 × 10 = 50
E−3 + E3 = EO
50E0 = 50 volts

Practice Problems: Arithmetic Operations

Perform the indicated operations with each of the following problems. Write the answer using the appropriate engineering notation, with three significant figures.

(1) 2.2 kilohms + 3.3 kilohms =
(2) 480 ohms + 620 ohms =
(3) 48 MW + 100 kilowatts =
(4) .250 kV − 150 volts =
(5) 1.5 amps + 250 milliamps =
(6) 6.8 mW − 3.5 mW =
(7) .35 millihenries + 100 μH =
(8) .01 microfarads + .001 μF =
(9) 10 kV − 10 mV =
(10) 5 uF + 25 picofarads =
(11) 15 amps × 10 ohms = (volts)
(12) 25 mA × 300 ohms = (volts)
(13) 50 mA × 1.2 kilohms = (volts)
(14) 30 mA × 25 volts = (watts)
(15) 50 μA × 10 volts = (watts)

(16) $\dfrac{100 \text{ volts}}{25 \text{ kilohms}}$ = (amps)

(17) $\dfrac{25 \text{ volts}}{10 \text{ milliamps}}$ = (ohms)

(18) $\dfrac{50 \text{ kilowatts}}{100 \text{ kilovolts}}$ = (amps)

(19) $\dfrac{430 \text{ milliwatts}}{4.3 \text{ microamps}}$ = (volts)

$$(20) \quad \frac{200 \text{ V} \times 200 \text{ V}}{4 \text{ kilohms}} = \text{(watts)}$$

PROGRAMS FOR THIS CHAPTER

The programs for this chapter are designed to quiz the student in the various concepts involved in rounding off, significant figures, scientific notation and engineering notation, with special emphasis placed on exponential notation.

The programs provide excellent practice after the student has mastered the rules. Whenever there is a wrong answer, the computer will offer a series of "helpful hints" for the purpose of reviewing the rules. Always keep in mind that the computer programs are only a supplement to the text and that they are not intended to replace proper study and practice with the practice problems.

This chapter is also a good place for the student to begin using an electronic calculator. It will be very important later to have a working knowledge of how the calculator uses exponential notation.

Figure 4-1 shows the program menu for scientific notation and a sample of the program to preview.

ENGINEERING
NOTATION COMPETENCY TEST

A. Round each of the following to three significant figures.

(1) 103,859
(2) 555,555
(3) 320.8
(4) 598.3
(5) 639.56
(6) 231.37
(7) 0.714285714
(8) .09090909
(9) .66666666
(10) .333333333

B. Write each of the following in scientific notation (as a number between 1 and 10 times the proper power of 10. Example: $57,000 = 5.7 \times 10^4$).

(11) 876,000
(12) 3,200
(13) 980,000,000
(14) 1,200,000
(15) 0.00000035
(16) 0.000189
(17) 0.0002
(18) 1.8
(19) 2500×10^3
(20) $.0036 \times 10^{-5}$

C. Write each of the following in exponential "E" notation (as a number between 1 and 10 followed by "E" and the power of 10. Example: $57,000 = 5.7E4$).

(21) 250,000
(22) 1,800
(23) 68,000,000
(24) 560
(25) 0.00000000025
(26) 0.00000357
(27) 0.0013
(28) 0.00098
(29) 560,000E-2
(30) 0.0000047E3

D. Convert each of the numbers on the left to the new units shown.

(31) 25000 V	_____	kV
(32) 1.25 A	_____	mA
(33) 25.5 mW	_____	W
(34) 3.5 kHz	_____	Hz
(35) .015 mH	_____	μH
(36) 680 μH	_____	mH
(37) 1500 μF	_____	pF
(38) 37,000 kΩ	_____	MΩ
(39) .000082 V	_____	μV
(40) .000960 A	_____	mA

E. Perform the indicated operations with each of the following problems. Write the answer using the most appropriate engineering notation, use three significant figures. The units shown in ( ) will be the resultant units without the engineering notation.

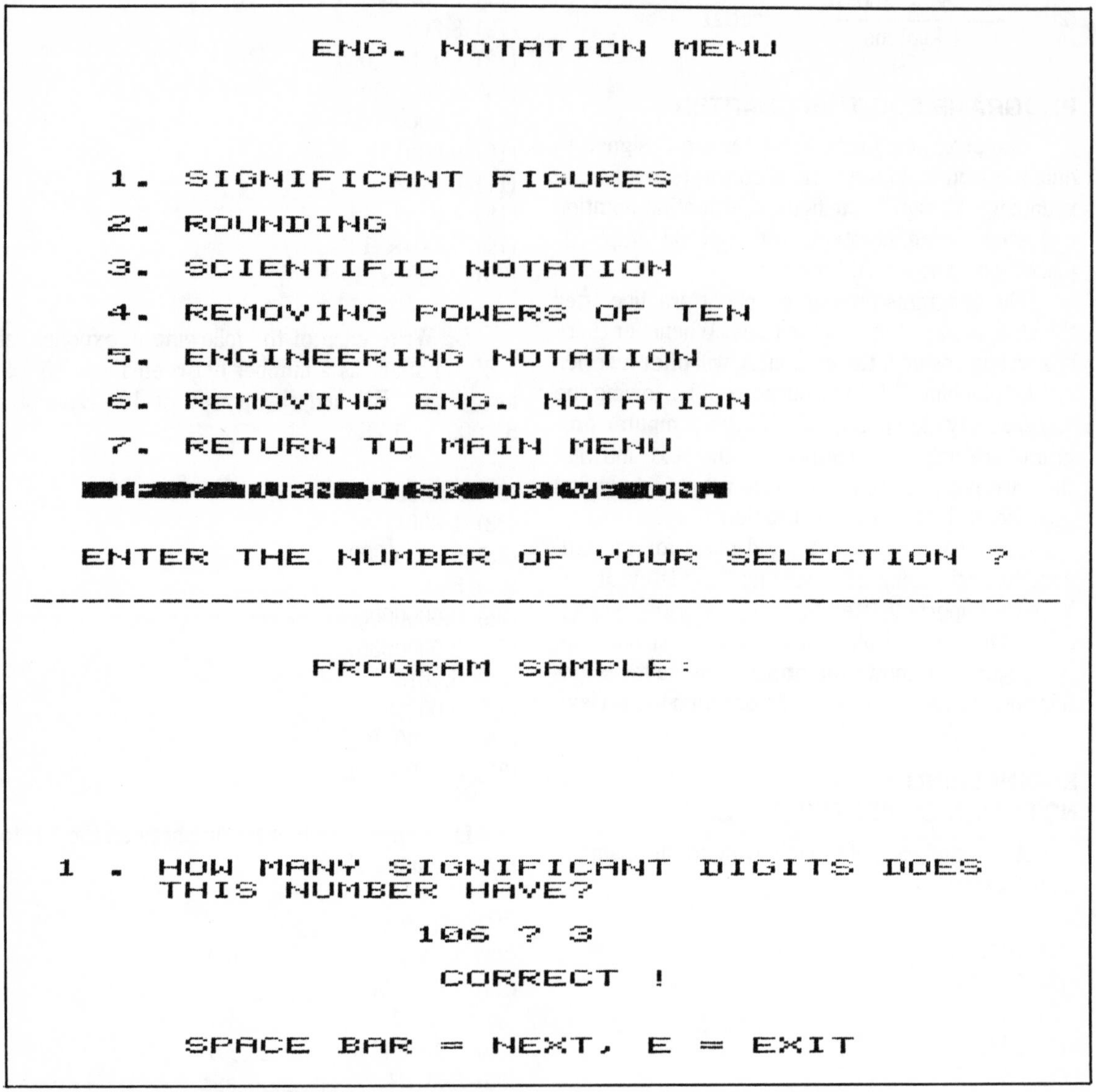

```
        ENG. NOTATION MENU


    1. SIGNIFICANT FIGURES

    2. ROUNDING

    3. SCIENTIFIC NOTATION

    4. REMOVING POWERS OF TEN

    5. ENGINEERING NOTATION

    6. REMOVING ENG. NOTATION

    7. RETURN TO MAIN MENU
    ████████████████████████

 ENTER THE NUMBER OF YOUR SELECTION ?
 ─────────────────────────────────────

          PROGRAM SAMPLE:




  1 . HOW MANY SIGNIFICANT DIGITS DOES
      THIS NUMBER HAVE?

           106 ? 3

          CORRECT !

   SPACE BAR = NEXT, E = EXIT
```

Fig. 4-1. Engineering notation program menu and program sample.

(41) 5.6 kilohms + 8.2 kilohms = (ohms)

(42) 280 ohms + 460 ohms = (ohms)

(43) 23 MW + 3500 kW = (watts)

(44) .250 mV − 125 μV = (volts)

(45) 25 amps × 20 ohms = (volts)

(46) 50 mA × 300 ohms = (volts)

(47) 20 mA × .125 kV = (watts)

(48) $\dfrac{200 \text{ volts}}{25 \text{ kilohms}}$ = (amps)

(49) $\dfrac{50 \text{ volts}}{10 \text{ milliamps}}$ = (ohms)

(50) $\dfrac{750 \text{ milliwatts}}{250 \text{ microamps}}$ = (volts)

44

Chapter 5

Introduction to DC Circuit Components

Chapter Objective: To learn the principles of basic components used in dc circuits. The components will each be examined as to how they are manufactured, rated and used.

This chapter will also introduce schematic symbols and schematic drawings.

Chapter Outline:

- ☐ Dc Voltage Sources
- ☐ Conductors
- ☐ Switches
- ☐ Fuses and Circuit Breakers
- ☐ Resistors
- ☐ Resistor Color Code
- ☐ Introduction to Schematic Diagrams
- ☐ Programs for this Chapter
- ☐ Dc Circuit Components Competency Test

INTRODUCTION

Circuits that use a dc voltage source are dc circuits. The dc stands for direct current. This simply means that the current flows only in one direction, versus ac voltage which alternates or reverses direction periodically.

The various circuit components discussed in this chapter all have very important roles in forming a complete circuit. The dc circuits form the basic rules for all circuits.

DC VOLTAGE SOURCES

The dc voltages can be produced from three general categories: power supplies, batteries and voltage cells. Power supplies are electronic circuits that change ac to dc through the use of rectifier diodes. Batteries produce a voltage through a chemical process. Voltage cells produce voltage by either light or heat striking the surface.

Power Supplies

A power supply is an electronic circuit that produces a dc voltage by converting ac to dc using rectifier diodes. Power supplies are rated according to their output voltage and output current handling capacity. The output voltage can be either fixed (unchangeable) or it can be variable over a wide range. The output current is determined by the manufacturer and will have a protective device, such as a fuse, to prevent damage in the event of overloading.

Examples of power supplies around the home are: a battery charger for a car; ac-dc converter for a radio. These two examples have two things in common—they both plug into the house electrical outlet and they both produce a dc voltage output.

Photo-Voltaic Cells

The most common type of photo-voltaic cell is the *solar cell*. When light energy strikes a solar cell, it causes the electrons inside the cell to move—current flows. More light causes more motion and so more current flows.

The actual voltage produced, and the output current capacity, depends upon the construction of the cell and how many cells are connected together. Normally, the voltage and current for any one cell is quite small, but several cells can be connected together to achieve the desired results.

Solar cells are in wide use with such items as pocket calculators, battery chargers, light-sensor switches, power for satellite stations, power for remote radios, etc.

Batteries

When a source of dc voltage is mentioned, usually a battery is the first thing to come to mind. "Storage batteries," as they are sometimes called, use chemical reactions to produce electricity. There are two basic types of batteries: wet cell and dry cell. Either type of battery operates in much the same manner. There are two electrodes, each made of different material, and an electrolyte.

Dry cell batteries are the type used in flashlights, portable radios, etc. The center terminal is the positive electrode and the flat back end is the negative electrode. The electrolyte is the chemical inside the battery that causes the reaction to produce electricity. The electrolyte can be an alkaline substance, or of various chemicals in a gel or paste form. The output voltage of a typical dry cell battery is approximately 1.5 volts. It is possible to connect several of these dry cells together to produce a higher voltage. Some batteries actually connect more than one cell with another inside the same container, such as the common 6 volt "lantern" battery.

Wet cell batteries are the type used in an automobile or motorcycle. The electrolyte in this type is a liquid, usually a strong acid. Each wet cell has the voltage output of approximately 2 volts. Therefore, a 12 volt car battery has 6 cells connected together. An important difference between wet cells and dry cells is their current handling ability. The wet cell can produce much more current than the dry cell.

Ampere-Hour Rating of Batteries

The ampere-hour rating of a battery is the rating of how long the battery will provide current before it is discharged. This is also known as the storage capacity of the battery. Usually this kind of rating is given to wet cells, especially car batteries.

If the ampere-hour rating of a particular battery is 60 ampere-hours; 60 amps of current can be drawn from the battery for 1 hour or 1 amp can be drawn for 60 hours.

Keep in mind that ratings of any product are stated for an item when it is new and under the most ideal of conditions. Temperature, for example, greatly affects the capacity of a battery. When it is cold, a battery loses much of its strength.

Schematic Symbols of DC Voltage Sources

Schematic symbols are used to represent different devices or components on a schematic drawing. A schematic drawing shows how an electric circuit is connected.

Figure 5-1 shows the schematic symbols for each of the three basic types of voltage sources. A dc voltage cell is represented by parallel lines with one shorter than the other. The longer of the two lines represents the positive terminal and the shorter of the two lines represents the negative terminal. It is not necessary to draw the positive sign next to the larger line, although it is a good practice.

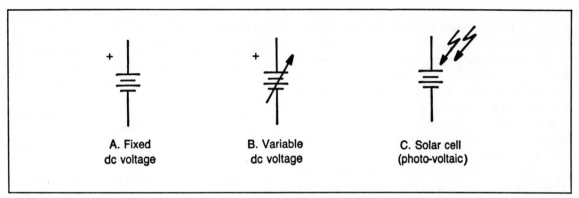

Fig. 5-1. Schematic symbols of dc voltage sources.

Figure 5-1A is the symbol for a fixed voltage source. This means that the voltage cannot be changed. This symbol would be used to represent a battery or any other fixed dc voltage source. Notice that the symbol contains two cells, back to back. This is the most common method of drawing the voltage symbol. Older books use several cells in the drawings.

Figure 5-1B is the symbol for a variable voltage source. This symbol would be used to represent a dc power supply whose output voltage can be varied. Notice that the symbol is the same as for the fixed voltage except that there is an arrow drawn through the cells. The arrow is used in many schematic symbols to signify "variable."

Figure 5-1C is the symbol for any photo-voltaic cell or solar cell. The basic voltage source symbol is shown with arrows pointing at the symbol. These arrows are used to represent light striking the cell's surface.

CONDUCTORS

The purpose of a conductor is to carry the electricity from one point to another. A good conductor has the least amount of resistance to the flow of electricity.

Conductor Materials

Generally speaking, metals make reasonably good conductors of electricity. Metals have a large number of electrons free to travel from one atom to the next. Since electrons are the current carriers, more free electrons mean electricity can flow more easily.

Insulators (such as plastic, rubber, wood, etc.) have very few free electrons and resist the flow of electricity.

At room temperature, all materials fall somewhere between a perfect conductor, which offers no resistance, and a perfect insulator, which offers infinite resistance. Most materials can be classified as either a conductor or an insulator.

The conductor material is important because so much of it is used, and it will determine cost, current carrying ability, ease of assembly and several other factors. The best conductor materials are:

☐ Silver
☐ Copper
☐ Gold
☐ Aluminum

Conductor Sizes

The physical size of the conductor must also be considered because it will have a great effect on the cost, current capacity, and ease of handling. The materials mentioned as the best choices for a conductor are all expensive and heavy in large quantities.

The larger wire size will have less resistance to the flow of electricity and can carry more current. Smaller wire sizes are cheaper and easier to work with (except very small wire). Every application of a wire is a compromise between these considerations.

In addition to the size, wire is also available in both solid and stranded wire. Stranded wire has an end result of being the same size as solid except that it is made of individual strands of wire twisted together. Stranding provides flexibility and the more strands used to make a particular wire, the more flexible it becomes.

Wire sizes are given as gauge numbers. The AWG (American Wire Gauge) number is the method by which wire is bought and sold. The following abbreviated list shows how the wires are numbered and their sizes. Note: smaller AWG numbers represent larger wires. Two examples of common uses of different size wires are; 14 gauge is common in household wiring, 22 gauge is common in electronic circuit wiring.

AWG #	Diameter (mils)
0000	460.0
2	258.0
6	162.0
10	102.0
14	64.0
18	40.0
20	32.0
22	25.3
36	5.0

Note: "mils" equals 1/1000 inches. 0000 AWG is approximately ½ inch in diameter, 18 AWG is about the thickness of the lead in a wooden pencil, 36 AWG is about the thickness of human hair.

SWITCHES

Switches are a very important part of any electrical circuit. They enable the user to control, not only off and on functions, but many other switching functions.

This section will deal with some of the more commonly used types of switches to allow the student to become familiar with the schematic symbols and to the operation of switches in circuits. Figure 5-2 shows several switches to be discussed.

Toggle Switches

A toggle switch is the type of switch often thought of as an "on/off" switch. For example, the switches used for the lights in a house are toggle switches. Figure 5-2A shows another type of toggle switch. This type is mounted through a panel with access to the switch lever from the front.

There are many different styles of switches that serve the same function as the toggle switch. The only difference is the style, and how it looks from the outside. Two of these styles are slide and rocker, and a drawing of these can be seen in Fig. 5-2.

Schematic Symbols

The schematic symbol of a switch shows that the switch "makes" or "breaks" the circuit. Often, the switch is drawn in an "open" position, with the switch line not making contact. When a switch is drawn in the open position, it symbolizes that the circuit is in a "break" condition and that the switch must be "closed" to "make" the current operate. Examine Fig. 5-3A. This simple switch is known as

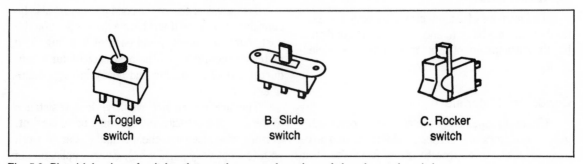

A. Toggle switch

B. Slide switch

C. Rocker switch

Fig. 5-2. Pictorial drawings of switches that use the same schematic symbol as the toggle switch.

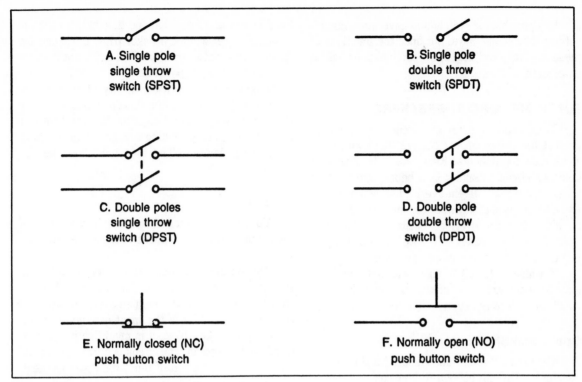

A. Single pole
single throw
switch (SPST)

B. Single pole
double throw
switch (SPDT)

C. Double poles
single throw
switch (DPST)

D. Double pole
double throw
switch (DPDT)

E. Normally closed (NC)
push button switch

F. Normally open (NO)
push button switch

Fig. 5-3. Schematic symbols of switches.

an on/off switch. It is a perfect example of make-break.

Figure 5-3A represents a single pole single throw (SPST) toggle switch. The straight lines with the small circles represent the wires and switch terminals. The line drawn at an angle represents the switch contact. This switch is drawn in the open position. It could also be drawn in a closed position. The SPST switch can be used only to control one circuit path.

Figure 5-3B shows the schematic symbol of a single pole double throw (SPDT) switch. Notice that there are places for three wires to be connected to the terminals of this switch. The center terminal is called "common." The left and right sides are two different circuits, with the center terminal common to both circuits. The switch is used to select which circuit, right or left, will be connected to the center common.

Figure 5-3C is the symbol of a double pole single throw (DPST) switch. This switch is two single throw (DPST) switch. This switch is two single

pole switches operated by the same switch level. Two circuit paths, usually the two wires of the same circuit, go to the switch terminals and the switch will turn on or off both of the wires at the same time.

Figure 5-3D shows a double pole double throw (DPDT) switch symbol. This switch is two SPDT switches connected together. Notice, there are six terminals available for wires. The three terminals on one side of the switch are completely separate from the terminals on the other side. The two commons are separate and each common is used with the circuit paths on its own side.

Figure 5-3E shows the symbol of a normally closed (N.C.) push button switch. This type of symbol means that the push button has its contacts closed until the button is pushed, at which time the contacts open.

Figure 5-3F shows the symbol of a normally open (N.O.) push button switch. This type of switch has its contacts open until the button is pushed, at which time, the contacts close.

It is possible for switches to have more combinations than shown here, but once the functions of these are mastered, any other combinations will be extensions of these.

FUSES AND CIRCUIT BREAKERS

The function of fuses and circuit breakers is to protect the circuit against current that could damage circuit components. Everyone is familiar with fuses or circuit breakers in a house circuit. In a house, the typical current overload situation results when too many appliances are connected to the same circuit. When the overload occurs, the fuse will "blow" or the breaker will "trip" and the circuit will cease to have any power available.

If a fuse or circuit breaker was not used, the excessive current would create excessive heat and could cause damage, even melt wires or start fires.

Opens and Shorts

The terms "open" and "short" are two fault conditions that can happen to a circuit.

An open circuit is a break in the circuit path, such as a wire becoming disconnected. In order for current to flow, there must be a complete circuit path, from the power source to the load, and back to the power source. If the circuit path is interrupted, current cannot flow and the load will not operate. This condition will not blow the fuse and there may still be voltage present that is a shock hazard.

A short circuit is the opposite of an open. In a short circuit, the circuit path is "short-cut" around the load causing an excessive amount of current to flow. A fuse or circuit breaker will respond to a short circuit and will break the circuit path, stopping the flow of current.

Resetting the Circuit

When a current overload protection device breaks the circuit, the overload or shorted condition must be resolved, before the circuit can be restored to normal.

A circuit breaker looks like a switch. To reset the circuit, it is a simple matter of switching the breaker to the off position and then back to the on position. Note: when a breaker trips, it will usually go to a state between off and on and must first be switched to the off position.

Fuses come in a wide variety of shapes and sizes, but they all have one thing in common; when the fuse blows, it is no longer useful. The fuse will open the circuit by melting a segment of the fuse conducting element. The fuse must then be replaced.

Ratings

Fuses and circuit breakers have two categories for the ratings: quickness of response and voltage/current.

The quickness of response is a very broad term stating if it is "quick blow" or "slow blow." A quick blow will respond the moment an overload situation is experienced. This is the most common type of current protection. Keep it in mind that if a fuse is rated for 15 amps and the circuit is drawing 14 amps for an extended period of time, the fuse may heat up enough to blow.

A slow blow device is used in situations where it is normal to have a momentary high current, then drop to a much lower value. An example of this is circuits with large motors. When the motor is first starting, there is a surge of current and quickly it drops to the lower current while the motor is running.

The voltage/current rating states the maximum voltage to safely use the device and the current which will cause the device to respond. When replacing a fuse, it is safe and acceptable to replace with a higher voltage rating. However, **Do Not** replace a fuse or breaker with a **Higher Current Rating**. The manufacturer of the circuit being protected selected the particular current rating to ensure protection of the circuit.

Schematic Symbols

Figure 5-4A is the schematic symbol of a fuse. Often the fuse current rating will be shown alongside the fuse symbol.

Figure 5-4B is the symbol for a circuit breaker. This symbol may also have the current rating.

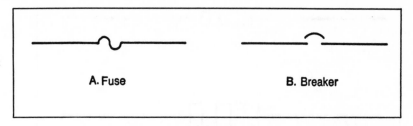

Fig. 5-4. Schematic symbols of current overload protection devices.

A. Fuse

B. Breaker

RESISTORS

Resistors come in many various sizes depending upon how they will be used in the circuit. Regardless of what type of electronic device they are in, the resistor is the most commonly used individual component.

The use of resistors will fall into one of two general categories: either limit the flow of current or provide a specified voltage drop. Even though the student may not understand these concepts at the present time, it is still important to examine the various types available.

The types of resistors available come under two very broad categories: either fixed or variable. Both fixed and variable resistors have essentially two general specifications: the ohmic value and the wattage rating. Therefore, when identifying a resistor, determine if it is fixed or variable and the ohmic value and wattage rating.

Ohmic Value

The unit of measure of resistance is the ohm. The symbol for ohm is the Greek letter omega Ω. Therefore, the ohmic value is another way of stating the resistor's value in ohms.

During the manufacture of resistors, there will be a tolerance allowed between the designed ohmic value and the actual value produced. Tolerances allowed will range from 0.5% to 20%. Naturally, the lower percent tolerance will require more expense during manufacture. Generally speaking, most circuits will be designed to use resistors with a 10% tolerance, which are the most common type available.

Wattage Rating

Whenever electricity passes through a resistor, heat will be produced. Some common examples of

heat produced from electricity are: incandescent light bulb, electric stove, electric heater, hair dryer, clothes dryer, etc.

The examples given produce enough heat for even a casual observer to feel the heat produced. Because electronic circuits use a number of resistors, and other components that produce heat, it is possible to feel a certain amount of heat radiating from electronic devices.

All components have a heat range in which they can safely operate. Excessive heat will destroy the component. Therefore, resistors and other components have an effective heat rating, stated in watts. Wattage is a unit of measure that is easily calculated and is therefore easy to work with.

When the wattage rating is stated for a resistor, it is stated for an ambient temperature much hotter than normal room temperature. In other words, its value is for a working circuit that is producing heat.

The wattage rating affects the physical size of the resistor since the surface area dissipates the heat. The lowest standard value of wattage rating is ⅛ watt. Carbon resistors are available in ⅛ watt, ¼ watt, ½ watt, 1 watt, and 2 watts. Larger wattage sizes are available with wire-wound resistors. A larger physical size will allow a resistor to dissipate more heat. Figure 5-5 shows some of the various sizes of carbon resistors.

Fixed Resistors

Most resistors are of the fixed type, which simply means that their ohmic value is determined during manufacture and cannot be varied.

The materials used to manufacture the resistors varies. Small fixed resistors are usually made of carbon or carbon with other various compositions. Resistors needing a higher wattage rating will often

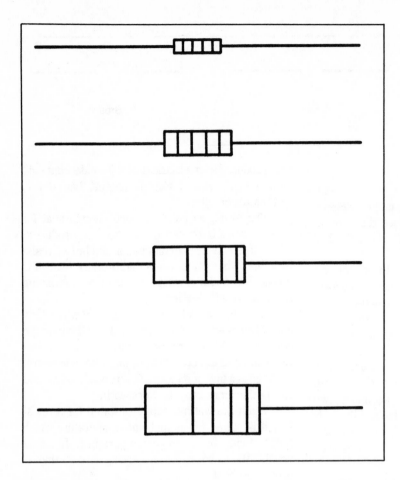

Fig. 5-5. Various sizes of resistors. Larger are higher wattage rating.

be wirewound, which means they are made of wire wrapped around a core.

The ohmic range of fixed resistors varies from 1 ohm to 100 megohms. It is possible to find precision resistors that have values of less than 1 ohm.

Fixed carbon resistors with a tolerance of 10 percent are the most common resistors available. The following series of numbers is used, with multiples of 10, to establish "standard values": 1.0, 1.2, 1.5, 1.8, 2.2, 2.7, 3.3, 3.9, 4.7, 5.6, 6.8, 8.2, 10.0.

The "standard values" series expands the basic series by using multiples of 10. For example, the value 1.8 can be used as: 1.8 ohms; 18 ohms; 180 ohms; 1800 ohms; 18 kilohms; 180 kilohms; 1.8 megohms; 18 meg ohms. Each of the "standard values" has a series similar to the one shown here and will therefore produce a very wide range of fixed resistance values.

Keep it in mind that the physical size of the resistor does not determine the ohmic value. The physical size determines the wattage rating.

Variable Resistors

A variable resistor is made in such a way that the ohmic rating can be varied. In a variable resistor, a sliding arm will slide over, and touch, the resistive element to allow the arm to select a portion of the full resistance available. The sliding arm is also called a "wiper" arm. An example of where a variable resistor is used is as a volume control. Variable resistors are also divided into two general categories: potentiometer and rheostat. The difference is in how they are wired and used.

A potentiometer is a variable resistor with three terminals. It is used in such a way that the variable arm divides the total resistance into two different, but connected, resistors. Often used as a voltage divider circuit. A "pot" can be connected as a rheostat.

A rheostat is a variable resistor with two terminals. It cannot be wired to have the effect of two connected resistors for a voltage divider effect.

Schematic Symbols

Figure 5-6 shows the three basic schematic symbols for resistors.

Figure 5-6A is the symbol for a fixed resistor. This symbol is used for any type of resistor that has a fixed value. The same symbol can also be used to show other types of circuit resistance, even if it is not a physical component. An example is the internal resistance of a power supply or the effective resistance of a long piece of wire.

Figure 5-6B is the symbol for a variable resistor. As with many other schematic symbols, the arrow is used to indicate variable. This symbol has three connections for wires, the two ends and the center contact (wiper), and is usually called a potentiometer.

Figure 5-6C is also a symbol used for a variable resistor, except this one has only two connections, one end and the center wiper. This symbol is used to show a rheostat.

RESISTOR COLOR CODE

Carbon resistors have color bands around the body of the resistor to identify the value of the resistor. Refer to Fig. 5-7.

The Colors

There are twelve colors used to identify the value of resistors. Refer to Table 5-1. The first 10 colors represent the digits 0-9 and the last two colors, silver and gold, are used to identify the per-

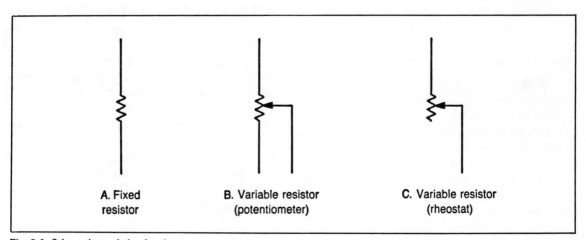

A. Fixed resistor   B. Variable resistor (potentiometer)   C. Variable resistor (rheostat)

Fig. 5-6. Schematic symbols of resistors.

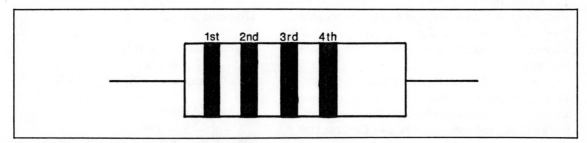

1st   2nd   3rd   4th

Fig. 5-7. Pictorial drawing of a carbon resistor to show the relationship of the color bands.

Table 5-1. Resistor Color Code.

Color	Value	
Black	0	
Brown	1	
Red	2	
Orange	3	
Yellow	4	
Green	5	
Blue	6	
Violet	7	
Gray	8	
White	9	
Gold	x0.1	(third band)
Silver	x0.01	(third band)
Gold	5%	(fourth band)
Silver	10%	(fourth band)
No color	20%	(fourth band)

cent tolerance. Silver and gold can also be used in the third band as a multiplier.

Color Bands

A resistor can have three, four or five color bands. A three band resistor is one of the older type, although there are some still in use. The four band resistor is the most commonly found type. The five band type is used for either precision resistors or to show a rating used for military standards. This chapter will deal with only the three and four band types because the five band types are special purpose resistors.

The first three color bands give the "nominal" value. Nominal means the "named" or ideal value. The fourth color band gives the tolerance, in percent. Keep in mind that all electronic components have a tolerance value. That is to say, the actual value can vary from the ideal value by that percent tolerance.

Bands 1 and 2 give the two significant figures. To achieve these two figures, the first two bands are directly translated into the digits they represent. For example, red-orange would give the first two significant figures of 23.

Band 3 is called the multiplier band. Each color represents the power of 10 multiplied times the significant figures. Gold is 0.1 times the significant figures and silver is 0.01 times the significant figures.

It is often easier to think of band 3 as representing the number of zeros that follow the significant figures. Gold and silver still remain multipliers.

Band 4 is the tolerance, stated in percentage. Gold is 5%, silver is 10% and if there is no fourth band, the tolerance is 20%. The tolerance is converted from percentage to a decimal and multiplied times the nominal value (found using the first three bands.) The result of multiplying the tolerance times the nominal is the ohmic value of the tolerance. The ohmic tolerance is *added* to the nominal for the *maximum* value and *subtracted* from the nominal for the *minimum* value. Note: an in-depth explanation of percent tolerance is given in Chapter 3.

Examples of Resistor Color Code

With the examples shown below, the first line is the colors given on the resistor. The second line is the value of each of the colors, as read from Table 5-1, the resistor color code. The third line is the nominal value of the resistor. The fourth line is the ohmic value of tolerance, based on the given percent tolerance. The fifth line is the max and min values of the resistor, based on the ohmic value of the tolerance. Note: the first few examples include only three lines—they do not show the results of tolerance calculations in order to best show examples of reading the color code.

yellow-violet-brown-gold
4 – 7 – 0 – 5%
470 ohms +/–5%

yellow-violet-orange-gold
4 – 7 – 3 – 5%
47,000 ohms = 47 kilohms +/–5%

red-red-red-silver
2 – 2 – 2 – 10%
2200 ohms = 2.2 kilohms +/–10%

54

red-red-yellow-silver
2 – 2 – 4 – 10%
220,000 ohms = 220 kilohms +/– 10%

blue-gray-orange-gold
6 – 8 – 3 – 5%
68,000 ohms = 68 kilohms +/–5%

blue-gray-brown-gold
6 – 8 – 1 – 5%
680 ohms +/–5%

blue-gray-blue-silver
6 – 8 – 6 – 10%
68,000,000 ohms = 68 megohms +/– 10%

brown-black-black-gold
1 – 0 – 0 – 5%
10 ohms +/–5%

brown-black-red-no color
1 – 0 – 2 – 20%
1,000 ohms +/–20%

brown-black-yellow-no color
1 – 0 – 4 – 20%
100,000 ohms = 100 kilohms +/–20%

brown-red-brown-silver
1 – 2 – 1 – 10%
120 ohms +/–10%
+/– 12 ohms tolerance
max = 132 ohms; min = 118 ohms

red-orange-yellow-gold
2 – 3 – 4 – 5%
230,000 ohms = 230 kilohms +/–5%
+/– 11500 ohms tolerance
max = 241500 ohms; min = 218500 ohms

orange-orange-silver-gold
3 – 3 – x.01 – 5%
0.33 ohms +/–5%
max = 0.3465 ohms; min = 0.3135 ohms

brown-black-gold-gold
1 – 0 – x.1 – 5%
1.0 ohms +/–5%
max = 1.05 ohms; min = 0.95 ohms

Practice Problems: Resistor Color Code

Part A. With each of the following, the first three color bands are given. Determine the nominal value of the resistor. Ignore the tolerance.

(1) brown-black-brown
(2) red-violet-brown
(3) brown-green-red
(4) red-red-red
(5) orange-white-red
(6) green-blue-red
(7) brown-black-orange
(8) brown-green-orange
(9) yellow-violet-orange
(10) Gray-red-orange
(11) brown-red-yellow
(12) blue-gray-yellow
(13) orange-orange-green
(14) brown-black-black
(15) brown-black-gold

Part B. With each of the following, the ohmic value of the resistor is given. Determine the colors of the first three color bands. Ignore the tolerance.

(16) 120 ohms
(17) 330 ohms
(18) 390 ohms
(19) 1000 ohms
(20) 1800 ohms
(21) 2.7 kilohms
(22) 4.7 kilohms
(23) 6.8 kilohms
(24) 8.2 kilohms
(25) 10 kilohms
(26) 12 kilohms
(27) 1 megohm
(28) 18 megohms
(29) 10 ohms
(30) 4 ohms

Part C. With each of the following, the first four color bands are given. Determine the nominal value and the maximum and minimum values.

(31) brown-green-brown-silver
(32) red-red-brown-gold
(33) yellow-violet-brown-no color
(34) green-blue-brown-silver
(35) orange-orange-red-gold
(36) blue-gray-red-no color
(37) brown-red-orange-silver
(38) brown-gray-orange-gold
(39) brown-red-green-no color
(40) orange-white-blue-silver

Part D. With each of the following, the ohmic value of the resistor is given, with the tolerance. Determine the first four color bands.

(41) 18 ohms +/−5%
(42) 180 ohms +/−10%
(43) 270 ohms +/−20%
(44) 680 ohms +/−5%
(45) 3900 ohms +/−10%
(46) 8.2 kilohms +/−10%
(47) 22 kilohms +/−10%
(48) 33 kilohms +/−5%
(49) 2.7 megohms +/−5%
(50) 15 megohms +/−20%

INTRODUCTION TO SCHEMATIC DIAGRAMS

A schematic diagram is a diagram showing the various connections in a circuit. In this section, simple schematics will be introduced to show the basic principles of drawing.

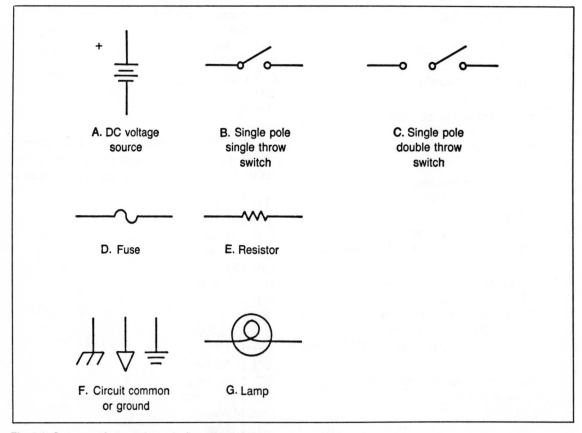

A. DC voltage source

B. Single pole single throw switch

C. Single pole double throw switch

D. Fuse

E. Resistor

F. Circuit common or ground

G. Lamp

Fig. 5-8. Summary of commonly used schematic symbols.

Using Schematic Symbols

Schematic symbols have been standardized in the electronics industry. There may be some slight variations with the standard symbols, but the symbols are the same on all drawings. Figure 5-8 shows the schematic symbols used in the circuits drawn for this section. Notice that there are some symbols added to this figure that were not shown previously in this chapter.

Figure 5-9 shows some examples of schematic diagrams that have been drawn correctly. Figure 5-9A is the simplest of all circuits possible—a voltage source and a load. Although a resistor is a specific electronic component, the resistor symbol can be used to represent any load. This drawing simply shows that the battery is connected to something.

Figure 5-9B is a schematic diagram with the four basic parts of a circuit: a voltage source; an on/off switch; a fuse for current protection; a load to use the electricity. Notice the wiring of the switch and the fuse. They are both in the direct path of the current. This is the correct way to connect these two devices.

Figure 5-9C demonstrates one possible use of a double throw switch. When the switch is in the right-hand position, the resistor load will be connected. When the switch is in the left-hand position, the lamp will be connected. Only one load at a time can be connected to the battery with the switch connected in this manner. Also, take note of the circuit common symbols. There are many types of circuit common or circuit ground symbols. They are often used to eliminate some of the lines on the schematic. Keep in mind that all commons are connected together.

The process of reading schematic diagrams and connecting wires in an actual circuit is a task that

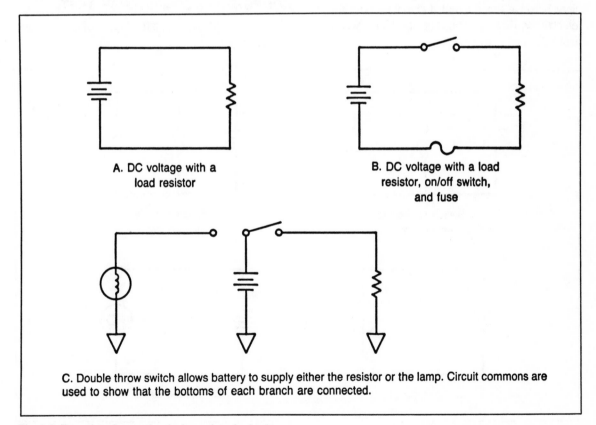

A. DC voltage with a load resistor

B. DC voltage with a load resistor, on/off switch, and fuse

C. Double throw switch allows battery to supply either the resistor or the lamp. Circuit commons are used to show that the bottoms of each branch are connected.

Fig. 5-9. Examples of correctly wired complete dc circuits.

takes a lot of practice. It is as important to recognize a correct circuit drawing, as it is to recognize an incorrect drawing. Figure 5-10 shows some common mistakes.

Figures 5-10A and 5-10B are incorrect because the switch and the fuse are connected "across" the battery instead of "in series with" the battery. When the switch is open, the battery will supply voltage to the resistor load. However, when the switch is closed, there will be a short circuit because the current will flow through the zero resistance path of the switch. This would cause serious problems. In Fig. 5-10B, the fuse is a zero resistance path. The moment the battery is connected, the fuse is a short circuit path and the battery will try to supply a large amount of current. This will instantly "blow" the fuse.

Figure 5-10C is an open circuit. This simply represents a broken connection. The lamp will not light because there is not a complete path for the electricity. However, no other problems will result from the open circuit.

Figure 5-10D has a short circuit. The diagonal line is the short circuit. Any circuit path that allows the electricity to bypass the load is considered a short circuit. The phrase "electricity takes the path of least resistance" applies to the short circuit.

PROGRAMS FOR THIS CHAPTER

There is one program for this chapter. It is for practice with the resistor color code.

The resistor color code is something that every student should memorize. The program provides practice in knowing the value of resistance when the colors are given.

Figure 5-11 is a preview sample of the color code program. This program may be used with either color or B&W monitors.

DC CIRCUIT COMPONENTS COMPETENCY TEST

1. What is the approximate output voltage of a single dry cell?

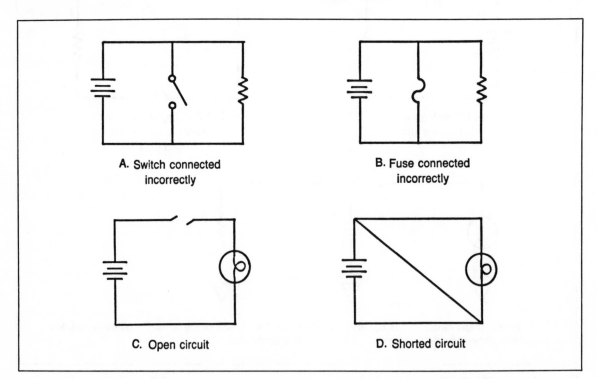

A. Switch connected incorrectly

B. Fuse connected incorrectly

C. Open circuit

D. Shorted circuit

Fig. 5-10. Schematic diagrams showing some common wiring errors.

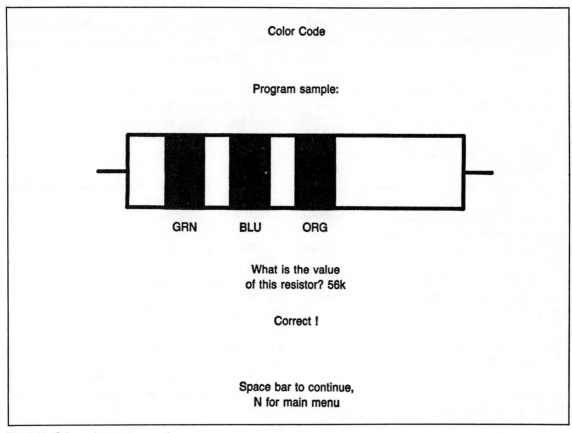

Color Code

Program sample:

GRN   BLU   ORG

What is the value
of this resistor? 56k

Correct !

Space bar to continue,
N for main menu

Fig. 5-11. Color code program sample.

2. Draw the schematic symbol of a fixed voltage source. Label positive and negative.
3. Draw the schematic symbol of a variable voltage supply.
4. Does a good conductor have low or high resistance?
5. Does a good insulator have low or high resistance?
6. Which wire size is larger; 18 AWG or 22 AWG?
7. Which wire size is more commonly used in house wiring; 14 AWG or 36 AWG?
8. When a switch is closed, does it have 0 resistance or infinite resistance?
9. When a switch is closed, is it an open circuit or a short circuit?
10. When a switch is open, does it have 0 resistance or infinite resistance?
11. When a switch is open, is it an open circuit or a short circuit?
12. Does electric current flow with an open or a closed switch?

With questions 13 to 18, draw the schematic symbols of these switches:

13. Single pole, single throw
14. Single pole, double throw
15. Double pole, single throw
16. Double pole, double throw
17. Normally open push button
18. Normally closed push button
19. Which over-current protection device needs to be replaced after use—fuse or circuit breaker?
20. Draw the schematic diagram of a fuse.

21. Draw the schematic diagram for a fixed resistor.
22. Draw the schematic diagram for a variable resistor.

With questions 23 to 30, convert the given value to the units shown.

23. 470 ohms   = _____ kilohms
24. 33 kilohms   = _____ ohms
25. 150 kilohms   = _____ megohms
26. 8.6 kilohms   = _____ ohms
27. 4.7 kilohms   = _____ ohms
28. 1.2 megohms   = _____ kilohms
29. 18 megohms   = _____ ohms
30. 220,000 ohms = _____ megohms

With questions 31 to 35, use the three colors given to determine the ohmic value of the resistor. Ignore the tolerance.

31. brown-black-brown
32. red-red-red
33. green-blue-orange
34. blue-gray-yellow
35. orange-white-green

With questions 36 to 40, use the four colors given to determine the nominal value, and maximum and minimum values.

36. brown-green-brown-silver
37. yellow-violet-red-gold
38. orange-orange-orange-no color
39. brown-black-yellow-silver
40. gray-red-blue-silver

With questions 41 to 49, determine the first four color bands of the resistor.

41. 10 ohms +/-10%
42. 270 ohms +/-5%
43. 330 ohms +/-20%
44. 1000 ohms +/-10%
45. 1800 ohms +/-5%
46. 4.7 kilohms +/-10%
47. 6.8 kilohms +/-20%
48. 10 kilohms +/-5%
49. 1 megohm +/-10%
50. Draw a complete schematic diagram of a simple flashlight (the type that uses 2 "D" cell batteries).

Chapter 6
Use of an Ohmmeter

Chapter Objective: A hands-on lesson to learn to operate an ohmmeter, correctly read the scale, use the range switch, and make resistance measurements.

Chapter Outline:
- ☐ Construction of an ohmmeter
- ☐ Ohmmeter range switch
- ☐ Ohmmeter scale
- ☐ Hands-on experience
- ☐ Programs for this chapter
- ☐ Ohmmeter written competency test

INTRODUCTION

An ohmmeter is used to measure resistance. It is usually part of a "multimeter", which is a combination meter containing an ohmmeter, voltmeter and ammeter. There are two general types of meters: analog, which uses a meter needle sweeping across the scale; digital, which uses electronic circuitry to convert the measurement to a digital readout.

Figures 6-1, 6-2, and 6-3 are models of multimeters. Figures 6-1 and 6-2 are analog meters and 6-3 is a digital meter.

CONSTRUCTION OF AN OHMMETER

All ohmmeters have their own internal power source. The internal power can come from being plugged into the wall socket or it can be from batteries. The purpose of the internal power source is to allow the meter to make measurements without voltage from the circuit.

The voltage from the meter is applied to the resistance to be measured. Current will flow from the meter, through the "circuit" being measured and allow the meter to measure the amount of current flowing. It is the amount of current flow that allows the meter to make the actual resistance measurement.

Simplified Schematic Drawing

Figure 6-4 shows a simplified schematic drawing of an ohmmeter. The three parts of this figure

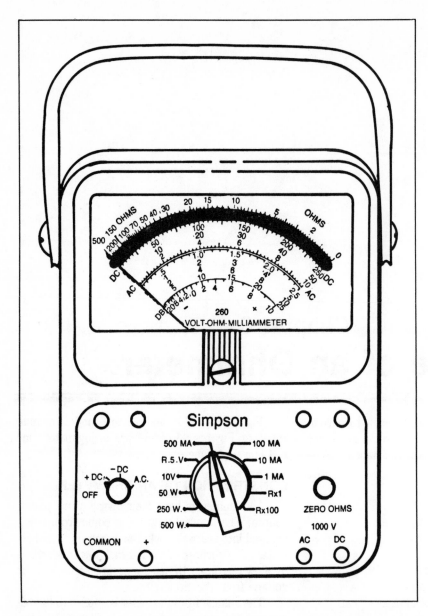

Fig. 6-1. Analog type multimeter.

show how the meter responds under different conditions.

Notice that each figure contains a meter movement, a battery, a variable resistor and a fixed resistor. The meter movement is represented as a 100 microammeter, which is typical. The battery is shown as 1.5 volts, since many meters use one flashlight battery to power the ohmmeter. The variable resistor is used to adjust the ohmmeter to zero. The fixed resistor is used to limit the current to the meter movement.

Figure 6-4A shows the meter terminals open. When the meter terminals of an ohmmeter are open, there will be no current flow because there is not a complete circuit. In this condition, the meter will read infinity which, for most meters, is the left side of the scale.

Figure 6-4B shows the test leads shorted to-

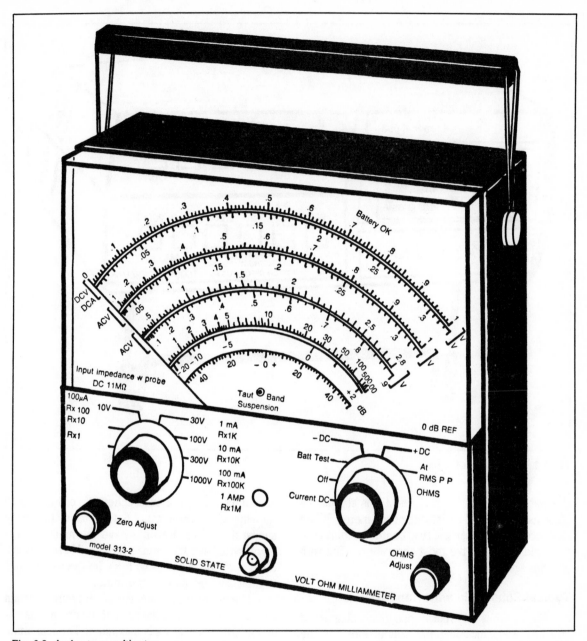

Fig. 6-2. Analog type multimeter.

gether. This connection makes a complete circuit. Current will flow from the battery, through the meter, and through R2 and R1. R1 can be adjusted to allow an amount of current to flow in the circuit to make the meter have full scale deflection. The test leads are considered to have zero ohms resistance and when the meter is adjusted for full scale, it will read zero ohms.

Figure 6-4C has the ohmmeter test leads connected to a resistor to measure its ohmic value. In

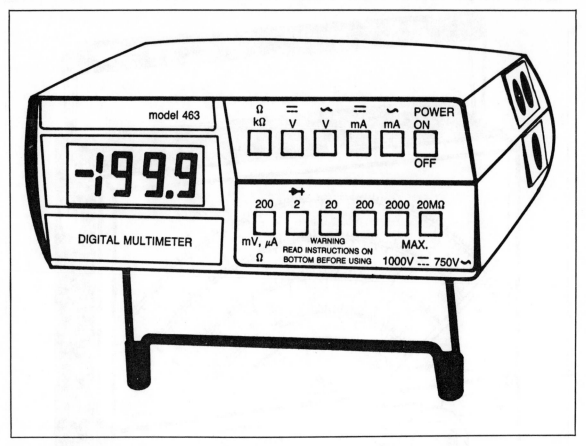

Fig. 6-3. Digital type multimeter.

this particular case, the test resistor is almost the same as the internal resistance of the meter. When this occurs, the meter will read center scale. A center scale reading is the most accurate reading with an ohmmeter.

Typical Schematic with Range Switch

Figure 6-5 is a "typical" schematic diagram of an ohmmeter, including the connections for the range switch. It is "typical" because, even if other meters are not exactly the same, the basic concept is.

This particular meter has a three-position range switch. The two rotary switches shown are connected together on the same shaft. When the knob on the meter front is turned, both rotary switches will turn at the same time.

Comparing the typical schematic of Fig. 6-5 to the simplified schematic of 6-4, compare the many similarities. Both drawings have the meter movement, both have R1, ohms adjust, and both have another resistor in series with R1 (in the same path) to limit current flow to the meter.

The meter movement can accept only a certain amount of current. In the case of the one in this example, 100 microamps is maximum. The maximum amount of current flows through the meter when the test leads are shorted together. When the range switch is in the highest range, in this case 10,000 ohms, R2 must limit the current to the maximum value.

When the range switch is moved to the next lower position, a much smaller resistor is connected. A smaller resistor is used because when the test

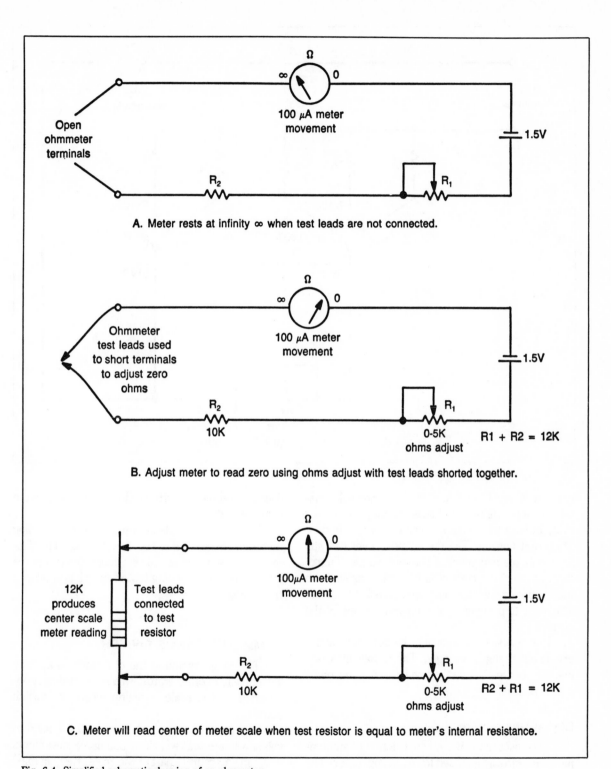

A. Meter rests at infinity ∞ when test leads are not connected.

B. Adjust meter to read zero using ohms adjust with test leads shorted together.

C. Meter will read center of meter scale when test resistor is equal to meter's internal resistance.

Fig. 6-4. Simplified schematic drawing of an ohmmeter.

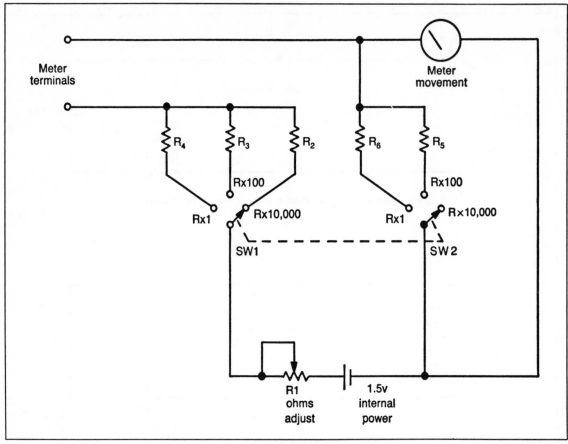

Fig. 6-5. Typical schematic of an ohmmeter, showing the range switch.

resistor is equal to the ohmmeter's internal resistance, there will be a mid-scale reading. A smaller value of internal resistance means a larger amount of current flowing. The meter movement can still have only the maximum of 100 microamps. Therefore, some of the current is by-passed around the meter movement. The purpose of SW2 is to select a resistor to provide a path to bypass some of the current.

It is necessary to readjust the zero setting every time the range is changed. This is done by shorting the test leads together and turning the ohms adjust control.

Digital Ohmmeters

This discussion of the construction of an ohmmeter is primarily intended for an analog meter. The digital meter uses electronic circuitry to perform the same operation.

The basic principles of operation of the analog meter can be applied to the digital meter. The digital meter uses an internal resistance and compares it to the resistance being tested, which is similar to the analog type.

OHMMETER RANGE SWITCH

The range switch of the ohmmeter is actually a multiplier. In other words, whatever reading is obtained from the scale is multiplied by the switch setting.

The range switch on the ohmmeter is used to select a range that will allow taking measurements in the most accurate part of the scale. Keep in mind that the best accuracy is obtained between zero and center scale.

Example: A 1000 ohm resistor is being measured. On the (R × 1) scale, the reading will be 1k—on the far left. On the (R × 100) scale, the reading will be 10—in the center. On the (R × 10,000) scale, the reading will be very close to zero. The best choice for the range switch setting in this example would be the (R × 100) scale.

OHMMETER SCALE

On a multimeter, the ohmmeter scale is quite different from the other scales. Even though it is different, it is no more difficult to read than a thermometer.

Each of the multimeters shown in Figs. 6-1, 2 and 3 have an ohmmeter scale. These three meters are different in how they look, but they accomplish the same function.

The multimeter shown in Fig. 6-1 is used as a model to explain the functions of the ohmmeter and how to read the scale. Figure 6-6 shows only the ohmmeter portion of the multimeter scales and the range switch. Note: the four needles shown are used as examples in reading the meter.

Nonlinear Scale

The ohmmeter scale is termed "nonlinear" because it is not the same size between the different divisions. The scale is nonlinear because the ohmmeter has an internal resistance to limit current flow. Keep in mind—the most accurate reading is found at exactly the center. Between the center and zero—the upper half of the scale—is the best place to make all resistance measurements. Adjust the range switch to make the reading fall into this range. The lower half of the scale is not very accurate because the divisions are squashed together.

Some ohmmeters have the zero on the left side, such as the one in Fig. 6-2. The most accurate part of the scale is still between zero and the center.

Reading the Ohmmeter Scale

For the purposes of learning to read the ohmmeter scale, Fig. 6-6 is used. Note: the four needles shown are used as examples in reading the meter.

The scale has zero on the right and infinity on the left. Therefore, keep in mind, that if the needle is between two divisions, then a lower number is on the right and a higher number is on the left.

When reading the ohmmeter scale, it is necessary to evaluate each place that the needle lands individually because the distance between the different scale markings is different.

Examples of Reading an Analog Ohmmeter

Table 6-1 shows the results of reading the four example needles of the ohmmeter in Fig. 6-6.

An analog ohmmeter reading *must be multiplied by the range switch setting*. The range switch setting for this example is (R × 100). The "resistance measurement" column of Table 6-1 has been multiplied by the range setting and is the final result of reading the analog example meter.

HANDS-ON EXPERIENCE

This section is designed to give the student hands-on experience using an ohmmeter. Any multimeter available will be adequate. Make sure the battery inside the meter is a fresh battery. Note: some meters that plug into the wall still need to have a battery inside.

Part A. Meter Adjustments

An ohmmeter needs two adjustments—they are adjustments for both ends of the scale. For the purposes of this lesson, it will be assumed that the meter in use has the ohms scale reading right to left. Zero on the right and infinity on the left.

Step 1. Meter Resting Position (left side of the scale). Refer to Fig. 6-4A.

   (a) Meter leads must not be shorted together.

   (b) Turn the meter range switch to select any ohms scale.

   (c) The meter should read exactly on the left side of the scale—infinity. If not, there is an adjustment screw at the point where the

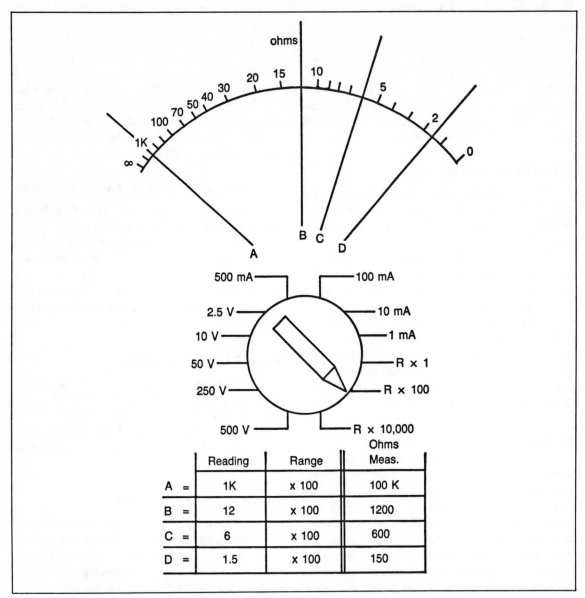

Fig. 6-6. Ohmmeter scale with examples.

Table 6-1. Ohmmeter Readings.

Needle	Reading	Resistance Measurement
A	1k	100 kilohms
B	12	1200 ohms
C	6	600 ohms
D	1.5	150 ohms

needle is attached. (This adjustment screw is usually plastic and not marked.) This screw is the "meter zero" and is used to adjust the meter in the resting position. Turn the screw to place the needle exactly over the left hand side of the scale.

(d) Turn the range switch to check the meter resting position on all scales—it should not change.

Step 2. Ohms Zero Adjustment. Refer to Fig. 6-4B.

(a) Short the test leads together.

(b) With the range switch on any ohms scale, the needle should swing to the far right side—0 ohms.

(c) Adjust the ohms adjust knob so that the needle falls exactly over zero. If this adjustment does not bring the needle to zero, it is probably because the battery is weak.

(d) The zero adjust must be checked every time a new range is selected.

Part B. Measuring Resistance

Select at least 10 different resistors to make measurements in this part of the hands-on experience. Use Table 6-2 to record the results of this exercise.

Step 1. Making the Measurement. Refer to Fig. 6-4C.

(a) Connect the test leads to the test resistor. With the range switch on any ohms scale, there should be a reading.

(b) Turn the range switch and make a mental note of the reading on each range. This can be done quickly without having to adjust the zero each time.

(c) Select the range that provides the best reading for accuracy—between zero and center scale.

(d) Adjust the zero for the range selected.

(e) Read the meter as accurately as possible. Record this reading in Table 6-2 under the heading "scale reading."

(f) Record the setting of the range switch in Table 6-2 under the heading "range switch".

(g) Multiply the scale reading by the range switch setting. Record the result of this multiplication in Table 6-2 under the heading "resist measure."

Step 2. Considering Tolerance.

(a) Determine the nominal value of the resistor under test by reading the resistor color code. Record this in Table 6-2 under the heading "nominal value."

(b) Calculate the maximum and minimum

Table 6-2. Measuring Resistance.

	Measured Values			Calculated Values			
	Scale Reading	Range Switch	Resist Measure	Nominal Value	Max Value	Min Value	Accept? yes/no
(1)							
(2)							
(3)							
(4)							
(5)							
(6)							
(7)							
(8)							
(9)							
(10)							

values, based on the resistor's tolerance. Record these values in Table 6-2 under the proper headings.

(c) Compare the resistance measurement to the calculated maximum and minimum values and determine if the test resistor is within acceptable tolerance and mark the "accept" column yes or no.

Part C. Measuring a Potentiometer

Measuring the resistance of a variable resistor (potentiometer) is a good demonstration in the proper use of an ohmmeter. Figure 6-7 shows a potentiometer schematic symbol and a pictorial

drawing. Figure 6-8 shows an ohmmeter connected to the potentiometer for testing.

Step 1. Measure Total Resistance. Connect the ohmmeter test leads to the two ends of the potentiometer, as shown in Fig. 6-8A. If the potentiometer has a resistance value marked on it, it should be equal to this measured value, within an acceptable tolerance. Turning the adjustment screw will have no effect on the measurement of total resistance. Record this measurement on the appropriate line in Fig. 6-9.

Step 2. Wiper to Either End. Connect the ohmmeter to the wiper and either end "a" or "b," as shown in Fig. 6-8B and 6-8C. Turning the adjust-

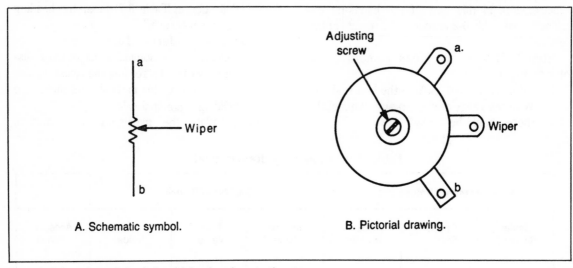

Fig. 6-7. Schematic symbol and pictorial drawing of a potentiometer.

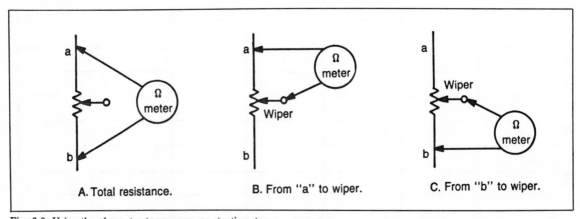

Fig. 6-8. Using the ohmmeter to measure a potentiometer.

ment screw will cause the resistance measurement to go up and down.

Step 3. Adding Resistor "a" and "b." With the ohmmeter connected to point "a," adjust the potentiometer to have a reading of approximately ⅓ of the total resistance. Record the actual measurement on the appropriate line in Fig. 6-9, and label it "resistor a." **Do not make further adjustments.**

Move the ohmmeter lead to point "b." **Do not adjust the potentiometer.** Record the reading on the appropriate line in Fig. 6-9, taken from the wiper to point "b," and label it "resistor b."

Add "resistor a" to "resistor b". Their sum should be equal to the measured value of total resistance.

Repeat this exercise for a second, different value potentiometer.

Part D. Measuring Continuity

The ohmmeter is a very useful instrument for measuring continuity. Continuity is considered a continuous path for the flow of electricity. Examples of checking continuity are:

- ☐ Checking for breaks in a wire.
- ☐ Determine if a fuse is good or bad.
- ☐ Locating which terminals of a switch go together.

Measurements for continuity can be made on any range setting. The readings will be either infinity, if the circuit is open, or zero, if the circuit is closed. Tests for this section will be made on switches.

The best type of switch for making this test is a single-pole double-throw toggle switch. Figure 6-10 shows the schematic symbol and a pictorial drawing of a SPDT toggle switch.

Figure 6-11 shows the readings at each terminal with the switch in either position.

Step 1. Locating Switch Terminals. Connect the ohmmeter test leads to the center terminal (common) and either outside terminal.

Note the reading at this outside terminal. Move the ohmmeter lead to the other outside terminal (the lead connected to common stays).

The reading from common to one terminal should be zero, and from common to the other terminal should be infinity.

The side with the zero reading is the closed contact and the side with the infinity reading is the open contact.

Step 2. Relating Terminals to Switch Position. With the ohmmeter connected to common and either terminal, record the reading on the appropriate line in Fig. 6-9. Move the ohmmeter to the other terminal and record this reading. Move the switch lever to the other position and note the effect on the ohmmeter reading. Record the readings.

PROGRAMS FOR THIS CHAPTER

The program for this chapter will provide experience with a digital ohmmeter.

There are 20 questions—each shows the face of a digital ohmmeter with 6 ranges. One of the ranges is selected for each question. The question is to state the meter reading, in ohms, without use of engineering notation in the answer.

If the range selected is 2 or 200, the measured value is read directly from the meter, with the decimal as shown.

If the range selected is 20k or 200k, the reading displayed on the meter is multiplied by 1000. Move the decimal 3 places to the right.

If the range selected is 2M or 20M, the reading displayed on the meter is multiplied by 1,000,000. Move the decimal 6 places to the right.

Each range setting is the maximum for that particular range. Digital meters use this method to improve accuracy.

Figure 6-12 shows a preview sample of the ohmmeter program.

OHMMETER WRITTEN COMPETENCY TEST

The 50 answers on this test are 2 points each.

Part A. Reading an Ohmmeter

With the 5 ohmmeters (scale/range switch) shown, determine the measurement with each needle.

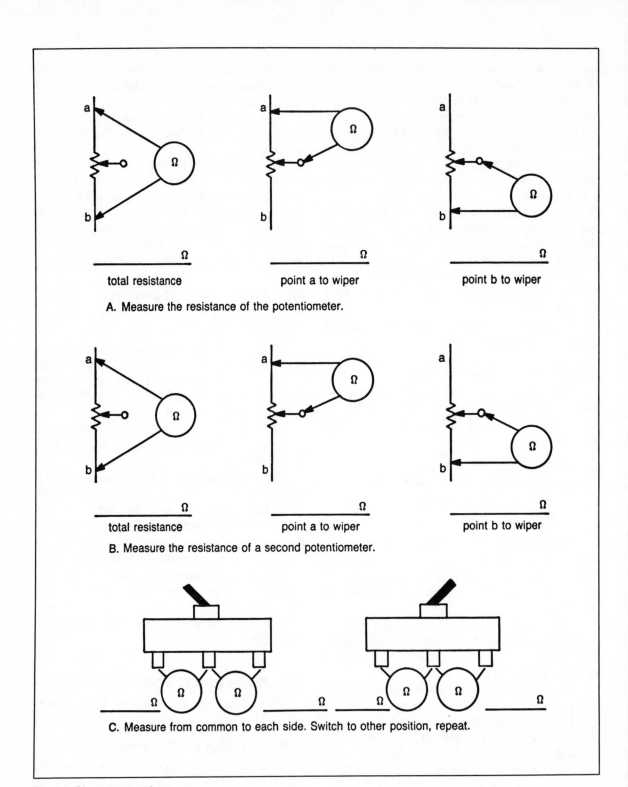

A. Measure the resistance of the potentiometer.

B. Measure the resistance of a second potentiometer.

C. Measure from common to each side. Switch to other position, repeat.

Fig. 6-9. Ohmmeter experience.

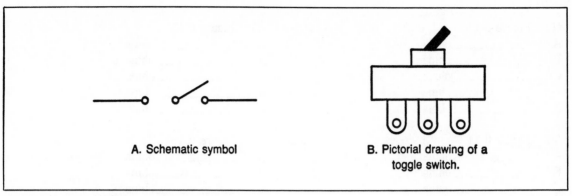

A. Schematic symbol

B. Pictorial drawing of a toggle switch.

Fig. 6-10. Single-pole double-throw (SPDT) switch.

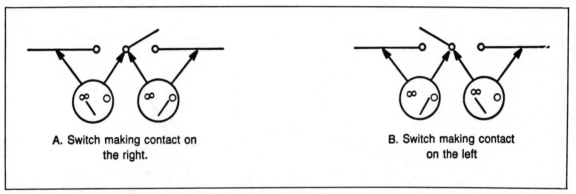

A. Switch making contact on the right.

B. Switch making contact on the left

Fig. 6-11. Ohmmeter showing the readings with the switch in both positions.

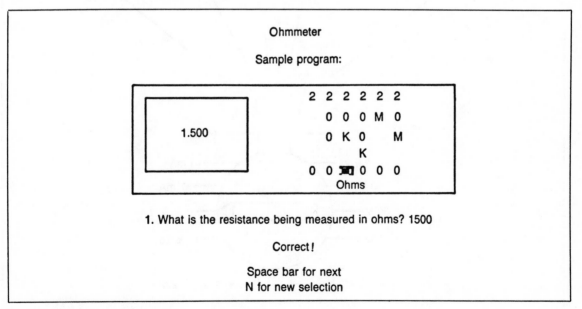

Ohmmeter

Sample program:

```
              2  2  2  2  2  2
              0  0  0  M  0
   1.500      0  K  0     M
                    K
              0  0 🔲 0  0  0
                  Ohms
```

1. What is the resistance being measured in ohms? 1500

Correct!

Space bar for next
N for new selection

Fig. 6-12. Ohmmeter program sample.

(1) Figure 6-13
A _____ohms
B _____ohms
C _____ohms
D _____ohms
E _____ohms

(3) Figure 6-15
A _____ohms
B _____ohms
C _____ohms
D _____ohms
E _____ohms

(2) Figure 6-14
A _____ohms
B _____ohms
C _____ohms
D _____ohms
E _____ohms

(4) Figure 6-16
A _____ohms
B _____ohms
C _____ohms
D _____ohms
E _____ohms

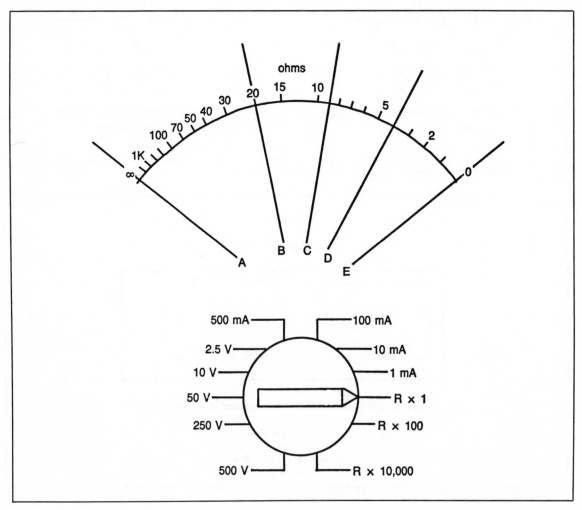

Fig. 6-13. Ohmmeter scale for question 1.

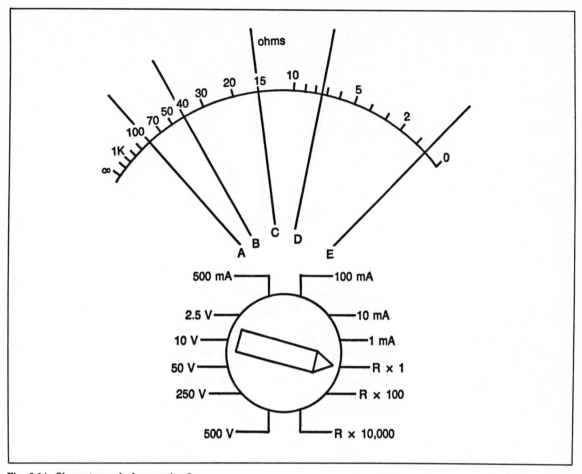

Fig. 6-14. Ohmmeter scale for question 2.

(5) Figure 6-17

A _____ohms
B _____ohms
C _____ohms
D _____ohms
E _____ohms

Part B. Ohmmeters; General Questions

(6) An ohmmeter is connected to both ends of a long piece of wire. The meter reads infinity. What is the condition on the wire? (good or bad)

(7) An ohmmeter is connected to both ends of a long piece of wire. The meter reads zero. What is the condition of the wire? (good or bad)

(8) When an ohmmeter is used to test a fuse, what should the reading be if the fuse is good?

(9) When an ohmmeter is used to test a fuse, what should the reading be if the fuse is bad?

(10) An ohmmeter is connected to a 200 ohm potentiometer, to one end and to the wiper. If the reading is 50 ohms, what would the reading be if it was connected from the wiper to the other terminal?

(11) An ohmmeter is connected to a 500 kilohm potentiometer, to the wiper and one end. If the reading is 50 on the (R × 100), what would be the reading if connected to the other end terminal?

(12) An ohmmeter is connected to a 100 kilohm

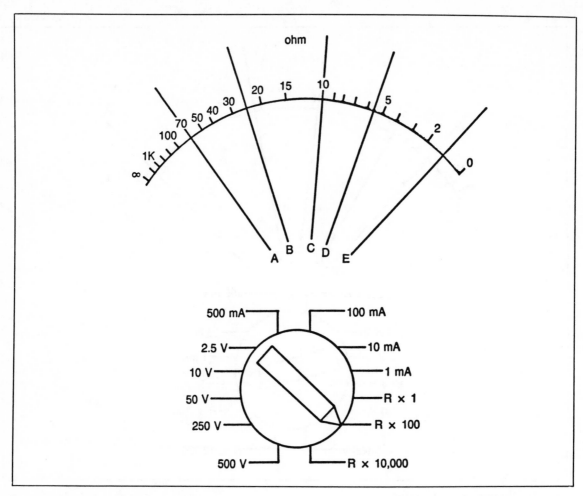

Fig. 6-15. Ohmmeter scale for question 3.

potentiometer, to the wiper and one end. If the reading is 3 on the (R × 10,000) scale, what would be the reading if connected to the other end terminal?

(13) What would the ohmmeter reading be if it were connected to the opposite terminals of a 1 kilohm potentiometer?

(14) If an ohmmeter is connected to the center terminal of a switch and to one end, what reading would be expected when there is continuity through the switch contacts?

(15) Describe the procedure for making the adjustment with the "ohms adjust" control.

Part C. Resistor Tolerance

Determine if the following resistors are within acceptable tolerance, based on the ohmmeter reading and color code. Answer yes or no.

	Reading	Scale	Colors
(16)	11	R × 10	brn-red-brn-gld
(17)	40	R × 100	org-whi-red-sil
(18)	3.5	R × 10,000	yel-vio-org-sil
(19)	9	R × 1	brn-blk-blk-gld
(20)	2.5	R × 100	red-red-brn-sil

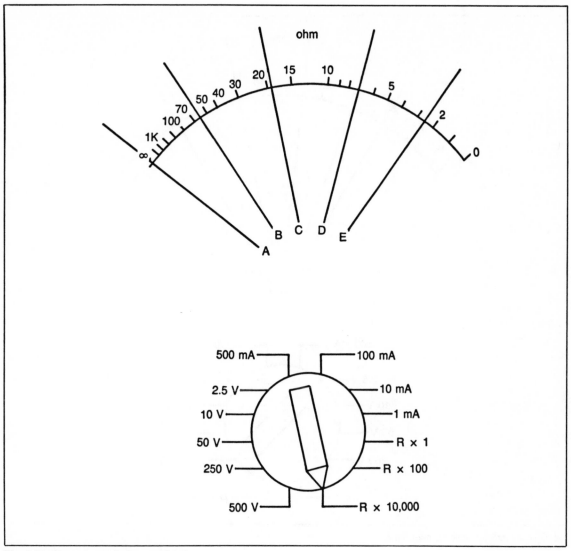

Fig. 6-16. Ohmmeter scale for question 4.

Part D. Converting in Engineering Notation

Convert the number on the left to the unit on the right.

(21)   1.2 MΩ =_____ kilohms
(22)   33 kΩ =_____ ohms
(23)   1500 mV =_____volts
(24)   0.5 W =_____ milliwatts
(25)   0.25 mA =_____ microamps

Part E. Draw the Schematic Symbols of the Following:

(26) single-pole double-throw switch
(27) double-pole double-throw switch
(28) potentiometer
(29) fuse
(30) a complete simplified schematic diagram of an ohmmeter (not including the range switch).

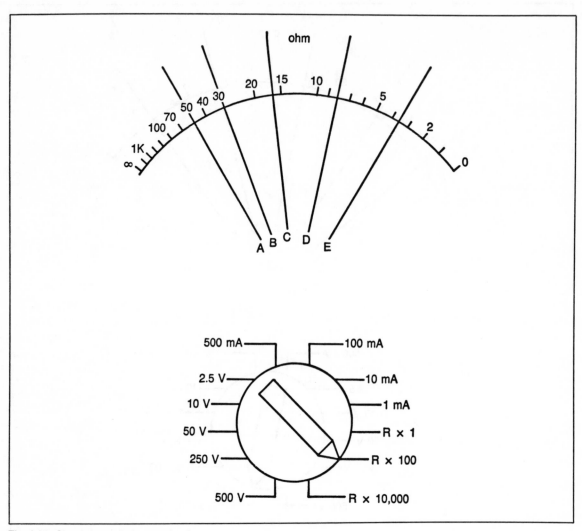

Fig. 6-17. Ohmmeter scale for question 5.

Chapter 7

DC Circuits: Relationships, Formulas and Measurements

Chapter Objectives: To define the relationships of voltage, current, resistance and power and to learn the mathematical formulas that apply to these relationships. Also, to learn to use a voltmeter and ammeter to measure circuit parameters.

Chapter Outline:
- ☐ Electrical relationships
- ☐ Ohm's law
- ☐ Power formulas
- ☐ Connecting single-load circuits
- ☐ Using a voltmeter
- ☐ Using an ammeter
- ☐ Meter construction
- ☐ Programs for this chapter
- ☐ Dc circuits, relationships, formulas and measurements competency test

INTRODUCTION

The terms voltage, current, resistance, power, amps, and watts are terms that many people use to describe electricity. Although these terms are fre-quently used, they are often misunderstood. This chapter will not only define these terms and their relationships to each other, but this chapter will also use mathematical formulas to calculate the rela-tionships.

ELECTRICAL RELATIONSHIPS

There are four types of measure of electrical energy and its effects and relationships. These four are voltage, current, resistance and power. Each of these have a particular unit of measure and a mathe-matical relationship.

Resistance

Resistance is a characteristic of a material in which electricity will or will not flow. Resistance can range from almost zero to an infinite amount. In this way, resistance is similar to friction.

In Chapter 5, the subjects of resistance and volt-age were discussed, and in Chapter 6 resistance was measured using an ohmmeter.

- The definition of resistance is: the opposition to the flow of electrical energy. It is the friction in an electrical circuit. The symbol for resistance is R.
- The unit of measure of resistance is ohms, symbol Ω, the Greek letter omega.

A good conductor should have as close to zero ohms resistance as possible. A closed switch allows current to flow and it should have zero resistance. An insulator does not allow the flow of electricity. Therefore, it should have resistance that is so high as to be considered infinity. An open switch has infinite resistance to stop the flow of electricity.

Those examples are the opposite ends of the resistance scale. Here are some examples of resistance not at the ends of the scale: a filament light bulb allows the flow of electricity, but offers a sufficient amount of resistance to cause the filament wire to heat to white hot and glow; the volume control knob on a radio or TV is a variable resistor—more resistance gives less volume and less resistance gives more volume.

Resistors are used for many purposes in controlling the flow of electricity or to provide work through the use of electricity.

Voltage

Voltage is the driving force behind electricity. It can range from a very small amount to a very large amount. In Chapter 5, batteries were discussed as a source of voltage. It was also stated that voltage sources can be added together to achieve a much larger voltage supply. Power companies send millions of volts along their long-distance lines. The larger the voltage, the harder the driving force and the more electrical energy that can flow.

- The definition of voltage is: force or pressure of electrical energy. The symbol for voltage is V. An older symbol is E (it stands for electro-motive force).
- The unit of measure of voltage is volt, symbol V.

A battery is a good example of a voltage source.

If the battery is disconnected or if there is an open switch, stopping the flow of electricity, the battery will still have its voltage. When the battery is allowed to supply energy, it will "push" electrons through the conductor. Another example is an electrical outlet. Even though there is nothing connected to the outlet, voltage is still present. This voltage can be measured with a voltmeter.

Current

Current is the flow of electricity. It is actually electrons flowing in the conductor, being pushed by the voltage. If there is no voltage to push the electrons, there will be no current flow. If the voltage applied is not strong enough to overcome the circuit resistance, such as an open switch, current cannot flow. It is the electrons flowing through the load device that performs the electrical work.

- The definition of current is: the flow of electrical energy. The symbol for current is I.
- The unit of measure of current is amperage (amp). The symbol is A.
- Current flows from negative to positive.

Most people are familiar with the term amperage from the fact that fuses are rated in amperage. The purpose of a fuse is to prevent too much current from flowing in a circuit. Resistance is similar to friction. Heat is produced due to the opposition to electron flow. Even wires will produce some heat. Too much heat in a wire can cause problems. Fuses "blow" because the heat from too much current melts the fuse.

Power

Power is the measure of work over time. An example is the term "horsepower." Horsepower is a standard measure of the amount of work a horse can produce in a specific amount of time. In terms of electrical work, the end result of the use of electricity is considered power. Regardless of how electricity is used, there will be power whenever there is both voltage and current.

□ The definition of power is: the measure of electrical work over time. The symbol of power is P.

□ The unit of measure of power is wattage (watt). The symbol is W.

The power company that supplies electricity measures the electricity used and sells it to the customer by the amount of work performed for a period of time. They charge by the "kilowatt-hour." In other words, one thousand watts used in one hour. The electric service meter measures in kilowatt hours.

In order for electricity to serve any useful purpose, it must perform some form of work. This work can be giving off light, heating a stove, or even operating a computer. The device that performs the work is considered the "electrical load." In direct current (dc) circuits, the load is often considered some form of resistance.

Relationships

The four units of electricity are all related together. An analogy that is often used to show the electrical relationships is water in a pipe. Figure 7-1 shows the relationships in a circuit and in a water pipe.

Voltage can be compared to water pressure. Even when there is no water flowing, the pressure is still there. Current is the water flowing in the pipe. In order to have flow, there must be pressure. Resistance can be compared to the friction in the pipes and a faucet that is partly open, so that it restricts the flow. Power can be compared to the result of the water flowing, such as spraying water on the grass.

Summary of Units

Quantity	Symbol	Unit	Symbol
Resistance	R	ohm	Ω
Voltage	V (or E)	volt	V
Current	I	amp	A
Power	P	watt	W

Direct Current/Alternating Current

The symbol dc stands for direct current and ac stands for alternating current. The definitions of the basic electrical relationships are the same regardless whether it is dc or ac. Up to this point, only dc has been discussed. Later in this book, ac will be discussed in detail.

□ With direct current (dc), the voltage, and current, will remain either always positive or always negative.

□ With alternating current (ac), the voltage, and current, will periodically alternate from positive to negative and negative to positive.

OHM'S LAW

A German scientist named Georg Ohm stated the electrical relationship between voltage, current and resistance as a mathematical formula. The formula is now called *Ohm's law*.

Ohm's Law Formulas

There are three formulas in Ohm's law, each solves for one of the three electrical quantities of voltage, current and resistance. Power is solved for by using a different formula, discussed later in this chapter.

When using formulas, the symbols representing the terms are used in place of the terms. Therefore, it is necessary to memorize the symbols:

R — resistance; measured in ohms (Ω)
I — current; measured in amps (A)
V — voltage; measured in volts (V)

Formula #1. Ohm's Law to Solve for Voltage.

$$V = I \times R$$
voltage = current × resistance
volts (V) = amps (A) × ohms (Ω)

Example of Solving for Voltage:

How much voltage is applied to a circuit if there are 2 amps of current flowing through 50 ohms of resistance?

Formula: $V = I \times R$

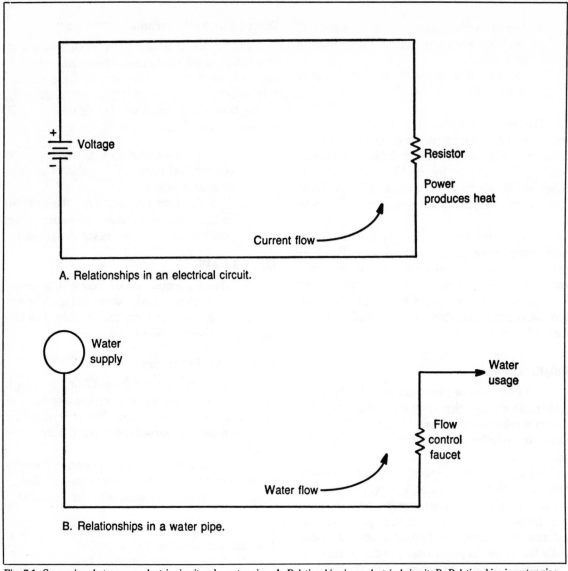

Fig. 7-1. Comparison between an electric circuit and a water pipe. A. Relationships in an electrical circuit; B. Relationships in water pipe.

Substituting: V = 2 amps × 50 ohms
Solving: V = 100 volts

Notice: when solving these formulas, always use the unit of measure for the value being solved for.

Formula #2. Ohm's Law to Solve for Current.

$$I = \frac{V}{R}$$

$$current = \frac{voltage}{resistance}$$

$$amps\ (A) = \frac{volts\ (V)}{ohms\ (\Omega)}$$

Example of Solving for Current:
Calculate the amount of current flowing in a circuit containing 80 volts and 20 ohms.

Formula: $I = \dfrac{V}{R}$

Substituting: $I = \dfrac{80 \text{ V (volts)}}{20 \text{ } \Omega \text{ (ohms)}}$

Solving: $I = 4$ amps

Notice: the answer is in the units for the value being found.

Formula #3. Ohm's Law to Solve for Resistance.

$$R = \dfrac{V}{I}$$

$$\text{resistance} = \dfrac{\text{voltage}}{\text{current}}$$

$$\text{ohms } (\Omega) = \dfrac{\text{volts (V)}}{\text{amps (A)}}$$

Example of Solving for Resistance:
Calculate the circuit resistance when there is 0.3 amp of current flowing with an applied voltage of 6.0 volts.

Formula: $R = \dfrac{V}{I}$

Substituting: $R = \dfrac{6.0 \text{ V (volts)}}{0.3 \text{ A (amps)}}$

Solving: $R = 20$ ohms

Notice: the answer is in the units for resistance.

Mathematical Relationships

When using a mathematical formula, it is very important to understand the relationships between all members of the formula. In other words, if one of the values is changed, how are the other values affected?

First, examine formula #1; $V = I \times R$ to see how each member relates. As with every formula, we are particularly concerned about the value that will be solved for, in this case, V. It is important to visualize how V will be affected if R or I were to go up or down.

If R is as a constant value (the circuit is built with a fixed value of resistance) and the current through the resistor changes, how does the voltage change? If I increases, voltage will also increase. If I decreases, V will also decrease. This is known as a "direct relationship."

If the current is held at a fixed value, and the resistance is changed, how does the voltage change? If the circuit resistance is increased, it will require more voltage to maintain the constant current. If R is decreased, V will also decrease. This is known as a "direct relationship."

□ A direct relationship is; when one value on one side of the equation changes, the value on the other side of the equation will change in the same direction. This will always occur when the operation side of the equation is multiplication, or a numerator of a fraction.

Examine formula #2; $I = V/R$ and determine how the values relate. In this formula, current is the value being solved for and voltage and resistance are allowed to vary to determine the circuit conditions.

If the circuit contains a fixed resistor and the voltage changes, how will the current change? If V increases, I will increase. If V decreases, I will decrease. Since they both change in the same direction, this is a "direct relationship." This occurs because V is the numerator of the fractional formula.

If the circuit voltage is maintained at a constant value and R is changed, how will the circuit current change? It should make sense that if the resistance is increased, the current will decrease. If the resistance is decreased, the current will increase. Since these values go in opposite directions, this is called an "inverse (or indirect) relationship."

□ An inverse (or indirect) relationship occurs when the value on one side of the equation is changed and the value on the other side is changed in the opposite direction. This occurs with division or with the denominator of a fraction.

Finally, examine formula #3: R = V/I to determine the relationships of the terms. V and I are related to R in this formula.

Since V is in the numerator of the fraction, it is a direct relationship. If V increases, R must also increase to maintain a constant I. If V decreases, R decreases to maintain I.

Since I is in the denominator of the fraction, it is an inverse relationship. If I increases, R will decrease to maintain a constant V and if I decreases, R will increase.

Practice Problems: Ohm's Law

With each of the following, use the given values to solve for the unknown value. The proper units must be included with each answer.

(1)	R = 100 ohms	I = 0.2 amps	Find: V
(2)	I = 500 mA	R = 250 ohms	Find: V
(3)	R = 1 kilohm	I = .03 amps	Find: V
(4)	I = 10 mA	R = 2.2 kΩ	Find: V
(5)	V = 100 volts	R = 25 ohms	Find: I
(6)	R = 0.5 kΩ	V = 50 volts	Find: I
(7)	V = 0.3 kV	R = 1 kΩ	Find: I
(8)	R = 30 ohms	V = 60 mV	Find: I
(9)	V = 60 volts	I = 3 amps	Find: R
(10)	I = 50 mA	V = 10 volts	Find: R
(11)	V = 25 mV	I = 5 μA	Find: R
(12)	I = 300 μA	V = 60 mV	Find: R
(13)	I = 25 μA	R = 2 MΩ	Find: V
(14)	R = 15 MΩ	I = 3 μA	Find: V
(15)	V = 3 mV	R = 10 ohms	Find: I

POWER FORMULAS

Power is considered one of the four basic circuit relationships. Calculations for power can be made using any two of the other three circuit values.

An important point to make is the fact that power is the measure of electrical work performed. It is a measure of electrical energy.

Voltage-Current Relationship

The power formulas start with the basic relationship of voltage and current. The unit of mea-sure of power is the watt, with the unit symbol of W. The symbol for power is P.

Formula #4. Power Formula Using the V×I Relationship.

$$P = V \times I$$
power = voltage × current
watts = volts × amps

Example of Solving for Power:

Determine the amount of power dissipated in a circuit with 0.5 amps of current and an applied voltage of 120 volts.

Formula: $P = V \times I$
Substituting: P = 120 volts × 0.5 amps
Solving: P = 60 watts

This same formula can be rearranged to solve for either voltage or current, similar to the manner in which Ohm's law was used.

Example of Solving for Voltage:

What is the applied voltage in a circuit that uses 20 milliwatts of power and has a current flow of 10 milliamps?

Formula: $V = \dfrac{P}{I}$

Substituting: $V = \dfrac{20 \text{ mA}}{10 \text{ mA}}$

Solving: V: 2 volts

Example of Solving for Current:

How much current flows in a circuit if 5 watts of power is dissipated, with an applied voltage of 20 volts?

Formula: $I = \dfrac{P}{V}$

Substituting: $I = \dfrac{5 \text{ W}}{20 \text{ V}}$

Solving: I = 0.25 amps

Combining the Power Formula with Ohm's Law

With the use of simple algebra, the three variations of Ohm's law can be combined with the three variations of the basic power formula. This is performed with algebra by substituting formulas in place of the different variables.

As a result of the combining of formulas, one of the four circuit values can be found, provided any two of the other values are known.

Solving for Power when R and I are Known:

Formulas needed: $P = V \times I$ and $V = I \times R$

Use the power formula and substitute Ohm's law in place of V.

Combining formulas: $P = (I \times R) \times I$

Formula #5. Power Formula Using I and R.

$$P = I^2 \times R$$

Example of Solving for Power When R and I are Known:

Find the power in circuit with 100 ohms resistance and 20 mA current flow.

Formula: $P = I^2 \times R$

Substituting: $P = (20 \text{ mA})^2 \times 100 \text{ ohms}$

Solving: $P = 40 \text{ mW}$

Note: $(20 \text{ mA})^2 = 20\text{E-}3 \times 20\text{E-}3 = 400\text{E}-6 = 0.0004$

Substituting: $P = .0004 \times 100 = .04 \text{ W} = 40 \text{ mW}$

Solving for Power when V and R are Known:

Formulas needed: $P = V \times I$ and $I = V/R$

Use the power formula and substitute Ohm's law in place of I.

Combining formulas: $P = V \times \left(\dfrac{V}{R}\right)$

Formula #6. Power Formula Using V and R.

$$P = \frac{V^2}{R}$$

Example of Solving for Power with V and R Known:

A circuit contains 2 kilohms resistance. What is the power dissipated with an applied voltage of 10 volts?

Formula: $P = \dfrac{V^2}{R}$

Substituting: $P = \dfrac{(10 \text{ V})^2}{2 \text{ kilohms}}$

Solving: $P = 50 \text{ mW}$

Table 7-1 shows all of the combined Ohm's law and power formulas. Keep in mind that it is much

Table 7-1. Combined Ohm's Law and Power Formulas.

Values Given	Unknown to Find	Formula to use
I, R	Voltage	• $V = I \times R$
I, R	Power	• $P = I^2 R$
V, R	Current	$I = \dfrac{V}{R}$
V, R	Power	• $P = \dfrac{V^2}{R}$
I, V	Resistance	$R = \dfrac{V}{I}$
I, V	Power	• $P = I \times V$
P, V	Current	$I = \dfrac{P}{V}$
P, V	Resistance	$R = \dfrac{V^2}{P}$
P, I	Voltage	$V = \dfrac{P}{I}$
P, I	Resistance	$R = \dfrac{P}{I^2}$
P, R	Current	$I = \sqrt{\dfrac{P}{R}}$
P, R	Voltage	$V = \sqrt{P \times R}$

* Note: these four formulas are the basic formulas. The others are re-arranged versions, to allow solving for any desired unknown.

better to learn how to re-arrange the formulas than to try and memorize each of the 12 different versions.

Practice Problems:
Ohm's Law and Power Formulas

Part A. With the table below, use the two given values to find the two unknown values. All answers must have the proper units.

	Voltage	Current	Resistance	Power
(1)	_____	15 amps	2 ohms	_____
(2)	_____	2 amps	_____	5 watts
(3)	100 volts	0.01 amps	_____	_____
(4)	250 volts	_____	5 ohms	_____
(5)	15 volts	_____	_____	100 mW
(6)	_____	_____	1 kilohm	10 mW
(7)	_____	25 mA	10 kilohms	_____
(8)	_____	2 mA	_____	25 mW
(9)	50 volts	5 mA	_____	_____
(10)	5 volts	_____	2500 ohms	_____

Part B. Use the information given in each of the following word problems to find the unknown values.

(11) A resistor with the color code brown-black-red-silver is connected to a 6 volt battery. Determine the current flowing from the battery and the power dissipated by the resistor.

(12) A particular light bulb in a car is rated at 36 watts. What is the resistance of the light and the current drain? (Assume a 12 volt battery.)

(13) A zener diode has a voltage dropped across it of 6 volts. The current through the diode is 2 amps. Determine the power-dissipation requirements and what value resistor could be used in its place.

(14) What is the resistance of a 60 watt/120 volt light bulb. Also determine the current requirement.

(15) A load resistor with the color code yellow-violet-orange-gold is connected to 2 "D-size" dry cell batteries. Determine the current flow and the power dissipated.

CONNECTING SINGLE-LOAD CIRCUITS

Whenever possible, all of the circuit parameters (voltage, current, resistance, power) should be calculated before making an attempt at measurements. This will ensure that the meters are used properly.

Wiring a Circuit

On paper, schematic diagrams are neatly drawn and a student quickly learns to read the schematics. However, when connecting a circuit with wires and components, things are not so neat and easy.

Figure 7-2 shows a schematic diagram and a pictorial drawing. The symbol for a battery is shown as a box. It is most common to use a variable power supply in a laboratory situation. If a variable power supply is not available, a 6 volt "lantern" battery will be adequate for the circuits presented here. Notice that the voltage source is labeled with + and − . This is the polarity of the voltage and is very important when working with dc.

All of the lines in a schematic diagram represent wires in an actual circuit. In Fig. 7-2, a wire runs from the + side of the voltage source to a switch. It is shown here as a two terminal on/off

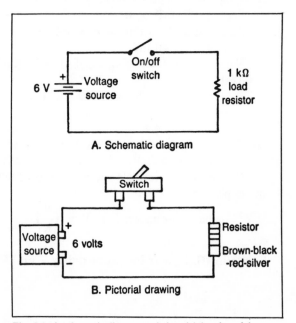

Fig. 7-2. A schematic diagram and pictorial drawing of the same dc circuit.

switch. Keep in mind, a double-throw switch works as well as a single-throw switch when it is used as on/off. A wire runs from the switch to the resistor. Resistors do not have a specific polarity, therefore, they can be connected in any direction. A wire then runs from the resistor back to the voltage source to complete the circuit.

It is best when connecting circuits to trace each wire as if it were a line on the schematic diagram.

Calculating the Circuit Parameters

It is very important to calculate the parameters of a circuit, whenever possible. By doing this, it will be seen immediately on the meters if all connections have been made correctly.

The circuit of Fig. 7-2 shows a 6 volt battery connected to a 1 kilohm resistor, through a switch. When the switch is closed, current will flow in the circuit and the voltage will be applied to the resistor. Using Ohm's law, if the voltage is known and the resistance is known, current and power can be calculated.

Calculating Current:

formula: $I = \dfrac{V}{R}$

substituting: $I = \dfrac{6 \text{ volts}}{1 \text{ kilohm}}$

solving: $I = 6$ milliamps

Calculating Power:

formula: $P = I \times V$
substituting: $P = 6 \text{ mA} \times 6 \text{ volts}$
solving: $P = 36$ milliwatts

Due to the nature of measuring instruments, meters to measure power are seldom used. The calculation for power is necessary only to ensure that the resistor connected will be a large enough wattage rating for the circuit. The calculation for current is much more important since a current meter (ammeter) will be used.

USING A VOLTMETER

The voltmeter most technicians use, and therefore most students, is the multimeter type. In other words, the same meter used as an ohmmeter will now change the range switch and become a voltmeter. Figure 7-3 shows two different multimeters, with quite different voltmeter scales.

Reading the Meter Scales

Always keep in mind that the range switch determines which scale is to be read.

Generally speaking, all meters will use the same scales for both voltage and current, and most meters will use a different scale for dc and ac, but usually they are marked with exactly the same numbers.

The meter on the left, in Fig. 7-3 has four scales. Ohms at the top, dc, ac and dB. The meter on the right has five scales, dc on the top, ac (RMS), ac (P-P), R and dB.

Using just the dc scale as a model, examine both meters. The scales are quite different, but consider the function of the range switch. The range switch determines the maximum or "full-scale" reading for each scale.

The meter on the left has scales for the ranges of 10, 50 and 250. The range switch for that same meter has those three positions, plus 2.5 and 500. That means the range switch also acts like a multiplier. The 50 scale is used for 500 and the 250 scale is used for the 2.5 range.

The meter on the right has its dc scale marked 1 and .3 and the range switch goes from .3 V to 1000 V. Notice, however, each step on the range switch is a multiple of the scales.

☐ The range switch of a voltmeter or ammeter selects the maximum for that range.

Connecting a Voltmeter

When connecting a voltmeter in a circuit, it is very important to remember that voltage will be applied to the meter. The meter must be properly connected and adjusted to ensure no damage will result from the applied voltage.

Polarity must be observed when using dc voltages. That means—connect the negative side of

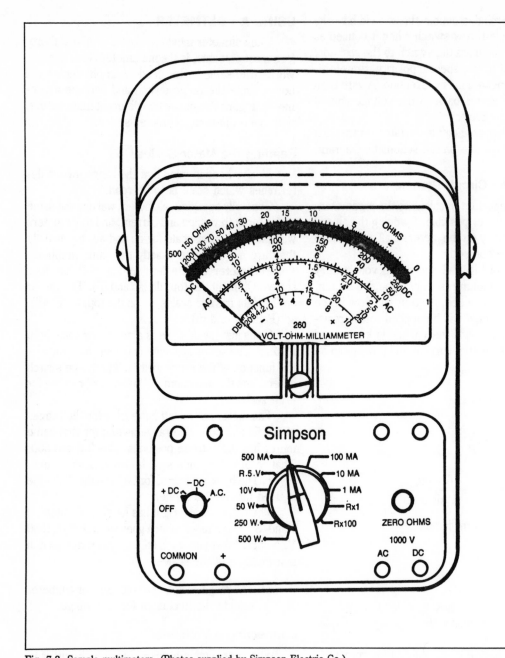

Fig. 7-3. Sample multimeters. (Photos supplied by Simpson Electric Co.)

the meter to negative and the positive side of the meter to positive.

When first connecting a meter, it is best to use a range higher than expected and then switch down to a lower range. In this way the meter is protected from over-voltage in the event that the voltage is higher than expected.

Voltmeters have a very high "input resistance." Although current flowing through the meter is required, voltmeters require a very small

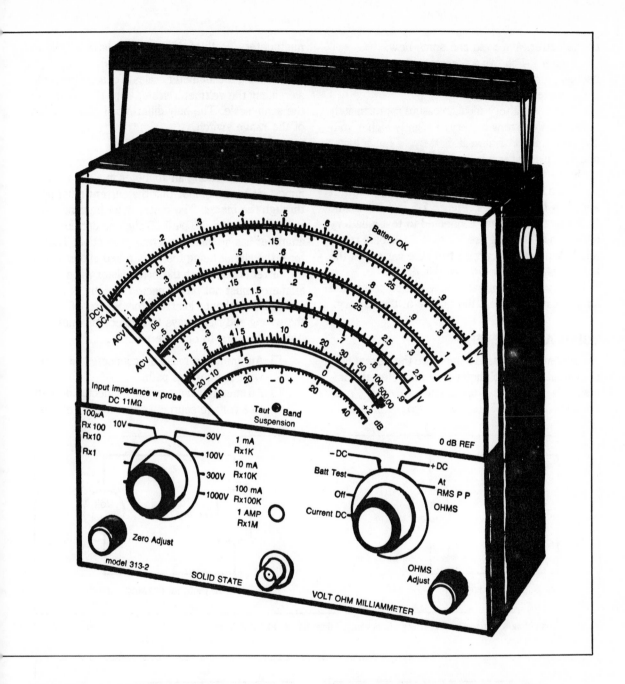

amount of current. Therefore, voltmeters are connected across (in parallel with) the voltage to be measured.

☐ Voltmeters are connected across (in parallel with) the voltage being tested.

Practice Voltmeter Measurements

In order to obtain practice with a voltmeter before making actual circuit measurements, dry cell batteries will be used.

Find several dry cell batteries. The type used in flashlights is good for a start. It is best if some of the batteries are old and some new.

Figure 7-4 shows a schematic diagram of connecting the voltmeter to the battery. Be sure to observe meter polarity.

A dry cell battery should measure approximately 1.5 volts. For a new battery, a slightly higher voltage is normal. For a weak battery, a much lower one is. This test will indicate the relative strength of the battery.

For a better test of a battery's quality, connect a load to the terminals. Figure 7-5 is a schematic diagram of a voltmeter connected to test a battery under load. The load used here is a 1 kilohm resistor. When drawing current from the battery, if the battery is weak, the voltage will drop.

The test demonstrated here can be performed on any battery to test the quality of the battery.

USING AN AMMETER

An ammeter is used to measure the current flow in a circuit. Like a voltmeter and ohmmeter, the ammeter is part of the one meter called a "multimeter." Figure 7-3 shows two examples of multimeters. Both of these meters have a scale to measure current (amps or milliamps).

Reading the ammeter scales is exactly the same as reading the voltmeter scale, since they both use the same scale. The only difference is the position of the range switch.

Connecting an Ammeter

When connecting an ammeter in a circuit, it is important to remember that the current must flow through the meter. The meter must be connected in series with (in the path of) the current flow. An ammeter has no built-in current protection. Therefore, the circuit being tested is relied upon to limit the current flow, which the load resistor will do. The ammeter must not be connected directly to a voltage source without a load resistor. Figure 7-6 shows the wrong and right ways to connect an ammeter. Always be sure to observe polarity.

☐ An ammeter must be connected in series with the current path.
☐ An ammeter must not be connected directly to a voltage source without a load resistor.

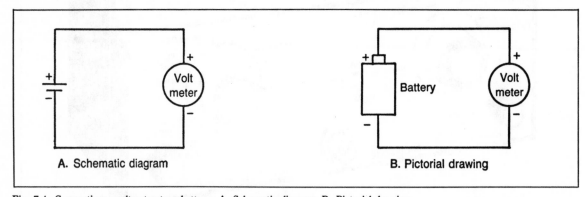

A. Schematic diagram   B. Pictorial drawing

Fig. 7-4. Connecting a voltmeter to a battery: A. Schematic diagram; B. Pictorial drawing.

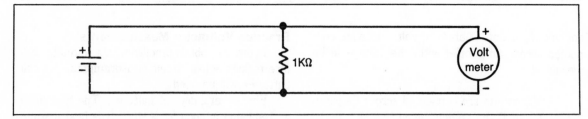

Fig. 7-5. Measuring the voltage of a battery with a 1 kilohm load resistor.

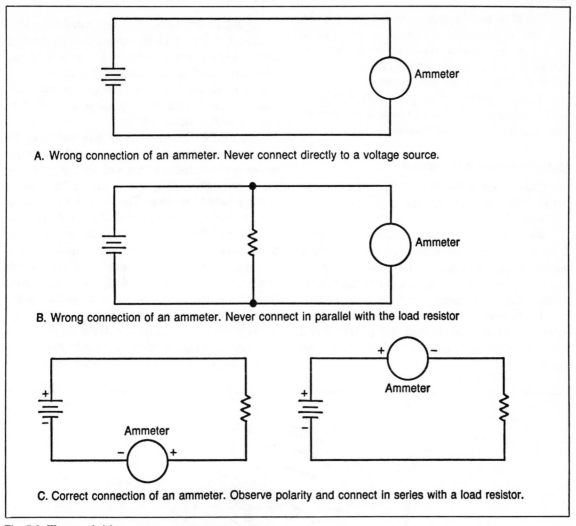

A. Wrong connection of an ammeter. Never connect directly to a voltage source.

B. Wrong connection of an ammeter. Never connect in parallel with the load resistor

C. Correct connection of an ammeter. Observe polarity and connect in series with a load resistor.

Fig. 7-6. Wrong and right ways to connect an ammeter.

Practice Ammeter Measurements

Using Fig. 7-6C as an example, connect a circuit with which to measure current. Any battery can be used, such as a 6 volt lantern battery. Any resistor can be used. A good size to start with is 1 kilohm.

Whenever connecting a circuit for practice, be sure to calculate the circuit parameters. Knowing the circuit parameters beforehand will ensure proper use of the meters. Notice that if the circuit is already built, it is necessary to disconnect one of the current paths to insert the meter. Make certain the negative side of the meter is connected toward the

negative side of the battery and the positive side of the meter is connected toward the positive side. Always observe the needle to make certain it does not go backwards or off the scale.

After making current measurements, reconnect the circuit and make voltage measurements to verify calculations.

METER CONSTRUCTION

The meter construction discussed here is of the analog-type meter. In other words, the type of meter that uses a needle.

Moving Coil

The most popular type of analog meter is the type with a moving coil. Figure 7-7 is a drawing of a meter movement using the moving coil. The moving coil is fixed on a pivot and is allowed to rotate inside the field of a permanent magnet.

When current flows through the coil, a magnetic field is developed which interacts with the permanent magnet and the coil rotates.

Meter Schematic Diagrams

Examination of the meter schematics helps to better understand how the meter will perform its functions.

When the ohmmeter was discussed in Chapter 6, its schematic diagram showed an internal battery was necessary for operation. That is because resistance is never measured when a circuit has voltage applied. The meter must supply its own voltage.

The voltmeter and ammeter use the electricity in the circuit to operate. In all three types of meters, it is current flowing through the coil that rotates the needle.

Voltmeter Schematic Diagram

A voltmeter allows only a very small amount of current to flow through the meter. Only the amount necessary to move the needle. In this way, it has almost no effect on the circuit being measured. A voltmeter should have a very large internal resistance, as close to infinity as possible and still allow current to the meter coil.

Figure 7-8 shows a simplified schematic diagram of a voltmeter. Notice the internal resistance of the meter is connected in series with the meter movement. This internal resistance is called a "multiplier" and is a very high value. The multiplier resistor is used to limit the current flow to the meter.

Figure 7-9 shows a complete schematic diagram of a voltmeter. The range switch is used to select different values of multiplier resistors. It takes a certain amount of current, typically 100 microamps, through the meter movement to make the needle go to "full scale." With each higher range, there will be more voltage, therefore, the multiplier resistor must be a higher value for each higher range. The lowest range will have the lowest multiplier and

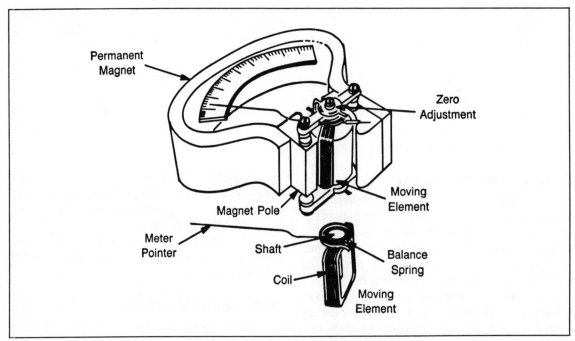

Fig. 7-7. Drawing of a meter movement showing the individual parts and the moving coil.

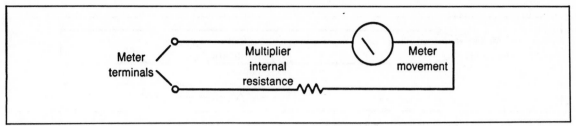

Fig. 7-8. Simplified schematic diagram of a voltmeter.

the highest range will have the highest value of multiplier resistor.

Ohms Per Volt Rating

Voltmeters have an "ohms per volt" rating. The "ohms per volt" rating states the input resistance of the voltmeter, which is based on the current through the meter. The "ohms per volt" rating is always stated for a full scale reading. For example: if a voltmeter has a rating of 1000 "ohms per volt," it will have an input resistance of 2500 ohms on the 2.5 volt scale, 10000 ohms on the 10 volt range, etc. This means that when the voltmeter is connected to a circuit, its resistance (which may affect the circuit) can be calculated, depending upon the range. Voltmeters with a high input resistance, therefore a high "ohms per volt" rating, will have less adverse effect on a circuit than a voltmeter with a lower rating.

Voltmeter Accuracy

The accuracy of a voltmeter is usually stated in percentage of full scale. If the voltmeter has a percent accuracy of 2%, and the range is 10 volts when the meter reads 10 volts, then the tolerance is from 9.8 volts to 10.2 volts (10 × .02 = .2). If this same meter is used on the same 10 volt range, but measures 2 volts, the tolerance is from 1.8 volts to 2.2 volts. It is obvious, then, that readings which are closer to full scale are less affected by the percent accuracy than lower readings in the same range.

Ammeter Schematic Diagram

Figure 7-10 shows a simplified schematic diagram of an ammeter. The meter terminals that connect to the circuit being measured go directly to the meter movement. There is no resistor in series to limit current flow. The shunt resistor is connected in parallel with the meter. The word "shunt" means

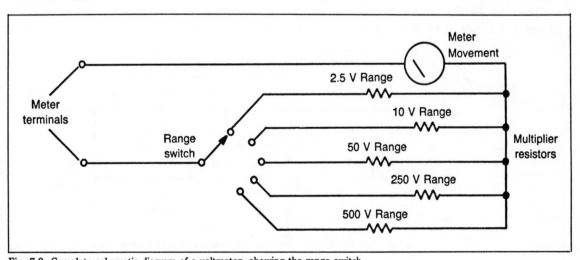

Fig. 7-9. Complete schematic diagram of a voltmeter, showing the range switch.

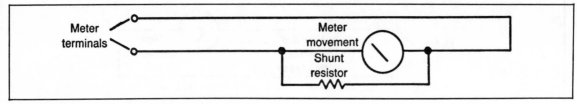

Fig. 7-10. Simplified schematic diagram of an ammeter.

parallel. The shunt resistor is in parallel with the meter movement to allow a percentage of the applied current to bypass the meter.

Figure 7-11 shows a complete schematic diagram of an ammeter. The range switch selects a shunt resistor. Therefore, each range has a percentage of current that bypasses the meter. Let's say, for example, that the meter movement is rated for 100 microamps (.1 milliamps) and the range selected is 1 milliamp. When the meter reads full scale, 1 milliamp flows through the meter terminals, but only 1/10 of that amount flows through the meter movement and the other 9/10 is bypassed through the shunt resistor.

Ammeters have very low resistance because they are connected in series in a circuit. The ideal situation is for the meter to have no more effect on the circuit than a piece of wire.

Ammeter Accuracy

The accuracy of an ammeter is based on a percentage of full scale, in the same manner as a volt-

meter. If the meter is rated as 1% of full scale accuracy, the tolerance on the 100 mA range (100 × .01 = 1), with a current of 100 mA is 99 mA to 101 mA. The same meter on the same 100 mA range, but measuring a current of 10 mA will have a range of 9.9 mA to 11 mA.

It is obvious then, meter readings are the most accurate when closest to full scale.

PROGRAMS FOR THIS CHAPTER

There are two programs for this chapter. The first is practice with Ohm's law and the power formulas and the second is practice with a voltmeter.

Figure 7-12 is a preview of the Ohm's law program. In this program two values are given and it is necessary for the student to calculate a third value. The student should make the actual calculations rather than just guessing at the answers.

Figure 7-13 is a preview of the V&A meter program. This program displays an analog-type meter scale. The student selects the meter range (either 30, 300, or 3000) then with the use of the computer

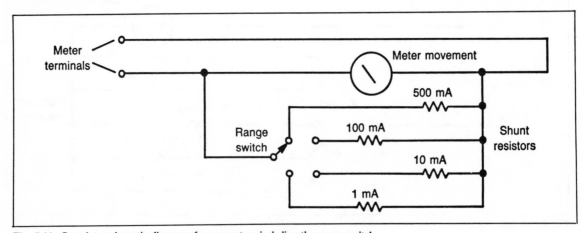

Fig. 7-11. Complete schematic diagram of an ammeter, including the range switch.

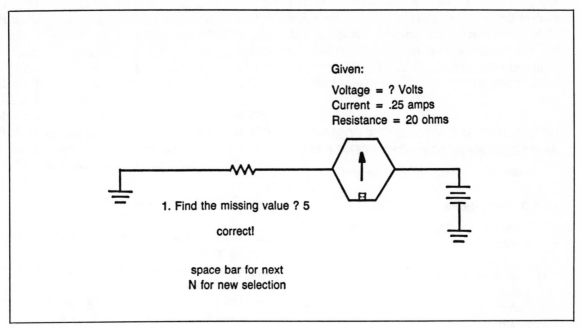

Fig. 7-12. Ohm's law program sample.

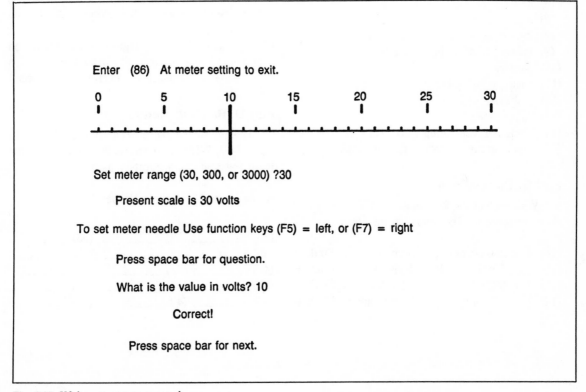

Fig. 7-13. V&A meter program sample.

keys, moves the needle. Once the meter is set, the student then has the opportunity to give the value of the meter reading. This program is unique in that it is a never-ending program, that is to say that the computer will continue to display the meter and allow for student response until the student ends the routine.

DC CIRCUITS: RELATIONSHIPS, FORMULAS AND MEASUREMENTS COMPETENCY TEST

A calculator is required for this test.

Part A. Definitions

Define the following terms. Whenever possible, give examples.

(1) resistance
(2) voltage
(3) current
(4) power
(5) direction of current flow
(6) dc
(7) ac
(8) direct relationship in a formula
(9) indirect relationship in a formula
(10) polarity
(11) analog-type meter
(12) multiplier resistor
(13) shunt resistor
(14) ohms per volt rating (give example)
(15) meter accuracy rating (give example)

Part B. Calculations

With each of the following, use the information given to solve for the unknown quantity.

(16) R = 200 ohms   I = 3 amps   Find: V
(17) I = 5 mA   R = 4 kilohms   Find: P
(18) I = 25 mA   V = 15 volts   Find: R
(19) V = 30 volts   I = 2 microamps   Find: P

(20) R = 2.2 kilohms   V = 44 volts   Find: I
(21) V = 60 volts   R = 250 ohms   Find: P
(22) P = 2 mW   R = 15 kilohms   Find: I
(23) R = 500 ohms   P = 20 mW   Find: V
(24) P = 4 watts   I = 2 amps   Find: V
(25) I = 50 mA   P = 1 watt   Find: R
(26) P = 100 milliwatts   V = 25 millivolts   Find: I
(27) V = 3 volts   P = 60 mW   Find: R
(28) R = 2 megohms   I = 5 microamps   Find: P
(29) I = 30 microamps   R = 4 megohms   Find: V
(30) P = 10 milliwatts   R = 25 megohms   Find: I

Part C. Schematic Diagrams

(31) Draw a simplified schematic diagram of an ohmmeter.
(32) Draw a simplified schematic diagram of a voltmeter.
(33) Draw a simplified schematic diagram of an ammeter.
(34) Draw a schematic diagram of a resistor connected to a battery. Show a voltmeter connected to measure the voltage applied to the resistor.
(35) Draw a schematic diagram of a resistor connected to a battery. Show an ammeter connected to measure the current in the circuit.

Part D. Reading Meters

Use the sample meter scales in Figs. 7-14, 7-15, 7-16, 7-17, 7-18; state the reading of each needle. Read the scale as accurately as possible.

All Answers Must Have Proper Units.

(36) _____ (37) _____ (38) _____
(39) _____ (40) _____ (41) _____
(42) _____ (43) _____ (44) _____
(45) _____ (46) _____ (47) _____
(48) _____ (49) _____ (50) _____

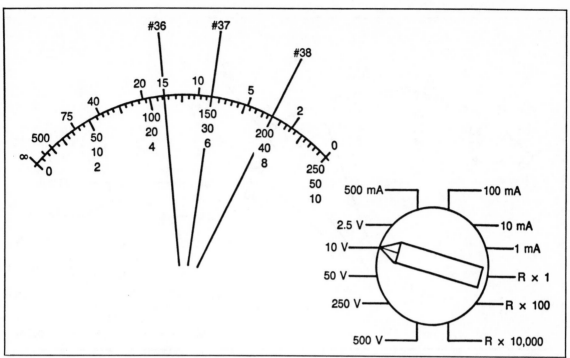

Fig. 7-14. Meter scale for test questions 36, 37, 38.

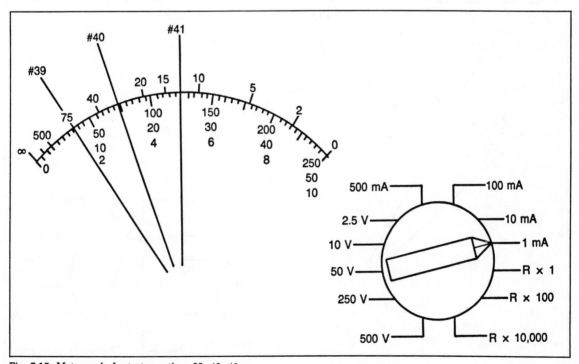

Fig. 7-15. Meter scale for test questions 39, 40, 41.

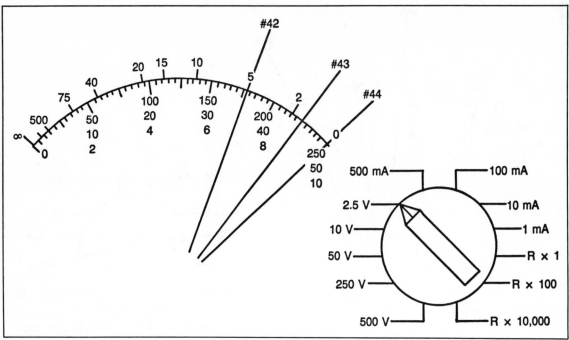

Fig. 7-16. Meter scale for test questions 42, 43, 44.

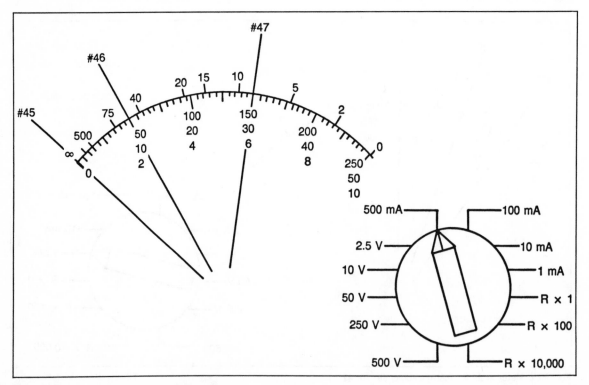

Fig. 7-17. Meter scale for test questions 45, 46, 47.

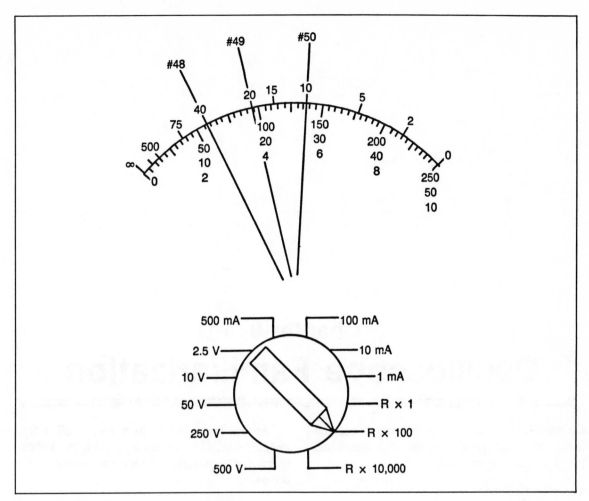

Fig. 7-18. Meter scale for test questions 48, 49, 50.

Chapter 8
Oscilloscope Familiarization

Chapter Objective: A hands-on lesson to become familiar with the operation of the oscilloscope and use it to measure dc voltages.

Chapter Outline:

- ☐ What an oscilloscope does
- ☐ Oscilloscope screen
- ☐ Understanding oscilloscope controls
- ☐ Measuring dc voltages
- ☐ Hands-on practice with dc voltages
- ☐ Programs for this chapter

INTRODUCTION

An oscilloscope, "scope" for short, is an electronic instrument used for making various voltage and waveform measurements. It is one of the most popular, and useful tools for troubleshooting a circuit.

Scopes have a cathode-Ray-Tube (CRT) screen similar to that of a TV for viewing the voltages being measured. It is this "picture" that makes the scope such a useful tool.

Scopes range in size from very small, a few inches across, with a screen area of only two inches, to quite large cabinets, with screens several inches across.

WHAT THE OSCILLOSCOPE DOES

In some ways, an oscilloscope is a voltmeter with a "picture" of the voltage as it varies over time.

In the field of electronics, there are many different types of waveforms that need to be measured and analyzed to determine if the electronic signal is correct for what is expected.

Therefore, it is very important for the student technician to gain experience with the oscilloscope as early as possible in the electronics training program.

The oscilloscope replaces a voltmeter in certain applications because of its capability to display a picture. However, it does not simply give an instant number reading of the measurement. In this way, the scope is harder to read and most technicians prefer using a voltmeter when all that is necessary is a number measurement.

One thing an oscilloscope cannot do is measure current or resistance. The voltage waveform can be thought of as a result of a current flowing and, therefore, the current waveform can be observed.

Voltage Measurements

The scope measures voltage by showing the relative size and shape of the waveform. The accuracy of the measurement can be seen on the screen. Voltage sizes are measured in comparison to a reference line, established with each measurement.

It is possible to display on the oscilloscope more than one voltage waveform at a time. Most scopes have "dual trace capability" and some have four or more traces. Each trace is a voltage measurement. A "dual trace" scope can measure two voltages at the same time.

The dual trace capability allows two voltages to be measured and observed at the same time. This means the voltages can be compared for both size (actual voltage measurement) and shape (what type of waveform it is). The dual trace capability is sometimes the only way to determine if a circuit is working correctly.

OSCILLOSCOPE SCREEN

The oscilloscope screen is usually rectangular and is divided into small squares. The squares are used to measure the size of the waveform measurements, both vertically and horizontally. Figure 8-1 is a drawing of a dual trace oscilloscope.

The scope screen is actually a cathode ray tube, like a TV screen. A beam of electrons strikes the back of the screen to form the trace.

Vertical Divisions

The lines going across the screen, forming the tops and bottoms of the squares, measure the wave-

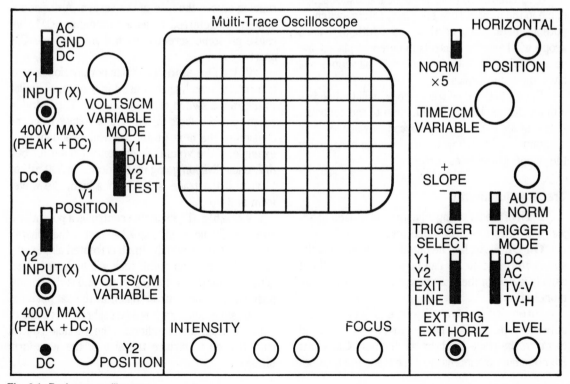

Fig. 8-1. Dual trace oscilloscope.

form in the vertical direction. Each of these lines is called a division. A voltage is measured by counting the number of divisions from the reference line.

Horizontal Divisions

The lines that run up and down on the screen, forming the sides of the squares are the divisions used to make measurements in the horizontal direction. These measurements are actually time measurements and can be used to determine frequency of the waveform.

This chapter will be mostly concerned with learning the controls and making measurements with a dc voltage. A dc voltage appears as a straight line on the screen. The horizontal divisions will not be of any major importance with dc voltages. In a later chapter, the horizontal, time per division, will be used for making measurements with ac voltages.

UNDERSTANDING OSCILLOSCOPE CONTROLS

The controls on the front of the oscilloscope come in the form of slide switches, rotary switches, potentiometers, connectors, etc. Although each scope will have the controls in different places and some will have a few extra controls, all scopes will have the same basics.

Figure 8-1, a dual trace scope, will be used as a model for explaining the function of the controls. If the student has an oscilloscope available, it is recommended to follow the explanation here, using the scope available as a model.

Trace Adjustments

Each of the following adjustments is used to adjust the trace for proper operation.

On/Off Switch. The on/off switch controls the power to the scope. It can be located by itself but usually is part of the intensity control, as it is in the model shown.

Intensity Control. The intensity control is a potentiometer, and is a control that turns. It is used to make the trace brighter on dimmer. **Caution:** Do not adjust the intensity of the trace too high be-

cause damage to the CRT can result. The correct and best adjustment is to have the intensity just high enough to comfortably see the trace.

Focus. The focus control is used to adjust the focus of the trace. When the intensity is low, it will be easiest to focus. A high intensity will be difficult to focus.

Astigmatism. This control is used in conjunction with the focus control. Most scopes have the astigmatism on the back, and accessible only to a screwdriver. This control is used only when the regular focus does not make a clear trace.

VERTICAL CONTROLS AND ADJUSTMENTS

Vertical deflection is the up and down movement of the oscilloscope trace. It is these controls and adjustments that affect the voltage measurements. Voltage is measured by its relative size or position to a reference and how the controls are set. When a scope is referred to as "dual trace", there is a separate vertical channel for each trace.

A division on an oscilloscope screen is each line running across the face of the screen. A division is sometimes referred to as a centimeter, CM, because on some screens, each division is one CM apart.

Volts/Division. The volts per division control is a rotary switch that is used in a manner similar to the range switch on a multimeter. The volts/division control selects the amount of voltage from one division to the next (in the vertical direction). For example, if the volts/division control is set for 500 mV, each division going up (or down) is 500 mV or ½ volt. If the trace is 4 divisions high, the waveform is 2 volts.

Variable. The variable control is a potentiometer, usually mounted to look like part of the volts/division control. When the knob is rotated all the way in one direction, an on/off click will be heard. That is the "calibrate" (or cal) position and is the normal position for this control. When in the cal position, the volts/division switch will be calibrated as labeled. Under certain test conditions, the variable control can be used to reduce the size of the waveform display.

AC/GND/DC. This slide switch is used to control how the input voltage is being measured.

GND blocks the input voltage waveform. In the GND position, the scope trace will be a straight line at the "ground reference level". The reference level is usually placed at a convenient line on the screen. (The position is adjusted using the position control.) The ground reference line must be adjusted each time the volts/division control is changed.

AC allows the scope to respond to only the ac content of a waveform. Any voltage waveform viewed in the AC position will center itself around the reference line. Most AC waveforms are symmetrical—that is, they have an equal amount of voltage above the reference as they have below. It is possible, however, for a voltage waveform not to be symmetrical and it would appear distorted if viewed in the AC position.

DC allows the scope to respond to both the dc and ac components of the waveform. It is very important to use dc with voltages that are unsymmetrical. When a dc voltage is measured, it must be performed in dc. Failure to do so will display only a straight line at the zero reference. Ac voltages that are symmetrical will appear exactly the same on either ac or dc. If a voltage has both a dc component and an ac component, it may be desired to measure only the ac portion, in which case ac must be used. Experience teaches the technician which setting to use for any given test.

Vertical Position. The position control is used to position the trace up and down on the screen. It is usually best to make this adjustment using the ground reference line—with the switch in GND.

HORIZONTAL CONTROLS

Regardless of how many voltage inputs a scope may have, there will only be one set of horizontal controls. These controls affect two functions—movement of the trace in the horizontal direction, and time measurements. All input channels are affected by these controls at the same time.

Horizontal Position. A potentiometer is used to adjust the horizontal position of the trace. When making time measurements, the waveform can be moved sideways to line it up exactly on a line to allow for each in making the measurements.

Time Per Division. The time per division control is a rotary switch used to adjust the speed of the beam across the screen. Time measurements are used to determine the frequency of a voltage waveform. Switching to a higher time setting will spread the width of a waveform and switching to a lower time setting will narrow the waveform. Most oscilloscopes have an added feature on the time per division control, a setting marked X-Y. When X-Y is selected, one voltage input controls the horizontal deflection and the other voltage input controls the vertical deflection. Although this is seldom used, its display can be useful for certain measurements.

Variable. The variable control is used to vary the time per division setting. Under normal conditions, the variable control is set to calibrate, cal. When an exact time measurement is not necessary, the variable control can be used to reduce the time/division. Sometimes a slight adjustment with the variable control will help make a voltage measurement.

Normal x5. Many scopes have a switch associated with the time/division control to allow an instant multiplication by 5 of the time/division setting. Under normal conditions, this switch would be left in normal. Under certain conditions, it is necessary to expand the size of the waveform for a closer look at a portion of it. This has the same effect as that of using a zoom lens on a camera.

TRIGGER

The trigger on an oscilloscope is used to allow for a stable trace. Since most waveforms that will be displayed have a continuously varying shape, it is necessary to have the same "starting point" each time the trace sweeps across the screen. The trace sweeps from left to right on the screen. Therefore, the "starting point" is on the left and is adjustable by selecting the trigger point—a voltage level. If the trigger point is not correctly set, then the waveform display will appear to move across the screen.

Trigger Select (Trigger Source). The trigger select or trigger source is a switch that selects which voltage will be used to trigger the display. There are usually four sources to choose from: channel 1; channel 2; external; line. For most applications, select the channel where the input voltage is connected. If both channels are used, the channel selected for trigger becomes a reference voltage. Under certain test conditions, a third voltage can be applied to the external trigger connector. This external voltage will be used as a reference. The fourth source, line, is used whenever the waveform displayed is 60 cycle (line frequency), in which case the trigger is internal to the scope.

Trigger Mode. The trigger mode selects the type of voltage to be used as the trigger. When dc is selected, it is a voltage level that triggers the scope. When ac is selected, it is a change in voltage that triggers the scope. Another choice available is TV which allows selecting a type of waveform, such as would be found in a TV receiver. For most test conditions, dc or ac is used.

Slope +/−. The slope switch is used to select whether the signal will trigger on a positive (+) or a negative (−) voltage. For most test conditions, select whichever provides the stable trace.

Auto/Normal. In the auto (automatic) mode, the scope will trigger on any voltage available. For many test conditions, auto is satisfactory, as long as the trace is stable. The auto mode bypasses the other trigger controls. Normal is used when it is desired to have control of the other trigger functions.

Level. The level control is a potentiometer that is turned to select the amount of voltage necessary to trigger the scope. Many level controls are labeled with − on the left and + on the right, which would be used in place of the slope control.

MEASURING DC VOLTAGES

Although the oscilloscope is primarily thought of as displaying waveforms, it is also very useful for measuring dc voltages. If a dc voltage is a pure dc voltage, it will appear as a straight line on the scope, at a height above (or below for negative voltages) the reference line. If it is a perfect straight line, that means it is a constant voltage. Remember, voltage is up and down on the screen, therefore a constant voltage does not change in height.

Scope Test Leads

The test leads connecting to an oscilloscope are made of coaxial wire. It has a center conductor, which is surrounded by an insulator. Wrapped around the insulator is a braided jacket and a final insulation is on the outside. One end of the test lead has a "BNC" connector which is connected to the BNC connector on the scope. The other end of the test lead has either alligator clips or a probe.

Connect the test lead BNC connector to the scope BNC connector to the channel 1 input. Notice that the center conductor of the test lead has a pin to fit into the connector on the scope. The braided jacket is connected to the metal portion of the connector, which clips onto the metal portion of the BNC connector on the scope. The connector on the scope is connected directly to the chassis of the scope (the electrical ground) from the three prong plug, is connected to the braided jacket of the test lead. The other end of the test lead is a black wire with an alligator clip. That is the ground wire.

Connecting a Scope to a Circuit

When connecting a scope to a circuit, it is very important to consider where the ground wire is connected. Where the ground is connected becomes zero volts reference in the circuit.

For example, if a flashlight battery is measured with the ground on negative and the probe to positive, the measurement will be positive 1.5 volts. However, if the leads are reversed and the ground is connected to the positive and the probe to the negative, then the measurement will be negative 1.5 volts.

Figure 8-2 shows the scope connected to a battery. The schematic diagram looks like a voltmeter

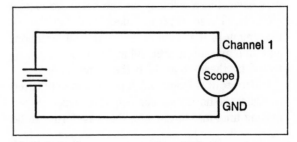

Fig. 8-2. Oscilloscope connected to a battery.

connected to a battery. The reason a scope and volt-meter have the same schematic diagram is because they both make the same measurement.

Preliminary Scope Adjustments

When a technician becomes familiar with the scope, it is not necessary to make preliminary adjustments. However, preliminary adjustments can be a great help to a student.

Scope adjustments come in four groups: beam (intensity and focus); time per division; trigger; volts per division. Preliminary adjustments are used with the trigger and time controls.

Trigger. When there is no voltage input signal, the scope must trigger on automatic. Select auto as a preliminary setting.

Beam. Once there is a trace on the screen, a straight line, adjust the intensity and focus to a normal level.

Time per Division. The time per division makes very little difference when a dc voltage is being measured. However, if the time is too slow, such as 100 ms, the trace will be a dot going across the screen. If it is too fast, such as 1 μs, the trace may appear dim and hard to trigger. The best preliminary setting before measuring dc voltages is a setting of approximately 1 ms. This setting should give a stable straight line.

Volts per Division. This control will be the primary control when making dc measurements. If the setting is too low, such as 10 mV, the line may jump off the screen when taking a measurement. If the setting is too high, such as 20 V, the line may appear not to move and make it impossible to take an accurate reading. Only experience and practice will dictate the setting of this control.

HANDS-ON PRACTICE WITH DC VOLTAGES

It is best with these practice dc measurements, to use both a scope and a dc voltmeter. In this way, the student gains more experience with the voltmeter and has more confidence in the measurements taken with the scope.

The hands-on practice for using a scope to measure dc voltages is designed as a step-by-step procedure to gain the most from the experience.

Step 1. Select a dc voltage source: a variable power supply or a 6 volts dry cell battery.

Step 2. Connect the ground lead from the scope and the negative voltmeter lead to the negative side of the battery.

Step 3. Connect the scope lead and the positive voltmeter lead to the positive side of the battery.

Step 4. Preadjust the scope settings as described in this chapter.

Step 5. Select the 1 volt per division setting. Make certain that the variable adjustment is set to cal. Use the GND switch and adjust the ground reference line to the bottom line on the screen. (Use the position control to adjust the trace to the desired position.)

Step 6. Move the AC/GND/DC switch to DC. The trace should jump up 6 divisions (1 volt per division). See Fig. 8-3. If the voltage of the battery is not exactly 6 volts, the trace will not fall exactly on the major division line. At the center of the oscilloscope screen, the divisions are divided with small lines to enable a more accurate reading. Use these minor divisions to read the screen as accurately as a voltmeter. The reading obtained in this step should be equal to the voltmeter connected.

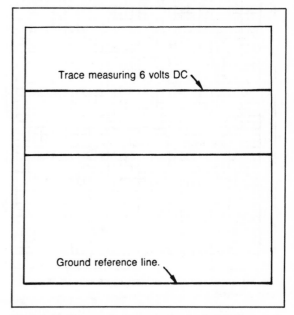

Fig. 8-3. Oscilloscope display measuring 6 volts DC. Scope setting: 1 volt/div.

Step 7. Change the volts/div setting to 2 volts/div. Make certain the variable control is set to cal. Use the GND switch and adjust the ground reference line to the bottom line on the screen.

Step 8. Move the AC/GND/DC switch to DC. The trace should now appear 3 divisions above the ground reference line (2 volts per division). See Fig. 8-4.

Step 9. Change the volts per division to 5 volts/div. Make certain variable is set at cal. Adjust the ground reference line.

Step 10. Move the AC/GND/DC switch to DC. The trace should now appear a little over 1 division above ground (5 volts/div).

Step 11. Change the volts/div to 500 mV/div. Make certain the variable control is set to cal. Use the GND switch and adjust the ground reference line to the bottom line on the screen.

Step 12. Move the AC/GND/DC switch to DC. The trace should disappear from the screen. The reason is that if each division is 500 mV (½ volt), there are not enough divisions on the screen to measure 6 volts.

Step 13. Select 1 volt per division, check the

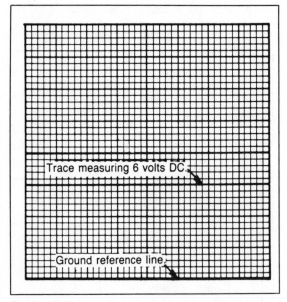

Fig. 8-4. Oscilloscope display measuring 6 volts DC. Scope setting: 2 volts/div.

variable and adjust the ground reference line. Select DC to verify the measurement is the same as step 6, above. In the next steps, the volts/div will remain on 1 volt/div.

Step 14. Move the AC/GND/DC switch to AC. The trace may jump up momentarily, but it will quickly go to the ground level and stay there. The scope does not recognize dc voltages when ac is selected.

Step 15. Return the AC/GND/DC switch to DC. (The trace should again appear at 6 volts). Turn the variable control. As the variable control is turned further from the cal position, the trace should move closer to the ground level. This control is valuable under certain conditions, but when measuring voltage, it must be set in the cal position.

Proper Selection of Volts/Div

It is very important to select the proper setting for the volts/div control. Too sensitive and the trace jumps off the screen; not sensitive enough and the voltage measurement is quite inaccurate. As a general rule, the best setting for the volts/div control is the setting that allows the maximum deflection of the trace, and still remain on the oscilloscope screen.

PROGRAMS FOR THIS CHAPTER

The program for this chapter is an opportunity for the student to learn and practice operation of the oscilloscope. The name is "Oscilloscope DC".

The screen is very similar to an actual oscilloscope screen. Refer to Fig. 8-5 for a sample of the oscilloscope dc program. The ground reference line has been placed at the center of the screen. Whenever counting divisions up or down, always begin counting from the center line.

On the right hand side of the computer, notice that there are three information blocks. The top info block is the setting for "time/division". Since all of the measurements in this program are dc, the time/division has no effect. The middle info block is the setting for "volts/division" for channel #1. This is the channel setting that will be in use throughout

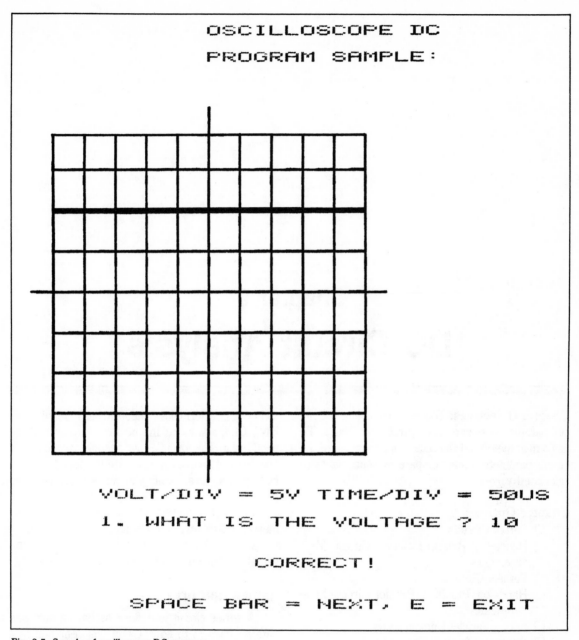

Fig. 8-5. Sample of oscilloscope DC program.

the program. The third info block is the setting for "volts/division" for channel #2. Channel #2 is not used at this time.

The middle information block with volts/div for channel #1 must be observed for each reading. This will change each time. Multiply the volts/div by the number of divisions away from the ground reference line, which is the center line in this program.

Chapter 9

DC Circuit Analysis

Chapter Objectives: To learn to calculate the circuit parameters of series and parallel dc circuits. To use a multimeter and an oscilloscope to measure the circuit parameters and compare measurements to calculated values.

Chapter Outline:

- ☐ Series Circuits
- ☐ Hands-On Practice: Series Circuit Measurements
- ☐ Parallel Circuits
- ☐ Hands-on Practice: Parallel Circuit Measurements
- ☐ Series-Parallel Combinations
- ☐ Programs for this Chapter
- ☐ Dc Circuit Analysis Competency Test

INTRODUCTION

This chapter will discuss dc circuits with more than one load resistor. The resistors can be connected in one of two manners, either series or parallel. They each have a set of rules to follow, including new formulas. The formulas learned in the past, Ohm's law and the power formulas, will be used again. The formulas and theory learned in this chapter will be used to calculate the four basic circuit parameters: voltage; current; resistance; power.

The three meters of the multimeter—ohmmeter, voltmeter, and ammeter—will be used to measure the circuit parameters. The oscilloscope will also be used for practice.

SERIES CIRCUITS

A series circuit is defined as having only one path for current to flow. Using this definition as a guideline, the following rules are established. Each rule will be explained in detail.

1. Current is the same throughout a series circuit.
2. Total resistance in a series circuit is the sum of the individual resistors.
3. The sum of the voltage drops in a series circuit equals the applied voltage.

(4) The sum of the individual powers equals the total applied power.

Current is the Same in Series

A series circuit has only one path for the flow of current. Therefore, the current must be the same at all points in the circuit. The current through one resistor is the same as the current in all resistors of the same circuit, and is equal to the total current flow.

In order for current to flow in a circuit, there must be a complete path for the electrons to leave the negative side of the voltage source, flow through the circuit, and for an equal number of electrons to return to the positive side of the power supply.

Figure 9-1 shows a circuit with three resistors connected in series. Notice that the arrow indicates the direction of current flow—from negative to positive. This arrow can be drawn at any location in this circuit, because current flow is the same throughout the circuit. The mathematics of calculating current will be demonstrated later.

Total Resistance is the Sum of Series Resistors

In a series circuit, the current flows through each resistor. Therefore, the total resistance imposed upon the current is equal to adding the individual resistors. This statement can be expressed as a formula.

Formula # 7. Total Resistance in a Series Circuit.

$$R_T = R_1 + R_2 + R_3 + \ldots$$

Resistance total = resistor 1 + resistor 2 + resistor 3 + all other series resistors.

Sample Circuit Calculation of Total Resistance

The total resistance can be calculated for the sample circuit of Fig. 9-1.

Formula:
$$R_T = R_1 + R_2 + R_3 + \ldots$$

Substituting:
$$R_T = 50 \text{ ohms} + 30 \text{ ohms} + 20 \text{ ohms}$$

Solving:
$$R_T = 100 \text{ ohms}$$

Calculating Total Current Using Total Resistance

Total current is calculated using the basic Ohm's law formulas with the applied voltage and the total resistance. The sample circuit, Fig. 9-1, is used to show the calculation of total current.

Applied voltage = 100 volts
Total resistance = 100 ohms
Formula:

$$I = \frac{V}{R}$$

Substituting:

$$I = \frac{100 \text{ volts}}{100 \text{ ohms}}$$

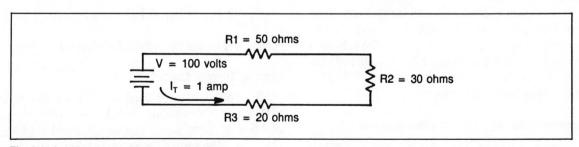

Fig. 9-1. A series circuit with three resistors.

Solving:

$$I = 1 \text{ amp}$$

The Sum of the Voltage Drops Equals the Applied Voltage

As current flows through a resistor, some of the voltage is dropped across the resistor. A portion of the voltage available from the voltage source will be "dropped" at each of the circuit resistors. The larger resistor will require more "voltage drop" and the smaller resistor will require a smaller "voltage drop." All of the voltage available will be distributed among the circuit resistors. This statement can be made with a mathematical formula.

Formula # 8. Voltage Drops in a Series Circuit

$$V_T = V_{R1} + V_{R2} + V_{R3} + \ldots$$

Voltage total equals the sum of the voltage drops across each resistor.

In order to calculate the voltage drop across each resistor in a series circuit, it is necessary to use Ohm's law to solve for voltage.

$$V = I \times R \text{ or } V = IR$$

It is very common, therefore, to rename the term "voltage drop" as the "IR drop." To reflect the "IR drop" phrase, the formula for voltage drops in a series circuit can be re-written.

Formula # 9. IR Drops in a Series Circuit

$$V_T = IR_1 + IR_2 + IR_3 + \ldots$$

Voltage total equals the sum of the IR drops of the individual resistors.

Comment: Both formulas for voltage drops have the same end result. The important point to remember is that the voltage drops of the individual resistors must add up to equal the total applied voltage. Always use this as a check to ensure calculations have been made correctly.

Sample Voltage Drops Calculations

Figure 9-1 will be used again here to demonstrate how to calculate voltage drops. In this sam-

ple, the voltage drop across each individual resistor will be calculated separately.

Current = 1 amp (same at all points in the circuit)

Voltage Across R_1
Formula: $V_{R1} = I \times R_1$
Substituting: $V_{R1} = (1 \text{ amp}) \times (50 \text{ ohms})$
Solving: $V_{R1} = 50 \text{ volts}$

Voltage Across R_2
Formula: $V_{R2} = I \times R_2$
Substituting: $V_{R2} = (1 \text{ amp}) \times (30 \text{ ohms})$
Solving: $V_{R2} = 30 \text{ volts}$

Voltage Across R_3
Formula: $V_{R3} = I \times R_3$
Substituting: $V_{R3} = (1 \text{ amp}) \times (20 \text{ ohms})$
Solving: $V_{R3} = 20 \text{ volts}$

Adding the Voltage Drops
Formula: $V_T = IR_1 + IR_2 + IR_3 + \ldots$
Substituting: $V_T = (50 \text{ volts}) + (30 \text{ volts}) + (20 \text{ volts})$
Solving: $V_T = 100 \text{ volts}$

Sum of the Powers Equals the Applied Power

Since the voltage source supplies both voltage and current to all parts of the circuit, it can be said that the voltage source also supplies power. All of the power supplied from the source is dissipated at the individual resistors. Therefore, the sum of the individual powers equals the total power. This can be expressed as a formula.

Formula #10. Total Power

$$P_T = 3 P_{R1} + P_{R2} + P_{R3} + \ldots$$

Total power equals the sum of the individual powers.

Sample Power Calculations

Figure 9-1 is again used to solve for the individual power dissipation of each resistor and the total power. Total power can be calculated in two ways: first, the sum of the powers and second, total current and applied voltage.

It is best to first calculate the power of the individual resistors.

Power of R_1
Formula: $P_{R1} = I \times V_{R1}$
Substituting: $P_{R1} = (1 \text{ amp}) \times (50 \text{ volts})$
Solving: $P_{R1} = 50$ watts

Power of R_2
Formula: $P_{R2} = I \times V_{R2}$
Substituting: $P_{R2} = (1 \text{ amp}) \times (30 \text{ volts})$
Solving: $P_{R2} = 30$ watts

Power of R_3
Formula: $P_{R3} = I \times V_{R3}$
Substituting: $P_{R3} = (1 \text{ amp}) \times (20 \text{ volts})$
Solving: $P_{R3} = 20$ watts

Sum of the Powers Equals Power Total
Formula: $P_T = P_{R1} + P_{R2} + P_{R3} + \ldots$
Substituting: $P_T = (50 \text{ watts}) + (30 \text{ watts}) + (20 \text{ watts})$
Solving: $P_T = 100$ watts

Power Total Using Power Formula
Formula: $P_T = I \times V$
Substituting: $P_T = (1 \text{ amp}) \times (100 \text{ volts})$
Solving: $P_T = 100$ watts

Summary of Solving a Series Circuit
The following procedure is intended as a general guideline for solving a series circuit. Some series circuit problems offer a different set of unknowns. However, an understanding of this guideline will help to solve any circuit.

(1) Find R_T. Finding the total resistance is the first step in solving a series circuit. Total resistance is the sum of the individual resistors.
(2) Find I_T. Remember, the current is the same throughout a series circuit. In order to calculate current, it is necessary to know the voltage and the resistance. Always use either total voltage and total resistance or the voltage drop across a resistor and its resistance.
(3) Find individual voltage drops. Voltage is calculated using Ohm's law with resistance and current. Make certain to add the individual voltage drops to check that they equal the applied voltage.
(4) Find power. Individual power of each resistor can be calculated by using the current and the individual voltage drops. Total power is the sum of the individual powers or use the power formula and total current with the applied voltage.

Practice Problems: Series Circuit
Part A. Use the information given in the schematic diagrams and in the problems to find the unknowns.

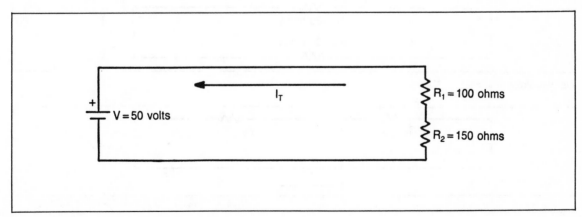

Fig. 9-2. Problem 1. Find: I_T, R_T, V_{R1}, V_{R2}, P_{R1}, P_{R2}.

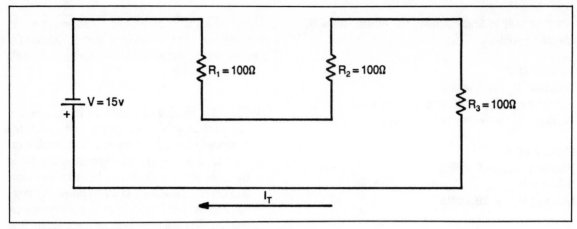

Fig. 9-3. Problem 2. Find: I_T, R_T, V_{R1}, V_{R2}, V_{R3}, P_{R1}, P_{R2}, P_{R3}.

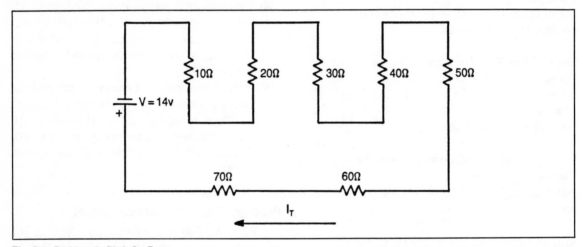

Fig. 9-4. Problem 3. Find: I_T, R_T.

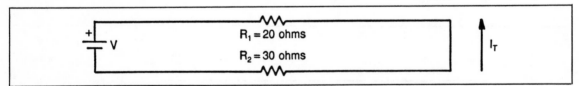

Fig. 9-5. Problem 4. Find: I_T, V.

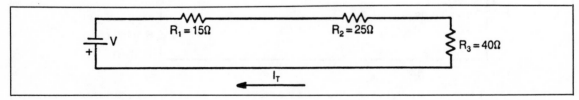

Fig. 9-6. Problem 5. Find: I_T, R_T, V.

112

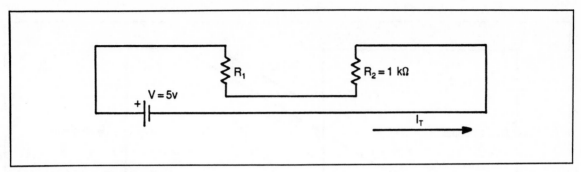

Fig. 9-7. Problem 6. Find: R_T, R_1.

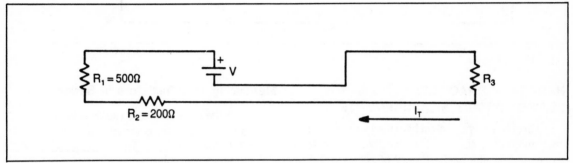

Fig. 9-8. Problem 7. Find: R_T, R_3, V.

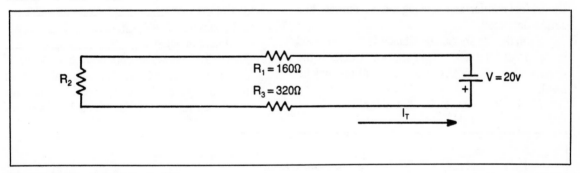

Fig. 9-9. Problem 8. Find: I_T, R_2, V_{R1}.

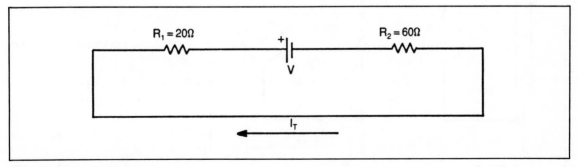

Fig. 9-10. Problem 9. V, I_T, R_2.

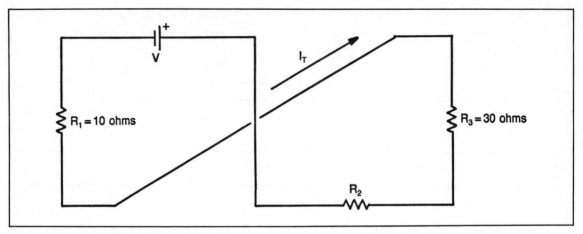

Fig. 9-11. Problem 10. V, I_T, R_2.

HANDS-ON PRACTICE:
SERIES CIRCUIT MEASUREMENTS

This section will contain both measurements and calculations of dc circuits. The objective is to achieve complete learning of the theory of series circuits. When the student completes this section he/she should feel comfortable making measurements in a series dc circuit.

Even though specific resistance values are used in this procedure, the values are not critical. If the specific values cannot be found, substitutes may be used.

R_1 = 330 ohms, R_2 = 220 ohms

Measuring Two Resistors in Series

(1) Use the color codes of the resistors to determine the tolerance range.
R1 Color Code: _____
R1 Maximum value = _____
R1 Minimum value = _____
R2 Color Code: _____
R2 Maximum value = _____
R2 Minimum value = _____

(2) Figure 9-12 shows an ohmmeter connected to a resistor. Figure 9-12A is a pictorial drawing to help "picture" the connection and Fig. 9-12B is a schematic. Use Fig. 9-12 as a refer-

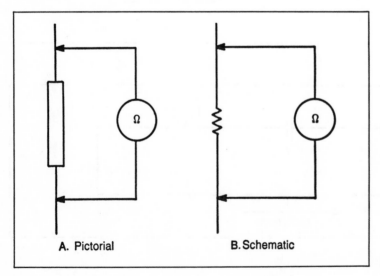

A. Pictorial   B. Schematic

Fig. 9-12. Using an ohmmeter to check the resistor's value.

ence and measure the actual values of the resistors.

R1 (measured) = _____

R2 (measured) = _____

Verify if the resistors are within tolerance. (y/n)

(3) Figure 9-13 shows the two resistors connected in series. First calculate the total resistance, showing the formula used, then measure the total resistance with the ohmmeter. (Use nominal values of the resistors for the calculations.)

Total resistance formula: _____

Calculated total resistance = _____

Measured total resistance = _____

(4) Figure 9-14 shows the two resistors connected to a power supply and a voltmeter. (A six volt

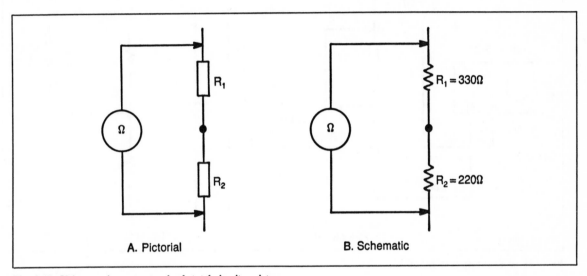

Fig. 9-13. Using an ohmmeter to check total circuit resistance.

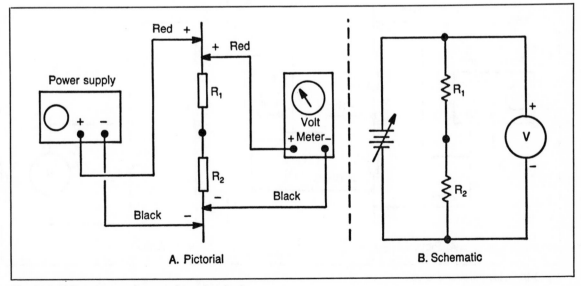

Fig. 9-14. Voltage measured across the entire circuit.

battery can be used in place of the power supply.) Notice the voltmeter is connected not only across the resistors, but also connected directly across the power supply. Use this arrangement to set the power supply voltage to 6 volts. **Be sure to observe meter polarity.**

(5) Using the nominal values of the resistors and an applied voltage of 6 volts; calculate total current and voltage drop across each resistor.

Formula for I_T = _____

I_T (calculated) = _____

Formula for voltage drop = _____

V_{R1} (calculated) = _____

V_{R2} (calculated) = _____

(6) Use Fig. 9-15 and 9-16 as samples to measure

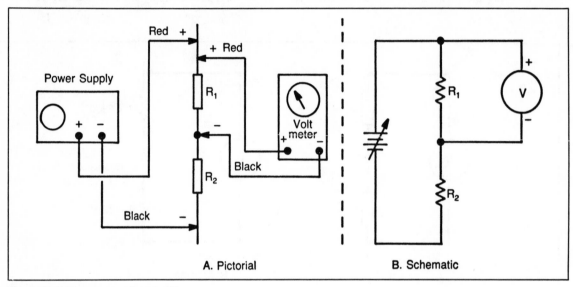

Fig. 9-15. Voltage measured across R1.

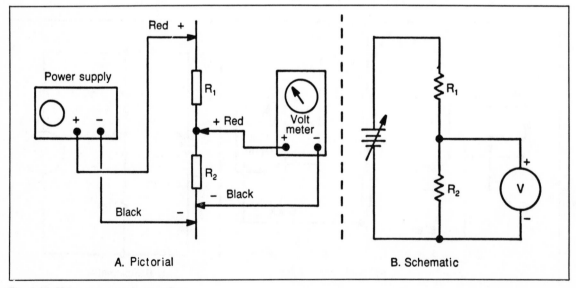

Fig. 9-16. Voltage measured across R2.

the voltage drop across each resistor.

V_{R1} (measured) = _____

V_{R2} (measured) = _____

(7) Compare the voltage readings of steps 5 and 6. It is normal for there to be a slight difference. Explain what causes this difference and how much is considered within acceptable tolerance.

(8) Use Fig. 9-17 as a sample to measure current flow in the circuit. An ammeter is connected in series. Therefore, it is necessary to place the meter directly in the path of current flow. Disconnect the wire from the negative side of the power supply to the resistor. Attach the negative side of the meter to the power supply and the positive side of the meter to the resistor. Remember to change the multi-meter to the current range.

I_T (measured) = _____

(9) Compare the measured value of current with the calculated value of step 5. Explain the difference and how to determine what is an acceptable tolerance range.

(10) In this step, the oscilloscope will be used to measure the total voltage in the circuit. Connect the oscilloscope probe to the top of R1, as shown in Fig. 9-18, and the ground lead connected to the negative side of the battery. Note: be sure the AC/GND/DC switch is in the DC position.

$V_{applied}$ (measured) = _____

(11) Connect the scope probe to the connection between the two resistors, as shown in Fig. 9-19, and the ground to the negative side of the battery. This connection will measure the voltage

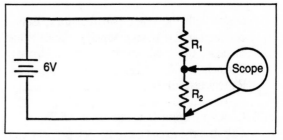

Fig. 9-18. Oscilloscope is used to measure total voltage.

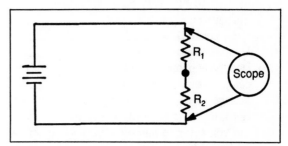

Fig. 9-19. Oscilloscope is used to measure voltage drop across R2.

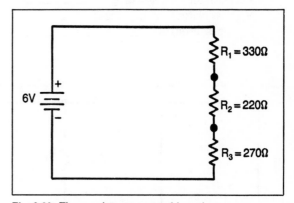

Fig. 9-20. Three resistors connected in series.

across R2. The voltage across R1 cannot be measured directly with the scope because the scope ground lead cannot be connected between two resistors in the circuit. Therefore, the voltage across R1 is found by subtracting the voltage across R2 from the applied voltage (this is still considered a measured value).

V_{R1} (measured) = _____

V_{R2} (measured) = _____

(12) The circuit that was used for steps 1 - 11 will now be expanded to have a third resistor. Refer to Fig. 9-20. Add the 270 ohm resistor in

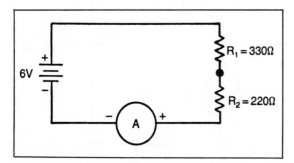

Fig. 9-17. Ammeter to measure total current.

117

series with the other two resistors. Before connecting the power supply, calculate and measure the total resistance of the circuit.

Formula for R_T = _____

R_T (calculated) = _____

R_T (measured) = _____

(13) Connect 6 volts dc to the circuit of Fig. 9-20. Calculate the circuit current, then properly connect an ammeter and measure the current flow. (Use Fig. 9-17 as a sample.)

Formula for I_T = _____

I_T (calculated) = _____

I_T (measured) = _____

(14) Use the nominal value of the resistors, the calculated value of total current and the applied voltage to calculate the voltage across each resistor. Using Fig. 9-21 as a reference, move the voltmeter to measure the voltage across each resistor.

Formula for voltage drop = _____

V_{R1} (calculated) = _____

V_{R1} (measured) = _____

V_{R2} (calculated) = _____

V_{R2} (measured) = _____

V_{R3} (calculated) = _____

V_{R3} (measured) = _____

(15) In Fig. 9-21, the voltage measurements across the resistors can all be made with reference to negative. When voltages are measured in reference to negative, the negative lead of the voltmeter remains attached to the negative of the power supply and the positive lead is moved to place the meter across the resistors.

V_{R3} = _____

$V_{R3} + V_{R2}$ = _____

V_{R2} = _____

V_{Total} = _____

V_{R1} = _____

(16) Repeat the measurements of step 15, this time using an oscilloscope.

V_{R3} = _____

$V_{R3} + V_{R2}$ = _____

V_{R2} = _____

V_{Total} = _____

V_{R1} = _____

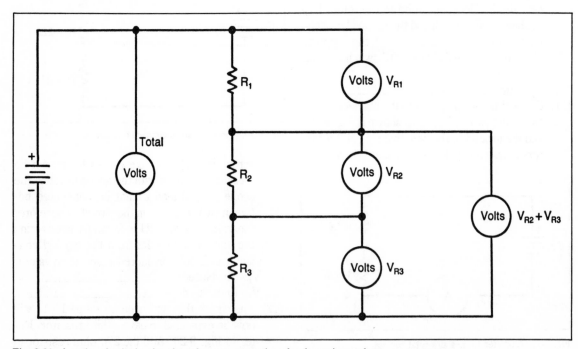

Fig. 9-21. A series circuit showing the voltmeter connections for the various voltage measurements.

PARALLEL CIRCUITS

A parallel circuit is defined as having more than one path for current to flow. With this definition, the following rules can be formed. Each of these rules will be discussed in detail.

(1) Voltage is the same throughout a parallel circuit.

(2) In a parallel circuit, current divides to the individual branches, indirectly proportional to the size of the branch resistance.

(3) Total current in a parallel circuit is the sum of the individual branch currents.

(4) Total resistance in a parallel circuit is found using the"reciprocal formula". Total resistance is always less than the smallest resistance connected in parallel.

(5) The sum of the individual powers in a parallel circuit is equal to the total power.

Voltage is the Same in a Parallel Circuit

Figure 9-22 shows a parallel circuit with three resistors. Notice, the wires from the power supply connect to each of the resistors. This means that each resistor will receive the same voltage.

Another example of a parallel circuit is the electrical outlets in a home. Each outlet supplies 120 volts. It doesn't matter which outlet is used or how many loads are connected, each receives the same voltage.

Current Divides to the Individual Branches

Figure 9-23 is a parallel circuit that shows how the current divides to the individual branches. The total current is supplied from the negative side of the power supply. The applied voltage supplies current to the individual parallel branches according to the amount needed for each branch. A smaller resistor will have more current than a larger resistor. The current flows through each branch and combines together to form the total current, to return to the positive side of the power supply.

Figure 9-24 has the branch currents labeled with the values of the branch currents. The branch currents are calculated as follows:

$$I = \frac{V}{R} \text{ (Ohm's law)}$$

Current in Branch #1:

Formula: $I_1 = \dfrac{V}{R_1}$

Substituting: $I_1 = \dfrac{12 \text{ volts}}{470 \text{ ohms}}$

Solving: $I_1 = 25.5 \text{ mA}$

Current in Branch # 2:

Formula $I_2 = \dfrac{V}{R_2}$

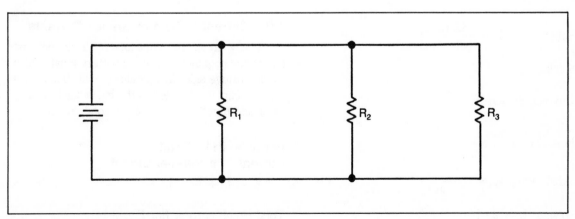

Fig. 9-22. A parallel circuit with three resistors.

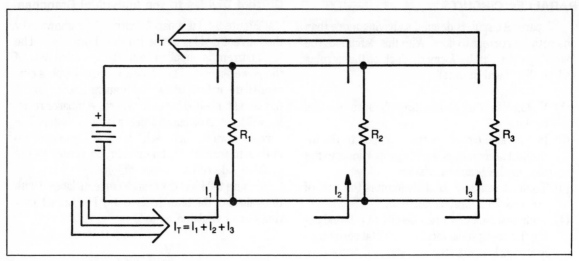

Fig. 9-23. A parallel circuit showing how the current divides.

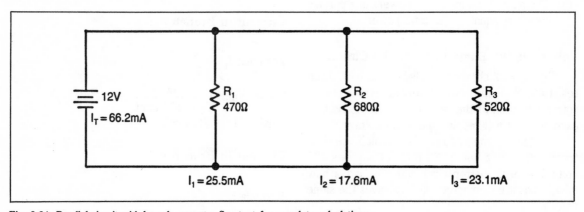

Fig. 9-24. Parallel circuit with branch currents. See text for complete calculations.

Substituting: $I_2 = \dfrac{12 \text{ volts}}{680 \text{ ohms}}$

Solving: $I_2 = 17.6$ mA

Current in Branch #3:

Formula: $I_3 = \dfrac{V}{R_3}$

Substituting: $I_3 = \dfrac{12 \text{ volts}}{520 \text{ ohms}}$

Solving: $I_3 = 23.1$ mA

Total Current is Sum of Branch Currents

In any circuit, the same amount of current that leaves the negative side of the battery must return to the positive side. In a parallel circuit, this means that the current supplied to the individual branches must add together to equal the total current.

Formula #11. Total Current in a Parallel Circuit

$$I_T = I_1 + I_2 + I_3 + \ldots$$

Total circuit current (for Fig. 9-14).

Formula: $I_T = I_1 + I_2 + I_3$
Substituting: $I_T = 25.5$ mA $+ 17.6$ mA $+ 23.1$ mA
Solving: $I_T = 66.2$ mA

Total Resistance in a Parallel Circuit

The total resistance in any circuit is a value of resistance "seen" by the power supply. The power supply must supply current to the circuit. The amount of current supplied to the circuit is determined by the applied voltage and the circuit resistance.

Total resistance in a parallel circuit can be found using either of two methods: total current or the reciprocal formula.

The total resistance in a parallel circuit must always be lower than the smallest branch resistance. This should make sense because the power supply must supply current to all branches. More current supplied appears to the power supply as lower resistance.

Formula #12. Total Resistance in a Parallel Circuit, Using Total Current

$$R = \frac{V}{I_T} \quad \text{(Ohm's law)}$$

Formula #13. Total Resistance in a Parallel Circuit, Reciprocal Formula

$$\frac{1}{R_T} = \frac{1}{R_1} + \frac{1}{R_2} + \frac{1}{R_3} + \dots$$

Total Resistance for Fig. 9-24. Total Current Method.

Formula: $R = \dfrac{V}{I}$

Substituting: $R_T = \dfrac{12 \text{ volts}}{66.2 \text{ mA}}$

Solving: $R_T = 181$ ohms

Using the Reciprocal Formula

To use the reciprocal formula follow these steps:

(1) Write down the formula.
(2) Substitute the known values into the formula in place of the variables.
(3) Take the reciprocal of each of the resistance values. Most calculators have a reciprocal key. Use this key rather than dividing into 1 each time. It is not necessary to write down the decimal equivalents. Simply press the + (addition) key after each reciprocal. After adding the decimal values of the reciprocals, the decimal total will be very small.
(4) Take the reciprocal of the sum of the reciprocals and this value will be the total resistance of the circuit. The total resistance will be lower than the lowest value of parallel resistor. Notice, only for extremely rare conditions, that the value of total resistance should not be less than 1. Use this as a check to be sure all steps have been followed.

Total Resistance for Fig. 9-24. Reciprocal Formula Method.

Formula: $\dfrac{1}{R_T} = \dfrac{1}{R_1} + \dfrac{1}{R_2} + \dfrac{1}{R_3}$

Substituting: $\dfrac{1}{R_T} = \dfrac{1}{470} + \dfrac{1}{680} + \dfrac{1}{520}$

Decimal equivalents of reciprocals:

$$\frac{1}{R_T} = .00213 + .00147 + .00192$$

Adding decimals: $\dfrac{1}{R_T} = .00552$

Final answer: $R_T = 181$ ohms

Short Cut Formulas

There are two short cut formulas available to calculate total resistance in a parallel circuit.

Formula #14. Short Cut Formula for Total Resistance With Two Resistors in Parallel

$$R_T = \frac{R_1 \times R_2}{R_1 + R_2}$$

This formula can be used only when there are two resistors in parallel. Notice the numerator is a multiplication and the denominator is an addition. Many students find that the calculators now available are so easy to use that it is not worth the effort to learn this so called "short cut" formula. It is presented here to be sure that the student has been exposed to all of the different formulas.

Formula #15. Short Cut Formula for Total Resistance with Equal Values of Resistors in Parallel

$$R_T = \frac{R}{n} \quad \begin{array}{l} \text{(resistance value)} \\ \text{(number of resistors)} \end{array}$$

This short cut formula is rather handy. The total re-sistance of a parallel circuit when the resistors are equal value is found by dividing the value of branch resistance by the number of equal resistors.

Example: Two 100 ohm resistors are connected in parallel, total resistance is 50 ohms (100 divided by 2).

Example: Three 600 ohm resistors are connected in parallel, total resistance is 200 ohms (600 divided by 3).

Total Power in a Parallel Circuit is the Sum of the Individual Powers

In all circuits, the total power is the sum of the individual powers dissipated by the individual loads. Power can also be calculated using the applied voltage and the total circuit current.

Practice Problems: Parallel Circuits

Use the information given in the schematic diagrams and the problems to find the unknown quantities.

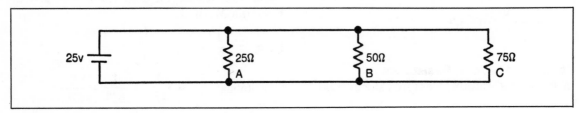

Fig. 9-25. Problem 1. Find: R_T, I_T, I_A, I_B, I_C (branch currents).

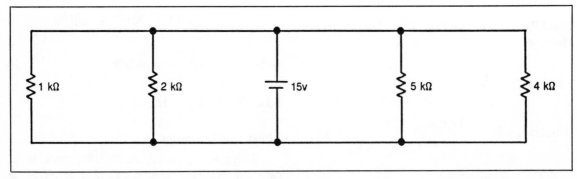

Fig. 9-26. Problem 2. Find: R_T, I_T.

122

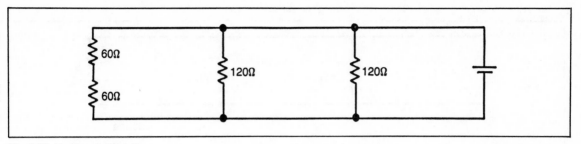

Fig. 9-27. Problem 3. Find: R_T.

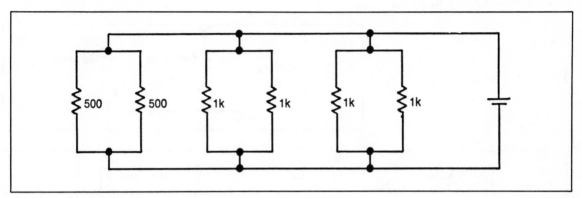

Fig. 9-28. Problem 4. Find: R_T.

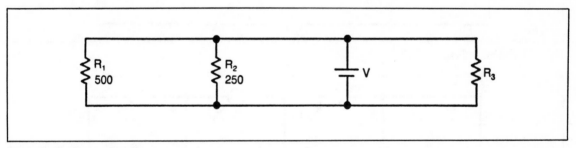

Fig. 9-29. Problem 5. Find: R_3.

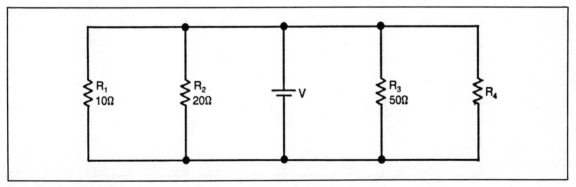

Fig. 9-30. Problem 6. Find: R_4.

123

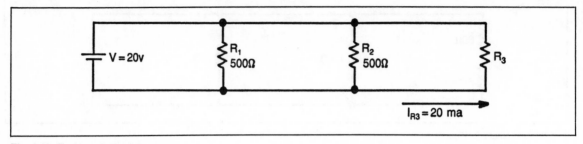

Fig. 9-31. Problem 7. Find: R_T, I_T, R_3.

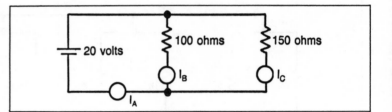

Fig. 9-32. Problem 8. Find: R_T, I_A, I_B, I_C.

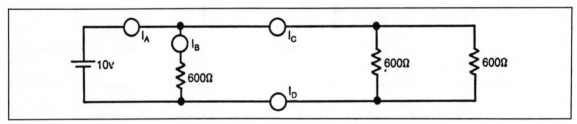

Fig. 9-33. Problem 9. Find: R_T, I_A, I_B, I_C, I_D.

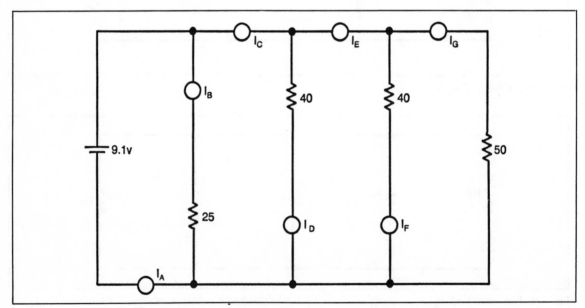

Fig. 9-34. Problem 10. Find: R_T, I_A, I_B, I_C, I_D, I_E, I_F, I_G.

HANDS-ON PRACTICE: PARALLEL CIRCUIT MEASUREMENTS

This section will contain both calculations and measurements of parallel circuits. When the student completes this section he/she should feel confident in making measurements in a parallel dc circuit.

Even though specific resistance values are given for these exercises, the actual values are not critical. Substitutes may be used.

Total Resistance of a Parallel Circuit

(1) Figure 9-35 shows three resistors connected in parallel. An ohmmeter is connected in place of the voltage source.Note: whenever using an ohmmeter, there must not be any other voltage connected to the circuit. First, calculate the total resistance of this circuit, then use the ohmmeter to measure the circuit resistance.
Total resistance formula: _____
R_T (calculated) = _____
R_T (measured) = _____

(2) Remove the ohmmeter and connect a dc power supply, as shown in Fig. 9-36. Connect a voltmeter across the power supply (with the circuit also connected) and set the power supply for 6 volts. Move the voltmeter to measure the voltage across each of the resistors.
V_{R1} = _____
V_{R2} = _____
V_{R3} = _____

(3) Remove the voltmeter and connect an oscilloscope in its place. Make the same voltage measurements with the oscilloscope that were made with the voltmeter.
V_{Total} = _____
V_{R1} = _____
V_{R2} = _____
V_{R3} = _____

(4) First, calculate total current and branch currents. Then, use Fig. 9-37 as a guide to connect an ammeter to measure circuit currents. Disconnect the wire from the positive side of the power supply to the circuit. Connect an ammeter in place of the wire. Remember: ammeters are connected in series with the current flow. Measure each branch current using the same technique. Disconnect a wire and connect the meter in its place. Be sure to observe meter polarity.
I_T (calculated) = _____
I_1 (calculated) = _____
I_2 (calculated) = _____
I_3 (calculated) = _____

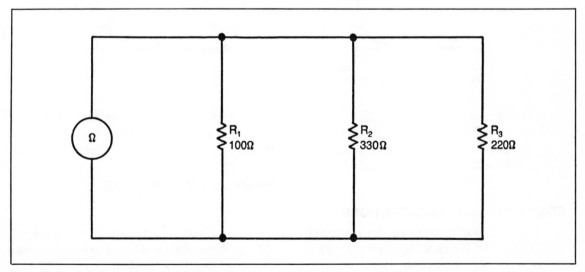

Fig. 9-35. An ohmmeter connected to a parallel circuit.

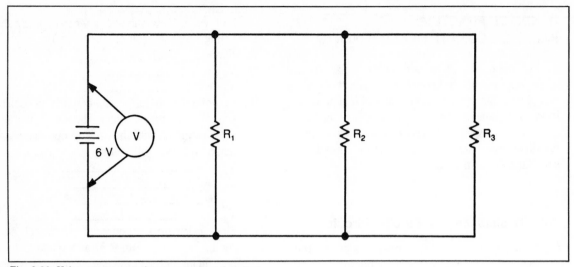

Fig. 9-36. Voltmeter connected to measure supply voltage.

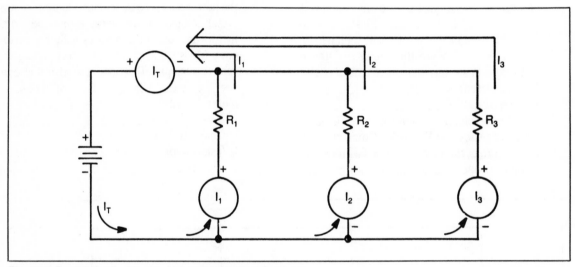

Fig. 9-37. Parallel circuit with ammeters to measure branch current.

I_T (measured) = _____

I_1 (measured) = _____

I_2 (measured) = _____

I_3 (measured) = _____

SERIES-PARALLEL COMBINATIONS

A series-parallel combination circuit, also called a *complex* circuit, is a circuit that contains both series resistors and parallel resistors.

To begin to analyze a complex circuit, it is necessary to separate the series from the parallel, because they require different rules and formulas.

Review of Series and Parallel

Series:

(1) Current is the same throughout a series circuit.
(2) Total resistance in a series circuit is the sum of the individual resistors.

126

(3) The sum of the voltage drops in a series circuit equals the applied voltage.

Parallel:

(1) Voltage is the same throughout a parallel circuit.
(2) Total resistance in a parallel circuit is found using the "reciprocal formula."
(3) Total current in a parallel circuit is the sum of the individual branch currents.

Solving a Complex Circuit

Figure 9-38 shows the three steps in solving a complex circuit. Figure 9-38A is the complete circuit.

Tracing the current flow, starting from the negative side of the battery, all of the current flowing from the battery, I_T, goes through R_4. Therefore, R_4 is a series resistor. The current flow then reaches point "b," where it divides to flow through the parallel branches of R_2 and R_3. The current flow from these two branches recombines at point "a" and becomes I_T, and flows through R_1 back to the positive side of the battery.

The following procedure is a suggested guideline for solving any complex circuit.

(1) Solve for total resistance, R_T. It is best to start from a point farthest from the power supply.
   a. Combine parallel branches into an equivalent series resistance.
   b. Combine the equivalent resistance with the series resistors.
   c. Continue this combination process until the entire circuit can be represented as one equivalent resistance.
(2) Use total resistance, R_T, to find I_T. $I = V/R$ (Ohm's law).
(3) Use I_T to find the voltage drop across resistors that are in series with I_T.
   a. Add the series voltage drops together.
   b. Subtract the total series voltage drops from the applied voltage.
   c. The result of the subtraction is the voltage remaining for the entire rest of the circuit

(the parallel circuits).

(4) Use the voltage drop for the parallel circuits to determine what the current flow is in each branch.

Steps in Solving Figure 9-38

(1) Find total resistance, R_T
   a. Determine which resistors are in series and which are in parallel. Combine the parallel resistors farthest from the power supply first.
   b. Combine resistors R_2 and R_3. This will be labeled R_{par}, short for parallel, as shown in Fig. 9-38B.

Formula: $\dfrac{1}{R_{par}} = \dfrac{1}{R_2} + \dfrac{1}{R_3}$

Substituting: $\dfrac{1}{R_{par}} = \dfrac{1}{100} + \dfrac{1}{100}$

Decimal equivalent of reciprocals:

$$\frac{1}{R_{par}} = 0.01 + 0.01$$

Adding decimals: $\dfrac{1}{R_{par}} = 0.02$

Final answer: $R_{par} = 50$ ohms

Note: since the two parallel resistors are exactly the same value, the short cut formula can be used.

Formula: $R_{par} = \dfrac{R}{n}$

Substituting: $R_{par} = \dfrac{100 \text{ ohms}}{2}$

Solving: $R_{par} = 50$ ohms

Re-draw the circuit diagram to show the parallel resistors replaced by the equivalent resistance, as shown in Fig. 9-38B.
   c. The circuit of Fig. 9-38B shows three resistors connected in series. Combine these

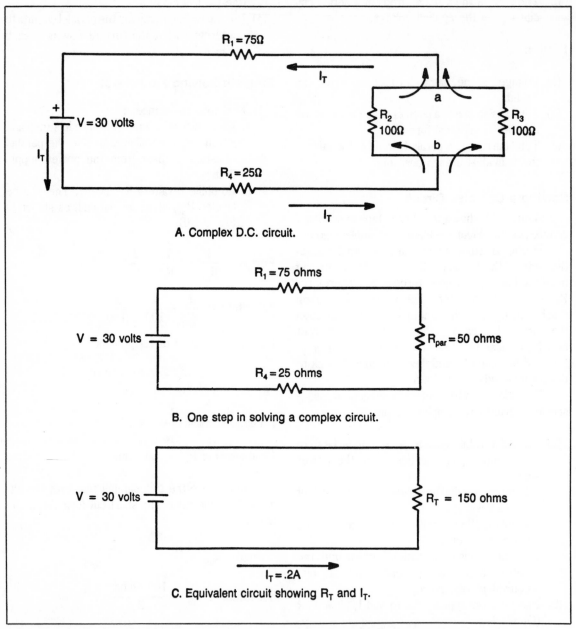

Fig. 9-38. Steps in finding total resistance and total current in a complex circuit. See text for calculations.

resistors to find one equivalent resistance, R_T.

Formula: $R_T = R_1 + R_{par} + R_4$

Substituting: $R_T = 75$ ohms $+ 50$ ohms $+ 25$ ohms

Solving: $R_T = 150$ ohms

Re-draw the circuit to show the one final equivalent resistance, R_T, as shown in Fig. 9-38C.

(2) Use the total resistance to find the total current.

Formula: $I = \dfrac{V}{R}$ (Ohm's law)

Substituting: $I = \dfrac{30 \text{ volts}}{150 \text{ ohms}}$

Solving: $I = 0.2$ amps

(3) Use I_T to find voltage drops across the series resistors.

Voltage Drop Across R₁

Formula: $V_{R1} = I_T \times R_1$

Substituting: $V_{R1} = 0.2$ amps $\times$ 75 ohms

Solving: $V_{R1} = 15$ volts

Voltage Drop Across R₄

Formula: $V_{R4} = I_T \times R_4$

Substituting: $V_{R4} = 0.2$ amps $\times$ 25 ohms

Solving: $V_{R4} = 5$ volts

Voltage drop across the parallel combination of R_2 and R_3, V_{par} is found by either of two methods. Either by finding the voltage drop across the equivalent resistance or by subtracting the other voltage drops from the applied voltage. The method used here will be the subtraction method.

Add the voltage drops of the series resistors.

Formula: $V_{series} = V_{R1} + V_{R4}$

Substituting: $V_{series} = 15$ volts + 5 volts

Solving: $V_{series} = 20$ volts

Subtract the series voltage drops from the applied voltage to find the voltage across the parallel branches.

Formula: $V_{par} = V_{applied} - V_{series}$

Substituting: $V_{par} = 30$ volts $-$ 20 volts

Solving: $V_{par} = 10$ volts

(4) Use the voltage across the parallel branches, V_{par} to find the current flow in each branch. Note: in this particular example, the branches have equal resistance. Therefore they will have an equal current flow. Since there are only two branches, each branch will have ½ of the total current. The method used as an example here will be to calculate the current flow. $I_{R2} = I_{R3}$ because they are equal in value of resistance.

Formula: $I = \dfrac{V}{R}$

Substituting: $I = \dfrac{10 \text{ volts}}{100 \text{ ohms}}$

Solving: $I = 0.1$ amps

This completes the analysis of the circuit shown in Fig. 9-38. Figure 9-39 is the schematic with all of the necessary information shown. It is also possible to continue the analysis by finding the power dissipated by each resistor. Power would be found by using the current through a resistor and the voltage across the resistor.

Solving for Total Resistance and Total Current of Figure 9-40

Figure 9-40 is a rather complicated looking circuit. The steps in solving this circuit are basically the same as any other complex circuit. Start from a point farthest from the power supply, combining series and parallel circuits individually. Remember, series circuits and parallel circuits cannot be combined together in one step.

(1) Combine the series resistors R8, R9 and R10 together. This will be labeled R_a.

Formula: $R_a = R_8 + R_9 + R_{10}$

Substituting: $R_a = 5 + 20 + 15$

Solving: $R_a = 40$ ohms

a. Re-draw the circuit diagram, shown in Fig. 9-40B, to show R_a as a single equivalent resistor to replace the combined resistors.

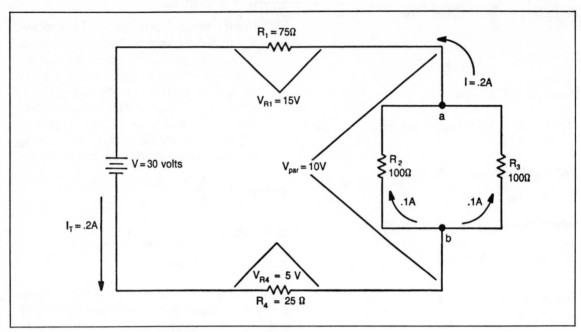

Fig. 9-39. Complex circuit showing voltage drops and current flow.

(2) Combine the series resistors R6 and R7. Note: this is not shown in the figure as a separate step. Combine the equivalent of these two resistors (40 ohms) in parallel with R_a. The result of this combination will be labeled R_b. Since the two branches are equal, the equivalent is the resistance value divided by 2.

Formula: $R_{par} = \dfrac{R}{n}$

Substituting: $R_b = 40/2$

Solving: $R_b = 20$ ohms

   a. Re-draw the circuit diagram, as shown in Fig. 9-40C, to show R_b as a single equivalent resistor to replace the combined resistors.

(3) Combine the series resistors R4, R5 and R6. Label this combination as R_c.

Formula: $R_c = R_4 + R_5 + R_6$

Substituting: $R_c = 20 + 10 + 20$

Solving: $R_c = 50$ ohms

   a. Re-draw the circuit diagram, as shown in Fig. 9-40D, to show R_c as a single equivalent resistor to replace the combined resistors.

(4) Combine the parallel resistors R3 and R_c. Label this combination as R_d.

Formula: $\dfrac{1}{R_d} = \dfrac{1}{R_3} + \dfrac{1}{R_c}$

Substituting: $\dfrac{1}{R_d} = \dfrac{1}{15} + \dfrac{1}{50}$

Decimal equivalents of reciprocals:

$$\frac{1}{R_d} = .0667 + .02$$

Adding decimals: $\dfrac{1}{R_d} = .0867$

Final answer: $R_d = 11.5$ ohms

   a. Re-draw the circuit diagram, as shown in Fig. 9-40E, to show R_d as a single equivalent resistor to replace the combined resistors.

(5) Combine the series resistors R1, R2 and R_d. This is the final combination and will be labeled R_T, to show it is the equivalent total circuit resistance.

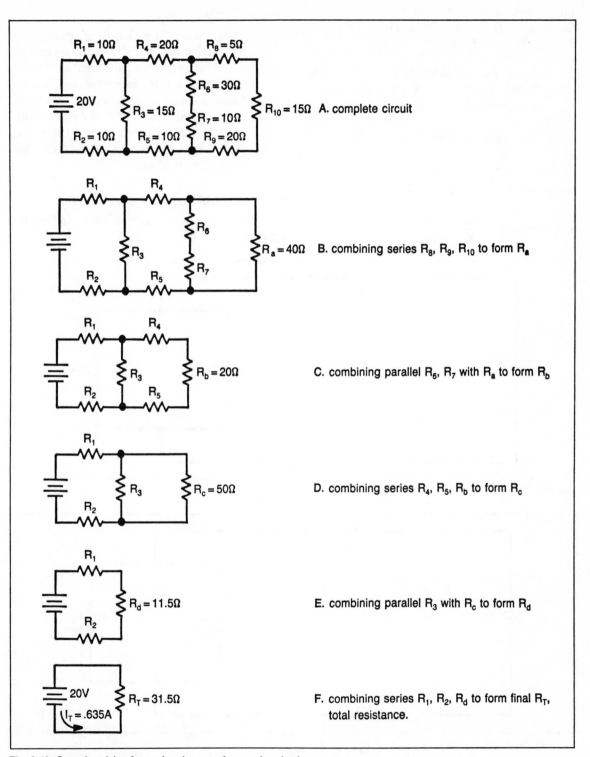

Fig. 9-40. Steps in solving for total resistance of a complex circuit.

Formula: $R_T = R_1 + R_2 + R_d$
Substituting: $R_T = 10 + 10 + 11.5$
Solving: $R_T = 31.5$ ohms

    a. Re-draw the circuit diagram, as shown in Fig. 9-40F, to show R_T as a single equivalent resistor to replace the entire circuit.

    b. Use the equivalent total resistance, R_T, and the applied voltage to calculate the total current.

Formula: $I = \dfrac{V}{R}$ (Ohm's law)

Substituting: $I = \dfrac{20 \text{ volts}}{31.5 \text{ ohms}}$

Solving: $I = 0.635$ amps

    c. Voltage drops for each resistor can be found by working backwards with the equivalent circuit diagrams. Use the current and the resistance value to determine the voltage drops. Where a parallel circuit is concerned, keep in mind that current divides, but voltage is constant. Where a series circuit is concerned, keep in mind that voltage drops, but current is constant.

Practice Problems: Complex Circuits

Use the schematic diagrams shown to find the unknown circuit parameters.

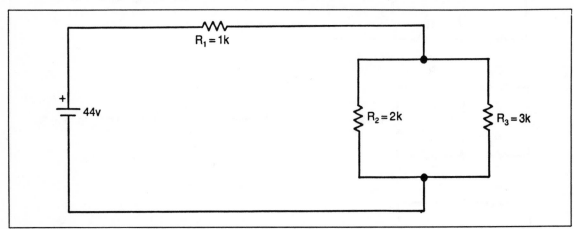

Fig. 9-41. Problem 1. Find: R_T, I_T, V_{R1}, V_{R2}, V_{R3}, I_{R2}, I_{R3}.

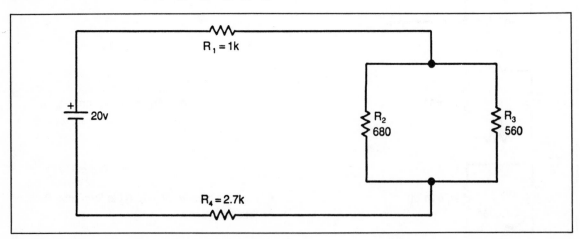

Fig. 9-42. Problem 2. Find: R_T, I_T, V_{R1}, V_{R2}, V_{R3}, V_{R4}, I_{R2}, I_{R3}.

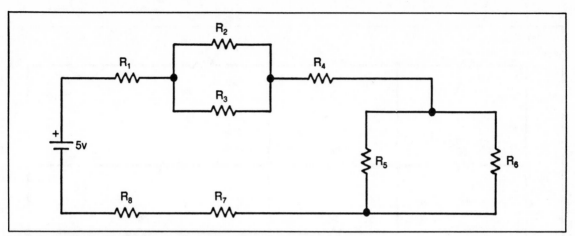

Fig. 9-43. Problem 3. Find: R_T, I_T, I_{R2}, I_{R5}, voltage drops for all resistors

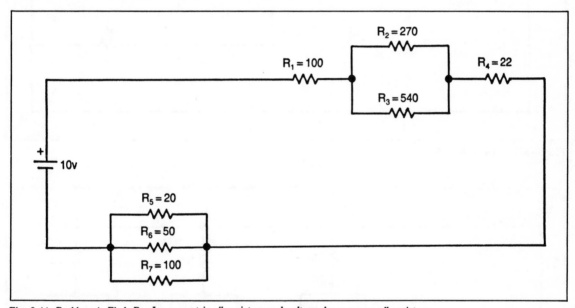

Fig. 9-44. Problem 4. Find: R_T, I_T, current in all resistors and voltage drops across all resistors.

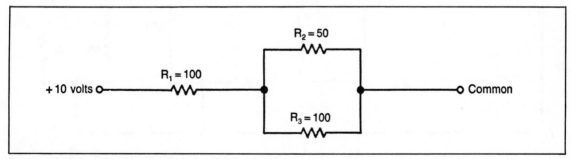

Fig. 9-45. Problem 5. Find: R_T, I_T, V_{R1}, V_{R1}, V_{R3}, I_{R1}, I_{R2}, I_{R3}.

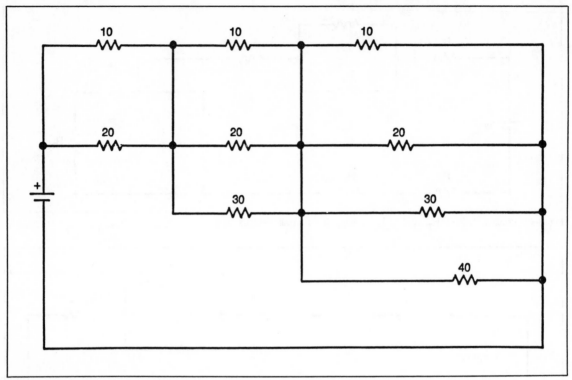

Fig. 9-46. Problem 6. Find: R_T.

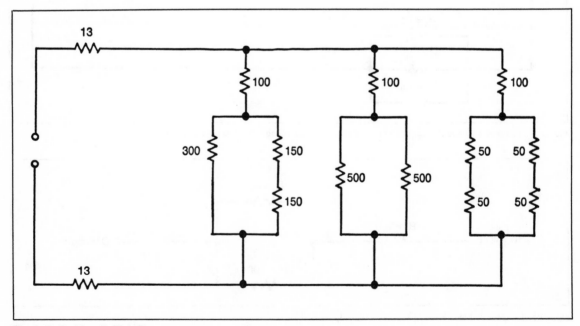

Fig. 9-47. Problem 7. Find: R_T.

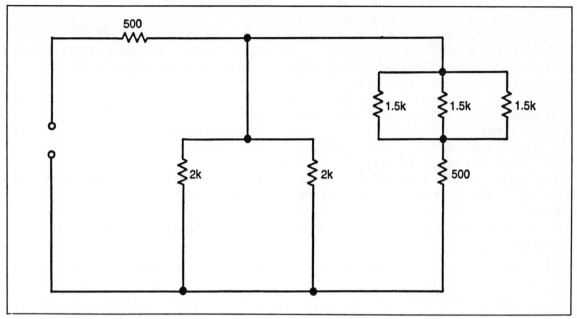

Fig. 9-48. Problem 8. Find: R_T.

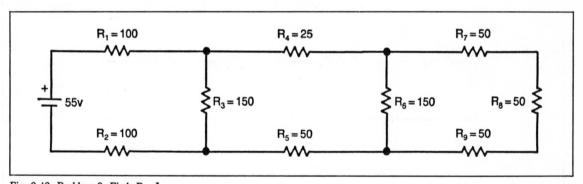

Fig. 9-49. Problem 9. Find: R_T, I_T.

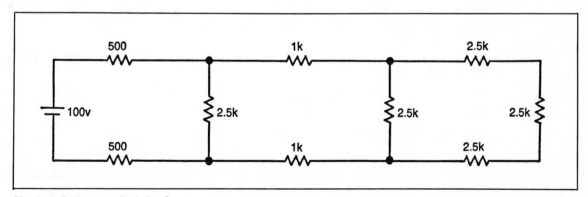

Fig. 9-50. Problem 10. Find: R_T, I_T.

135

PROGRAMS FOR THIS CHAPTER

The program for this chapter is a set of dc circuits to allow the student to further practice the rules of series and parallel circuits.

It would be best for the student to use a calculator when solving these circuits. By using the calculator, two very important concepts will be practiced: solving with the calculator and review of the circuit rules.

Use the help hints when you have a wrong answer. It is also a good idea to review the book when any concept is not fully understood. Keep in mind that the computer programs provide valuable practice, when used properly.

Figure 9-51 shows a sample of the dc analysis program.

DC CIRCUIT ANALYSIS TEST

Part A. Circuit Analysis Theory

(1) In a series circuit, which circuit parameter is common at all points in the circuit?

    a. voltage
    b. current
    c. resistance
    d. power

(2) Which value of resistor will have the largest voltage drop?

    a. small ohmic value
    b. large ohmic value

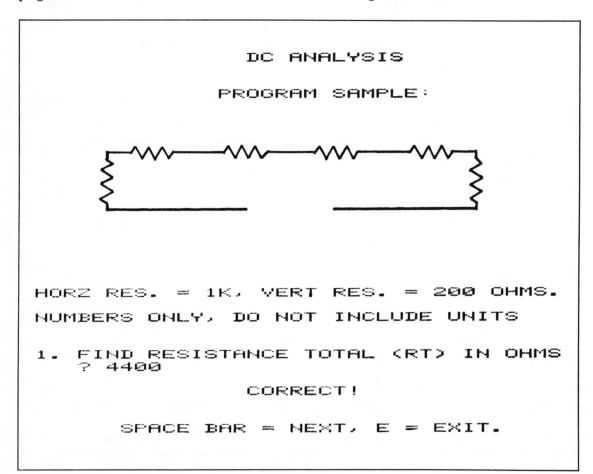

Fig. 9-51. DC analysis program sample.

c. size makes no difference
d. not enough information given

(3) In a parallel circuit, which circuit parameter is common throughout the circuit?

a. voltage
b. current
c. resistance
d. power

(4) Which value of resistor will have the largest current flow?

a. small ohmic value
b. large ohmic value
c. value makes no difference
d. not enough information given

(5) In a parallel circuit, the total resistance is:

a. larger than the largest value resistor
b. smaller than the smallest value resistor
c. one-half the value of the two resistors
d. the sum of all resistors

(6) In a series circuit the total resistance is:

a. larger than the largest value resistor
b. smaller than the smallest value resistor

c. one-half the value of the two resistors
d. the average of the resistor values

(7) The formula for total resistance in a parallel circuit is:

a. $\dfrac{1}{R_T} = \dfrac{1}{R_1} + \dfrac{1}{R_2} + \dfrac{1}{R_3} + \ldots$

b. $R_T = \dfrac{R_1 \times R_2}{R_1 \times R_2}$

c. $R_T = R_1 + R_2 + R_3 + \ldots$
d. none of the above

(8) The formula for total resistance in a series circuit is:

a. $\dfrac{1}{R_T} = \dfrac{1}{R_1} + \dfrac{1}{R_2} + \dfrac{1}{R_3} + \ldots$

b. $R_T = \dfrac{R_1 \times R_2}{R_1 \times R_2}$

c. $R_T = R_1 + R_2 + R_3 + \ldots$
d. none of the above

(9) A voltmeter is connected in:

a. series
b. parallel
c. series-parallel

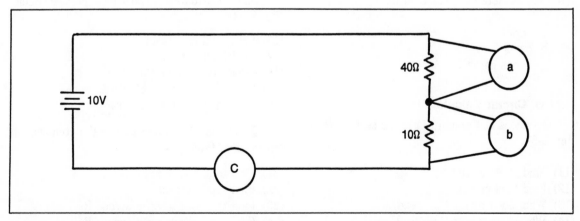

Fig. 9-52. Circuit for questions 11-15.

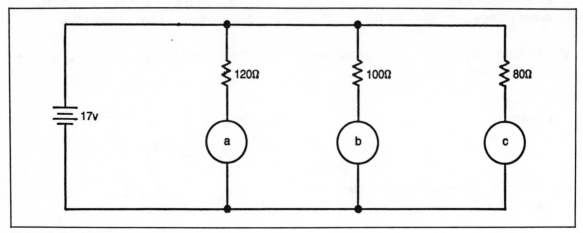

Fig. 9-53. Circuit for questions 16-20.

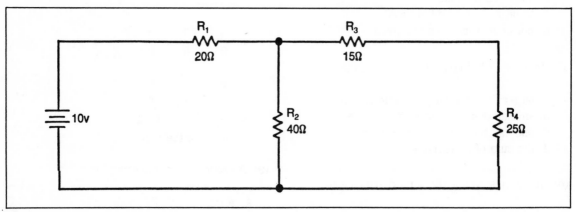

Fig. 9-54. Circuit for questions 21-25.

(10) An ammeter is connected in:

    a. series
    b. parallel
    c. series-parallel

Part B. Circuit Calculations

Questions 11 through 15 use the series circuit, Fig. 9-52.

(11) Find total resistance
(12) Find total current
(13) What does meter "a" read?
(14) What does meter "b" read?
(15) What does meter "c" read?

Questions 16 through 20 use the parallel circuit, Fig. 9-53.

(16) Find total resistance
(17) Find total current
(18) What does meter "a" read?
(19) What does meter "b" read?
(20) What does meter "c" read?

Questions 21 through 25 use the combination circuit, Fig. 9-54.

(21) Find total resistance
(22) Find total current
(23) Find the voltage drop across R_1
(24) Find the voltage drop across R_2
(25) Find the voltage drop across R_4

Exam #1. DC Building Blocks

- ☐ Safety
- ☐ Engineering Notation
- ☐ Resistor color code
- ☐ Schematic symbols
- ☐ Use of an ohmmeter
- ☐ Ohm's law
- ☐ Power formulas
- ☐ Use of a multimeter and an oscilloscope
- ☐ DC circuits

SAFETY

(1) Shop safety is the responsibility of:
 a. the teacher
 b. the school principal
 c. the student
 d. all of the above

(2) In order to determine if a soldering iron is hot enough to use for soldering:
 a. sprinkle water on the tip
 b. melt a piece of solder on the tip to see if it flows freely
 c. touch tip with your fingers

(3) In the event of an injury, you should:
 a. allow another student to administer first aid
 b. inform the instructor
 c. disregard a small injury

(4) If you witness a person being electrocuted, the best action is:
 a. pull the person from the source of electricity
 b. turn off the source of electricity before touching the person
 c. call for the instructor

(5) Severe electrical shock results from:
 a. only large voltages
 b. only large currents
 c. small amounts of current passing through the body

ENGINEERING NOTATION

Convert the given numbers to the units shown.

(6) 5,600,000 hertz   _____ kHz
(7) 15 amps   _____ mA
(8) 0.0035 volts   _____ mV

(9) 250 milliwatts _____ W

(10) 25 microvolts _____ mV

RESISTOR COLOR CODE

Use the colors given to determine the resistance value.

(11) brown - black - black

(12) red - violet - brown

(13) green - blue - red

(14) yellow - violet - orange

(15) blue - gray - yellow

SCHEMATIC SYMBOLS

Draw the following schematic symbols:

(16) Dc power supply (show + and −)

(17) Single pole, single throw switch in the closed position

(18) fuse

(19) potentiometer

(20) fixed value resistor

USE OF AN OHMMETER

(21) What will the ohmmeter reading be with a good fuse?

(22) What will the ohmmeter reading be with an open wire?

(23) Read the meter in Fig. Ex1-1, needle #23

(24) Read the meter in Fig. Ex1-1, needle #24

(25) Read the meter in Fig. Ex1-1, needle #25

OHM'S LAW

Use Ohm's law to find the unknown value. The proper unit **must** be included with each answer. If the answer is over 1000 or less than $1/1000$, answer **must** be written in the proper form of engineering notation.

(26) R = 100 ohms I = 0.2 amps Find: V

(27) V = 100 volts R = 25 ohms Find: I

(28) V = 60 volts I = 3 amps Find: R

(29) I = 500 mA R = 250 ohms Find: V

(30) R = 30 ohms V = 60 mV Find: I

POWER FORMULAS

Use the power formulas to find the unknown value. The proper unit **must** be included with each answer. If the answer is over 1000 or under $1/1000$, answer **must** be written in the proper form of engineering notation.

(31) V = 100 volts I = 0.02 amps Find: P

(32) I = 15 amps R = 2 ohms Find: P

(33) I = 2 amps P = 5 watts Find: V

(34) V = 15 volts P = 100 mW Find: I

(35) P = 5 watts I = 2 amps Find: R

USE OF A MULTIMETER AND AN OSCILLOSCOPE

(36) Draw a schematic diagram of a voltmeter connected to measure voltage across a resistor.

(37) Draw the schematic diagram of an ammeter connected to measure current flow in a circuit with one resistor.

(38) Draw the schematic diagram of an oscilloscope connected to measure the voltage of a dc voltage source.

(39) An oscilloscope is adjusted to measure dc voltages and the volts/division is set at 2 v/d. How many divisions will the trace "jump" for a voltage of 7 volts?

For questions 40 - 45, read the multimeter scales in the appropriate figures.

Figure Ex1-2

(40) _____

(41) _____

(42) _____

Figure Ex1-3

(43) _____

(44) _____

(45) _____

DC CIRCUITS

In the questions below, the term "parameters" refers to: resistance, current, voltage, power.

(46) Which parameter is the same at all points in a series circuit?

(47) Which parameter is the same throughout a parallel circuit?

(48) Use the circuit in Fig. Ex1-4 to find total resistance.

(49) Use the circuit in Fig. Ex1-5 to find total current.

(50) Use the circuit in Fig. Ex1-6 to find total resistance.

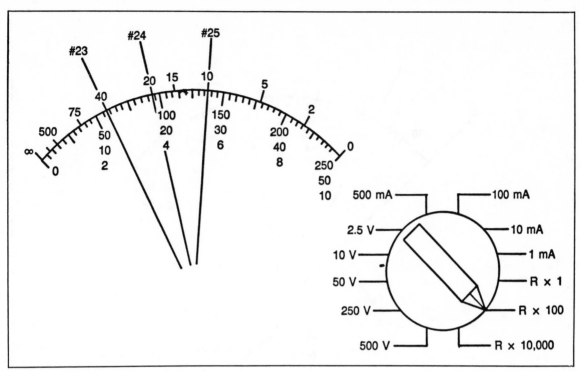

Fig. Ex1-1. Ohmmeter scale for questions 23-25.

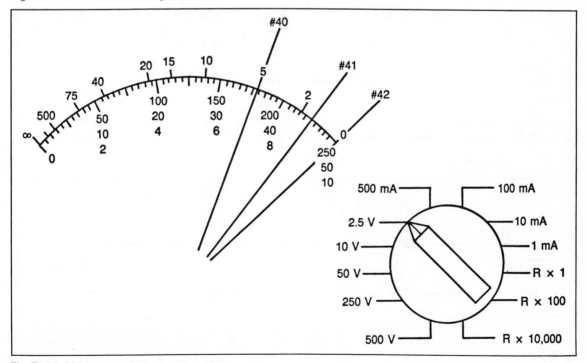

Fig. Ex1-2. Multimeter scale for questions 40-42.

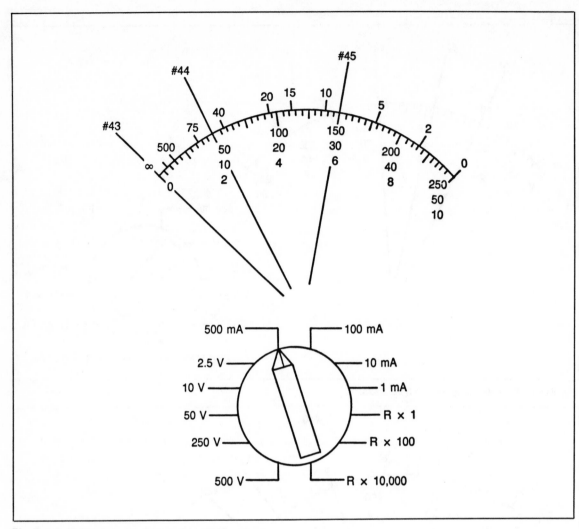

Fig. Ex1-3. Multimeter scale for questions 43-45.

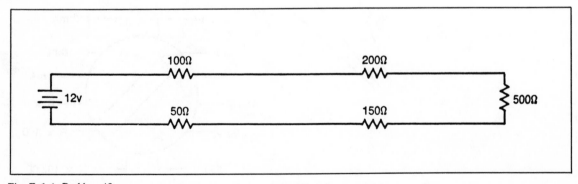

Fig. Ex1-4. Problem 48.

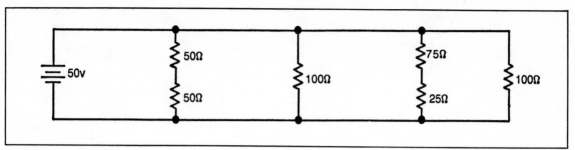

Fig. Ex1-5. Problem 49.

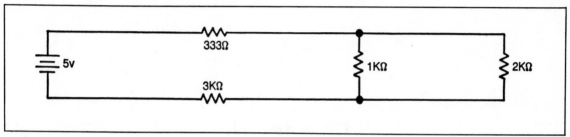

Fig. Ex1-6. Problem 50.

Chapter 10

Magnetism and Inductance

Chapter Objectives: to become familiar with the characteristics of magnetic fields and magnets. To learn how voltage is induced in a wire within a magnetic field and how electric current flow produces magnetism. To examine inductance, as a property, and as a circuit component.

Chapter Outline:

☐ Magnetism
☐ Inducing Voltage
☐ Electro-Magnets
☐ Applications of Electro-Magnets
☐ Properties of Inductance
☐ Inductors in Series
☐ Inductors in Parallel
☐ Programs for This Chapter
☐ Magnetism and Inductance Competency Test

INTRODUCTION

Magnetism is a subject that almost everyone is familiar with. Magnetism and magnetic fields have

a very important place in the field of electricity and electronics. When a wire is moved through a magnetic field, voltage will be induced in the wire. When electric current flows through a wire, a magnetic field is developed around the wire. An electro-magnet has a very wide range of applications—some of which will be examined in this chapter and others in later chapters.

MAGNETISM

Magnetism, as defined in general terms is: a force of attraction or repulsion.

Magnetic Fields

A magnetic field is an invisible area of force surrounding a magnet. The magnetic field effectively starts from the ends of the magnet, called poles. A magnet has a north and a south pole. Figure 10-1 shows how the magnetic field goes from the north to the south pole, with no lines of force in the center. If a small magnet, such as a compass, were placed within the magnetic field, the lines of force

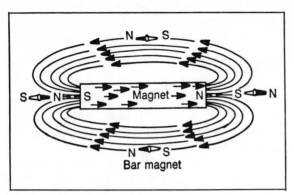

Fig. 10-1. Magnetic lines of force.

would align it so that the opposite poles would face each other.

Magnetic Terms and Definitions

The list of terms and definitions shown here is to familiarize the student with the terminology. In the study of electronics, a familiarization with the terminology of magnetism is satisfactory since an in-depth study isn't required.

Magnetic Field. The area around a magnet that has the effects of magnetism.

Magnetic Lines of Force. The force of the magnet forms lines from the north to the south pole.

Flux. Another term used to describe the magnetic lines of force. A stronger flux means a stronger magnetic field.

Retentivity. The ability of a material to retain magnetism.

Residual Magnetism. Magnetism that remains in a material.

Temporary Magnet. A material with poor retentivity and low residual magnetism, an example is soft iron. This type of material loses its magnetic properties soon after the magnetizing force is removed. Used for electro-magnets.

Permanent Magnet. A material with good retentivity and high residual magnetism—examples are hard steel and alloys containing nickel. This type of material will hold its magnetic properties for long periods of time.

Permeability. The ease with which magnetic lines pass through a material. Materials with high permeability are classified as magnetic materials. This is the type of material that will be attracted to a magnet.

Reluctance. The opposition to the passage of magnetic lines of force.

Magnetic Shield. Stops the magnetic field from affecting an object by absorbing the magnetic field and allowing it to pass around the object being protected.

Law of Attraction. Unlike magnetic poles are attracted to each other, see Fig. 10-2A.

Law of Repulsion. Like magnetic poles repel, see Fig. 10-2B.

INDUCING VOLTAGE

The purposes of magnets in the field of electronics are: using a magnet to produce voltage or using voltage to produce magnetism.

A Conductor in a Magnetic Field

When a conductor is moved through a magnetic field, electrons will move in the conductor and pro-

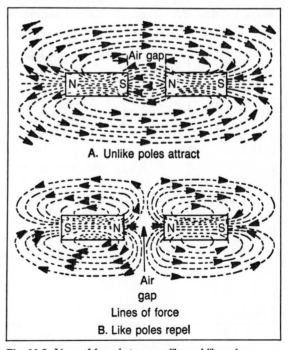

A. Unlike poles attract

Air gap
Lines of force
B. Like poles repel

Fig. 10-2. Lines of force between unlike and like poles.

duce a voltage. The voltage is referred to as an induced voltage. The amount of induced voltage is determined by:

1. Speed of cutting the magnetic lines of force. Faster movement will increase the induced voltage.
2. Strength of the magnetic field. A stronger field will induce a stronger voltage.
3. Angle of cutting the magnetic lines. When the magnetic lines of force are cut by the conductor at right angles, maximum voltage will be induced in the conductor. When the conductor is moving in the same direction as the magnetic lines, no voltage will be induced.

This chapter will also discuss in further detail the effects of inducing voltage in a conductor, when it is passed through a magnetic field.

ELECTRO-MAGNETS

When electric current flows through a conductor, a magnetic field is developed around the conductor, and an electro-magnet is formed. The strength of the magnetic field depends on the amount of current flow and the concentration of the lines of force. A coil of wire will concentrate the lines of force and produce a stronger magnet.

Magnetic Cores

An iron bar can be used as a magnetic core by wrapping the coil around it. The purpose of the core is to concentrate the lines of force and produce a stronger magnet than can be achieved with the coil with no core.

An example of a large electro-magnet is the magnets used in a commercial application (such as auto-parts salvage) where it is necessary to lift or move very heavy metallic objects.

Solenoids

A solenoid is an application of an electro-magnet where the core has a moveable portion, called a plunger, see Fig. 10-3A. When electrical current flows through the coil, it generates a magnetic field. The iron core acts as both a support frame and as a core to strengthen the magnetic field. The magnetic field will draw the plunger in to fill the hollow portion of the core. When the magnetic field is released, the return spring will pull the plunger back to its resting position.

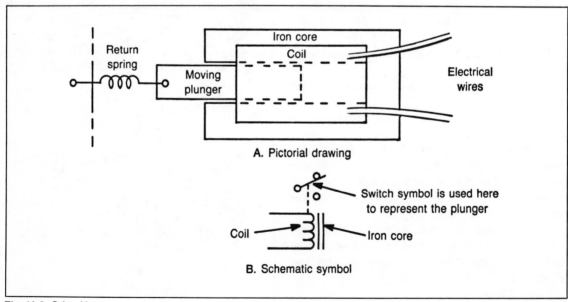

Fig. 10-3. Solenoid.

Figure 10-3B shows the schematic diagram of a solenoid. The symbol represents a coil of wire. The two straight lines next to the coil represent an iron core. It is not always necessary for a solenoid to have an iron core. The dotted line indicates a magnetic connection to the plunger. In this particular drawing, a switch is used to show the plunger, for lack of a better symbol.

A solenoid is used to perform work by the fact that the plunger can move. For example, the plunger could be attached to a door latch. The solenoid would be used to electrically open the door latch. Another example is in a washing machine. Solenoids are used to turn the water on and off, change speeds of the motor and go from wash cycle to spin cycle.

To test a solenoid, usually checking the continuity of the coil is enough. An ohmmeter applied to the coil wires should indicate low resistance if the coil is electrically good.

Relays

A relay is a form of solenoid. Instead of a plunger, an armature is used, which is a moveable plate that is attracted by the magnetic field. The spring returns the armature to its resting position. Refer to Fig. 10-4A. Also notice, attached to the moveable armature is a set of electrical switch contacts. These are also referred to as relay contacts. The switch contacts are separated from the metal plate with an insulator.

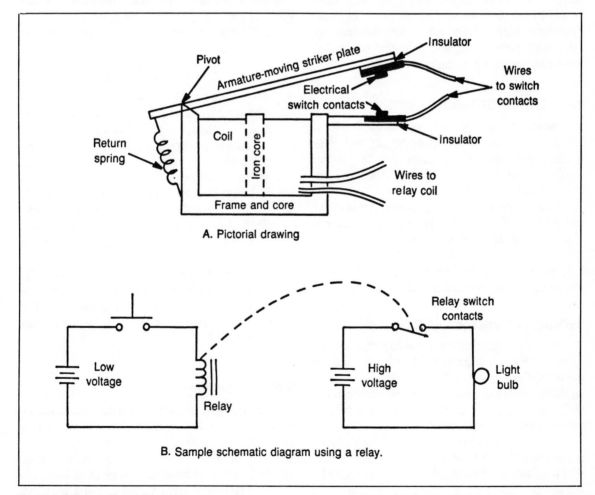

A. Pictorial drawing

B. Sample schematic diagram using a relay.

Fig. 10-4. Relay: A. Pictorial drawing.

Figure 10-4B is a sample circuit to show a possible application for a relay. The relay coil is connected to a voltage source, through a push button switch. When the switch is pressed, the relay will develop a magnetic field. The magnetic field will operate the switch contacts attached to the moveable armature.

Notice in particular, in Fig. 10-4B, the dotted line indicates that only the magnetic field is used to operate the second circuit. When the relay is energized, the relay switch contacts will close, which allows the high voltage battery to supply electricity to the light bulb.

Like toggle switches, a relay can have many different sets of switch contacts. Each set of contacts can be used to operate different circuits. Therefore, one relay can control many different circuits, with only the magnetic field common to the relay and the switch contacts.

PROPERTIES OF INDUCTANCE

Inductors and capacitors, as well as resistors, are the basic components of electricity and electronics. Inductors and capacitors have the unique capability of storing electrical energy. Also, both can be used with ac and dc.

Transformers work by inductance. Another example of an inductor is the ignition coil for an engine. The coil stores energy and uses it to fire the spark plug. Capacitors can be used for filter circuits in a power supply, for timing circuits, and for energy stored in an electronic flash on a camera.

Self-Induced Voltage and Back-EMF

Whenever electrical current is flowing in a piece of wire, there is a magnetic field developed around the wire. The strength of the magnetic field depends on the amount of current flowing. Inductance is the ability of a conductor to use the magnetic field to induce a voltage within itself.

It is important to note that even though there is a magnetic field developed whenever there is current flow, the only time there can be "self-induced" voltage is when there is a changing current. This changing current does not need to be ac. Ac current can also change. This self-induced voltage is known as "back EMF". The term EMF stands for "Electro-Motive-Force", which is a term used to describe voltage. The strength or amount of self-induced voltage, back EMF, is determined by the amount of current flow and the size of inductance.

The size of inductance is determined by several factors, the most important being the number of turns in the coil and the core material. An inductor can be thought of as an electro-magnet, and the factors that produce more magnetism will also produce more inductance.

An inductor, as a component, is a coil of wire that is essentially an electro-magnet. The main "property" of inductance is the back-EMF, which opposes any change in current flow.

Let's examine the effects of current flowing in a coil of wire:

1. When current first starts to flow, it will start developing the magnetic field.
2. The developing magnetic field causes a back-EMF, which opposes the changing current. This opposition to current flow is the property of inductance.
3. When the current reaches a point where it is no longer changing, then the magnetic field will be steady, and there will no longer be any back-EMF. In other words, when current is not changing, there is no back-EMF and no opposition to the current flow.
4. When the current starts to decrease, the magnetic field will start to collapse, which will induce a back-EMF that will actually aid the current, therefore opposing any further change in current.

Unit of Inductance

The unit of inductance is the henry. An inductor can be rated from very small to very large. The unit henry, symbol H, is the base unit for inductance. The symbol for an inductor, as a component, is L.

The ratings of inductors range from less than 1 mH (milli-henry) for a tuning coil in a radio, to several henrys for a strong solenoid. An electro-magnet, such as the one in a junk yard, might be several hundred henrys.

Key Points of Inductance

- [ ] A magnetic field is produced whenever current flows in a wire.
- [ ] Self-induced voltage is produced in an inductor when there is changing current.
- [ ] Back-EMF is another term for self-induced voltage.
- [ ] Inductance is the characteristic that opposes any change in current.
- [ ] Henry is the base unit for inductance, symbol for Henry is H and symbol for inductor is L.

INDUCTORS IN SERIES

Like resistors, inductors (and capacitors) can be connected in series or parallel. There are different reasons for doing this, such as two solenoids connected together, two electro-magnets connected, etc. Another reason might be simply to use two or more component values to form a new value.

Mutual Inductance

Mutual inductance is a term used to describe two coils that are physically close enough together for their magnetic fields to interact.

In the case of a transformer, it is desired to have a maximum amount of mutual inductance. In fact, the ideal situation is a mutual coupling of 1:1, which means every magnetic line of force from one coil interacts with the other coil's line.

Two completely separate inductors could have their coils close enough together so some of the magnetic lines of force interact. The interaction between coils could result in an aiding condition or an opposing condition.

Normally, mutual inductance is considered only when the inductors are connected in series. It is possible with the inductors in parallel but the calculations would be very difficult. Because mutual inductance is only considered in series and since it can be aiding or opposing, there are four formulas possible for calculating series inductance.

Formula #16. Series Inductors, No Mutual Inductance

$$L_T = L_1 + L_2 + L_3 + \ldots$$

Total inductance equals the sum of the individual inductors in series. The same type of formula is used for series resistors.

Formula #17. Series Inductors, Aiding Mutual Inductance

$$L_T = L_1 + L_2 + 2L_M$$

Total inductance equals the sum of the inductors plus 2 times the amount of mutual inductance.

Formula #18. Series Inductors, Opposing Mutual Inductance

$$L_T = L_1 + L_2 - 2L_M$$

Total inductance equals the sum of the inductors minus 2 times the amount of mutual inductance.

Formula #19. Series Inductors, with Aiding or Opposing Mutual Inductance

$$L_T = L_1 + L_2 +/- 2L_M$$

Total inductance equals the sum of the inductors plus (for aiding) or minus (for opposing) 2 times mutual inductance.

Schematic Diagrams

Figure 10-5 shows the three possible conditions for two inductors in series.

Figure 10-5A shows the schematic diagram for two inductors in series, with no mutual inductance. Notice the schematic symbol for an inductor represents a coil.

Figure 10-5B shows the schematic diagram of two inductors in series, with their "phasing dots" in the same direction. The phasing dots are schematic symbols that are added to the inductor symbol to show the direction of the turns, or magnetic field. When the phasing dots are drawn in the same direction, they represent an aiding mutual inductance.

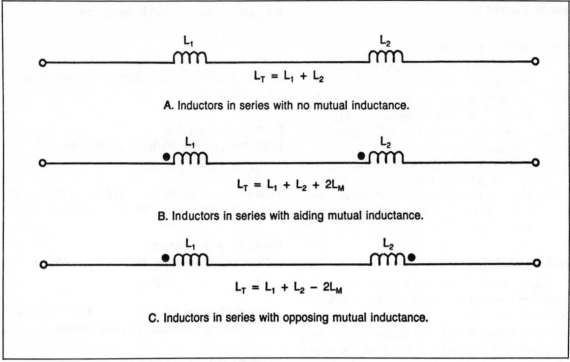

L₁ **L₂**

$L_T = L_1 + L_2$

A. Inductors in series with no mutual inductance.

$L_T = L_1 + L_2 + 2L_M$

B. Inductors in series with aiding mutual inductance.

$L_T = L_1 + L_2 - 2L_M$

C. Inductors in series with opposing mutual inductance.

Fig. 10-5. Series inductors showing the possible combinations of mutual inductance.

Figure 10-5C shows the schematic diagram for two inductors in series, with their phasing dots in opposite directions. This represents opposing mutual inductance.

Key Points of Mutual Inductance

Mutual inductance is the result of the magnetic fields of inductors interacting.

Phasing dots show the polarity of magnetic fields.

Sample Problems: Inductors in Series

SP#10-1 Determine the equivalent inductance of three inductors connected in series, no mutual inductance and their values are; 25 mH, 50 mH, 75 mH.

Formula: $L_T = L_1 + L_2 + L_3$
Substituting: $L_T = 25$ mH + 50 mH + 75 mH
Solving: $L_T = 150$ mH

SP#10-2 Two 100 mH coils are connected in series. What is the total inductance with 10 mH aiding mutual inductance.

Formula: $L_T = L_1 + L_2 + 2 L_M$
Substituting: $L_T = 100$ mH + 100 mH + (2 × 10 mH)
Solving: $L_T = 220$ mH

SP#10-3 A 5 H inductor is connected in series with a 4 H inductor, with 0.5 H opposing mutual inductance. What is the effective inductance?

Formula: $L_T = L_1 + L_2 - 2 L_M$
Substituting: $L_T = 5$ H + 4 H − (2 × .5 H)
Solving: $L_T = 8$ H

INDUCTORS IN PARALLEL

Inductors are connected in parallel for different reasons, such as: the value of circuit inductance needed is not available, but by connecting them in parallel, the value can be achieved. This is similar to connecting resistors in parallel when a different value is needed. Another example of inductors in parallel is when several electric motors are connected across the same power line.

It can be seen, then, that there are times when it is desirable to have inductors connected in parallel and it might be required to know the value of the total circuit inductance.

Reciprocal Formula

To calculate the total inductance of inductors connected in parallel, use the reciprocal formula. This is essentially the same formula used to calculate resistors in parallel. Any of the "short-cut" formulas used with resistance can be used for calculating inductance in parallel.

Formula #20. Inductors in Parallel, Reciprocal Formula

$$\frac{1}{L_T} = \frac{1}{L_1} + \frac{1}{L_2} + \frac{1}{L_3} + \dots$$

Mutual Inductance in Parallel

Mutual inductance occurs anytime the magnetic field from one inductor interacts with the magnetic field of another inductor.

Even though mutual inductance is quite possible in parallel circuits, the necessary mathematics to calculate it would be extremely difficult due to the reciprocal formula. Because of this, mutual inductance in parallel is not used.

Sample Problem: Inductors in Parallel

SP#10-4 Two 250 mH inductors are connected in parallel. Determine the total circuit inductance.

Formula: $\dfrac{1}{L_T} = \dfrac{1}{L_1} + \dfrac{1}{L_2}$

Substituting: $\dfrac{1}{L_T} = \dfrac{1}{250 \text{ mH}} + \dfrac{1}{250 \text{ mH}}$

Solving: $L_T = 125$ mH

PROGRAMS FOR THIS CHAPTER

This chapter has one multiple-choice quiz. This is an excellent method of reviewing the theory of magnetism and inductance.

Figure 10-11 shows a sample of the program. There are no hints with this program because there is no mathematics.

Practice Problems: Inductance

Determine the total inductance of each of the following combinations. Assume no mutual inductance when no value is given.

(1) Series circuit; 500 μH, 700 μH
(2) Series circuit; 10 mH, 50 mH, 30 mH
(3) Series circuit; 100 mH, 0.2 H, 0.15 H, L_M = 10 mH aiding
(4) Series circuit; 1 H, 1.5 H, 1200 mH, L_M = 25 mH opposing
(5) Parallel circuit; 100 mH, 200 mH
(6) Figure 10-6
(7) Figure 10-7
(8) Figure 10-8
(9) Figure 10-9
(10) Figure 10-10

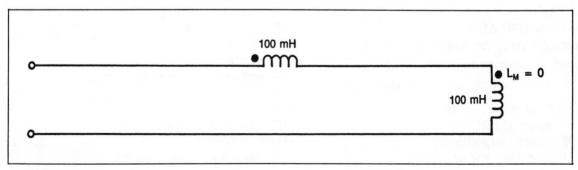

Fig. 10-6. Problem 6.

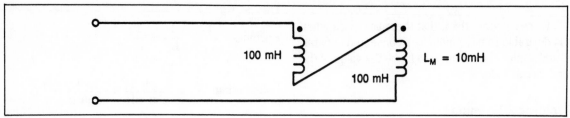

Fig. 10-7. Problem 7.

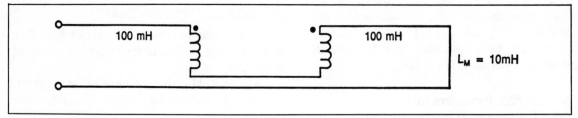

Fig. 10-8. Problem 8.

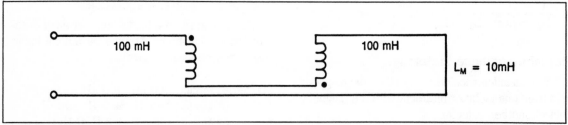

Fig. 10-9. Problem 9.

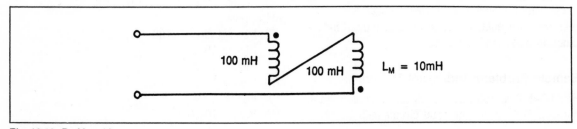

Fig. 10-10. Problem 10.

MAGNETISM AND
INDUCTANCE COMPETENCY TEST
Part A. Definitions

Questions 1-20, define the following terms.

(1) magnetic lines of force
(2) magnetic field
(3) residual magnetism
(4) temporary magnet
(5) permanent magnet
(6) reluctance
(7) electro-magnet
(8) magnetic core (state its purpose)
(9) solenoid
(10) relay
(11) self-induced voltage
(12) back EMF
(13) opposes a change in current

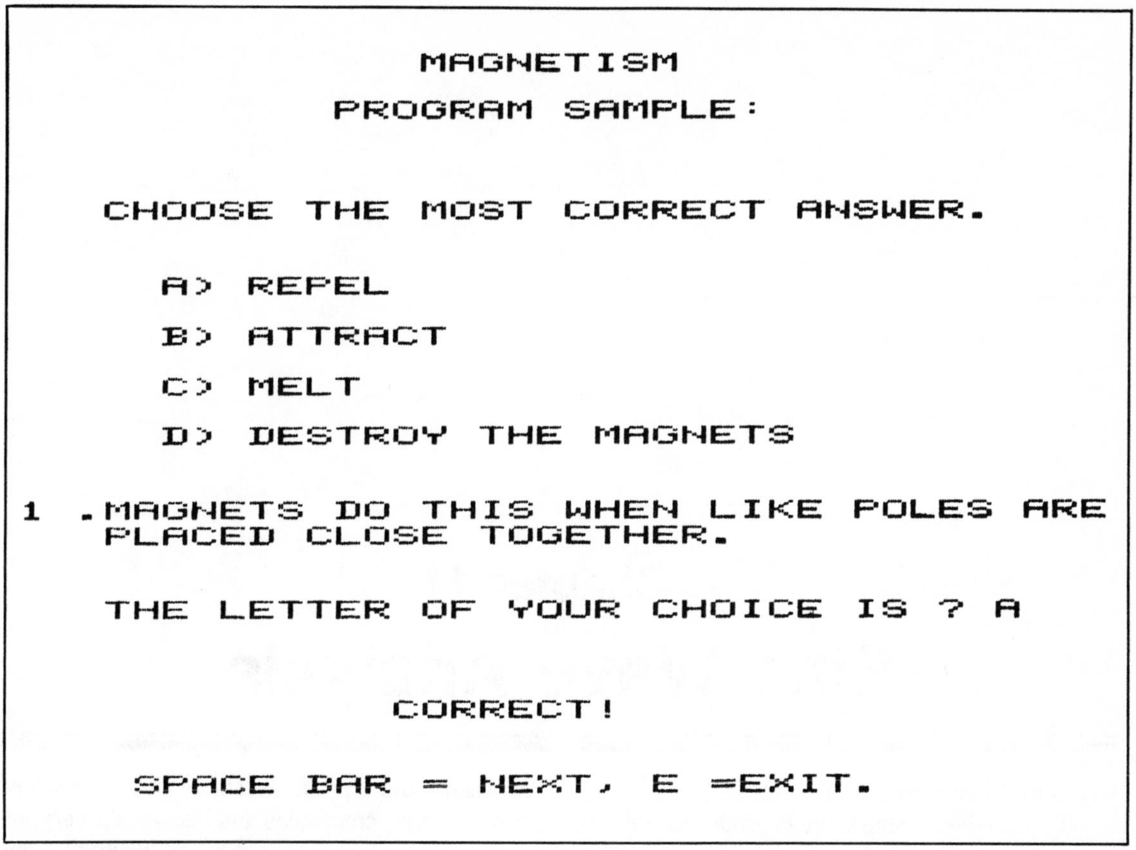

```
          MAGNETISM
       PROGRAM SAMPLE:


   CHOOSE THE MOST CORRECT ANSWER.

      A> REPEL

      B> ATTRACT

      C> MELT

      D> DESTROY THE MAGNETS

 1 .MAGNETS DO THIS WHEN LIKE POLES ARE
    PLACED CLOSE TOGETHER.

    THE LETTER OF YOUR CHOICE IS ? A


           CORRECT!

    SPACE BAR = NEXT, E =EXIT.
```

Fig. 10-11. Magnetism program sample.

(14) basic unit for inductance
(15) inductance
(16) mutual inductance
(17) phasing dots
(18) formula for inductors in series
(19) formula for inductors in parallel
(20) henry

Part B. Calculations

(21) Determine the total inductance of two inductors (50 mH and 80,000 μH) connected in series, with no mutual inductance.

(22) Determine the total inductance of two inductors (.350 H and 250 mH) connected in series with 100 mH aiding mutual inductance.

(23) Determine the total inductance of two inductors (10 H and 5 H) connected in series with 2 H opposing mutual inductance.

(24) Determine the total inductance of two inductors (75 mH and 100 mH) connected in parallel.

(25) Determine the total inductance of three inductors (each 150 mH) connected in parallel.

Chapter 11

Sine Wave Analysis

Chapter Objectives:

To learn how a sine wave is produced and plot its waveform. Also, to learn to calculate, measure and analyze the parameters of sine waves and other waveforms. This chapter included hands-on practice with an oscilloscope and ac voltmeter.

Chapter Outline:

☐ Alternating current (ac)
☐ AC Line Voltage
☐ Producing a Sine Wave
☐ Plotting a Sine Wave
☐ Units of Amplitude
☐ Units of Time
☐ Using an Oscilloscope to Measure a Sine Wave
☐ Hands-On Practice with Sine Waves
☐ Programs for This Chapter
☐ Sine Wave Analysis Competency Test

INTRODUCTION

The sine wave is a naturally occurring waveform that is found in all fields of science. The sine wave represents the type of electricity that is produced by the electric companies and becomes a very important subject in the study of electricity and electronics—it is also referred to as ac.

ALTERNATING CURRENT (AC)

Alternating current, abbreviated ac, is electricity that periodically changes its direction of current. Although it uses the term "current," it also effects voltage and power. An ac voltage produces a waveform that has a definite pattern that repeats itself periodically. The sine waveform is an example of ac. Ocean waves are like sine waves. The waves in an ocean go from high to low, back to high, and then the pattern is repeated.

DC Compared to AC

Previous chapters of this book have dealt with dc (direct current). The formulas and circuit theory are almost identical for both dc and ac. The major difference is the fact that dc has a voltage that is fairly constant at all times (although there are certain exceptions) and ac has a constantly changing voltage.

A dc voltage is necessary to operate almost all electronic circuitry, such as radios, TV's, computers, etc. In cases where an electronic device is plugged into the wall socket, which supplies ac, the electronic circuitry will convert the ac to dc.

A dc voltage is not practical for long distances on wire because it produces a large voltage drop on the wire. Ac is much better for travel over long wires because it does not cause an excessive voltage drop.

A dc voltage is the type stored in batteries. When it is used to power a motor, the speed of the motor will be determined by the amount of voltage applied. Therefore, dc is used quite extensively with motor speed controls.

An ac voltage is the electricity supplied from the household wall socket. It is easy for the power companies to produce and distribute. Many motors operated in a house are operated directly from the ac line: refrigerators, furnaces, electric clocks, fans, air conditioners, etc. All of these motors are called "synchronous" because the speed of the motor is determined by the frequency of the ac supply voltage. Under normal conditions, the speed of the motor cannot be changed.

An ac voltage cannot be stored for future use, dc can be stored in a battery, although ac is easy to produce for use at that moment.

Waveforms

Figure 11-1 shows four different types of waveforms. Figure 11-1A shows a dc voltage waveform. There are two dc voltages shown in the same drawing, positive and negative.

Figure 11-1B is a sine wave. This is the most commonly found waveform. Figure 11-1C is a sawtooth and 11-1D is a square wave. These are also a form of alternating current.

AC LINE VOLTAGE

The electricity available from the wall socket is referred to in this book as the ac line voltage. It can also be called household electricity. Regardless of what it is called, a student of electronics must be-come familiar with the characteristics of the electricity in use.

Nominal Voltage

The nominal voltage of household electricity is 120 volts at 60 cycles per second. Each of these terms will be explained as the chapter is further developed.

The actual voltage can range from about 110 volts to about 120 volts. The exact value of voltage is of little concern, normally, because most equipment that an electronics technician will deal with changes the ac line voltage to dc.

The 60 cycles per second frequency is exact and the power companies constantly monitor it to ensure that it remains exact.

3 Wire System

The ac line voltage is supplied with a 3 wire system. The wires are: hot, neutral and ground. Refer to Fig. 11-2.

The ground wire in a standard system is a green wire and is the semi-round hole/prong. This wire is not intended to be a current carrying wire. Instead, it is used to provide protection in the event that the hot wire was to become disconnected or faulty in some way. It is becoming increasingly more popular to have a "ground fault indicator" (GFI) connected to certain types of circuits. These sense extremely small amounts of current in the ground wire and disconnect the circuit. In this manner, electric shock is avoided.

The neutral wire is white and is the larger flat blade/hole. The neutral wire is intended to be a current carrying wire. However, by itself, it has no voltage potential. In many cases, it is actually connected to ground. Its function is to be the "return" wire to the voltage supply. In a household fuse panel, all of the white wires in the house are connected to a center "buss-bar," which is then connected to the in-coming supply wires. The white wire should not be used for switching. In other words, it should not be the one connected to turn on/off an electric circuit. The electricity in the circuit will stop flowing, and the light will go out, but there will still be volt-

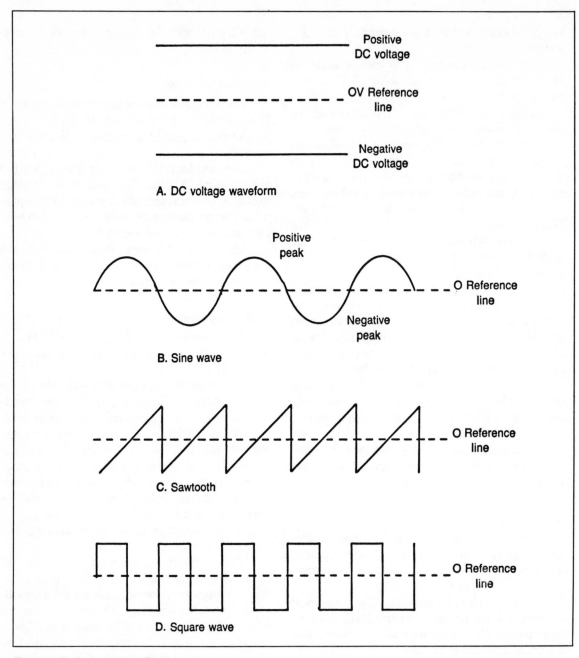

Fig. 11-1. Various waveform displays:

age available. In this case, the circuit is still considered "live" and can cause a shock. With proper electrical connections, the white wire itself cannot cause shock.

The hot wire is the smaller flat blade/hole and is the black wire. This is the wire that supplies voltage to the circuit. It is the hot wire that should be used to switch the circuit on/off. At the fuse panel,

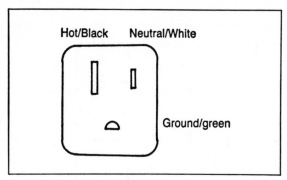

Fig. 11-2. Pictorial drawing of a wall socket.

the black wires individually go to separate fuses/circuit breakers. Each fuse is a separate circuit rated to carry a certain amount of current. If a person touches the black wire and is in any way grounded (by touching something metal, bare feet, wet surfaces, etc.) there will be potential for an electric shock. If the hot wire becomes loose in an electric appliance and touches the side of the box, the appliance could become a shock hazard. The green ground wire is usually attached to the box to prevent this.

If an appliance or electric device is wired for three wire operation, then the green (ground) wire will be attached to the outside case. Often the neutral wire is also attached to the outside metal case. A very dangerous thing that some people will do is interrupt the three wire system. Sometimes the round ground prong is cut off because the outlet to be used has only two holes. Sometimes an extension cord with only two wires is used. Whatever the fault, if the third wire is not connected, the device will still operate, but it is possible (50% chance) to reverse the two wires. In other words, the hot wire may be connected to the outside metal case and the neutral wire may be connected to the machine. The machine will still operate, but there will be an extreme danger of electric shock. Therefore, it is very important to be sure that the three wire system in use remains as intended.

PRODUCING A SINE WAVE

A sine wave can be produced by different methods. This chapter will discuss the method of generating a sine wave through the use of a generator. Examining how the generator produces a sine wave will tie together the concepts of magnetic fields and inducing a voltage, and how and why the sine wave is shaped the way it is.

The Sine Wave Generator

A sine wave generator is made with magnetic poles, producing a magnetic field and wire rotating through the magnetic field to induce voltage in the wire.

As a wire is moved through a magnetic field, voltage will be induced. The strongest voltage will be induced when the wire is moving perpendicular (at right angles) to the magnetic lines of force. This will occur when the wire moves past the pole of the magnet.

Zero voltage will occur when the wire is moving in the same direction as the lines of force. This will occur when the wire is between the magnetic north and south poles.

A reference of positive and negative voltage is established when the wire is first started to rotate. If north is said to produce a positive voltage, then south must produce a negative voltage. When the wire passes a north pole, a positive voltage will be induced in the wire and when it passes a south pole, a negative voltage is induced.

Rotating a Wire in the Generator

Figure 11-3 shows a loop of wire rotating in the magnetic field of a two pole generator. Note: actual generators have many more than one pole and many turns of wire, but the principle is the same.

The loop of wire in this drawing will make a complete revolution of 360 degrees, with check points every 90 degrees.

Point "a" is the start of the rotation. This point marks 0 degrees. At this point, the wire is exactly in line with the magnetic lines of force, therefore, no voltage is induced in the wire. The graph shows a point of zero volts, marked at 0 degrees.

Point "b" shows the wire has moved counterclockwise to a position directly perpendicular to the magnetic lines of force. The wire is marked with a

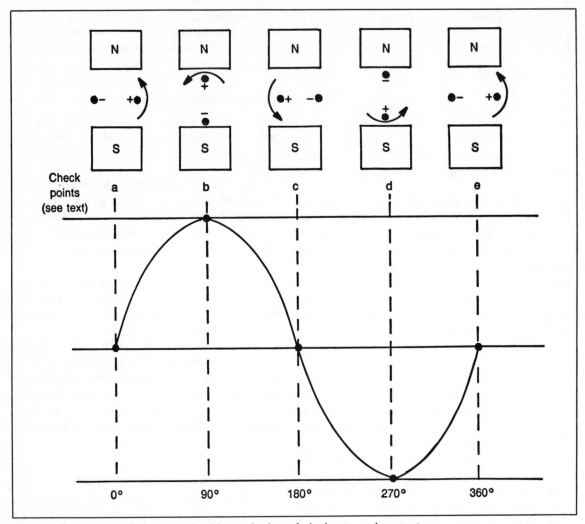

Fig. 11-3. One cycle of a sine wave produced by rotating loop of wire in a two pole generator.

+ at north and a − at south to indicate the polarity of the voltage. Notice, on the graph, that the voltage increased from the zero position, in a positive direction, to maximum voltage at point "b." This point occurs at 90 degrees and is ¼ of the way through the cycle.

Point "c" marks the wire at a point where it is again exactly in line with the lines of force. Again, the induced voltage is zero. Notice the curve as it drops from maximum to zero. This zero point occurs at 180 degrees, ½ way through the complete cycle. As the wire leaves the 180 degree point, it is traveling towards the south pole.

Point "d" shows the wire exactly perpendicular to the lines of force and directly in line with the south pole. Notice the polarity markings on the wire. The + is now at the south and the − is at the north. This is a condition that is opposite from point "b." The voltage in this direction produces a negative polarity. The graph shows a maximum voltage developed at point "d," but it is in the negative direction. This maximum negative voltage occurs at 270 degrees of rotation, ¾ of a complete cycle.

Point "e" is where the wire returns to the starting position and the cycle repeats itself.

How often the cycle repeats itself depends upon

two factors: the number of poles in the generator and the speed of rotation. The actual voltage developed depends on two factors: the strength of the magnetic fields and the speed of rotation. It is not necessary for an electronics student to be concerned about the operation of a generator other than the basic principles of operation.

PLOTTING A SINE WAVE

Plotting the shape of the sine wave can be performed with a mathematical formula. In this way, it is possible to determine the voltage at any instant in time, based on the electrical degrees of the cycle.

Note: electrical degrees means how many degrees of a cycle. Mechanical degrees means how many degrees of rotation. When dealing with electricity, the number of degrees will be the electrical degrees.

Instantaneous Voltage

There are several points along the sine wave that have significant value. Instantaneous voltages are found at any instant along the sine wave, based on the number of degrees.

Formula #21. Instantaneous Voltage of a Sine Wave

$$v = V_{max} \times sine\ \theta$$

v (lower case v) is the instantaneous voltage, or the voltage at an instant.

V_{max} (upper case V) is the maximum voltage the sine wave reaches.

Sine θ (or sin θ) is the trigonometric function, which can be calculated on a calculator. It is multiplied times the maximum voltage. θ is the Greek letter theta and it represents the number of degrees of the cycle.

Calculating and Plotting One Cycle

Formula #21, the instantaneous voltage formula will be used to plot one cycle of a sine wave. The calculations are performed on an electronic calculator for every 15 degrees. This will provide points for the graph to plot a fairly nice curve.

For this sample, the sine wave has a maximum voltage of 100. This value is selected to simplify the calculations. Any value of maximum voltage can be used.

Results of the calculations are shown in Table 11-1. One sample calculation is shown below for 45 degrees. The graph of these sample calculations is shown in Fig. 11-4.

Formula: $v = V_{max} \times sine\ \theta$
Substituting: v = 100 volts × sine 45°
Find the sine of 45 degrees on the calculator.
Sine 45° = .707
Substituting: v = 100 volts × .707
Solving: v = 70.7 volts

Note: this sample calculation is the point on a sine wave called the rms value, to be discussed later.

UNITS OF AMPLITUDE

Amplitude is a term used to describe a waveform in terms of its height. It must be clearly understood that a particular waveform can be either voltage or current, although voltage is the most common form of waveforms. Therefore, to simplify the discussion, when dealing with amplitude, it will be described as voltage.

Amplitude is a term used to describe the quantity, or amount, of voltage. Keep in mind how the oscilloscope is used to measure dc voltages, although dc voltages are a straight line, the line "jumps" to

Table 11-1. Voltage Formula.

Degrees	Voltage	Degrees	Voltage
0	0	180	0
15	25.9	195	−25.9
30	50.0	210	−50.0
45	70.7	225	−70.7
60	86.6	240	−86.6
75	96.6	255	−96.6
90	100	270	−100
105	96.6	285	−96.6
120	86.6	300	−86.6
135	70.7	315	−70.7
150	50.0	330	−50.0
165	25.9	345	−25.9
180	0	360	0

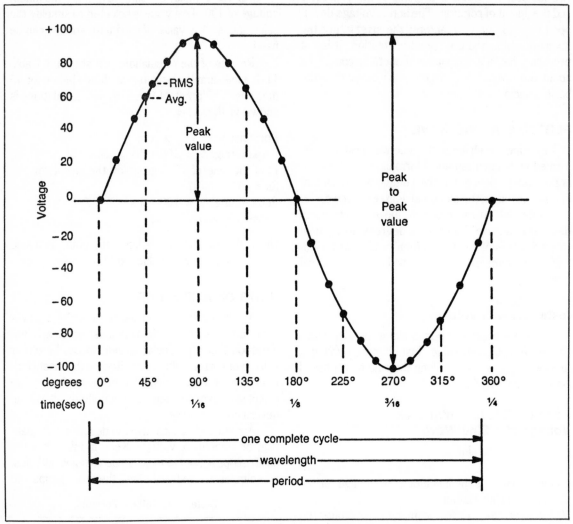

Fig. 11-4. Plotting one cycle of a sine wave using the formula: $v = V_{max} \times sine\ \theta$.

a certain amplitude. Therefore, the oscilloscope measurement of dc voltage is a measure of the height, or amplitude of the wave (straight line) above a reference line.

The amplitude of a sine wave can be described by any of four terms: average, rms, peak, peak to peak. These four terms can be interchanged mathematically. Refer to Fig. 11-4 and Table 11-1 to examine the four values of amplitude.

Peak

The peak value is the maximum height of the waveform. This measurement is made in reference to the center/zero reference line. The peak value can be measured as either positive or negative.

Although it is possible to have waveforms that have the positive peak a different value from the negative peak, that is not the case with a sine wave. A sine wave is a symmetrical waveform, with the positive peak equal to the negative peak.

The sine wave in Fig. 11-4 has a peak value of 100 volts. Figure 11-5 shows five different sine waves. Each sine wave in this figure has a peak amplitude of 6 volts.

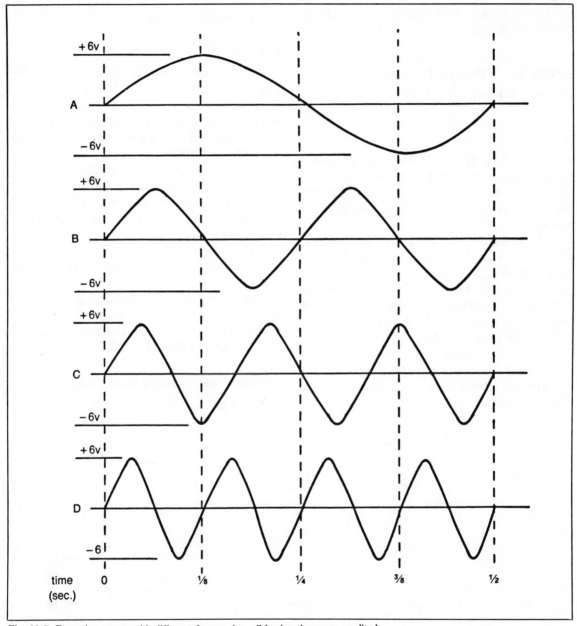

Fig. 11-5. Four sine waves with different frequencies, all having the same amplitude.

The basic formulas to convert from one value to the next are based on the peak value.

Peak to Peak

The peak to peak value is a measurement from one peak to the other.

Quite often this is the easiest measurement to make on the oscilloscope because it is sometimes hard to determine the exact center to make a peak measurement. It is always relatively easy to simply count the divisions from one peak to the other.

Because a sine wave is symmetrical, the peak

to peak value is always twice the peak value. Figure 11-4 is 200 volts peak to peak and Fig. 11-5 is 12 volts peak to peak.

Formula #22. Peak to Peak from Peak.

peak to peak = 2 × peak

RMS

Rms is a significant value because that is what an ac voltmeter will read. It is also the "effective" value, which means that an ac rms voltage will have the same results as an equivalent amount of dc voltage.

The rms is the effective value of the sine wave and occurs at 70.7% of the peak value. The rms value is at 45 degrees, half way between 0 degrees and 90 degrees. Even though it is half way in degrees, the instantaneous voltage at this point is 70.7% of the maximum. The sine of 45 degrees is .707 for the purpose of making the calculation.

The rms stands for the "root mean square" which is a mathematical expression.

The rms value of the sine wave in Fig. 11-4 is 70.7 volts and Fig. 11-5 is 4.24 volts.

Formula #23. Rms from Peak.

rms = .707 × peak

Average

The average value of ½ the sine wave is 63.6% of the peak value.

In order to determine the average, the instantaneous value of every point along ½ of the sine wave would have to be considered and the average taken of those values.

It is very important to notice that a sine wave is equal in both negative and positive. Therefore, if the average of the entire sine wave were to be considered, the result would be zero. Whenever the term average is used for a sine wave, it considers only ½ of the waveform.

The average value becomes a very important calculation in advanced electronics. For example, it is used to calculate the output voltages of power supplies.

The average value of the sine wave in Fig. 11-4 is 63.6 volts and Fig. 11-5 is 3.82 volts.

Formula #24. Average from Peak

Average = .636 × peak

Table 11-2. Summary of Amplitude Formulas.

Given Value	Peak	Peak to Peak	RMS	Average
Peak	—	mult. by 2	mult. by .707	mult. by .636
Peak to Peak	divide by 2	—	mult. by $\frac{.707}{2}$	mult. by $\frac{.636}{2}$
RMS	divide by .707	peak × 2	—	mult. by .9
Average	divide by .636	peak × 2	peak × .707	—

Note: to use the conversion factors in this table; first find the given value in the left hand column, then find the desired value to be converted to by looking in the top row. The given value is multiplied or divided by the conversion factor.

Sample Problems: Converting Amplitudes

SP#11-1. Given: 20 volts peak; convert to rms.

Formula: rms = peak × .707
Substituting: rms = 20 × .707
Solving: rms = 14.14 volts

SP#11-2. Given: 20 volts peak; convert to peak to peak.

Formula: p-to-p = 2 × peak
Substituting: p-to-p = 2 × 20
Solving: p-to-p = 40 volts

SP#11-3. Given: 20 volts peak; convert to average.

Formula: avg = peak × .636
Substituting: avg = 20 × .636
Solving: avg = 12.72 volts

SP#11-4. Given: 280 volts p-to-p; convert to peak.

Formula: peak = $\dfrac{\text{p-to-p}}{2}$

Substituting: peak = $\dfrac{280}{2}$

Solving: peak = 140 volts

SP#11-5. Given: 156 volts rms; convert to peak.

Formula: peak = $\dfrac{\text{rms}}{.707}$

Substituting: peak = $\dfrac{156}{.707}$

Solving: peak = 220 volts

SP#11-6. Given: 63.6 volts average; convert to peak.

Formula: peak = $\dfrac{\text{avg}}{.636}$

Substituting: peak = $\dfrac{63.6}{.636}$

Solving: peak = 100 volts

Practice Problems: Units of Amplitude

For problems 1-10, use the given value to find the others.

(1) Given: 30 volts peak
    Find: a) rms   b) p-to-p   c) avg
(2) Given: 100 volts peak
    Find: a) p-to-p b) avg   c) rms
(3) Given: 80 volts p-to-p
    Find: a) rms   b) peak   c) avg
(4) Given: 260 volts p-to-p
    Find: a) peak   b) avg   c) rms
(5) Given: 70 volts rms
    Find: a) peak   b) p-to-p   c) avg
(6) Given: 12 volts rms
    Find: a) avg   b) p-to-p   c) peak
(7) Given: 16 volts avg
    Find: a) rms   b) peak   c) p-to-p
(8) Given: 120 volts avg
    Find: a) peak   b) p-to-p   c) rms
(9) Given: 85 volts rms
    Find: a) peak   b) p-to-p   c) avg
(10) Given: 70 volts peak
    Find: a) p-to-p b) avg   c) rms

With problems 11-15, the drawing will supply either peak or p-to-p. State which is given and find the other three values.

(11) Figure 11-6. Given?
    Find: a) p-to-p   b) peak c) rms d) avg
(12) Figure 11-7. Given?
    Find: a) p-to-p   b) peak c) rms d) avg
(13) Figure 11-8. Given?
    Find: a) p-to-p   b) peak c) rms d) avg
(14) Figure 11-9. Given?
    Find: a) p-to-p   b) peak c) rms d) avg
(15) Figure 11-10. Given?
    Find: a) p-to-p   b) peak c) rms d) avg

UNITS OF TIME

When a waveform is measured in the horizontal direction, the measurements can have many different names. Refer to Fig. 11-4. There are five different ways to measure in the horizontal direc-

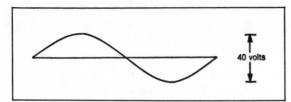

Fig. 11-6. Problem 11.

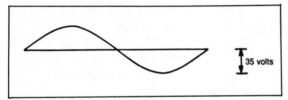

Fig. 11-7. Problem 12.

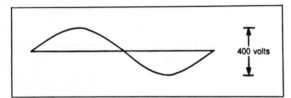

Fig. 11-8. Problem 13.

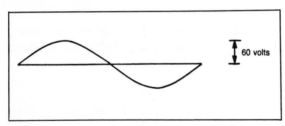

Fig. 11-9. Problem 14.

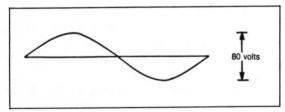

Fig. 11-10. Problem 15.

tion: degrees, time, one cycle, wavelength, period and frequency (not shown in this figure).

Each of these measurements have very specific purposes and relationships in describing and understanding the nature of the waveform.

Degrees

As discussed earlier in this chapter, degrees are used to measure a particular point in the cycle with 360 degrees being a complete cycle. There are several key points which are usually described in terms of degrees, for example; 180 degrees is ½ cycle, which is the point where the sine wave crosses from a positive voltage to a negative voltage. At 180 degrees, the voltage is zero. At 90 degrees, the sine wave is at its positive peak value and at 270 degrees, the sine wave is at its negative peak value. 45 degrees is rms and 39.5 degrees is average.

Cycle

One complete cycle is the point where the waveform repeats itself. Notice that the sine wave starts at a point of zero volts and goes in a positive direction. The next time the waveform is again at this point is at 360 degrees.

With each successive cycle, the waveform again starts at zero degrees and ends at 360 degrees.

Figure 11-5 shows four different waveforms, all with the same frequency. Figure 11-5A shows a sine wave that is only one cycle. Notice that at no point does the sine wave repeat itself. In this figure, the time reference is ½ second. Frequency is a calculation that uses time.

Figure 11-5B is two complete cycles. In the same length of time as Fig. 11-5A, the sine wave repeats itself. There are two cycles in ½ second, one cycle takes place in ¼ second.

Figure 11-5C is three complete cycles and Fig. 5-11D is four complete cycles.

To determine the number of cycles, count how many times the sine wave crosses the zero point with the voltage increasing in the positive direction. Do not count when the wave crosses zero in the negative direction.

Period

The period of a waveform is the length of time it takes to complete one cycle. It has been demonstrated that a cycle can be measured in degrees, with 360 being a complete cycle. There is no specific length of time to complete a cycle. The length of time is based on the frequency of the waveform.

Using the wire and two pole generator as a sample, if the wire makes one complete revolution in one second, then the sine wave will have a period of one second. If the speed is increased, the wire will pass by the magnetic poles more often and the length of time will decrease to complete one cycle.

The term period is measured in time units.

Time

The time required for a sine wave to complete its cycle is a measurement that can be made on an oscilloscope to determine the frequency of the waveform. The oscilloscope is calibrated in the horizontal direction in units of time.

Frequency

Frequency is the number of times a waveform repeats itself in one second. Frequency is measured in cycles per second (cps), also called Hertz (Hz). Frequency can be calculated as the inverse (reciprocal) of time.

Formula #25. Frequency as the Reciprocal of Time Period.

$$f = \frac{1}{t}$$

The sine wave plotted in Fig. 11-4 has a period of ¼ second. Therefore, the frequency is:

Formula: $f = \frac{1}{t}$

Substituting: $f = \frac{1}{.25 \text{ seconds}}$

Solving: $f = 4$ hertz

The four sine waves shown in Fig. 11-5 have different frequencies. Figure 11-5A; period of ½ second, frequency of 2 Hz. Figure 11-5B; period of ¼ second, frequency of 4 Hz. Figure 11-5C; period of .1667 seconds (½ second divided by 3), frequency

of 6 Hz. Figure 11-5D; period ⅛ second, frequency of 8 Hz.

Wavelength

Wavelength is a term used especially with radio waves. It is the length of a sine wave when it travels through air. A low frequency will have a much longer wavelength than a high frequency sine wave. Further discussion of wavelength is beyond the scope of a book on dc and ac building blocks.

Practice Problems: Units of Time

Part A. Calculate the period of the following frequencies.
(1) 10 Hz
(2) 50 Hz
(3) 60 Hz
(4) 100 Hz
(5) 500 Hz
(6) .7 kHz
(7) 1 kHz
(8) 1.5 kHz
(9) 7.5 kHz
(10) 10 kHz
(11) 12 kHz
(12) 15 kHz
(13) 20 kHz
(14) 50 kHz
(15) 75 kHz
(16) 100 kHz
(17) .5 MHz
(18) 1 MHz
(19) 1.5 MHz
(20) 100 MHz

Part B. Calculate the frequency of the following periods.
(21) 5 sec
(22) 10 sec
(23) .1 s
(24) .5 s
(25) .01 s.
(26) .02 s
(27) .05 s
(28) .001 s
(29) .003 s

(30) .005 s
(31) 15 ms
(32) 16.67 ms
(33) 20 ms
(34) 60 ms
(35) 100 ms
(36) .1 ms
(37) .01 ms
(38) 20 μs
(39) 5 μs
(40) 1 μs

USING AN OSCILLOSCOPE TO MEASURE A SINE WAVE

The oscilloscope is the best instrument available for measuring a sine wave, or any other waveform. The oscilloscope can show exactly what the waveform looks like, to detect any distortion. The scope measures voltage and time. The time measurement makes it possible to calculate the frequency.

At this point, the student is familiar with most of the controls on the scope. This section will examine the remainder of the scope controls and introduce a new piece of test equipment, the signal generator.

Before making any connections, read the following subsections for the necessary background information. It will make it much easier to follow the step by step hands-on procedure.

Signal Generator

A signal generator is an instrument that will generate different types of waveforms. The frequencies produced are in the audio range (unless the generator produces radio frequencies, which should not be used for this exercise). The audio range of frequencies is from 10 Hz to 20,000 Hz.

The signal generator, or audio generator, can produce sine waves, square waves, and triangular waves. For this exercise, it is best to start with the sine waves. The student should examine the effects of the other waveforms available, at a later date.

The output of the signal generator has two controls: frequency and amplitude. The frequency control determines the output frequency. The amplitude control determines the amount of output voltage.

Ac Voltmeter

The ac voltmeter is usually part of a multimeter. In fact, the multimeter that has been used as an ohmmeter, dc voltmeter and dc milliammeter is the same one that will now be used as an ac voltmeter.

The ac voltmeter will measure the rms value of a sine wave. It is important to remember that the rms value is calculated with an oscilloscope measurement, because scopes measure peak to peak. The ac voltmeter measures rms values. Because of these differences between instruments, it is important to learn both.

Oscilloscope Controls

When using a signal generator with the scope, it is necessary to trigger the waveform properly or it will not be possible to view a steady waveform.

The trigger must be adjusted to trigger on the channel in use. If the signal is connected to channel 1, it is necessary to trigger on that channel. It will be best to trigger on ac mode and adjust the level for a stable trace (waveform).

The scope's AC-GND-DC switch is best used in the ac position. It is possible to view an ac signal in the dc position, and it will be best for some test conditions, but for now, it should be used in the ac position. The ground reference line should be adjusted to the exact center of the screen.

The volts/div control is a very important control in obtaining a useful and accurate display of the waveform. Figures 11-11, 11-12 and 11-13 show the effects of adjusting the volts/div control. Figure 11-11 is the correct adjustment. Figure 11-12, the volts/div control is set too low. This adjustment allows the waveform to go off the screen. Figure 11-13, the volts/div is set too high. In this case, the waveform is too small to make accurate measurements.

Measuring Frequency on an Oscilloscope

Since an oscilloscope can make measurements in time, it is necessary to use those time measure-

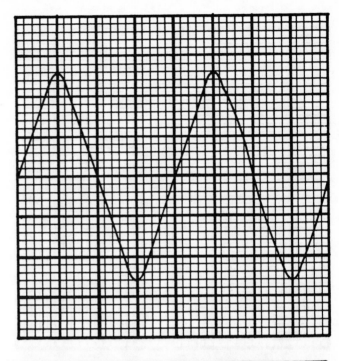

Fig. 11-11. Representation of an oscilloscope display showing a sine wave with the volts per division and time per division correctly adjusted.

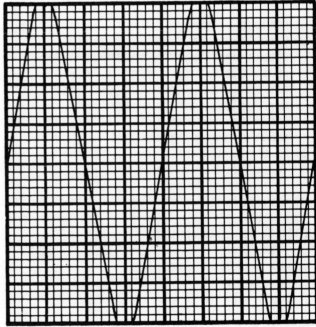

Fig. 11-12. Volts per division expanded too much.

ments and calculate the frequency of a waveform.

Remember, frequency is the reciprocal of time. $f = 1/t$. Once a time measurement is made, simply take the reciprocal to find the frequency.

In order to measure time of a waveform on an oscilloscope, there are a few simple steps to follow:

(1) Determine the time/div setting. The variable

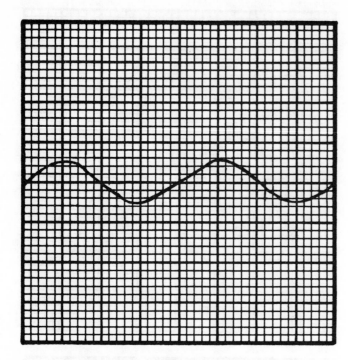

Fig. 11-13. Volts per division not expanded enough.

control must be set to calibrate.

(2) Count the number of divisions from the start of one cycle to the start of the next cycle. The start of a cycle is the point where the waveform crosses the zero axis in the positive direction. It is best to adjust the ground reference line to the exact center of the screen, this makes the center the zero point.

(3) Multiply the number of divisions by the time/division. This will result in the time for one cycle, also called the period.

(4) Calculate frequency by taking the reciprocal. f = 1/t.

SP#11-7. Scope setting: 2 ms/div.

No. of div.: 5 div

Period = 2 ms/div × 5 div

Period = 10 ms

Frequency = 100 Hz (f = 1/t)

HANDS-ON PRACTICE WITH SINE WAVES

Equipment needed:
    Oscilloscope
    Signal generator
    Ac voltmeter

Step 1. Connect a test lead cable to the output of the signal generator. Connect test leads to the input of the scope and an ac voltmeter. Connect all ground wires together, then connect all the "hot" wires together.

Step 2. Adjust the signal generator for an output frequency of approximately 100 Hz. (Other frequencies will be examined later.) The output amplitude will be adjusted using the scope.

Step 3. Adjust the oscilloscope time/div control to 2 ms per div. This setting will enable a display of approximately two cycles, depending on the actual input frequency.

Step 4. Adjust the scope trigger for a stable display of the waveform. If necessary, adjust the volts/div to enable a proper setting of the trigger. The volts/div will be readjusted after the trigger is set.

Step 5. Set the volts per division to 1 volts/div. Use the amplitude adjust on the signal generator for a peak to peak voltage of 5 volts. Be sure the variable control is set to calibrate, the AC/DC/GND switch is on ac, and the ground reference line is set in the center (using the GND switch). There should be 2½ divisions on each side of the center line.

Step 6. Calculate the rms value of the sine wave now on display. Use the ac voltmeter to measure the rms value.

Rms formula _____

Calculated rms_____ (volts)

Measured rms _____ (volts)

Step 7. Change the volts/div setting to .5 volts/div. Adjust the amplitude to 3 volts peak to peak.

Peak formula_____

Calculated peak _____ (volts)

Measured peak_____ (volts)

Rms formula _____

Calculated rms_____ (volts)

Measured rms _____ (volts)

Step 8. Using the ac voltmeter, adjust the signal generator to an output voltage of 4 volts rms. Note: if necessary, adjust the oscilloscope volts/div control.

p-to-p formula _____

Calculated p-to-p_____ (volts)

Measured p-to-p_____ (volts)

Peak formula_____

Calculated peak _____ (volts)

Measured peak_____ (volts)

Step 9. Using the ac voltmeter, adjust the signal generator to an output voltage of 1 volt rms. Adjust the volts/div, if necessary.

p-to-p formula _____

Calculated p-to-p _____ (volts)

Measured p-to-p _____ (volts)

Peak formula_____

Calculated peak _____ (volts)

Measured peak _____ (volts)

Step 10. Adjust the output frequency of the signal generator until the oscilloscope displays exactly two full cycles. Adjust the amplitude to 1 volt rms (Step 9). Be sure the variable control is set to calibrate. Time/div was set to 2 ms/div in Step 3. Determine the period (time) of one cycle

by counting the divisions between the start of one sine wave and the start of the next sine wave. Note: use the horizontal position control to move the waveform so that the display has the start of the waveform at exactly the left side of the screen. Record the period and calculate the frequency. Draw on graph paper exactly what is displayed on the scope. Label the drawing with: p-to-p, peak, rms, period and 0, 90, 180, 270, 360 degrees.

Period_____(time in ms)

Frequency formula _____

Calculated freq _____ (Hz)

Step 11. Adjust the time/div to 1 ms/div. Adjust the signal generator for two full cycles.

Period _____(time in ms)

Frequency formula _____

Calc. freq _____ (Hz)

Step 12. Adjust the time/div for .5 ms/div. Adjust the signal generator for three full cycles.

Period _____(time in ms)

Frequency formula _____

Calc. freq _____ (Hz)

Step 13. Pre-calculate the period for the following frequencies. Pre-determine the number of divisions for one cycle. Adjust the signal generator for the desired frequency, based on the pre-determined calculations. Check the frequency dial on the signal generator to verify results of calculations. The scope time/div may have to be adjusted for the different frequencies, which will change the number of divisions, but not the period in time.

Period formula _____

1000 Hz

Period _____ (ms)

time/div _____ (setting)

divisions _____ (number)

1500 Hz

Period _____ (ms)

time/div _____ (setting)

divisions _____ (number)

2000 Hz

       Period _____ (ms)
       time/div _____ (setting)
       divisions_____ (number)

10,000 Hz

       Period _____ (ms)
       time/div _____ (setting)
       divisions_____ (number)

PROGRAMS FOR THIS CHAPTER

There is one program for this chapter. It is a graphical representation of an oscilloscope. The program will provide practice in using and interpreting the information using oscilloscope waveforms.

As shown in Fig. 11-14, the computer will show the oscilloscope screen, with a waveform. To the right are three blocks giving the setting of time/div and volts/division. To answer the questions, it is necessary to use these settings.

In the time/div block, the unit "MS" is used to stand for milliseconds and "US" is used to stand for microseconds. This is necessary because the computer does not allow lower case letters.

It is necessary to use a calculator to answer many questions. Make certain to use the proper units with each answer. Some waveforms shown are the "sawtooth" type. Use caution with these when answering questions about time or frequency because these waveforms show two cycles rather than one cycle, like all of the others.

SINE WAVE ANALYSIS COMPETENCY TEST

Part A. Definitions

Define the Following. (2 points each.)
(1) alternating current (ac)
(2) direct current (dc)
(3) ac line voltage (give nominal voltage and frequency)
(4) instantaneous voltage
(5) amplitude
(6) peak
(7) peak to peak
(8) rms

(9) average
(10) degrees (in reference to a sine wave)
(11) cycle
(12) period
(13) frequency
(14) hertz
(15) wavelength

Part B. Units of Amplitude Calculations

Use the information given to calculate the unknown values. (Answers are 1 point each.)

(16) Given: 25 volts peak
    Find: a) rms   b) p-to-p

(17) Given: 15 volts peak
    Find: a) avg   b) rms

(18) Given: 40 volts p-to-p
    Find: a) peak   b) rms

(19) Given: 240 volts p-to-p
    Find: a) rms   b) avg

(20) Given: 120 volts rms
    Find: a) peak   b) p-to-p

(21) Given: 45 volts rms
    Find: a) peak   b) avg

(22) Given: 15 volts avg
    Find: a) peak   b) rms

(23) Given: 90 volts avg
    Find: a) p-to-p   b) peak

(24) Given: 100 volts peak
    Find: a) rms   b) avg

(25) Given: 160 volts p-to-p
    Find: a) rms   b) avg

Part C. Units of Time Calculations

Use the value given to find the unknown. When a time is given, it is the period of one cycle. (2 points each.)

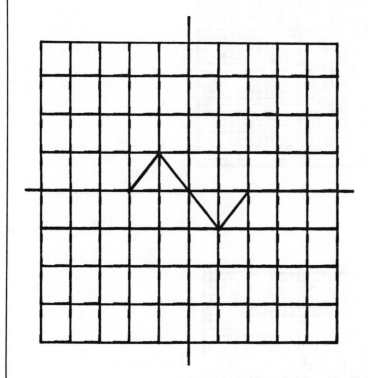

OSCILLOSCOPE AC
PROGRAM SAMPLE:

VOLT/DIV = 5V TIME/DIV = 50US
INCLUDE UNITS
1. WHAT IS THE VOLTAGE PP ? 10 V

CORRECT!

SPACE BAR = NEXT, E = EXIT

Fig. 11-14. Sample of Oscilloscope ac program.

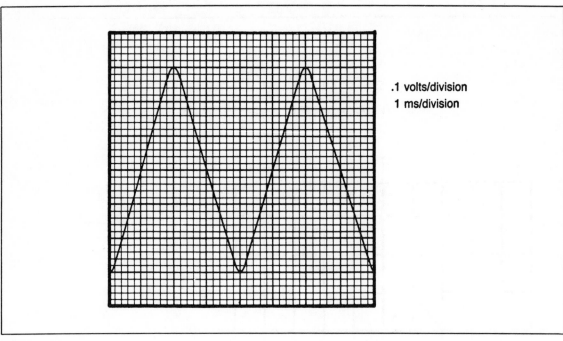

.1 volts/division
1 ms/division

Fig. 11-15. Problem 31.

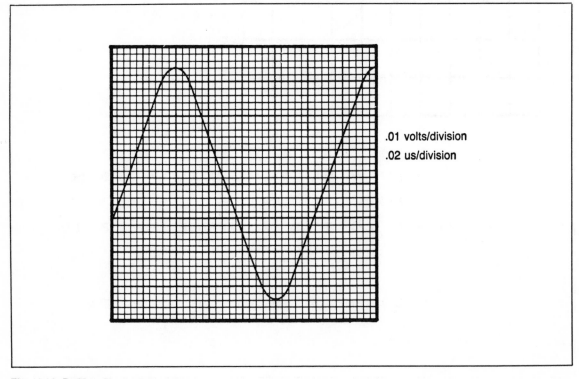

.01 volts/division
.02 us/division

Fig. 11-16. Problem 32.

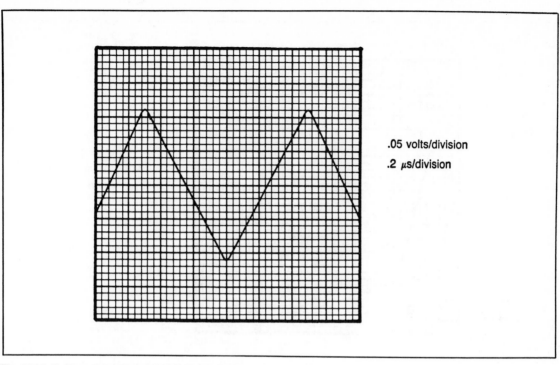

.05 volts/division

.2 μs/division

Fig. 11-17. Problem 33: .05 volts/division .2 μs/division.

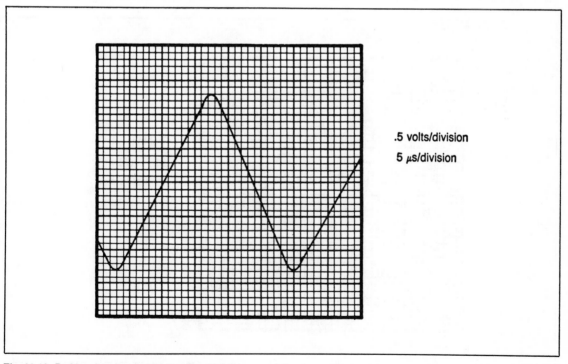

.5 volts/division

5 μs/division

Fig. 11-18. Problem 34: .5 volts/division; 5 μs/division.

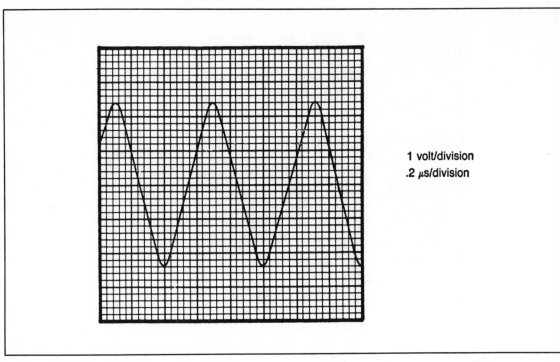

1 volt/division
.2 µs/division

Fig. 11-19. Problem 35: 1 volt/division; .2 µs/division.

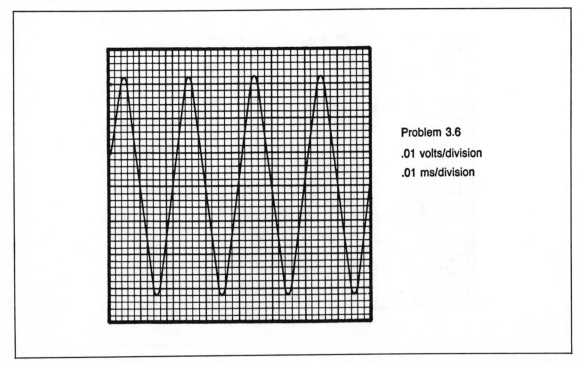

Problem 3.6
.01 volts/division
.01 ms/division

Fig. 11-20. Problem 36: .01 volts/division; .01 ms/division.

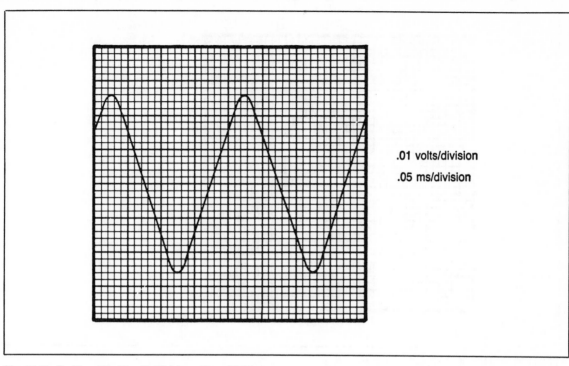

.01 volts/division

.05 ms/division

Fig. 11-21. Problem 37: .01 volts/division; .05 ms/division.

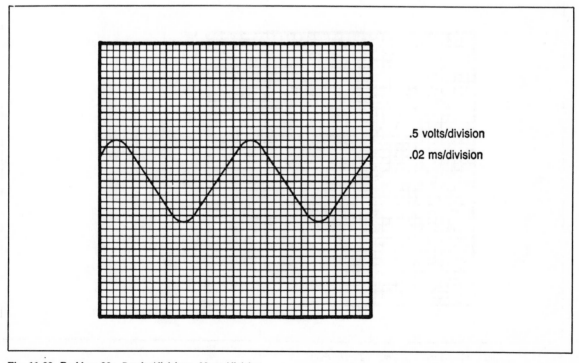

.5 volts/division

.02 ms/division

Fig. 11-22. Problem 38: .5 volts/division; .02 ms/division.

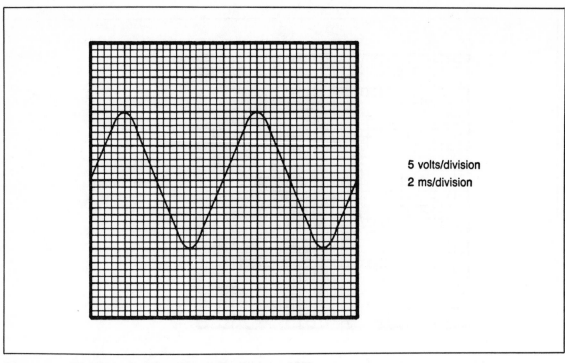

5 volts/division
2 ms/division

Fig. 11-23. Problem 39: 5 volts/division; 2 ms/division.

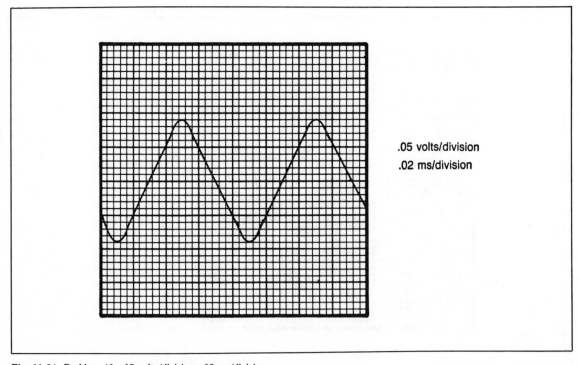

.05 volts/division
.02 ms/division

Fig. 11-24. Problem 40: .05 volts/division; .02 ms/division.

176

(26)	Given: 60 Hz	Find: period	
(27)	Given: 50 ms	Find: frequency	
(28)	Given: 200 Hz	Find: period	
(29)	Given: 1 ms	Find: frequency	
(30)	Given: 2 μs	Find: frequency	

Part D. Waveform Analysis

Find the frequency and peak to peak voltage of the sine waves drawn in Figs. 11-15 to 11-24. (Each answer 2 points.)

(31) Figure 11-15; a) p-to-p voltage b) frequency
(32) Figure 11-16; a) p-to-p voltage b) frequency
(33) Figure 11-17; a) p-to-p voltage b) frequency
(34) Figure 11-18; a) p-to-p voltage b) frequency
(35) Figure 11-19; a) p-to-p voltage b) frequency
(36) Figure 11-20; a) p-to-p voltage b) frequency
(37) Figure 11-21; a) p-to-p voltage b) frequency
(38) Figure 11-22; a) p-to-p voltage b) frequency
(39) Figure 11-23; a) p-to-p voltage b) frequency
(40) Figure 11-24; a) p-to-p voltage b) frequency

Chapter 12

Transformers

Chapter Objectives: To learn what transformers are, how they are constructed and their function. To learn how to calculate transformer relationships and how to perform measurements of voltage, current and resistance.

Chapter Outline:

- ☐ Transformer Construction
- ☐ Transformer Ratios
- ☐ Power and Efficiency
- ☐ Variations of Transformers
- ☐ DC Voltage with the Transformer
- ☐ Hands-On Testing of Transformers
- ☐ Programs for this Chapter
- ☐ Transformer Competency Test

INTRODUCTION

A transformer is a device that allows an ac voltage, usually a sine wave, to pass from the input to the output through magnetism. The output voltage, compared to the input, has three different possibilities: higher than the input; lower than the input;

same as the input.

Because the transformer can be used to change the level of the voltage, it has a very important role in the fields of electricity and electronics. For example, the power company uses a transformer to change the very high voltage used for long distance transmission, to the voltage used in the house. Nearly all electronic devices have a cord to plug into the ac line. When the ac line voltage enters the device, it goes through a transformer to lower the voltage before it goes to the power supply, where it is then changed to a dc voltage.

TRANSFORMER CONSTRUCTION

A transformer is constructed in such a way that magnetism is used to induce voltage in a second wire. The input of the transformer is called the primary and the output is called the secondary. Both the primary and secondary are each a coil of wire (referred to as a winding). When current flows in a coil, magnetism is developed and when magnetic lines of force cross a coil, voltage is developed.

Primary and Secondary Windings

Figure 12-1 is a set of three simplified drawings of a transformer. Figure 12-1A shows a primary winding alongside a secondary winding. The two windings are not physically connected, but they are connected by the magnetic flux. Figure 12-1B shows the windings wrapped around an iron core. The core is used to concentrate the magnetic lines of force to achieve more complete magnetic coupling. Figure 12-1C is the schematic drawing. Also, in all three drawings of Fig. 12-1, the primary is shown connected to an ac voltage source. The symbol for this is a sine wave inside of a circle. The load is represented by a resistor.

When an ac voltage is applied to the primary of a transformer, current will flow in the primary winding (coil). The ac current in the primary develops a magnetic field. The primary and secondary windings are made in such a way that the magnetic field overlaps the secondary completely.

The magnetic field from the primary induces a voltage in the secondary. The amount of induced voltage in the secondary is determined by the size of the secondary coil as compared to the primary coil.

Transformer Core

The purpose of the transformer core is to concentrate the magnetic field. Thus, it allows more complete coupling of the magnetic lines of force (flux) between the primary winding and the secondary winding.

The core of a transformer is made of soft iron. Soft iron is used because it is an excellent conductor of magnetic flux, and can magnetize and demagnetize very quickly. In the schematic symbol shown in Fig. 12-1C, the two parallel lines between the windings represent the iron core.

Core Losses

There are two types of losses in the core of a transformer that are of particular importance: hysteresis loss, and eddy current loss.

Hysteresis loss is caused by residual magnetism. This is the magnetism that is left over after a material has been magnetized, then demagnetized. With alternating current, the polarity of the voltage is continuously changing. Since the polarity of the voltage changes, the polarity of the magnetic field also changes. In order to change the polarity of the magnetic field, the magnet must be magnetized, then demagnetized. The frequency of the voltage will affect the severity of the hysteresis loss.

Hysteresis loss is minimized by selecting a material that can magnetize and demagnetize very quickly, with a minimum amount of residual magnetism. Soft iron is a good material for this reason.

Eddy current loss is caused by an electrical current being developed in the core, because the core is a conductor. The eddy currents will produce a back-EMF and will have severe effects on allowing the coupling of magnetic flux.

Eddy current loss is minimized by laminating the core. The core is manufactured in layers, with the layers separated by an insulating material. In this way, the magnetic flux can pass through, but the electrical current cannot.

An iron core can only be used with relatively low frequencies, usually in the audio range (20 Hz to 20,000 Hz). High frequency transformers use an air core in order to eliminate the core losses. At low frequencies, the core losses are not severe enough to offset the advantages.

TRANSFORMER RATIOS

There are four ratios involved with transformers: turns ratio, voltage ratio, current ratio and impedance ratio. These four ratios are used to describe what takes place between the primary and secondary.

Turns Ratio

The turns ratio describes the number of turns of the primary compared to the number of turns of the secondary, or vise-versa. The turns ratio is stated by the formula:

Formula #26. Transformer Turns Ratio

$$Np : Ns \text{ (or) } \frac{Np}{Ns}$$

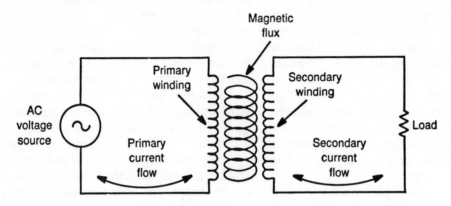

A. Pictoral drawing showing how the magnetic field of the primary induces voltage in the secondary which causes current to flow.

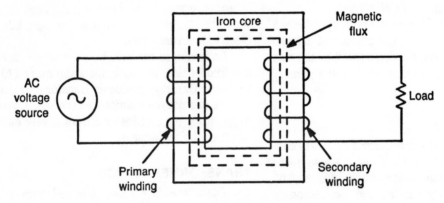

B. Pictorial drawing showing the primary winding and secondary windings wrapped around an iron core.

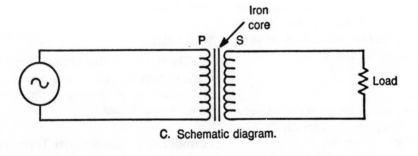

C. Schematic diagram.

Fig. 12-1. Simplified drawings of a transformer.

Np stands for turns of the primary.
Ns stands for turns of the secondary.
: (colon) is the symbol for a ratio.

The ratio is stated as primary to secondary, unless otherwise specified.

The turns ratio statement is read as "turns of the primary to turns of the secondary." Example: Np = 10 and Ns = 1

The turns ratio of this example transformer is 10:1, and is read as "10 to 1, primary to secondary."

Usually the turns ratio is stated as part of the specifications of the transformer. It is this ratio that determines how the transformer will operate.

Keep in mind when dealing with the transformer turns ratio that the turns ratio does not state the actual number of turns of wire, it is only a ratio. For example, a ratio of 10:1 is not an actual 10 turns in the primary and 1 in the secondary. The actual number of turns could be 4000 in the primary and 400 in the secondary. Remember, the size of the wire used to make the coil is very small. A small wire is used because it takes up less space and allows a large number of turns to produce a strong enough magnetic field.

Step-Up/Step-Down

The terms "step-up" or "step-down" refer to the results of the transformer action.

- ☐ If the number of turns of the primary is larger than the number of turns of the secondary, then the transformer is considered a "step-up" transformer.
- ☐ If the number of turns of the primary is smaller than the number of turns of the secondary, then the transformer is considered a "step-down" transformer.

Voltage Ratio

The voltage ratio is probably the most important of the four ratios. It is a direct relationship to the turns ratio and is used to calculate the amount of voltage that will be produced by the secondary with a certain voltage applied to the primary. The voltage ratio allows the turns ratio to be used as an equation:

Formula #27. Transformer Voltage Ratio

$$\frac{Np}{Ns} = \frac{Vp}{Vs}$$

Np is turns of the primary
Ns is turns of the secondary
Vp is voltage of the primary
Vs is voltage of the secondary

The voltage ratio formula is read: "turns of the primary is to turns of the secondary as voltage of the primary is to voltage of the secondary."

The voltage ratio lends itself to easily determine if the transformer is step-up or step-down. If the voltage of the primary is higher than the voltage of the secondary, the transformer is step-up, and if the primary voltage is lower than the secondary voltage, it is step-down.

In order to use the voltage ratio as a formula, three of the four quantities must be known, leaving only one unknown. The equation is then rearranged using "cross multiplication". Shown below are the four possible ways the formula can be used.

$$Np = \frac{Vp}{Vs} \times Ns$$

$$Ns = \frac{Vs}{Vp} \times Np$$

$$Vp = \frac{Np}{Ns} \times Vs$$

$$Vs = \frac{Ns}{Np} \times Vp$$

Sample Problems: Voltage Ratios

SP#12-1.

Given: primary voltage = 60 volts, secondary voltage = 15 volts, secondary turns = 2.

Find: primary turns and determine if it is step-up or step-down.

Formula: $Np = \dfrac{Vp}{Vs} \times Ns$

Substituting: $Np = \dfrac{60}{15V} \times 2$

Solving: $Np = 8$, step-down.
Note: there are no units with the answer because it is a ratio. The term "turns" may be used, if desired, but it is not technically correct because the ratio is not the actual number of turns of wire in the winding.

SP#12-2.

Given: Primary turns = 20, primary voltage = 10 volts, secondary voltage = 30 volts.
Find: secondary turns and if it is step-up or step-down.

Formula: $Ns = \dfrac{Vs}{Vp} \times Np$

Substituting: $Ns = \dfrac{30\ V}{10\ V} \times 20$

Solving: $Ns = 60$, step-up

SP#12-3.

Given: primary turns = 2, secondary turns = 1, secondary voltage = 20 volts.
Find: primary voltage and if it is step-up or step-down.

Formula: $Vp = \dfrac{Np}{Ns} \times Vs$

Substituting: $Vp = \dfrac{2}{1} \times 20$ volts

Solving: $Vp = 40$ volts, step-down

SP#12-4.

Given: primary voltage = 120 volts, primary turns = 1, secondary turns = 4.
Find: secondary voltage and if it is step-up or step-down.

Formula: $Vs = \dfrac{Ns}{Np} \times Vp$

Substituting: $Vs = \dfrac{4}{1} \times 120V$

Solving: $Vs = 480$ volts, step-up

Current Ratio

The current ratio of a transformer is the inverse of the turns ratio. This means a step-up transformer will step-up the voltage but step-down the current. A step-down transformer will step-up the current.

When a transformer is being selected for a particular circuit, usually the voltage is the determining factor. However, extreme caution must be exercised in terms of current. Keep in mind that fuses, which protect a circuit, have current ratings. In order to correctly determine the proper size fuse, the current of both the primary and secondary must be considered.

The current ratio, stated as a formula:

Formula #28. Transformer Current Ratio

$$\frac{Np}{Ns} = \frac{Is}{Ip}$$

Np is turns of the primary.
Ns is turns of the secondary.
Is is turns of the secondary.
Ip is turns of the primary.
Notice the inverse relationship.

Impedance Ratio

Impedance is a term used to describe the ac resistance. There are times in electronic circuits where it is necessary to use a transformer to "match impedances". For example, in an audio amplifier, the output impedance of the amplifier might be as high as 5,000 ohms. The amplifier will supply power to an 8 ohm speaker. If this connection were made directly, the 8 ohm speaker would short-out the amplifier because it is such a low resistance. A transformer should be used with a 5,000 ohm primary and an 8 ohm secondary.

When the impedances of input and output are matched, there is a maximum transfer of power.

This application of a transformer is beyond the scope of the contents of this book. The impedance ratio is presented here as a means of future reference. Most applications of transformers involve the voltage and current ratios.

Formula #29. Transformer Impedance Ratio

$$\frac{Zp}{Zs} = \left[\frac{Np}{Ns}\right]^2$$

Zp is impedance of the primary.
Zs is impedance of the secondary.
Np is turns of the primary.
Ns is turns of the secondary.
Note that the entire turns ratio is squared.

Calculating the Turns Ratio

The turns ratio can be calculated using the voltage ratio, current ratio, or impedance ratio.

Each of these ratios can be thought of as a fraction. Like common fractions, the size of the numbers in the numerator and denominator can be changed without changing the value of the fraction. For example, each of the following fractions are equal:

$$\frac{1}{2} = \frac{2}{4} = \frac{4}{8} = \frac{10}{20} = \frac{30}{60}$$

Keep in mind that the numerator and denominator can be multiplied or divided by the same number and the value of the fraction remains the same. When reducing the turns ratio of a transformer, do not use decimals in the final ratio.

Sample Problems: Calculating Turns Ratio

SP#12-5.

Given: primary voltage = 36 volts, secondary voltage = 9 volts.
Find: turns ratio.

Formula: $\dfrac{Np}{Ns} = \dfrac{Vp}{Vs}$

Substituting: $\dfrac{Np}{Ns} = \dfrac{36\ V}{9\ V}$

To solve: (reduce the voltage ratio to lowest terms)

Solving: $\dfrac{Np}{Ns} = \dfrac{4}{1}$ (step-up)

SP#12-6.

Given: primary voltage = 60 volts, secondary voltage = 120 volts.
Find: turns ratio.

Formula: $\dfrac{Np}{Ns} = \dfrac{Vp}{Vs}$

Substituting: $\dfrac{Np}{Ns} = \dfrac{60\ V}{120\ v}$

Solving: $\dfrac{Np}{Ns} = \dfrac{1}{2}$ (step-down)

SP#12-7.

Given: primary current = .06 amps, secondary current = .02 amps.
Find: turns ratio.

Formula: $\dfrac{Np}{Ns} = \dfrac{Vs}{Ip}$

Substituting: $\dfrac{Np}{Ns} = \dfrac{.02\ A}{.06\ A}$

Solving: $\dfrac{Np}{Ns} = \dfrac{1}{3}$

Practice Problems: Transformer Ratios

Use the information given to complete the table on page 184.

Prob. Number	Turns Ratio (P:S)	Primary Voltage (volts)	Second. Voltage (volts)	Primary Current (amps)	Second. Current (amps)	Step up or Step down
1	10:1	120 v	—	.1 A	—	—
2	6:1	—	20 V	—	.6 A	—
3	1:5	30 v	—	—	.2 A	—
4	1:7	17 v	—	.03 A	—	—
5	—	24 V	96 v	—	1 A	—
6	—	—	27 v	.2 A	.6 A	—
7	—	120 v	60 v	.3 A	—	—
8	—	45 v	—	.1 A	.02 A	—
9	—	300 v	50 v	1 A	—	—
10	—	6 v	120 v	—	1 A	—

POWER AND EFFICIENCY

Power and efficiency are terms used to describe how well work is performed, taking into account losses in the system.

Power

Power is the term used to describe electrical work performed. In order to have power, there must be both voltage applied and current flow.

Power is a form of energy, which cannot be created or destroyed. Electrical work can be found in many forms, with heat being one of the most common. If heat is produced when it is not desired, then it is considered a loss.

The transformer changes the voltage applied to the primary winding into a magnetic field. The magnetic field is used to induce voltage in the secondary winding and allow current to flow.

If the transformer is assumed to be 100% efficient (that is, perfect), then the power applied to the primary of the transformer must equal the power available at the secondary. Another way of stating this is "power in equals power out".

Using the turns ratio, voltage ratio and current ratio, the power of a transformer can be proven to be $P_{in} = P_{out}$:

Voltage ratio: $\dfrac{Np}{Ns} = \dfrac{Vp}{Vs}$

Current ratio: $\dfrac{Np}{Ns} = \dfrac{Is}{Ip}$

Combining ratios: $\dfrac{Vp}{Vs} = \dfrac{Is}{Ip}$

Using cross-multiplication: $Vp \times Ip = Vs \times Is$
Basic power formula: $P = I \times V$
Therefore: $P_{pri} = P_{sec}$

The purpose of the above mathematical demonstration is to prove that if a transformer is 100% efficient, there will be no loss of power between the input and the output. It makes sense, therefore, that if the power out is less than the power in, the loss of power is due to transformer losses. Keep in mind that the output power can never be greater than the input power.

Efficiency

Efficiency describes how well work can be performed in a system that is not 100% efficient. A transformer has losses in the core—losses due to heat, losses in the wire itself, losses due to imperfect magnetic coupling, etc.

Even though the list of losses seems long, modern transformers are manufactured in such a way that they are able to reduce the losses to a minimum. An efficiency of 80 to 90 percent is common.

It is interesting to note that the efficiency of any system (such as an oil furnace, gasoline engine, solar energy, etc.) can be calculated using the same formula:

Formula #30. Efficiency

$$\% \text{ eff} = \frac{P_{out}}{P_{in}} \times 100\%$$

Efficiency is measured in percent.
P_{out} is the power of the secondary.
P_{in} is the power of the primary.
Multiply by 100 to convert to percent.

Sample Problems: Efficiency

SP#12-8.

Given: secondary power = 10 watts, primary power = 12 watts.
Find: efficiency.

Formula: $\% \text{ eff} = \frac{P_{out}}{P_{in}} \times 100$

Substituting: $\% \text{ eff} = \frac{10 \text{ W}}{12 \text{ W}} \times 100$

Solving: % eff = 83.3%

SP#12-9.

Given: efficiency = 85%, primary power = 20 watts.
Find: secondary power.

Formula: $\% \text{ eff} = \frac{P_{out}}{P_{in}} \times 100$

Substituting: $85\% = \frac{P_{out}}{20 \text{ W}} \times 100$

Rearranging: $P_{out} = \frac{85\% \times 20 \text{ W}}{100}$

Solving: P_{out} = 17 watts

SP#12-10.

Given: efficiency = 80%, secondary power = 25 watts.

Find: primary power.

Formula: $\% \text{ eff} = \frac{P_{out}}{P_{in}} \times 100$

Substituting: $85\% = \frac{25 \text{ W}}{P_{in}} \times 100$

Rearranging: $P_{in} = \frac{25 \text{ W}}{85\%} \times 100$

Solving: P_{in} = 29.4 watts

Loaded and Unloaded

The loading of a transformer is determined by the amount of current flow in the secondary.

The transformer is considered unloaded if there is no current flow in the secondary. Voltage will still be developed in the secondary windings, but with no current flow, there is no power developed, therefore, efficiency is zero.

If the transformer is fully loaded, it is drawing a current in the secondary equal to an amount that would be produced by 100% efficiency. It is impossible for the transformer to ever reach a 100% loaded condition.

As the secondary current increases, toward maximum, the losses in the transformer will start to increase. The result of this increase in losses will cause the voltage of the secondary to decrease.

Practice Problems: Power and Efficiency

1. Given: eff = 85%, primary power = 5 watts
   Find: secondary power
2. Given: eff = 80%, primary power = 6 mW
   Find: secondary power
3. Given: eff = 90%, secondary power = 10 watts
   Find: primary power
4. Given: eff = 75%, secondary power = 80 mW
   Find: primary power
5. Given: pri. power = 40 watts, sec. power = 36 watts
   Find: efficiency
6. Given: primary power = 100 mW, secondary power = 60 mW
   Find: efficiency
7. Given: sec. power = .08 watts, pri. power = 120 mW
   Find: efficiency

8. Given: primary voltage = 120 volts, primary
   current = 2 amps, secondary voltage = 60
   volts, efficiency = 80%
   Find: secondary current
9. Given: primary voltage = 80 volts, primary
   current = 1 amp, secondary voltage = 20
   volts, secondary current = 3 amps
   Find: efficiency
10. Given: primary voltage = 10 volts, primary
    current = 1 amp, secondary voltage = 80
    volts, secondary current = .1 amps
    Find: efficiency

VARIATIONS OF TRANSFORMERS

There are many variations of the basic transformer. However, in all cases, current flowing in the
primary develops a magnetic field. The magnetic
field of the primary is coupled to the secondary,
where it induces a voltage in the secondary and allows current to flow.

The various types of transformers to follow are
representative of the wide range of possibilities.

Nonisolated Transformer

Figure 12-2 shows the schematic diagram of a
nonisolated transformer. Notice how, the bottom
line, labeled ground, is common to both the primary
and secondary.

This type of transformer has a very distinct disadvantage, if it is not clear which wire in the secondary is grounded, the hot wire might be connected

to the metal chassis of the electric device. In an
event like this, it does present a shock hazard.

To check if a transformer is a non-isolation type,
use an ohmmeter. Connect one ohmmeter test lead
to one wire in the secondary. Touch the other ohmmeter test lead to the primary wires. Then check
the other secondary wires in the same manner. If
the ohmmeter shows any continuity between the primary and the secondary, it is a non-isolation type.

Isolation Transformer

Figure 12-3 shows the schematic diagram of an
isolation transformer. Under normal conditions, most
transformers are of the isolation type. A transformer
manufactured in this manner has no connections between the primary and secondary, except the magnetic field.

The term ''isolation transformer'' can also refer to a transformer with a 1:1 turns ratio. This type
of transformer does not step-up or step-down the
voltage, it only provides isolation. Because of the
fact that the line voltage available has one side
grounded, there are often times when it is necessary not to have one side of the line grounded. The
isolation transformer with a 1:1 turns ratio provides
the same voltage as the line, except that one side
is not grounded.

Autotransformer

The autotransformer can be either step-up or
step down, as shown in Fig. 12-4. This type of transformer uses only one coil of wire. Taps are made
into the coil to provide the primary and secondary.

Fig. 12-2. Non-isolation transformer.

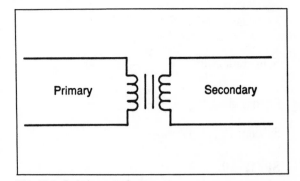

Fig. 12-3. Isolation transformer.

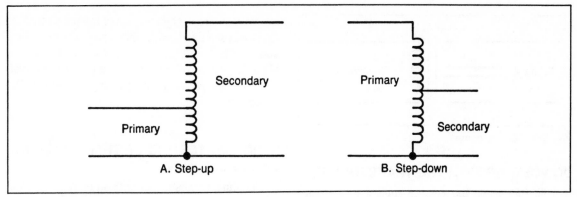

Fig. 12-4. Autotransformer.

The autotransformer works the same way as any other transformer, with a magnetic field from the primary inducing a voltage in the secondary. The autotransformer is a nonisolation type.

Center-Tap Transformer

The schematic diagram of a center-tap transformer is shown in Fig. 12-5. With this type, the turns ratio is stated for the entire secondary. A wire tap is placed at the center of the transformer's secondary. This has the effect of providing three possible connections: 1) across the entire secondary, 2) from the top to the center, 3) from the bottom to the center.

The voltage available from one side to the center is ½ of the full secondary voltage.

Multi-Tap Secondary

The schematic diagram of a transformer with a multi-tap secondary is shown in Fig. 12-6. This transformer has two secondaries, with only one pri-mary. The secondary can be used as a center-tap by connecting the two windings together. By not connecting, the one primary can supply the two separate windings and they would remain completely separate, with only magnetism in common.

Multi-Tap Primary

A multi-tap primary is shown in Fig. 12-7. Although not shown, it is possible for the secondary to have any of the other combinations.

The multi-tap primary is used when it is necessary to have a device that can be wired to either of two voltages. Sometimes, when a device is manufactured, it is not known if it will be used on 120 volts or 240 volts. In this case, the multi-tap primary can be wired to either.

The secondary of the transformer will produce the same voltage with either voltage on the primary (assuming the wiring connections are made correctly). Since the secondary voltage is the same, the rest of the circuit will be the same, even though the input voltage can be different.

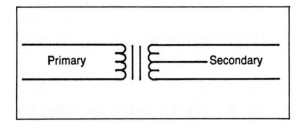

Fig. 12-5. Center-tap transformer.

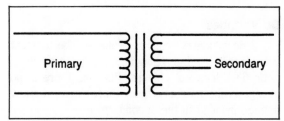

Fig. 12-6. Multi-tap secondary.

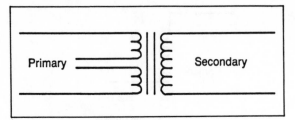

Fig. 12-7. Multi-tap primary.

DC VOLTAGE WITH THE TRANSFORMER

To this point, the voltage applied to a transformer has been an ac sine wave. Other ac waveforms may be used with a transformer, but the transformer action may not permit the wave to have the exact same shape at the secondary, as it did at the primary.

A Changing Voltage is Necessary

When a voltage is to be induced by placing a wire in a magnetic field, it is necessary for the wire to be moving across the magnetic lines of force. The wire must be moving.

When a voltage is developed in an inductor, the voltage only has an effect when the voltage in the coil is changing.

With a transformer, it is necessary to have the changing voltage that is found with a sine wave. The sine wave has a continuously changing voltage. The continuously changing voltage of the sine wave produces the same effect as the wire moving through the lines of force of a magnet.

Therefore, the sine wave will cause a continuously changing magnetic field and will allow a voltage to be developed. The shape of the sine wave will be exactly the same at the secondary as it was at the primary.

Dc Voltages

A dc voltage is a constant voltage. The constant voltage will develop a magnetic field, but its magnetic field does not change. Because there is no change in the magnetic field, there cannot be any voltage induced in the secondary.

If a dc voltage is present at the same time as the ac voltage applied to the primary, the dc volt-age will cause a certain portion of the magnetic field to remain at a fixed level. This is called "saturation" and results in a great deal of distortion. It is possible to have a dc voltage so strong that it will not allow the sine wave to induce any voltage in the secondary.

HANDS-ON TESTING OF TRANSFORMERS
Ohmmeter Testing

Testing a transformer with an ohmmeter prior to applying a voltage ensures that there is continuity in the coils. In other words, it ensures that the coils are good—with no breaks.

1. Set the ohmmeter to the $R \times 100$ scale. Connect the test leads to the primary. Note: the primary usually has two red wires. The reading should be low, of not more than a few hundred ohms. If the reading is high, the coil may be defective. If it is very high, the coil is open. A defective coil in a transformer cannot be fixed unless the break is in the heavier lead wire.

   Primary _____ (ohms)

2. Connect the ohmmeter to the secondary. Once again, it should be a low reading. If the secondary has more than two wires, be sure and check each wire.

   Secondary _____ (ohms)

3. Connect the ohmmeter leads from one of the primary wires to both of the secondary wires. The ohmmeter should read infinity, indicating that there is no connection. Try this same measurement with the other primary wire.

   Primary to secondary _____ (ohms)

Voltage Tests

4. For this test, it is best if the transformer selected has an input voltage of 120 volts. If so, connect it directly to the ac line.

Use Caution.

Note: the primary is usually two red wires.

Use an ac voltmeter to measure the actual voltage present on the line, connected to the primary of the transformer. **Do not use the oscilloscope on the primary.**

Primary voltage _____ (volts)

5. With nothing else connected to the secondary of the transformer, connect the voltmeter to measure the secondary voltage.

Secondary voltage _____ (volts)

6. Based on the results of the voltage measurements, determine the turns ratio of the transformer being tested.

Turns ratio _____ (pri : sec)

7. Remove the voltage applied to the transformer and connect the resistors to the secondary, as a load. Then measure the voltage of the secondary. It is normal for the secondary voltage to decrease slightly with a larger current load, i.e.; lower resistance. Caution: continuously check the transformer and resistor for heat. If either begins to heat up, discontinue testing. Use both an ac voltmeter and oscilloscope to measure the secondary voltage.

Secondary Voltage

Load (ohms)	AC voltmeter (rms)	Oscilloscope (p-to-p)
a) 47 k	_____	_____
b) 33 k	_____	_____
c) 22 k	_____	_____
d) 10 k	_____	_____
e) 1 k	_____	_____

PROGRAMS FOR THIS CHAPTER

There is one program for this chapter. It contains problems in transformer ratios: turns, voltage, current and problems dealing with efficiency. Figure 12-8 shows a sample of the program.

TRANSFORMERS COMPETENCY TEST
Part A. Definitions

Give a brief description of each of the following terms.

(1) transformer
(2) primary of a transformer
(3) secondary of a transformer
(4) transformer core (state the function)
(5) magnetic coupling
(6) name one of the transformer losses
(7) transformer turns ratio
(8) step-up transformer
(9) step-down transformer
(10) transformer efficiency

Part B. Transformer Ratios

Use the information given to find the unknown. Note: all turn ratios are stated primary:secondary.

(11) Given: turns ratio = 10:1
            primary voltage = 100 v
      Find: secondary voltage

(12) Given: turns ratio = 6:1
            secondary voltage = 18 v
      Find: primary voltage

(13) Given: turns ratio = 1:5
            primary voltage = 12 v
      Find: secondary voltage

(14) Given: turns ratio = 1:8
            secondary voltage = 160 v
      Find: primary voltage

(15) Given: turns ratio = 5:1
            primary current = 1 amp
      Find: secondary current

```
            TRANSFORMERS

         SAMPLE PROGRAM:

  NOTE:  UNITS ARE GIVEN, JUST GIVE
  THE NUMERIC VALUE.

  GIVEN:

         TURNS RATIO = 10 TO 1

         PRIMARY VOLTAGE = 120 V

         SECONDARY VOLTAGE = ? V

  1 .FIND THE UNKNOWN ?   12

         ▧◫▨▨=◫◢▦

      SPACE BAR = NEXT, E = EXIT
```

Fig. 12-8. Transformers program sample.

(16) Given: turns ratio = 7:1
              secondary current = 14 mA
      Find: primary current

(17) Given: turns ratio = 1:3
              primary current = .6 amps
      Find: secondary current

(18) Given: turns ratio = 1:4
              secondary current = 2 amps
      Find: primary current

(19) Given: primary voltage = 120 V
              secondary voltage = 12 V
      Find: turns ratio

(20) Given: primary voltage = 30 V
              secondary voltage = 270 V
      Find: turns ratio

Part C. Transformer Efficiency

Use the information given to find the unknown.

Note: answers for efficiency must be in percent.

(21) Given: efficiency = 85%
              primary power = 6 watts
      Find: secondary power

(22) Given: efficiency = 80%
              secondary power = 10 watts
      Find: primary power

(23) Given: primary power = 3 watts
              secondary power = 2 watts
      Find: efficiency (in percent)

(24) Given: primary power = 10 watts
              . secondary power = 9 watts
      Find: efficiency (in percent)

(25) Given: primary voltage = 120 V
              primary current = 2 amps
              secondary voltage = 30 V
              secondary current = 6 amps
      Find: efficiency (in percent)

Chapter 13

Capacitors and Time Constants

Chapter Objectives: To learn the properties of capacitance and to learn how capacitors behave in series and parallel.

To plot and understand the universal time constant curve and examine the effects on inductors and capacitors as they charge and discharge.

To perform calculations with time constants and to apply time constants to RC waveshaping circuits.

Chapter Outline:

INTRODUCTION

The chapter will discuss two very important concepts—capacitance and time constants. Capacitance is a characteristic of electron behavior, and it is an electronic component. A time constant is a method of measuring the effects of either an inductor or capacitor as it charges or discharges. The time constant has many practical applications in electronic circuitry.

PROPERTIES OF CAPACITANCE

The property of capacitance is the ability to store a charge, using conductors and an insulator.

Capacitors are one of the most commonly used components in electronics. Capacitors are used in such applications as: power supply filters, radio tuning circuit filters, electronic timers and timing circuits, waveshaping circuits, electronic flash for cameras, electronic ignition in automobiles, etc. Capacitors can be used in applications using dc or ac voltages, and the size of the capacitors range from very small to very large.

Unit of Capacitance

The base unit of measure of capacitance is the "farad," symbol F. The farad, as a base unit, is much too large for use in measuring practical capacitors. Capacitors will be measured in either microfarads (μF, 10^{-6}) or picofarads (pF, 10^{-12}). Millifarads (mF, 10^{-3}) and nanofarads (nF^{-9}) are generally not used.

The actual size of a capacitor ranges from a small of about 1 pF, used in radio circuits, to a large of about 5000 μF, used as power supply filters.

Schematic Symbol of a Capacitor

When a capacitor is used in a schematic diagram, or in a formula, the symbol is C.

Figure 13-1 shows four different schematic symbols for the capacitor. It is important to note that the capacitor can be used with both ac and dc voltages. When it is used with ac, the capacitor must be nonpolarized. When the capacitor is used with dc, it is best to use one that is polarized.

If a capacitor is polarized, it works best when the positive is connected to the positive side and the negative connected to the negative side. Polarized capacitors can be manufactured with a higher value of capacitance. If a reverse voltage or ac is connected to a polarized capacitor, it could be destroyed.

A "disk" capacitor is the most common type, they are usually round and flat, small in size, $\frac{1}{8}$ to 1 inch in diameter and used for ac. An "electrolytic" capacitor is the next most common type, they are

fairly large physically, cylindrical in shape, $\frac{1}{2}$ inch to several inches long and used for dc voltages. Other types of capacitors are made of various materials, each for different applications.

Electrolytic capacitors are a polarized capacitor that can be used only in dc circuits. They look like a small metal cylinder, with the polarity + or − marked at one end. It is essential that the electrolytic capacitor be connected properly and only in dc circuits. The main advantage of electrolytic capacitors is that they can be manufactured to have a small physical size, with a large value of capacitance. They also have a voltage rating of the maximum allowable voltage.

Figure 13-1A shows the schematic symbol of a nonpolarized capacitor. This symbol, with two straight parallel lines, is an older symbol that is now considered obsolete, although it is still used in some books and schematics. The same symbol is also used to represent switch contacts.

Figure 13-1B shows another non-polarized capacitor with the bottom line curved. This is the more accepted symbol for a nonpolarized capacitor.

Figure 13-1C is a polarized capacitor, using the same symbol as Fig. 13-1B, except the straight line is marked with a positive sign. Figures B and C are the most commonly used symbols.

Figure 13-1D is a symbol that is sometimes used to represent an electrolytic capacitor.

Forming Capacitance

In order to form capacitance, the only requirement is to have two conductors separated by an insulator. The amount of capacitance is determined by the material's ability to store electrical energy.

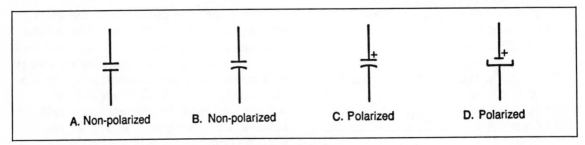

A. Non-polarized   B. Non-polarized   C. Polarized   D. Polarized

Fig. 13-1. Schematic symbols of capacitors, non-polarized and polarized.

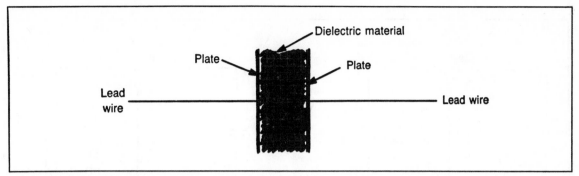

Fig. 13-2. A drawing of a capacitor, showing the plate area and dielectric material.

To build relatively large amounts of capacitance, the size and materials of the conductors and insulator must be considered.

Figure 13-2 is a pictorial drawing of a capacitor. The conductors are not simply two pieces of wire. The lead wires are used to connect the capacitor to the circuit. The conductors of the capacitor are called plates. The plates are parallel to each other and because they are conductors, they provide electrons.

The insulating material of a capacitor is called the dielectric and is shown in Fig. 13-2. The dielectric serves two purposes: it keeps the conductors separated, and stops the electrons from traveling between the plates.

☐ Larger value capacitance is produced by either a larger plate area or thinner dielectric.

Charging/Discharging a Capacitor

Figure 13-3 shows a simple dc circuit to demonstrate how a capacitor charges and discharges.

Figure 13-3A is drawn with the switch in the "off" position. No current flows in this circuit. The switch has three positions, "off," "a," and "b." The dc voltage source is shown as a 10 volt supply. The amount of voltage used here is of little importance; 10 volts was selected just to have a number to use. The capacitor shown is a polarized type to have a larger value capacitance. The resistor can be any value for this exercise. Later in this chapter, the actual values of capacitance and resistance will be discussed along with their effects.

In Fig. 13-3B—the switch is placed in position "a." With the switch in this position, the current path is around the outside of the drawing. Current will flow from the negative side of the battery, through the resistor, to the negative side of the capacitor. Since the capacitor plates are separated by a dielectric (insulator), current flow cannot pass through the capacitor. The negative plate and dielectric will collect electrons, giving the negative plate a negative charge.

The negative charge on the negative plate will produce a field, referred to as an electrostatic field, that will repel electrons from the positive side of the capacitor. At the same time, the positive side of the battery will draw electrons from the positive side. Therefore, for every electron that goes to the negative plate, there will be an equal number of electrons that leave the positive plate. This is called "charging the capacitor."

As current flows to charge the capacitor, a voltage will develop across the capacitor. If the charge process is allowed to continue for a long enough period of time, the capacitor will reach a voltage equal to the applied voltage. When the voltage across the capacitor reaches the applied voltage, there will no longer be any current flow because there is no difference in potential between the applied voltage and the capacitor voltage.

The actual amount of current flowing during charge is determined by the difference in voltage between the battery and the capacitor and the amount of resistance in the circuit.

Figure 13-3C, the switch is moved to the "off" position again. The circuit now has no current path,

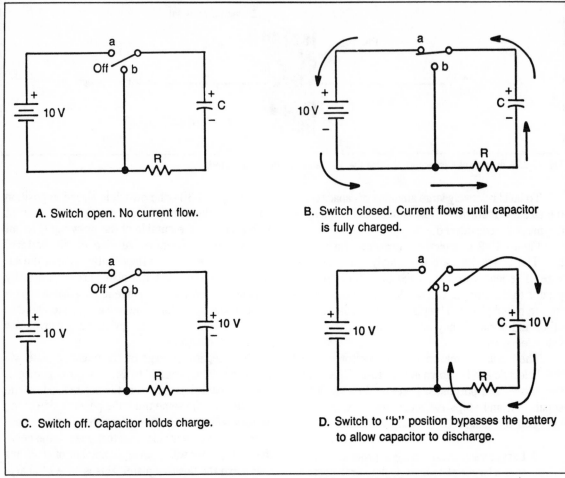

A. Switch open. No current flow.

B. Switch closed. Current flows until capacitor is fully charged.

C. Switch off. Capacitor holds charge.

D. Switch to "b" position bypasses the battery to allow capacitor to discharge.

Fig. 13-3. A simple dc circuit to show how a capacitor charges, stores voltages, and discharges.

either for the battery or for the capacitor. The circuit in this position does not allow the capacitor to equalize the excess of electrons on one side and the lack of electrons on the other side. The capacitor will remain charged until a path is provided for the electrons to flow from one side to the other. In actual practice, the dielectric will leak somewhat and allow the plates to eventually equalize themselves. A good quality electrolytic capacitor can hold a charge for long periods of time, even days.

Figure 13-3D shows the switch moved to the "b" position. In this position, the battery is not in the circuit at all. The capacitor will supply voltage and current flow to the resistor, through the switch contacts. Current will flow from the negative side

of the capacitor to the positive side. As the electrons flow, the charge across the capacitor will decrease until there is no longer a difference between the two plates.

Current flow during discharge is determined by the voltage on the capacitor and the resistance in the circuit.

Notice that the direction of current flow, in relation to the capacitor, is opposite during charge and discharge.

Due to the fact that the charge and discharge of a capacitor does not happen instantly, the voltage across the capacitor cannot change instantly.

□ A capacitor opposes any change in voltage.

CAPACITORS IN PARALLEL AND SERIES

Capacitors, like resistors and other components, can be connected in series and parallel. There are different reasons for wanting to do this, such as changing the value of the component, or improving the voltage or current capabilities.

Capacitors in Parallel

Figure 13-4 shows two capacitors connected in parallel. With the capacitors connected in this way, the two positive plates and the two negative plates will both receive the same charge.

The parallel connection has the effect of increasing the plate area. An increase in plate area will produce a larger capacitance. Therefore, the values of the capacitors are simply added as in the following formula:

Formula #31. Capacitors in Parallel

$$C_T = C_1 + C_2 + C_3 + \ldots$$

When capacitors are connected in parallel, the result, in addition to the values adding, is an increase in current capability. Because they are connected in parallel, they both receive the same applied voltage. Each capacitor will store a charge of electrons based on its own capacitance value. The current capacity is also based on the capacitance value since that is what determines the amount of electrons stored.

Batteries that are connected in parallel will have the same resultant effect as capacitors in parallel. For example, if two flashlight batteries are connected in parallel, the voltage will still be 1.5 volts, but the total current capability will be doubled. For example, if each battery could supply current to light a bulb for 3 hours, then two of these in parallel would supply current to the same light for 6 hours.

Capacitors in Series

Figure 13-6 shows two capacitors connected in series. When capacitors are connected in this manner, the net result is reduced capacitance. The result can be calculated using the reciprocal formula—the same formula used by resistors in parallel.

Formula #32. Capacitors in Series

$$\frac{1}{C_T} = \frac{1}{C_1} + \frac{1}{C_2} + \frac{1}{C_3} + \ldots$$

Figure 13-6 shows how the electrons flow in a circuit with two capacitors in series.

The charge or discharge of capacitors in series is similar to that of a single capacitor. When the electrons leave the negative side of the battery, during charge, they are collected to the negative plate of the closest capacitor. The positive side of the battery will attract electrons from the positive plate of the capacitor closest to that battery terminal. As electrons are collected on one plate and removed from another plate, there is an electro-static field developed that will allow the plates that are on the "inside of the circuit" to equalize themselves ac-

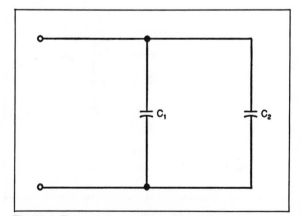

Fig. 13-4. Two capacitors connected in parallel.

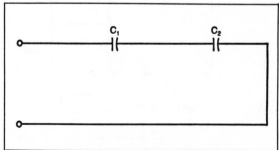

Fig. 13-5. Two capacitors connected in series.

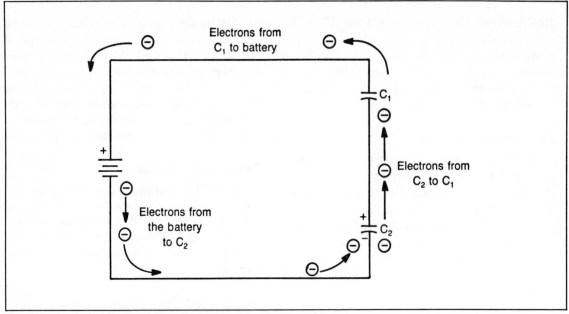

Fig. 13-6. Circuit showing the electron flow with two capacitors in series.

cording to the charge on their own capacitor. As a result, both capacitors will charge, but the voltage developed across each depends on the actual capacitance value. Capacitor voltage dividers will explain this point in further detail.

Capacitor Voltage Dividers

A capacitive voltage divider is a circuit with capacitors in series. Figure 13-7 shows two capacitive voltage divider circuits. A capacitive voltage divider can be used to distribute the voltage in a dc circuit.

Notice that in Fig. 13-7A the two capacitors have the same value, therefore they have the same voltage dropped across them. In Fig. 13-7B, the capacitors have different values. Notice in particular that the larger value capacitor has the smaller voltage drop.

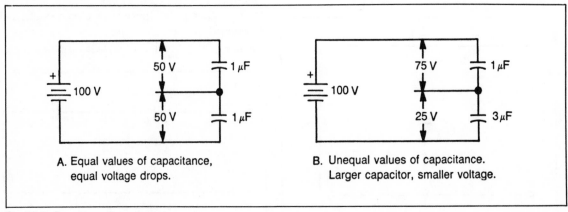

A. Equal values of capacitance, equal voltage drops.

B. Unequal values of capacitance. Larger capacitor, smaller voltage.

Fig. 13-7. Capacitive voltage dividers.

The voltage drop across a capacitor in a voltage divider can be calculated based on a ratio between the opposite capacitor and the total capacitance, as follows:

Formula #33. Capacitive Voltage Divider

$$V_{C1} = \frac{C_2}{(C_1 + C_2)} \times V$$

$$V_{C_2} = \frac{C_1}{(C_1 + C_2)} \times V$$

V_{C1} is the voltage across C_1.
V_{C2} is the voltage across C_2.
V is the voltage applied to the voltage divider.

Calculations for V_{C1} in Figure 13-7B

Formula: $V_{C1} = \dfrac{C_2}{(C_1 + C_2)} \times V$

Substituting: $V_{C1} = \dfrac{3\ \mu F}{(1\ \mu F + 3\ \mu F)} \times 100v$

Simplifying: $V_{C1} = \dfrac{3}{4} \times 100v$

Solving: $V_{C1} = 75$ volts

Calculations for V_{C2} in Figure 13-7B

Formula: $V_{C1} = \dfrac{C_2}{(C_1 + C_2)} \times V$

Substituting: $V_{C2} = \dfrac{1\ \mu F}{(1\ \mu F + 3\ \mu F)} \times 100v$

Simplifying: $V_{C2} = \dfrac{1}{4} \times 100v$

Solving: $V_{C2} = 25$ volts

PRACTICE PROBLEMS: CAPACITANCE

Part A. Parallel Capacitance

Determine the total capacitance of the following capacitors connected in parallel.

(1) 1 μF and 3 μF
(2) 5 pF and .001 μF and 10 pF
(3) 0.01 μF, 0.001 μF, 0.22 μF
(4) 47 μF, 47 μF, 47 μF
(5) 500 μF, 100 μF, 200 μF, 300 μF, 400 μF

Part B. Series Capacitance

Determine the total capacitance of the following capacitors connected in series. Also, use the supply voltage given to determine the voltage drops across each capacitor.

(6) C1 = 1 μF, C2 = 2 μF, V = 10 volts
(7) C1 = 5 pF, C2 = 10 pF, V = 10 volts
(8) C1 = 0.01 μF, C2 = 0.1 μF, V = 5 volts
(9) C1 = 10 μF, C2 = 10 μF, V = 15 volts
(10) C1 = 0.1 μF, C2 = 0.2 μF, V = 20 volts

UNIVERSAL TIME CONSTANT CURVE

The time constant is a means of calculating the voltage that will be developed across a capacitor or inductor during either charge or discharge.

A universal time constant curve can be calculated and plotted based on the fact that the charge and discharge pattern will always be the same.

In order to make matters as simple as possible, time constants are always considered for only dc voltages.

Definition of a Time Constant

☐ One time constant is defined as the time required to reach 63% of full charge or discharge.

☐ Five time constants are defined as the time required to reach full charge or discharge.

The definitions for time constants apply to both inductors and capacitors. Keep in mind that when a dc voltage is applied to an inductor, the current will start to flow in the coil and it will begin to develop a magnetic field. With a capacitor, the current flow will store a charge of electrons. Inductors oppose a change in current—capacitors oppose a change in voltage. In either case, the energy being stored, the magnetic field or the electrons, does not develop instantly. The time required to develop the stored energy is the time constant.

Based on the definition of time constants, the universal time constant curve is developed. See Fig. 13-8. The calculations for this graph will be presented in a moment. Notice that there are two curves: charge and discharge. The horizontal base line is labeled in time constants. Note: actual time is determined by the circuit conditions. The vertical axis is labeled in percentage of full charge. Note: actual voltage along the curve is based on the circuit conditions.

Plotting the Charge Curve

Calculating the values along different points along the curve can be performed using two methods:

Method 1. Based on the definition that one time constant is 63% of full charge, it is possible to calculate each of the five time constants in a full charge. The disadvantage of this method is the fact that the 63% is actually an approximation and it can be used only with whole number time constants (1, 2, 3, 4, 5).

Method 2. Calculations can also be made using the instantaneous charging formula, which will be demonstrated later.

Both methods of calculations will be presented. A summary of the results of these calculations can be found in Table 13-1.

The following are the calculations to plot the charge curve based on one time constant being 63%.

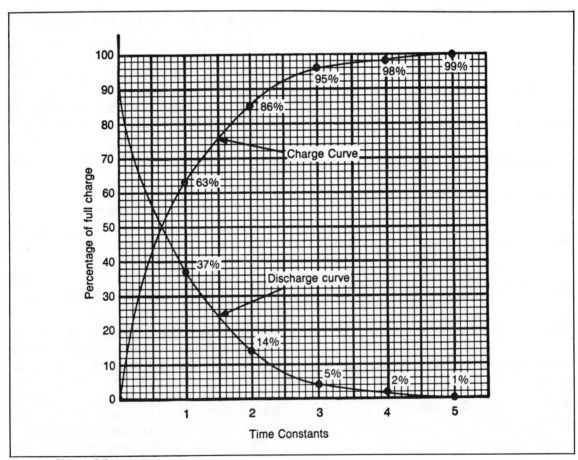

Fig. 13-8. Universal time constant curve.

Table 13-1. Plotting the Universal Time Constant Curve.

	Percent of Full Charge			
	CHARGING		DISCHARGING	
Time C.	63%	Instan	63%	Instan
0	0%	0%	100%	100%
1	63%	63.2%	37%	36.8%
2	86%	86.5%	14%	13.5%
3	95%	95.0%	5%	5.0%
4	98%	98.2%	2%	1.8%
5	99%	99.3%	1%	0.67%

Results are summarized in Table 13-1 and dots are shown on the curve in Fig. 13-8.

Plotting the Charge
Curve with Time Constants

(0) Time 0 is considered the starting point. At this moment, the switch is closed and the circuit receives the applied voltage. Current begins flowing.

(1) First time constant. 63% of the full charge has been completed, leaving 37%.

(2) Second time constant. Because this has a time of one time constant, the charge during this time is 63% of the charge remaining: 37%. Therefore, during this time constant, there is 23% of the charge (.63 × .37 = .23). If this portion of the charge is added to the first time constant (63% + 23%), the charge so far is 86% with 14% remaining.

(3) Third time constant. This time constant allows 63% of the amount remaining: 14%. Therefore, during this portion of the charge curve, the charge is 9% of the total charge (.63 × .14 = .09). After completion of the third time constant, 5% of the full charge remains (63% + 23% + 9% = 95%).

(4) Fourth time constant. This time constant charges 63% of the charge remaining: 5%. During this portion of the charge is 3% of the total amount (.63 × .05 = .03). After completion of this time constant, there is 2% of the full charge remaining (63% + 23% + 9% + 3% = 98%).

(5) Fifth time constant. Again, 63% of the remaining is charged (.63 × .02 = .01). This portion brings the completed charge to within 1% of the applied voltage. This is considered full charge because it is necessary to take into account that circuit losses will not allow the charged voltage to ever reach the applied voltage.

Charge Curve with Instantaneous Values

Analysis of the charge curve using instantaneous values is considerably more accurate than only at the points of a time constant.

Plotting the curve using the time constants is acceptable because it does provide enough points to determine the shape of the curve. If the voltage at a certain point in time is desired, it can be found reasonably close using the curve.

If it is necessary to determine the exact value of charge at any point in time, calculate it using the instantaneous charge formula:

Formula #34.
Instantaneous Charging Voltage

% of full charge = $(1 - e^{-T}) \times 100\%$ e is the natural log. T is the time constant.

This formula can be used for any point along the charge curve. It is not necessary to use whole numbers as the time constant.

The following is a sample calculation showing how to use the formula. Results in Table 13-1 are for each of the five time constants. The sample calculation is performed for 1 time constant.

Example of Instantaneous Charge Voltage

Formula: % charge = $(1 - e^{-T}) \times 100\%$
Substituting: % = $1 - e^{-1} \times 100\%$
Simplifying: % = $(1 - .368) \times 100\%$
Simplifying: % = $.632 \times 100\%$
Solving: % of full charge = 63.2%

The advantage of using this formula is the fact that it will find the value of any point along the curve. The disadvantage is that it is more difficult to use and harder to remember than the 63% method.

Plotting the Discharge Curve Using 63%

(0) At time zero, the discharge is about to start. At this time it is considered a full charge, regardless of the voltage present. Current starts to flow allowing the discharge to begin.

(1) First time constant. 63% of the voltage has now been discharged, leaving 37% of the full charge.

(2) Second time constant. 63% of the remaining will be discharged here. 23% of the complete discharge occurs during this period (.63 × .37 = .23), leaving the remaining charge at 14% of the starting point (100% − [63% + 23%] = 14%).

(3) Third time constant. (.63 × .14 = .09). Charge remaining after the third time constant is 5% (100% − [63% + 23% + 9%] = 5%).

(4) Fourth time constant. (.63 × .05 = .03). Charge after the fourth time constant is 2% (100% − [63% + 23% + 9% + 3% = 2%).

(5) Fifth time constant. Less than 1 percent remains to be discharged, therefore, this is considered fully discharged.

Discharge Curve with Instantaneous Values

The discharge curve can also be calculated using an exponential formula. This method produces very accurate results and it is possible to make the calculations of instantaneous values at any point along the discharge curve. The formula is as follows:

Formula #35.
Instantaneous Discharge Voltage

% of full charge = $e^{-T} \times 100\%$

Example of Instantaneous Discharge Voltage:

Sample is for second time constant.
Formula: $\% = e^{-T} \times 100\%$
Substituting: $\% = e^{-2} \times 100\%$
Simplifying: $\% = .135 \times 100\%$
Solving: $\% = 13.5\%$ remaining after 2 time constants

L/R TIME CONSTANT

The L/R time constant is used when there is an inductor in the circuit. The actual circuit values will determine the length of time for an inductor to charge or discharge. Keep in mind that when an inductor charges, then current flows through the coil of wire and a magnetic field is developed. The building of the magnetic field to full strength does take time.

Calculating the L/R Time Constant

The definition of one time constant is 63% of full charge. The actual length of time of one time constant depends on the values of inductance and resistance in the charge and discharge paths.

Formula #36. L/R Time Constant

$$T = \frac{L}{R}$$

T is time in seconds of one time constant
L is inductance in Henrys
R is resistance in Ohms

Figure 13-9 is an inductive circuit that demonstrates the use of the L/R time constant. Notice that in Fig. 13-9 there are two paths for current to flow. The current paths are in opposite directions and labeled charge and discharge.

The charge path of the inductor in Fig. 13-9 is from the negative side of the battery, through the inductor, through the resistor, through the switch in position "a," and returns to the positive side of the battery. Notice that the inductor is labeled with a polarity. This shows the polarity of the magnetic field in relation to the charging voltage.

To calculate the value of a time constant in this circuit, use the circuit values as follows:

Formula: $T = \frac{L}{R}$

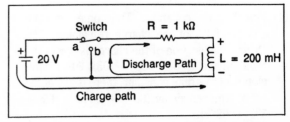

Fig. 13-9. A circuit to demonstrate the L/R time constant.

Substituting: $T = \dfrac{200 \text{ mH}}{1 \text{ kilohm}}$

Solving: $T = .2$ ms
One time constant $= .2$ ms
Five time constants $= 1$ ms (full charge)

This circuit, like all circuits, follows the universal time constant curve. Knowing the value of one time constant provides the curve with a relationship to actual time.

After a period of 1 ms (five time constants) the inductor is fully charged. If voltage is applied after this time, then the charge current will be limited by only the resistor. This full charge current can be calculated using Ohms' law, as follows:

Formula: $I = \dfrac{V}{R}$

Substituting: $I = \dfrac{20 \text{ v}}{1 \text{ kilohm}}$

Solving: $I = 20$ mA

The current flowing, after full charge is reached, will remain constant as long as the voltage is applied. If the switch is placed in position "b," then the charging voltage is removed and a discharge path is provided.

The magnetic field needs a path to release its energy. The discharge of energy is opposite to the charge path because it must flow from negative to positive of the polarity on the inductor. The circuit shown in Fig. 13-9 has the same value resistance in both the charge and discharge paths. The time constant for charge and discharge will be the same since the value of resistance is the same.

Different Charge and Discharge Resistances

Figure 13-10 is an inductive circuit with different values of resistance in the charge and discharge paths. Having the different values of resistance allows for a different time constant for both charge and discharge.

The time constant for charge is:

Formula: $T = \dfrac{L}{R}$

Substituting: $T = \dfrac{200 \text{ mH}}{10 \text{ Ohms}}$

Solving: $T = 20$ ms (charge)

The time constant for discharge is:

Formula: $T = \dfrac{L}{R}$

Substituting: $T = \dfrac{200 \text{ mH}}{1000 \text{ Ohms}}$

Solving: $T = .2$ ms (discharge)

Notice that the time constant of an inductive circuit is lowered by a larger value resistance. Keep in mind that the full period of time for charge or discharge is 5 time constants.

When the discharge resistance is larger than the charge resistance, then a voltage larger than the supply voltage will develop across the discharge resistor.

Charging current for Fig. 13-10 can be calculated as follows:

Formula: (Ohm's law) $I = \dfrac{V}{R}$

Substituting: $I = \dfrac{20 \text{ volts}}{10 \text{ Ohms}}$

Solving: $I = 2$ amps

The current calculated is after a full charge of at least 100 ms. (5×20ms). If, after full charge

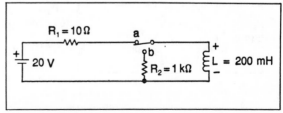

Fig. 13-10. An inductive circuit with different time constants for charge and discharge.

is reached, the switch is moved from the charging position "a" to the discharge position "b," then the magnetic field of the inductor will try to maintain the same amount of current flow.

During discharge, the magnetic field of the inductor will supply current to resistor R_2. The amount of current flow during discharge starts at the maximum charge current and drops at a rate that follows the universal time constant curve.

The discharge current will cause a voltage drop across the discharge resistor equal to an amount as calculated by Ohm's law, as follows:

Formula: (Ohm's law) $V = I \times R$
Substituting: $V = 2$ amps $\times 1$ kilohm
Solving: $V = 2,000$ volts

The calculated 2,000 volts is an instantaneous voltage developed for a very short period of time at the start of discharge.

High Voltage Developed By Opening an L/R Circuit

Figure 13-11 shows a representational diagram of the older-type ignition system of an automobile. R1 represents the dc resistance of the ignition coil, L is the ignition coil, the switch is the points contacts, and R2 represents the resistance of the spark plug gap. This figure is only for the purpose of understanding circuit concepts.

As we know, there must be an extremely large voltage developed across the spark plug in order to cause a spark to jump the gap. To determine how much voltage will be developed, first calculate the full charge current, then use the charge current, with

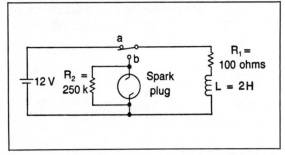

Fig. 13-11. High voltage developed by opening an R-L circuit.

Ohm's law, to calculate the discharge voltage developed.

Charge current:

Formula: $I = \dfrac{V}{R}$

Substituting: $I = \dfrac{12 \text{ volts}}{100 \text{ Ohms}}$

Solving: Full charge current $= .12$ amps

Voltage developed:

Formula: $V = I \times R$
Substituting: $V = .12$ amps $\times 250$ kilohms
Solving: $V = 30,000$ volts

The principle of a high voltage developed when opening an inductive circuit must be taken into consideration when wiring such devices as large electric motors. A large electric motor has a very large inductor for its windings. When the power is switched off, a large voltage will be produced across the switch. When this happens, a spark will jump across the switch contacts. A situation like this can cause severe damage to the switch. A capacitor can be placed in parallel with the switch contacts to absorb the spark.

RC TIME CONSTANT

In the field of electronics, when the term "time constant" is used, it will usually bring to a technician's mind a circuit with a resistor and capacitor. Although a capacitor is used in applications other than just time constant circuits, the time constant is a very important application.

The universal time constant curve applies to capacitive circuits as well as it does to inductive circuits. The definition of one time constant is 63% of full charge (or discharge). Full charge or discharge is reached after a period of five time constants.

Formula #37. RC Time Constant

$T = R \times C$
T is 1 time constant in seconds

R is resistance in Ohms
C is capacitance in farads

Figure 13-12 shows a circuit to demonstrate the principle of the RC time constant. This circuit has the same value of resistance for both the charge and discharge paths. Therefore, the circuit has the same value of time constant for both charge and discharge.

When the switch is placed in position "a", the capacitor is allowed to charge. The charge current is determined, along with the circuit resistance, by the difference between the applied voltage and the capacitor's voltage. Initially, the charge current is highest, determined by only circuit resistance. As the charge continues, the current will decrease.

As a capacitor stores electrons, a voltage develops across the capacitor terminals. The full charge voltage will be equal to the applied voltage.

Time constant of Fig. 13-12:
Formula: T = R × C
Substituting: T = 100 Ohms × 10 μF
Solving: T = 1000 μs or 1 ms
Full charge = 5 ms

Notice that in Fig. 13-12, the discharge path has the same value of resistance. Current flow during discharge is opposite to the current flow during charge.

High Current by Shorting a Capacitor

The electronic flash units used with modern cameras require a high amount of current for a very short period of time. Shorting a charged capacitor is the method used to produce this high current even though small batteries are used in the flash unit.

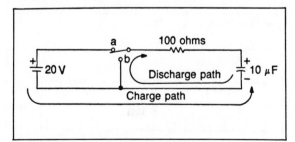

Fig. 13-12. A circuit to demonstrate the R-C time constant.

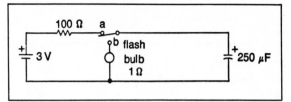

Fig. 13-13. Schematic for an electronic flash unit in a camera.

Figure 13-13 is a representative schematic diagram of an electronic flash unit. The battery shown is 3 volt. This represents two "AA" batteries. The 100 ohm resistor is only in the charge path. It is used to limit the current drain from the batteries. Changing the size of this resistor will affect the battery's current drain, during charge, and the amount of time required to charge the capacitor each time the flash is fired. The size of the capacitor is limited by the physical size of the flash unit.

When the capacitor is fully charged, it will have 3 volts across it. When triggered, the capacitor will discharge through the 1 Ohm flash bulb, which produces a current of 1 amp (using Ohm's law). This high current can be produced for only a very short period of time. The capacitor will be fully discharged in only 1.25 ms, but the flash bulb will produce a very high intensity light from the high current for that short period of time.

Practice Problems: Time Constants

Use the schematic diagrams in Figs. 13-14 to 13-23 to solve the following time constant problems:

Part A. Inductive time constant circuits.
In problems 1 through 5, find:

    a. one time constant during charge
    b. full charge time
    c. full charge current
    d. one time constant during discharge
    e. full discharge time
    f. voltage developed at first instant of discharge

Part B. Capacitive time constant circuits.
In problems 6 through 10, find:

    a. one time constant during charge

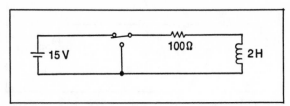

Fig. 13-14. Problem 1.

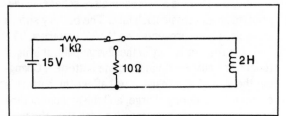

Fig. 13-15. Problem 2.

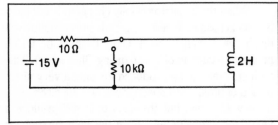

Fig. 13-16. Problem 3.

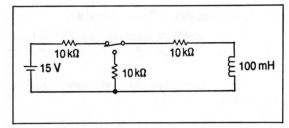

Fig. 13-17. Problem 4.

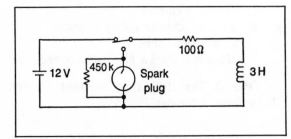

Fig. 13-18. Problem 5.

b. full charge time
c. full charge voltage
d. one time constant during discharge
e. full discharge time
f. current developed at first instant of discharge

RC WAVESHAPING

Waveshaping circuits are a useful application of the RC time constant. Waveshaping with a square wave presents a very dramatic application to show the effects of capacitor action and time constants.

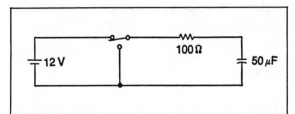

Fig. 13-19. Problem 6.

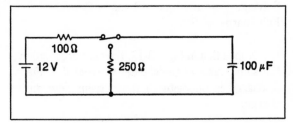

Fig. 13-20. Problem 7.

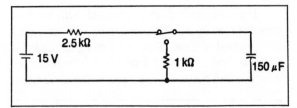

Fig. 13-21. Problem 8.

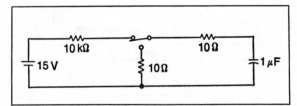

Fig. 13-22. Problem 9.

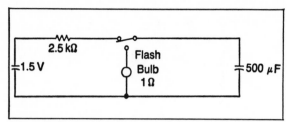

Fig. 13-23. Problem 10.

Differentiation and Integration

Differentiation and integration are words used to label the series RC circuits used in waveshaping. The only difference between the two circuits is where the output is taken. Although it is possible to use any type of waveform, a square wave is usually used. The results with a square wave are more pronounced and easier to predict. The square waves used are a type that will switch from zero to a positive peak—this makes calculations much easier.

A differentiator is identified as having the output taken across the resistor, as shown in Fig. 13-24. An integrator is identified as having the output taken across the capacitor, as shown in Fig. 13-25.

A differentiator usually has a short time constant. The primary used for this type of circuit is to produce positive and negative spikes. This will be discussed in further detail later in this chapter.

An integrator usually has a medium-to-long time

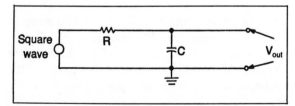

Fig. 13-24. Differentiator.

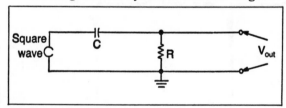

Fig. 13-25. Integrator.

constant. Because the output is taken across the capacitor, it will result in a waveform that represents the capacitor charging and discharging. The integrator is used to modify the shape of the input square wave.

Waveshaping Circuits

The following sections discuss waveshaping circuits with short, medium, long and very long time constants. The circuits and their respective waveforms are found in Figs. 13-26 through 13-29. Each circuit has an output across both the capacitor and resistor and the respective waveforms are drawn. It is presented in this manner to simplify the discussion.

To further simplify the understanding of the circuit, each of the four circuits to be discussed will use the same 1 kHz square wave input. They all have the same value capacitor. The only change between the circuits is the value of the resistor, which changes the time constant.

It is necessary to determine the "on" and "off" times of the square wave. In the case of this demonstration, the square wave input is symmetrical—the "on" and "off" switch times are the same. The period of a 1 kHz waveform is 1 ms (period = 1/frequency). The period is one full cycle. Therefore, the "on" time is .5 ms and the "off" time is .5 ms.

The "on" time is the period of time when the square wave is producing a positive voltage. During this time, the capacitor will receive a charging voltage. The "off" time is the period of time when the square wave is not producing any voltage. During this time, the capacitor will supply voltage to the circuit using the power supply as a discharge path.

Short Time Constant

A short time constant is defined as allowing the capacitor more than enough time to reach full charge during the "on" time of the input square wave. Since the square wave is symmetrical, the capacitor will also have more than enough time to fully discharge during the "off" time.

Figure 13-26 is the short time constant circuit. The input square wave is plotted with the times

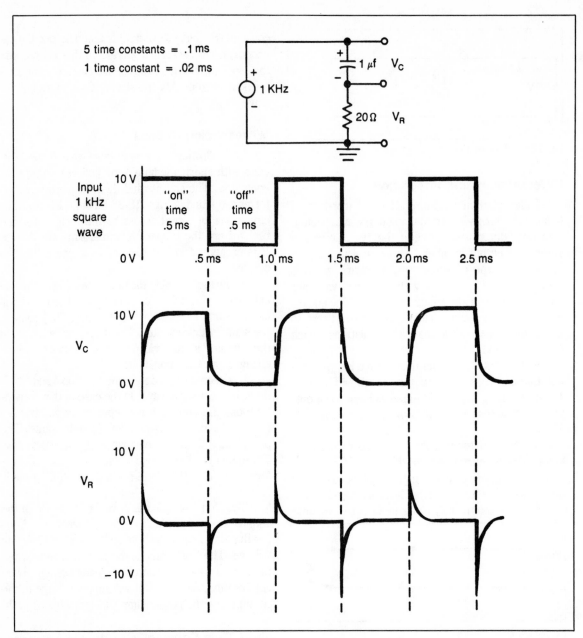

Fig. 13-26. Short time constant.

marked off when the changes occur. V_C, the middle waveform is the voltage across the capacitor, as seen with an oscilloscope. V_R, the bottom waveform is the voltage developed across the resistor, as seen with an oscilloscope.

The time constant of this circuit is 20 microseconds. The capacitor is fully charged in 100 microseconds, or .1 milliseconds. Therefore, the capacitor reaches full charge in approximately one-fifth of the time allowed by the input square wave.

Whatever voltage, of the applied square wave, that is not dropped across the capacitor is dropped across the resistor: $V_C + V_R = V_{Applied}$. Then, as the capacitor charges, the voltage potential in the circuit will decrease and the current flow will also decrease. Finally, when the capacitor is fully charged, the circuit will have no current flow, therefore no voltage will be developed across the resistor.

Examining the first "on" time, the capacitor very quickly charges, then holds a constant 10 volts for the remainder of the "on" time. The resistor initially has the applied 10 volts dropped across it. But as the capacitor charges, the voltage across the resistor drops to zero.

When the input square wave switches to "off," the capacitor is allowed to discharge through the power supply and circuit resistance. At the first instant of the "off" time, the capacitor is fully charged and is the only source of voltage in the circuit. The capacitor has a voltage polarity that is opposite to the polarity of the power supply. Therefore, the voltage applied to the resistor will be of an opposite polarity. The voltage across the resistor will be a negative voltage equal to the capacitor voltage, at every instant of the discharge. The resistor voltage is therefore plotted as a negative spike.

The square wave then repeats the cycle: it switches to "on"; the capacitor charges; the resistor voltage is positive; the square wave switches to "off"; the capacitor becomes the supply for the circuit voltage with an opposite polarity; the resistor voltage is negative.

Medium Time Constant

A medium time constant circuit is defined as having a time constant that allows the capacitor to reach full charge during the "on" time, with little or no time to spare. Figure 13-27 shows a medium time constant circuit. Only the resistor value is changed from the previous circuit. The time constant in this circuit is 100 microseconds. Full charge is 500 microseconds (.5 milliseconds) which is the "on" time.

The square wave will allow the capacitor to charge during the "on" time. The resistor will have a voltage equal to the applied voltage minus the capacitor voltage. When the square wave switches to the "off" time, the capacitor will supply voltage to the circuit, with a negative polarity. The resistor during the "off" time will have a negative voltage.

Long Time Constant

Both the long time constant circuit, shown in Fig. 13-28, and the extra long time constant circuit, shown in Fig. 13-29, have time constants that are longer than the time allowed by the input square wave. The capacitor does not have enough time to fully charge or discharge. The capacitor will store a small amount of the charge voltage and will eventually reach a level where it is very close to the applied voltage. When this happens, the resistor voltage will be centered around the center line. This type of circuit uses the capacitor as a "dc blocking capacitor." It allows the changing voltage to pass through, but blocks the steady dc voltage.

Voltage calculations for the long and extra long time constant circuits must be performed using the instantaneous charge and discharge formulas.

HANDS-ON PRACTICE: TIME CONSTANTS AND WAVESHAPING

This hands-on experience will apply the knowledge learned about: a) the universal time constant curve, b) charge and discharge of capacitors, c) RC time constants, d) RC waveshaping. The student will also be required to use a dual trace oscilloscope and a signal generator.

The actual component values of the resistor and capacitor may vary, depending on the components available.

The short and medium time constant circuits shown in Fig. 13-26 and 13-27 are to be used as samples. There are some differences, however. Notice that the circuits shown in the sample figures use different resistor values to produce different time constants. This exercise will maintain constant circuit values and allow the frequency of the signal generator to change to produce a different on/off time.

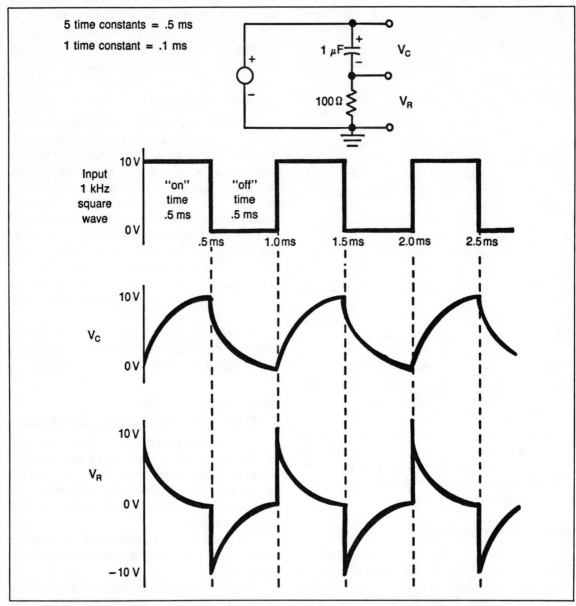

Fig. 13-27. Medium time constant.

COMPONENT VALUES

	Recommended	Actual
Resistor:	10 kilohms	_____
		_____
Capacitor:	.001 μF	_____
		_____

Step 1. Connect the leads of the capacitor and resistor together, as shown in the sample figures, so that they are in series. Record the actual component values in the space provided, above.

Step 2. Connecting test equipment:

a. Connect the ground wires from the dual

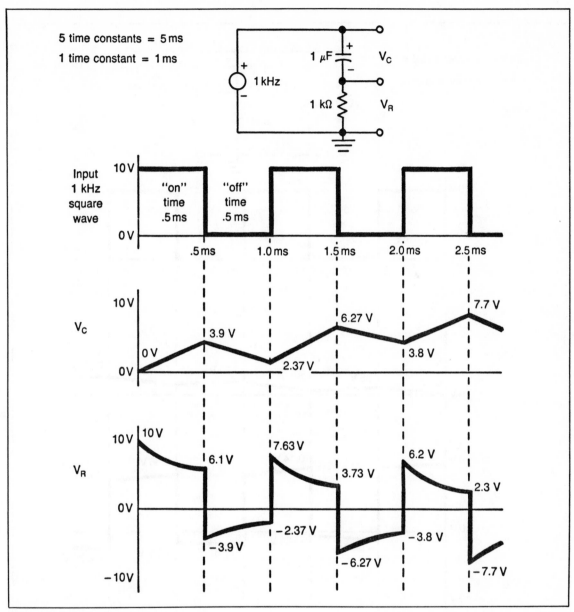

Fig. 13-28. Long time constant.

trace oscilloscope and signal generator to the bottom of the capacitor (opposite to the schematic shown). It is absolutely necessary to have all of the grounds connected together.

b. Connect the "hot" lead from the signal generator to the top of the resistor.

c. Adjust the oscilloscope for dual trace operation. Trigger on channel 1.

d. Adjust the signal generator for square wave operation with a frequency of approximately 20 kHz. (Note: later in this exercise, the frequency will be set to a different value.)

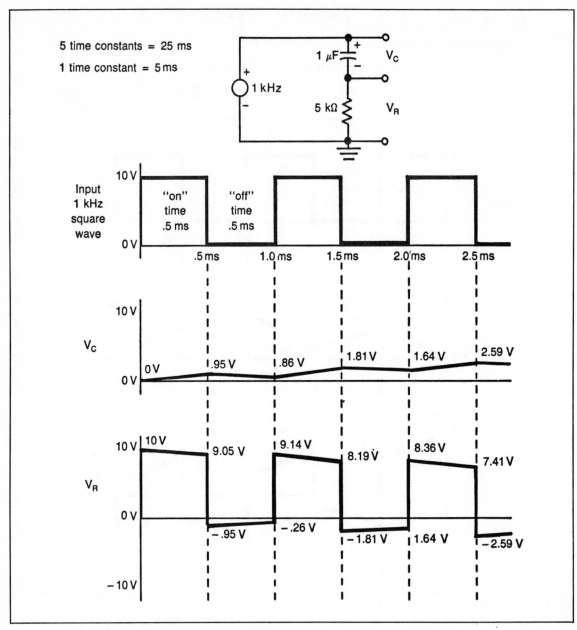

Fig. 13-29. Very long time constant.

e. Connect channel 1 of the scope to the top of the resistor. This will measure the square wave from the generator.

f. Connect channel 2 of the scope to the junction between the resistor and capacitor. This will measure the voltage

across the capacitor.

g. Adjust the scope's time/div for approximately 3 full cycles of the input square wave. Be sure that the scope is properly triggered.

h. Adjust the scope's volts/div on each

channel to allow each channel to use only ½ of the screen: channel 1 on top and channel 2 on the bottom.

Step 3. If the test equipment is properly set up and adjusted, then the top waveform (channel 1) should display the square wave. The bottom waveform (channel 2) should display the voltage across the capacitor, labeled V_c in the sample figures. The following will be on the same sheet of graph paper, using the samples provided as a guide.

  a. Draw the schematic diagram of the circuit connected (note: it is slightly different from the sample). Show the connections for the scope and generator. Include component values.

  b. Measure (using the oscilloscope) the actual period and frequency of the square wave and record below.

period = _____

frequency = _____

"on" time = _____

"off" time = _____

  c. Draw the square wave shown on the scope. Label the "on" and "off" times.

  d. Draw the capacitor voltage as shown on the scope. Make certain it is drawn correctly with respect to the square wave.

  e. With the component values used in the circuit, calculate the value of one time constant and the value for full charge/discharge. Record below and on the graph paper.

one time constant = _____

full charge time = _____

  f. On the back of the graph paper, give a brief explanation of the capacitor voltage curve.

Step 4. Changing test equipment connections. *Do not change oscilloscope or generator settings. If necessary, check settings by adjusting according to step 3a.*

  a. Disconnect the circuit used in the previous steps.

  b. Connect the ground wires to the bottom of the resistor.

  c. Connect the signal generator "hot" lead to the top of the capacitor.

  d. Connect the scope, channel 1 to the top of the capacitor to measure the square wave.

  e. Connect the scope, channel 2 to the junction between the resistor and the capacitor, to measure the voltage developed across the resistor.

Step 5. If the test equipment has been properly connected, the same square wave used in previous steps should be present on channel 1. Channel 2 should display a waveform similar to the one shown in the sample labeled V_R. Using the same graph paper as in step 3:

  a. Again, using the square wave as a reference, draw the curve of the resistor voltage.

  b. On the back of the graph paper, explain the shape of the waveform. Explain why the resistor voltage is negative during the capacitor discharge time (square wave "off" time).

  c. Label this completed graph paper "Medium Time Constant," as shown in Fig. 13-27.

Step 6. Adjust the frequency of the signal generator to approximately 4000 Hz. This will produce "on" and "off" times approximately 5 times longer than is necessary to charge and discharge the capacitor.

  a. Repeat the entire procedure. The frequency change will change the "on" and

211

"off" times of the square wave, which will produce a different set of curves since the capacitor will have more than enough time to charge and discharge. Be sure to draw the curves as described. Use Fig. 13-26 as a sample.

b. Label the completed graph "short time constant."

PROGRAMS FOR THIS CHAPTER

There is one program for this chapter, called "Time constants." It is divided into two types of problems. The first 10 questions deal with calculations using the two time constant formulas. The second 10 questions require the use of the universal time constant curve found in this chapter. The help hints discuss the various methods of dealing with problems and how to make the calculations.

Figure 13-30 is the program sample.

CAPACITORS AND TIME CONSTANTS COMPETENCY TEST

Part A. Definitions

Define the following terms:

1. basic unit of measure of capacitance
2. dielectric
3. one time constant
4. full charge (in terms of time constants)
5. universal time constant curve

Part B. Formulas

State the formula for each of the following:

6. Total capacitance for capacitors in series.

```
            TIME CONSTANT

          SAMPLE PROGRAM:


   NOTE: UNITS ARE GIVEN, JUST GIVE
   THE NUMERIC VALUE.


   GIVEN:

           TIME CONSTANT = ? US

           INDUCTOR = 2 MH

           RESISTANCE = 1 KOHM


 1 .CALCULATE THE UNKNOWN ?   2


           ▓▓▓▓▓▓▓▓▓
         SPACE BAR = NEXT, E = EXIT
```

Fig. 13-30. Time constant program sample.

7. Total capacitance for capacitors in parallel.
8. Voltage across C_1 of a two-capacitor voltage divider.
9. Voltage across C_2 of a two-capacitor voltage divider.
10. Inductive time constant.
11. Capacitive time constant.
12. Period when given frequency.
13. Frequency when given period.
14. "on" time of a square wave.
15. "off" time of a square wave.

Part C. General Questions

16. Describe how a capacitor is formed.
17. If the dielectric is made thinner, does the value of capacitance increase or decrease?
18. Describe how a capacitor charges and discharges.
19. A capacitor opposes any change in (voltage or current).
20. An inductor opposes any change in (voltage or current).

Part D. Capacitors in Parallel

Determine the total capacitance of the following capacitors connected in parallel.

21. 2 μF and 5 μF
22. 30 μF and 30 μF and 30 μF
23. .01 μF and .05 μF and .02 μF
24. 10 pF and 25 pF and 100 pF
25. 1 μF and 220,000 pF

Part E. Capacitors in Series

Determine the total capacitance of the following capacitors connected in series.

26. 2 μF and 5 μF
27. 30 μF and 30 μF and 30 μF
28. .01 μF and .05 μF and .02 μF
29. 10 pF and 25 pF and 100 pF
30. 1 μF and 220,000 pF

Part F. Capacitive Voltage Dividers

Determine the voltage drop across each of the following capacitors, connected as a voltage divider. The voltage given is the supply voltage. (Note: there are two answers required for each problem, 1 test point each.)

31. V = 10 volts, C_1 = 2 μF, C_2 = 3 μF
32. V = 15 volts, C_1 = 1 μF, C_2 = 2 μF
33. V = 20 volts, C_1 = 3 μF, C_2 = 4 μF
34. V = 25 volts, C_1 = 6 pF, C_2 = 9 pF
35. V = 30 volts, C_1 = 10 pF, C_2 = 20 pF

Part G. Time Constant Circuits

Problems 36 through 40 use the inductive circuit in Fig. 13-31.

36. 1 time constant of charge
37. time for full charge
38. full charge current
39. time for full discharge
40. voltage developed at first instant of discharge

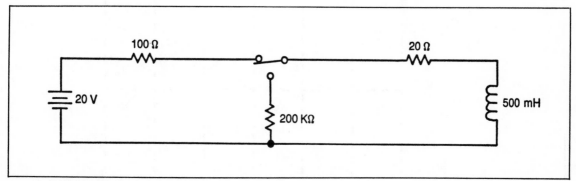

Fig. 13-31. Problems 36-40.

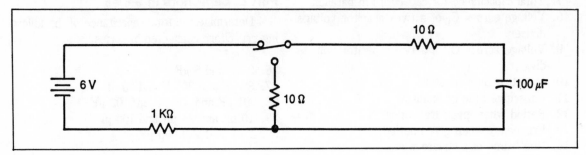

Fig. 13-32. Problems 41-45.

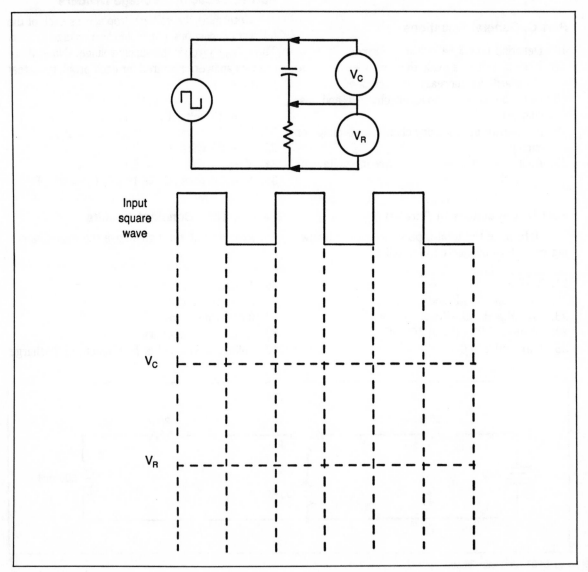

Input
square
wave

V_C

V_R

Fig. 13-33. Problems 46-50.

214

Problems 41 through 45 use the capacitive circuit in Fig. 13-32.

41. 1 time constant of charge
42. time for full charge
43. full charge voltage
44. time for full discharge
45. current developed at first instant of discharge

Part H. Waveshaping

Figure 13-33 is a schematic diagram of a waveshaping circuit and its graph. Use the information given to answer the following questions.

Given: square wave frequency = 5000 Hz

resistance = 200 ohms
capacitance = 0.1 microfarads

Find:

46a. "on" time
46b. "off" time
47a. 1 time constant
47b. full charge time
48. How is this circuit classified?

a. short time constant
b. medium time constant
c. long time constant

49. Draw the curve of the capacitor voltage.
50. Draw the curve of the resistor voltage.

Chapter 14

AC Circuits

Chapter Objectives: To make calculations with inductive and capacitive reactance. To use phasors to solve for impedance in circuits containing both resistance and reactance. To analyze the effects of reactance on power dissipation.

Chapter Outline:
- ☐ Reactance
- ☐ Phasor Analysis
- ☐ Reactive Circuits
- ☐ Ac Power
- ☐ Measuring Phase Angle On an Oscilloscope
- ☐ Hands-On Practice Measuring Phase Angle
- ☐ Programs for This Chapter
- ☐ Ac Circuits Competency Test

INTRODUCTION

A circuit containing an inductor and/or a capacitor with a resistor will respond somewhat differently when an ac voltage is applied, than if the circuit had only resistance.

Inductors and capacitors are classified as reactive components because an ac voltage will cause them to have resistance that will vary with the frequency of the ac voltage. A combination of reactance and resistance is called impedance.

Power in an ac circuit will also be affected by the presence of reactive components. The phase angle of a circuit is the relationship between voltage and current in an ac circuit.

This chapter will also present a hands-on exercise with the oscilloscope to gain experience in measuring phase angle.

REACTANCE

Reactance is defined as the ac resistance of an inductor or capacitor. Reactance is measured in ohms, as is resistance. Since inductors and capacitors are devices that store energy, they cannot simply charge and discharge instantly. It is the charging and discharging that acts like a form of resistance to the ac signal. This section deals with calculating the reactance in both inductive and capacitive circuits.

☐ Reactance has the unit of measure of ohms.

Inductive Reactance

Inductive reactance is the reactance in a circuit containing an inductor. There are two factors that effect the amount of reactance: frequency of the ac signal and the value of the inductor. When the frequency and/or the value of inductance is lowered, the inductive reactance becomes lower, to the point where the frequency is 0 Hz (dc) and the inductive reactance is 0 ohms. Inductive reactance uses the symbol X_L.

Formula #38. Inductive Reactance, X_L

$$X_L = 2\ (\pi)\ f\ L$$

Note: all terms are multiplied on the right side of the equation.

$2\ (\pi)$ is 2 times the Greek letter (π). $(\pi) = 3.14$, therefore 6.28 can be substituted for $2(\pi)$ in the formula.

f is frequency, measured in hertz.
L is inductance, measured in henrys.

Sample Problems: Inductive Reactance

Note: in the problems below, parentheses ( ) are used around a number to indicate multiplication.

SP#14-1.

Given: frequency = 10 kHz
         inductance = 5 mH
Find: inductive reactance

Formula: $X_L = 2\ (\pi)\ f\ L$
Substituting: $X_L = (6.28)\ (10\ kHz)\ (5\ mH)$
Solving: $X_L = 314$ ohms

SP#14-2.

Given: frequency = 2000 Hz
         inductive reactance = 800 ohms
Find: inductance

Formula: $X_L = 2\ (\pi)\ f\ L$

Rearranging: $L = \dfrac{X_L}{2(\pi)\ fL}$

Substituting: $L = \dfrac{800\ ohms}{(6.28)\ (2000\ Hz)}$

Solving: $L = 63.7$ mH

SP#14-3.

Given: inductive reactance = 15 kilohms
         inductance = 2 henrys
Find: frequency

Formula: $X_L = 2\ (\pi)\ f\ L$

Rearranging: $f = \dfrac{X_L}{2(\pi)\ fL}$

Substituting: $f = \dfrac{15\ kilohms}{(6.28)(2H)}$

Solving: $f = 1200$ Hz

Capacitive Reactance

Capacitive reactance is the ac resistance from a capacitor and is measured in ohms. The value of capacitive reactance is affected by two quantities: frequency and value of capacitance. When the frequency and/or the capacitance is reduced, the capacitive reactance becomes larger, to a point where the frequency is 0 Hz (dc)—the reactance is infinity. Capacitive reactance uses the symbol X_C.

Formula #39. Capacitive Reactance, X_C

$$X_C = \dfrac{1}{2\ (\pi)\ f\ C}$$

X_C is capacitive reactance, measured in ohms.
$2(\pi) = 6.28$

f is frequency, measured in hertz (Hz).
C is capacitance, measured in farads.

Sample Problems: Capacitive Reactance

Note: in the problems below, parentheses ( ) are used around a number to indicate multiplication.

SP#14-4.

Given: frequency = 10 kHz
capacitance = .5 μf
Find: capacitive reactance

Formula: $X_C = \dfrac{1}{2\,(\pi)\,f\,C}$

Substituting: $X_C = \dfrac{1}{(6.28)\,(10\text{ kHz})\,(.5\ \mu F)}$

Solving: $X_C = 31.8$ ohms

SP#14-5.

Given: frequency = 25 kHz
capacitive reactance = 1.2 kilohms
Find: capacitance

Formula: $X_C = \dfrac{1}{2\,(\pi)\,f\,C}$

Rearranging: $C = \dfrac{1}{2\,(\pi)\,f\,X_C}$

Substituting: $C = \dfrac{1}{(6.28)\,(25\text{ kHz})\,(1.2\text{ kilohms})}$

Solving: $C = .005\ \mu F$

SP#14-6.

Given: capacitive reactance = 100 ohms
capacitance = .47 μF
Find: frequency

Formula: $X_C = \dfrac{1}{2\,(\pi)\,f\,C}$

Rearranging: $f = \dfrac{1}{2\,(\pi)\,X_C\,C}$

Substituting: $f = \dfrac{1}{(6.28)\,(100\text{ ohms})\,(47\ \mu F)}$

Solving: f = 3390 Hz

Practice Problems: Reactance

Part A. Inductive Reactance.

Use the information given to calculate the inductive reactance.

1. f = 1000 Hz, L = 100 mH; find X_L
2. X_L = 1000 ohms, f = 10 kHz; find L
3. X_L = 200 ohms, f = 10 kHz; find L
4. X_L = 200 ohms, L = 16 mH; find f
5. X_L = 600 ohms, L = 16 mH; find f
6. f = 5000 Hz, L = 2 H; find X_L
7. X_L = 400 ohms, f = 10 kHz; find L
8. X_L = 1000 ohms, L = 16 mH; find f
9. L = 50 μH, f = 3 MHz; find X_L
10. L = 50 mH, f = 0 Hz (dc); find X_L

Part B. Capacitive Reactance.

Use the information given to calculate the capacitive reactance.

11. f = 1000 Hz, C = .001 μF; find X_C
12. X_C = 1.59 kilohms, f = 1000 Hz; find C
13. X_C = 15.9 ohms, C = 1 μF; find f
14. X_C = 15.9 kilohms, f = 1000 Hz; find C
15. X_C = 159 ohms, C = 1 μF; find f
16. f = 10 kHz, C = 150 μF; find X_C
17. f = 0 Hz (dc), C = 10 μF; find X_C
18. f = 100 MHz, C = 1 μF; find X_C
19. f = 1 GHz, C = 1 pF; find X_C
20. f = 1 Hz, C = 1 pF; find X_C

PHASOR ANALYSIS

Phasor analysis is a method of solving ac circuits using a combination of vectors and trigonometry. (This sounds more complicated than it really is.)

The word "phasor" is a combination of two words: vector and phase. A vector is a line that represents the magnitude (size) and direction of some number, phase is the resultant angle.

Reactance, either inductive or capacitive, causes a phase shift between the circuit voltage and current. This phase shift is called the phase angle or operating angle of the circuit. To determine the phase shift and to show the relationship between resistance and reactance, a right triangle can be drawn. The sides of the triangle represent the relative sizes of resistance and reactance, and the hypotenuse represents the relative size of the impedance: the combined total ac resistance. The enclosed angle becomes the phase shift.

Drawing a Phasor Triangle

When solving electrical circuits, there are three types of phasor triangles: impedance, voltage and current. When drawing these triangles, there are certain basic rules to follow (Note: sample problems will be shown later in this chapter with the triangles drawn.):

Resistance. Plotted on the horizontal. All values dealing with resistance, such as resistance (in ohms), voltage drop across the resistor, or current through the resistor.

Reactance, X (X_L or X_C). Plotted vertically, forming a right angle with resistance. All values dealing with reactance, such as: reactance (in ohms); voltage drop across the reactive component; current through the reactive component. The phasor for reactance can be plotted either up or down, depending upon if the circuit is series or parallel, and if it is inductive or capacitive.

Totals. The hypotenuse of the right triangle. The hypotenuse is always longer than either of the other two sides and will be at some angle between 0 and 90 degrees. The totals are: total ac resistance (impedance, Z, measured in ohms); total applied voltage; total circuit current.

Phase Angle. Phase angle is represented by the Greek letter theta, θ, and is measured in degrees. The phase angle is the phase shift in the circuit, between the resistive and reactive components. It is the angle in the triangle formed between the resistance and the hypotenuse.

Calculations with Phasor Triangles

There are two basic calculations to be made with the phasor triangles: hypotenuse and angle theta. These two basic calculations can be rearranged to allow solving for all quantities of the triangles, but it is not necessary.

Hypotenuse. Pythagorean's theorem ($a^2 = b^2 + c^2$) is used to solve for the magnitude of the hypotenuse. Using the impedance triangle for an example: $Z^2 = R^2 + X^2$

The formula can be simplified by taking the square root of both sides.

Formula #40. Hypotenuse of a Right Triangle

a. Impedance triangle.
$$Z = \sqrt{P^2 + X^2}$$

b. Voltage triangle.
$$V_T = \sqrt{V_R^2 + V_X^2}$$

c. Current triangle.
$$I_T = \sqrt{I_R^2 + I_X^2}$$

Phase Angle. Tan θ = opposite/adjacent. This is the trigonometric function used to find theta.

Formula #41. Phase Angle, Theta, θ

$$\tan \theta = \frac{\text{opposite}}{\text{adjacent}}$$

a. Impedance triangle.
$$\theta = \tan^{-1} \frac{X}{R}$$

b. Voltage triangle.
$$\theta = \tan^{-1} \frac{V_X}{V_R}$$

c. Current triangle.
$$\theta = \tan^{-1} \frac{V_X}{V_R}$$

Note: $\tan^{-1}$ is the same as the arctan. It is expressed as "the angle whose tangent is . . ."

Note: to find $\tan^{-1}$ on a calculator; first press the 2nd function key (2nd F or INV or ARC), then the tan key.

Note: to properly use this formula, first divide X (reactance) by R (resistance) and then find $\tan^{-1}$.

REACTIVE CIRCUITS

There are four basic types of reactive circuits: inductance in series with resistance; inductance in parallel with resistance; capacitance in series with resistance; capacitance in parallel with resistance. It is also possible, as will be examined in the next chapter, to have combinations of these basic circuits.

Although each type of circuit has a different set of characteristics, the phasor diagrams and calculations are quite similar, which will simplify the circuit analysis.

Inductive Reactance in Series with Resistance

In any series circuit, current is the same throughout the circuit. An inductor causes the current to "lag" the voltage by 90 degrees. It is this "lagging" current that makes it necessary to plot a voltage triangle and impedance triangle for series circuits. The resultant voltage (total circuit voltage) will be the hypotenuse of the triangle and will be at an angle equal to the phase angle, also called the operating angle.

When solving a series inductive circuit, follow these guidelines:

1. Solve for impedance, Z, using an impedance triangle. Inductive reactance, X_L, phasor is plotted at a positive 90 degrees (up), resistance, R, phasor is plotted at 0 degrees (horizontal), impedance phasor is the hypotenuse.
2. Circuit current is found using Ohm's law with impedance and total voltage.
3. Voltage drops, V_R and V_L are found using Ohm's law with circuit current and the values of resistance and inductive reactance.
4. Solve for total circuit voltage, V_T, using a voltage triangle. The inductive voltage, V_L (or

V_{XL}), phasor is plotted at a positive 90 degrees (up), and the resistive voltage, V_R, phasor is plotted at 0 degrees. The total voltage, V_T, is the hypotenuse.

5. Phase angle, theta, θ, is the angle of the hypotenuse of either triangle. The phase angle in a series inductive circuit will be positive.

Sample Problem: Series Inductive Reactance

SP#14-7. Series circuit, schematic diagram, Fig. 14-1.

Given: R = 350 ohms, X_L = 500 ohms
V = 100 volts
Find: Z, θ, I, V_R, V_L

Step 1. Impedance triangle, Fig. 14-2.

    a. Plot the phasors using the given values of R and X_L

    b. Pythagorean's theorem to solve for Z.

Formula: $Z = \sqrt{R^2 + X_L^2}$

Substituting: $Z = \sqrt{350^2 + 500^2}$

Solving: Z = 610 ohms

Step 2. Theta, θ, using the impedance triangle.

Formula: $\theta = \tan^{-1} \dfrac{X_L}{R}$

Substituting: $\theta = \tan^{-1}\dfrac{500}{350}$

Solving: θ = 55 degrees

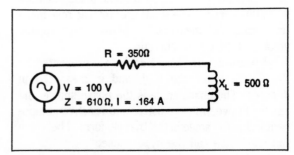

Fig. 14-1. Schematic diagram for sample problem 14-7.

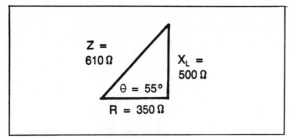

Fig. 14-2. Impedance triangle for sample problem 14-7.

Step 3. Circuit current using Ohm's law.

Formula: $I = \dfrac{V}{Z}$

Substituting: $I = \dfrac{100 \text{ volts}}{610 \text{ ohms}}$

Solving: $I = .164$ amps

Step 4. Voltage triangle, Fig. 14-3.
- a. Voltage drop across the resistor, V_R, using Ohm's law.
  Formula: $V = I \times R$
  Substituting: $V_R = .164$ amps $\times$ 350 ohms
  Solving: $V_R = 57.4$ volts
- b. Voltage drop across the inductor, V_L, using Ohm's law.
  Formula: $V = I \times X_L$
  Substituting: $V_L = .164$ amps $\times$ 500 ohms
  Solving: $V_L = 82.0$ volts
- c. V_R and V_L do not simply add to equal the total voltage, as would be the case in a dc circuit. The voltages must be ad-

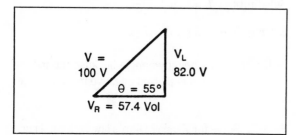

Fig. 14-3. Voltage triangle for sample problem 14-7.

ded using phasors, Pythagorean's theorem.

Formula: $V = \sqrt{V_R^2 + V_L^2}$
Substituting: $V = \sqrt{57.4^2 + 82.0^2}$
Solving: $V = 100$ volts

Inductive Reactance in Parallel with Resistance

Voltage is the same throughout a parallel circuit. In a parallel circuit, the current divides to the individual branches according to the size of the resistance, or impedance, of each branch. In a parallel circuit with inductive reactance, the current in the inductive branch will "lag" the resistive branch by 90 degrees. This means that there is a 90 degree phase shift between the two currents. Because of the 90 degree phase shift, it is necessary to calculate total current using a phasor triangle.

When solving a parallel circuit with inductive reactance, follow these guidelines:

1. Calculate individual branch current, using Ohm's law with the applied voltage and branch resistance or reactance.
2. Draw the current triangle with resistive current, I_R at zero degrees (horizontal) and inductive reactance current, I_L at -90 degrees (down). The vector drawn down represents the lagging phase shift. The hypotenuse of the triangle is total current, I_T.
3. Calculate total circuit impedance using Ohm's law with total circuit current and applied voltage.
4. Calculate phase angle theta using the current triangle. The phase angle in a parallel inductive circuit is negative.

Sample Problem: Parallel Inductive Reactance

SP#14-8. Parallel circuit, Fig. 14-4.

Given: $R = 200$ ohms, $X_L = 150$ ohms
           $V = 25$ volts
Find: I_R, I_{XL}, I_T, Z, theta

Step 1. Current triangle, Fig. 14-5.

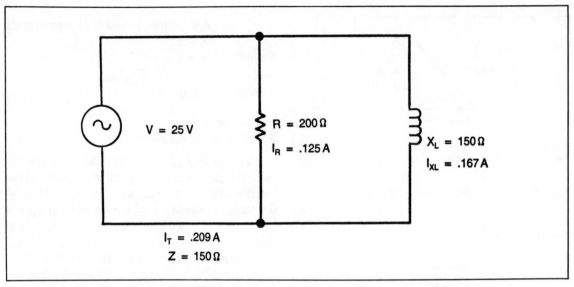

Fig. 14-4. Schematic diagram for sample problem 14-8.

a. Calculate resistive current, I_R.

Formula: $I = \dfrac{V}{R}$

Substituting: $I = \dfrac{25 \text{ volts}}{200 \text{ ohms}}$

Solving: $I_R = .125$ amps

b. Calculate inductive current, I_{XL}.

Formula: $I = \dfrac{V}{X_L}$

Substituting: $I = \dfrac{25 \text{ volts}}{150 \text{ ohms}}$

Solving: $I_{XL} = .167$ amps

c. Solve for current total, I_T, using Pythagorean's theorem.

Formula: $I_T = \sqrt{I_R^2 + I_{XL}^2}$
Substituting: $I_T = \sqrt{.125^2 + .167^2}$
Solving: $I_T = .209$ amps

d. Solve for theta, θ, using the current triangle.

Formula: $\theta = \tan^{-1} \dfrac{I_{XL}}{I_R}$

Substituting: $\theta = \tan^{-1} \dfrac{.167}{.125}$

Solving: $\theta = -53.2$ degrees

Note: theta is a negative angle because the inductive current is plotted negative in the current triangle.

Step 2. Solve for Z using Ohm's law with total current and applied voltage.

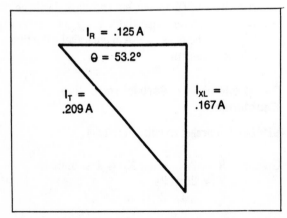

Fig. 14-5. Current triangle for sample problem 14-8.

Formula: $Z = \dfrac{V}{I}$

Substituting: $Z = \dfrac{25 \text{ volts}}{.167 \text{ amps}}$

Solving: $Z = 150$ ohms

Capacitive Reactance in Series with Resistance

As in any series circuit, current is the same throughout the circuit. In a circuit with capacitance, the capacitor stores voltage, which causes the voltage across the capacitor to "lag" the voltage across the resistor. Therefore, when solving a series capacitive circuit, it is necessary to draw the voltage triangle and the impedance triangle.

To solve a series capacitive circuit, follow these guidelines:

1. Solve for impedance, Z, using an impedance triangle. Capacitive reactance, X_C, phasor is plotted at a negative 90 degrees (down), resistance, R, phasor is plotted at 0 degrees (horizontal), impedance phasor is the hypotenuse.
2. Circuit current is found using Ohm's law with impedance and total voltage.
3. Voltage drops, V_R and V_C are found using Ohm's law with circuit current and the values of resistance and capacitive reactance.
4. Solve for total circuit voltage, V_T, using a voltage triangle. Capacitive voltage, V_C (or V_{XC}), phasor is plotted at a negative 90 degrees (down), resistive voltage, V_R, phasor is plotted at 0 degrees, total voltage, V_T, is the hypotenuse.
5. Phase angle, theta, θ, is the angle of the hypotenuse of either triangle. The phase angle in a series capacitive circuit will be negative.

Note: Capacitive reactance has properties that are opposite the properties of inductive reactance. Solving the two types of circuits is very similar, bearing in mind opposite phasors.

Sample Problem: Series Capacitive Reactance

SP#14-9. Series circuit, schematic diagram, Fig. 14-6.

Given: R = 500 ohms, X_C = 500 ohms
   V = 20 volts
Find: Z, θ, I, V_R, V_C

Step 1. Impedance triangle, Fig. 14-7.
   a. Plot phasors using given values of R and X_C.
   b. Pythagorean's theorem to solve for Z.

Formula: $Z = \sqrt{R^2 + X_C^2}$

Substituting: $Z = \sqrt{500^2 + 500^2}$

Solving: $Z = 707$ ohms
   c. Theta, θ, using the impedance triangle.

Formula: $\theta = \tan^{-1} \dfrac{X_C}{R}$

Substituting: $\theta = \tan^{-1} \dfrac{500}{500}$

Solving: $\theta = -45$ degrees

Step 2. Circuit current using Ohm's law.

Formula: $I = \dfrac{V}{Z}$

Substituting: $I = \dfrac{20 \text{ volts}}{707 \text{ ohms}}$

Solving: $I = 28.3$ mA

Step 3. Voltage triangle, Fig. 14-8.
   a. Voltage drop across the resistor, V_R, using Ohm's law.

Formula: $V = I \times R$
Substituting: $V_R = 28.3$ mA $\times$ 500 ohms
Solving: $V_R = 14.2$ volts
   b. Voltage drop across the inductor, V_C, using Ohm's law.

Formula: $V = 1 \times X_C$

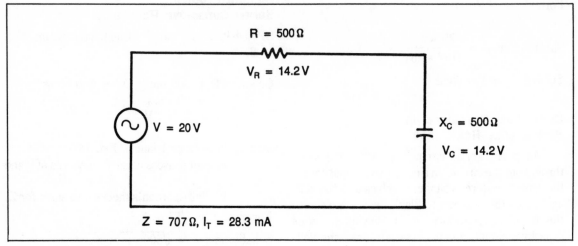

Fig. 14-6. Schematic diagram for sample problem 14-9.

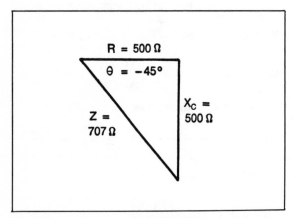

Fig. 14-7. Impedance triangle for Fig. 14-9.

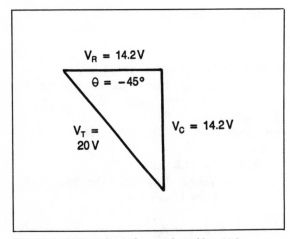

Fig. 14-8. Voltage triangle for sample problem 14-9.

Substituting: V_C = 28.3 mA × 500 ohms

Solving: V_C = 14.2 volts

    c. V_R and V_C do not simply add to equal the total voltage, as would be the case in a dc circuit. The voltages must be added using phasors, Pythagorean's theorem.

Formula: $V = \sqrt{V_R^2 + V_C^2}$

Substituting: $V = \sqrt{14.2^2 + 14.2^2}$

Solving: V = 20 volts

Capacitive Reactance in Parallel with Resistance

As in any parallel circuit, voltage is the same throughout the circuit. This means that the voltage applied to each branch of the parallel circuit is the same. Reactance in a parallel circuit causes a phase shift in the branch current and the resultant total current. A parallel circuit with capacitance will have the capacitive current "lead" the resistive current. The phase shift between reactance and resistance is always 90 degrees.

To solve a circuit with capacitance in parallel with resistance, follow these guidelines:

1. Calculate individual branch currents, using Ohm's law with the applied voltage and branch resistance or reactance.

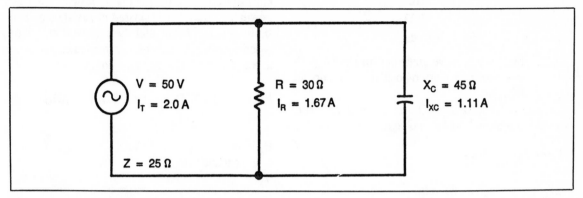

Fig. 14-9. Schematic diagram for sample problem 14-10.

2. Draw the current triangle with resistive current, I_R at zero degrees (horizontal) and capacitive reactance current, I_C at +90 degrees (up). The vector drawn up represents the leading phase shift. The hypotenuse of the triangle is total current, I_T.
3. Calculate total circuit impedance using Ohm's law with total circuit current and applied voltage.
4. Calculate phase angle theta using the current triangle. The phase angle in parallel capacitive circuit is positive.

Sample Problem:
Parallel Capacitive Reactance

SP#14-10. Parallel circuit, Fig. 14-9.

Given: R = 30 ohms,
          V = 50 volts
Find: I_R, I_{XC}, I_T, Z, theta

Step 1. Current triangle, Fig. 14-10.
a. Calculate resistive current, I_R.

Formula: $I = \dfrac{V}{R}$

Substituting: $I = \dfrac{50 \text{ volts}}{30 \text{ ohms}}$

Solving: $I_R = 1.67$ amps
b. Calculate capacitive current, I_{XC}.

Formula: $I = \dfrac{V}{X_C}$

Substituting: $I = \dfrac{50 \text{ volts}}{45 \text{ ohms}}$

Solving: $I_{XC} = 1.11$ amps
c. Solve for current total, I_T, using Pythagorean's theorem.

Formula: $I_T = \sqrt{I_R^2 + I_{XC}^2}$
Substituting: $I_T = \sqrt{1.67^2 + 1.11^2}$
Solving: $I_T = 2.0$ amps
d. Solve for theta, θ, using the current triangle.

Formula: $\theta = \tan^{-1} \dfrac{I_{XC}}{I_R}$

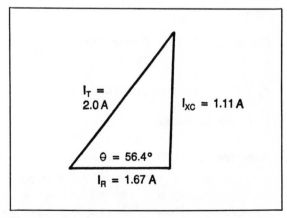

Fig. 14-10. Current triangle for sample problem 14-10.

Substituting: $\theta = \tan^{-1} \dfrac{1.67}{1.11}$

Solving: $\theta = +56.4$ degrees

Note: theta is a positive angle because the capacitive current is plotted positive in the current triangle.

Step 2. Solve for Z using Ohm's law with total current and applied voltage.

Formula: $Z = \dfrac{V}{I}$

Substituting: $Z = \dfrac{50 \text{ volts}}{2.0 \text{ amps}}$

Solving: $Z = 25$ ohms

AC POWER

Having reactance in an ac circuit changes the relationship of power dissipated. There are four quantities related to the power in an ac circuit: true power; reactive power; apparent power; power factor.

True Power, P_R, Watts

True power, also called real power, is the power dissipated in pure resistance. This is the power that is not affected by the reactive component and is measured in watts. It is calculated using the same method in any type of circuit. The calculation for true power is current through the resistor, times the voltage across the resistor. It is also possible to use all of the same formulas for power as were used in dc circuits.

Formula #42. True Power, Watts.

$$P_R = I_R \times V_R$$

P_R is true power (real power), in watts
I_R is resistor current
V_R is resistor voltage

Reactive Power, P_X, VARS

Reactive power, measured in VAR, is the power in a reactive component. The unit VAR stands for "Volt-Ampere-Reactive." In a purely reactive cir-

cuit, there is no power actually dissipated because power can only be dissipated in resistance. Since there is current flow and voltage even in a purely reactive circuit, it is necessary to calculate the power associated with the reactive component.

Formula #43. Reactive Power, VARS

$$P_X = I_X \times V_X$$

P_X is reactive power in VAR
I_X is reactive current
V_X is reactive voltage

Apparent Power, P_A, VA

Apparent power is the total circuit power in an ac circuit containing both resistance and reactance. It is called apparent power because it is the calculated power using total current and total voltage. The units VA comes from "Volt-Ampere."

Formula #44. Apparent Power, VA

$$P_A = I_T \times V_T$$

P_A is apparent power in VA
I_T is total current
V_T is total applied voltage

Power Factor, PF, No Units

The power factor is the ratio of real power to apparent power. It is a pure number, with no units. The easiest method of calculating power factor is to find the cosine of the phase angle, theta.

Formula #45. Power Factor, PF

$$PF = \text{cosine } \theta$$

Practice Problems:
Reactance, Impedance, Ac Power

Part A. Use Fig. 14-11 for problems 1-5. Find: Z, I, V_R, V_L, theta, P_R, P_X, P_A, PF.

1. R = 450 ohms, X_L = 600 ohms
2. R = 825 ohms, X_L = 550 ohms
3. R = 250 ohms, X_L = 300 ohms

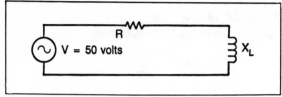

Fig. 14-11. Problems 1-5.

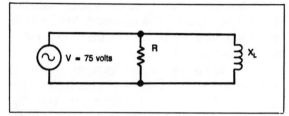

Fig. 14-12. Problems 6-10.

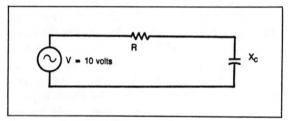

Fig. 14-13. Problems 11-15.

4. R = 375 ohms, X_L = 375 ohms
5. R = 600 ohms, X_L = 450 ohms

Part B. Use Fig. 14-12 for problems 6-10. Find: I_R, I_L, I_T, Z, theta, P_R, P_X, P_A, PF.

6. R = 250 ohms, X_L = 300 ohms
7. R = 450 ohms, X_L = 300 ohms
8. R = 125 ohms, X_L = 275 ohms
9. R = 750 ohms, X_L = 500 ohms
10. R = 450 ohms, X_L = 450 ohms

Part C. Use Fig. 14-13 for problems 11-15. Find: Z, I, V_R, V_C, theta, P_R, P_X, P_A, PF.

11. R = 300 ohms, X_C = 325 ohms
12. R = 250 ohms, X_C = 450 ohms
13. R = 500 ohms, X_C = 300 ohms
14. R = 750 ohms, X_C = 800 ohms
15. R = 250 ohms, X_C = 250 ohms

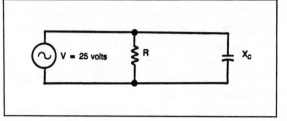

Fig. 14-14. Problems 16-20.

Part D. Use Fig. 14-14 for problems 16-20. Find: I_R, I_C, I_T, Z, theta, P_R, P_X, P_A, PF.

16. R = 350 ohms, X_C = 325 ohms
17. R = 200 ohms, X_C = 325 ohms
18. R = 500 ohms, X_C = 425 ohms
19. R = 775 ohms, X_C = 900 ohms
20. R = 100 ohms, X_C = 325 ohms

MEASURING PHASE ANGLE WITH AN OSCILLOSCOPE

To measure the phase angle with an oscilloscope, it is necessary to compare the voltage across the reactive component to the circuit voltage. A dual trace oscilloscope is necessary.

Review of the Oscilloscope Screen

Reading the scope screen is critical when making measurements. The screen is divided into "blocks," with the lines going up used for voltage measurements and the lines going across used for time measurements.

Each "block" on the screen represents 1 division as related to the volts/division and the time/division controls.

Each division is sub-divided into subdivisions, with four subdivisions per division. The subdivisions allow reading to one decimal place (.2, .4, .6, .8, 1.0).

Degrees per Division

When measuring frequency on a scope, it is necessary to measure the time of one cycle. This is done by counting the number of divisions in one cycle and multiplying by the time per division.

When measuring phase angle on the scope, it is not necessary to measure time, but only the number of divisions in one cycle. Since one cycle contains 360 degrees and the number of divisions can be counted, it is possible to determine the number of degrees per division.

Keep in mind that phase angle measurements require comparing the difference between two sine waves. The phase angle is measured in degrees, but the measurement is the number of divisions difference between the two waveforms.

Formula #46. Degrees per Division, From an Oscilloscope

$$\frac{\text{deg}}{\text{div}} = \frac{360 \text{ degrees}}{\text{\# divisions}}$$

Phase Angle

Once it is known how many degrees per division there are for a sine wave, then the phase angle is found by determining the # of divisions difference between the two waveforms and multiplying by the deg/div.

Formula #47. Phase Angle, from an Oscilloscope

$$\theta = \text{\# div} \times \frac{\text{deg}}{\text{div}}$$

Triggering the Oscilloscope

When using a dual trace oscilloscope with two different waveforms, it is necessary to determine which waveform will be used by the scope to start the trace on the left.

Refer to Fig. 14-15. This figure shows a scope with two sine waves. One wave is the applied voltage, V_A, and the other is the inductor voltage, V_L. Here, the scope is triggered on the input voltage. Notice that V_a starts at the zero axis line, while V_L looks like it started prior to this point.

Refer to Fig. 14-16. This figure shows a scope with two sine waves, but this drawing has the scope triggered on V_L, and V_A looks like it started late.

Figures 14-15 and 14-16 are of the same circuit. In fact, the values of R and X_L are equal, giving a 45 degree phase angle. The phase angle is positive because V_L leads V_A, as would be ex-

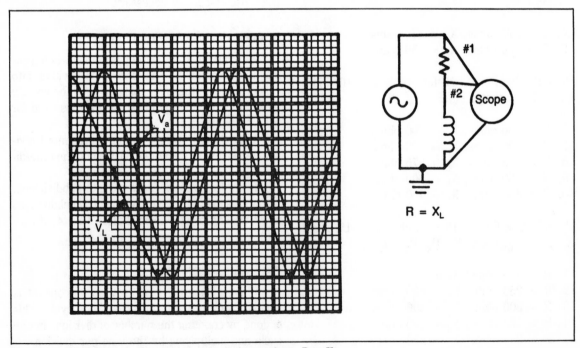

Fig. 14-15. 45° phase angle. Scope triggers on the input voltage. $R = X_L$.

pected in a series inductive circuit. One difference between these two figures is that 14-15 has the time per division control set faster than 14-16. Notice that although the degrees per division is different, the measurement of phase angle is the same.

Sample Problems:
Phase Angle Measurements

SP#14-11. Refer to Fig. 14-15.

Note: count the divisions at the center, ground reference line.

Step 1. Count the number of divisions in one complete cycle. In this sample, the applied voltage, V_A, is the trigger voltage and would be the best waveform to use.
1 cycle = 4 divisions

Step 2. Divide the number of degrees in one cycle by the number of divisions in one cycle.

$$\frac{deg}{div} = \frac{360 \text{ degrees}}{4 \text{ divisions}}$$

$$\frac{deg}{div} = 90$$

Step 3. Determine the difference between the two waveforms by counting the number of divisions between the two waveforms, accurate to one decimal place.

.5 div diff

Step 4. Multiply the divisions difference by the degrees per division to determine the degrees difference between the sine waves—the phase angle.

$$.5 \text{ div} \times 90 \ \frac{deg}{div} = 45 \text{ deg}$$

phase angle = 45 degrees

SP#14-12. Refer to Fig. 14-16.

Step 1. Divisions in 1 cycle.
1 cycle = 8 divisions

Step 2. Degrees per division

$$\frac{deg}{div} = \frac{360 \text{ degrees}}{8 \text{ divisions}}$$

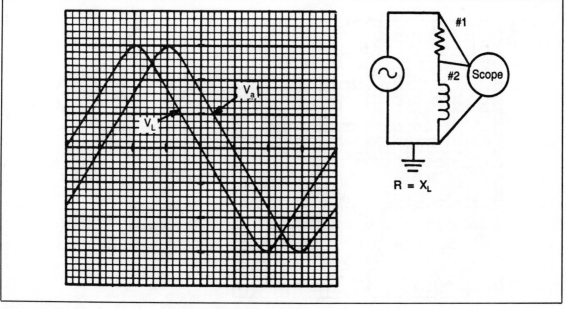

Fig. 14-16. 45° phase angle. Scope triggers on the inductor voltage. $R = X_L$.

$$\frac{\text{deg}}{\text{div}} = 45$$

Step 3. Number of divisions difference.
1 div diff

Step 4. Div diff × deg/div
1 div × 45 deg/div
phase angle = 45 degrees

SP#14-13. Refer to Fig. 14-17.
Step 1. Divisions in 1 cycle.
1 cycle = 8 divisions

Step 2. Degrees per division

$$\frac{\text{deg}}{\text{div}} = \frac{360 \text{ degrees}}{8 \text{ divisions}}$$

$$\frac{\text{deg}}{\text{div}} = 45$$

Step 3. Number of divisions difference.
0 div diff

Step 4. Div diff × deg/div
1 div × 45 deg/div
phase angle = 0 degrees (in phase)
(reactance value very small)

SP#14-14. Refer to Fig. 14-18

Step 1. Divisions in 1 cycle.
1 cycle = 8 divisions

Step 2. Degrees per division

$$\frac{\text{deg}}{\text{div}} = \frac{360 \text{ degrees}}{8 \text{ divisions}}$$

$$\frac{\text{deg}}{\text{div}} = 45$$

Step 3. Number of divisions difference.
2 div diff

Step 4. Div diff × deg/div
2 div × 45 deg/div
phase angle = 90 degrees
(resistance value very small)

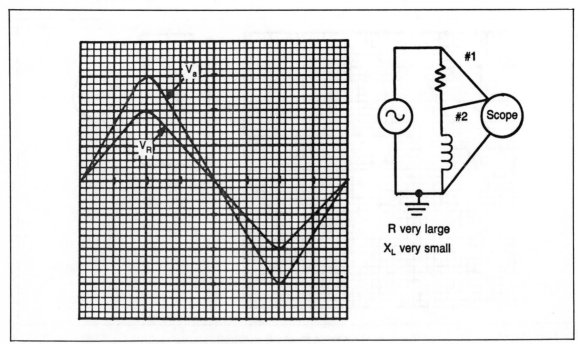

Fig. 14-17. 0° phase angle. R very large compared to X_L.

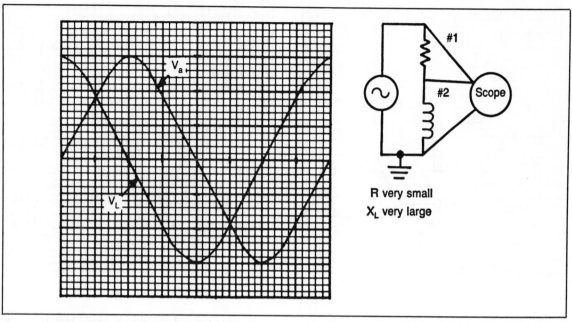

Fig. 14-18. 90° phase angle. R very small compared to X_L.

Practice Problems: Phase Angle

Figures 14-19 to 14-28 are practice problems in reading an oscilloscope screen to measure phase angle. To simplify matters, all 10 drawings are from circuits containing inductive reactance. The scope is triggered on the applied voltage. The phase angles are all positive, and the inductor voltage leads the applied voltage.

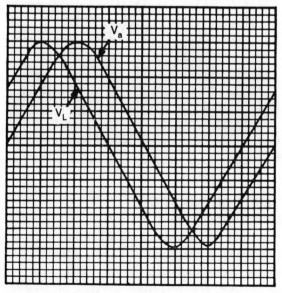

Fig. 14-19. Problem 1. a) _____ b) _____ c) _____ d) _____

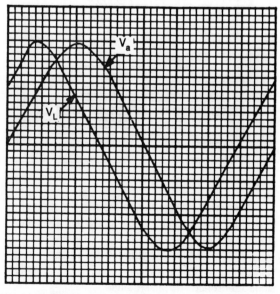

Fig. 14-20. Problem 2. a) _____ b) _____ c) _____ d) _____

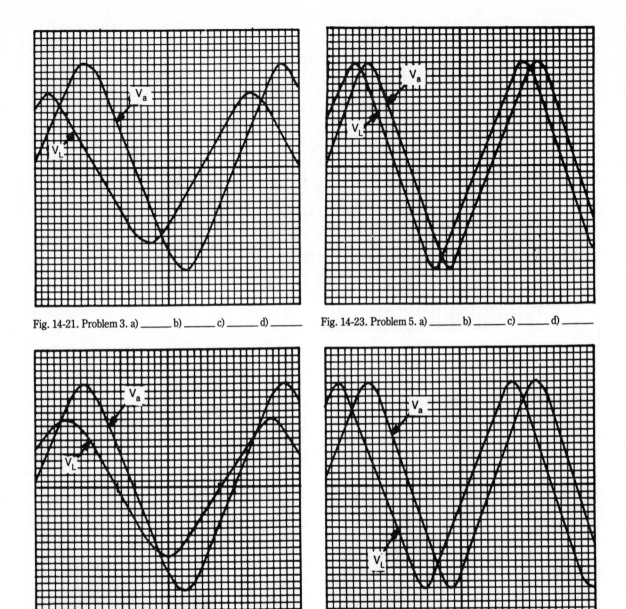

Fig. 14-21. Problem 3. a) _____ b) _____ c) _____ d) _____

Fig. 14-23. Problem 5. a) _____ b) _____ c) _____ d) _____

Fig. 14-22. Problem 4. a) _____ b) _____ c) _____ d) _____

Fig. 14-24. Problem 6. a) _____ b) _____ c) _____ d) _____

The hands-on practice in the next section contains capacitive circuits, which have a negative phase angle.

Determine the following for each figure: a. divisions in 1 cycle. b. degrees per division. c. # divisions difference. d. phase angle.

HANDS-ON PRACTICE: MEASURING PHASE ANGLE

This hands-on experience is intended to serve two purposes: first, practice with phasor analysis and second, measurements of the phase angle using the oscilloscope. The two parts to this exercise will give

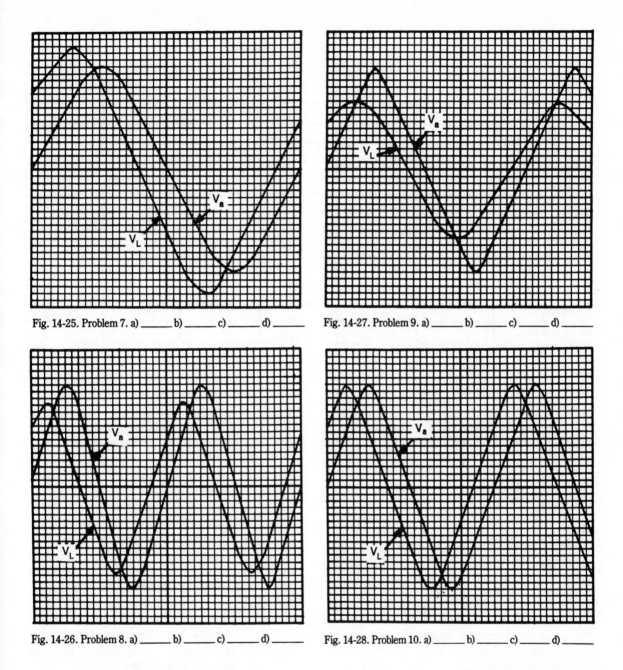

Fig. 14-25. Problem 7. a) _____ b) _____ c) _____ d) _____

Fig. 14-27. Problem 9. a) _____ b) _____ c) _____ d) _____

Fig. 14-26. Problem 8. a) _____ b) _____ c) _____ d) _____

Fig. 14-28. Problem 10. a) _____ b) _____ c) _____ d) _____

both a theoretical and a visual demonstration of the effects on phase angle as the reactance is varied.

A series resistor/capacitor circuit has been chosen for this exercise because this is the simplest type of circuit to use for phase angle measurements. The actual value of the components is not critical because the frequency will be varied to change the capacitive reactance.

Before proceeding with the hands-on portion of this exercise, the student should complete the list of formulas and the calculated values in Table 14-1. This is necessary to provide the needed information

233

Table 14-1. Calculated Values.

FREQUENCY	X_c	Z	I	V_R	V_c	θ
15,000 Hz						
20,000 Hz						
25,000 Hz						
30,000 Hz						
35,000 Hz						
40,000 Hz						
45,000 Hz						
50,000 Hz						
••••••••••						
10,000 Hz						
7,500 Hz						
5,000 Hz						
2,500 Hz						

and background to obtain maximum learning efficiency.

Examine the schematic diagram and sample drawing of an oscilloscope display in Fig. 14-29. Note the relationship of the two sine waves in the drawing.

CIRCUIT VALUES

Recommended: Actual:
Resistor: 10 kilohms   _____
Capacitor: 0.001 μF   _____
Applied voltage: 10 volts peak to peak

FORMULAS: (to be supplied by the student)

Capacitive reactance (ohms): X_C =
Impedance (ohms): Z =
Current (amps): I =
Voltage across the resistor (volts): V_R =
Voltage across the capacitor (volts): V_C =
Phase angle, theta (degrees): θ =
Degrees/division on scope: deg/div =
# of divisions difference between waveforms:
   # div =
Phase angle, theta, on scope (degrees): θ =

Step 1. Observations made from calculations at the frequency of 15,000 Hz.
  a. What is the approximate relationship between resistance and reactance?
  b. What is the approximate relationship of voltage drops across the resistor and capacitor?
  c. What is the approximate value of theta?
  d. What is the approximate shape of the voltage and impedance triangles?

Step 2. Observations made from the calculations as the frequency increases ABOVE 15,000 Hz.
  a. How does the relationship between resistance and reactance change?
  b. How does the relationship of the voltage drops change?
  c. How does theta change?
  d. How does the shape of the triangles change?

Step 3. Observations made from the calculations as the frequency decreases BELOW 15,000 Hz.

234

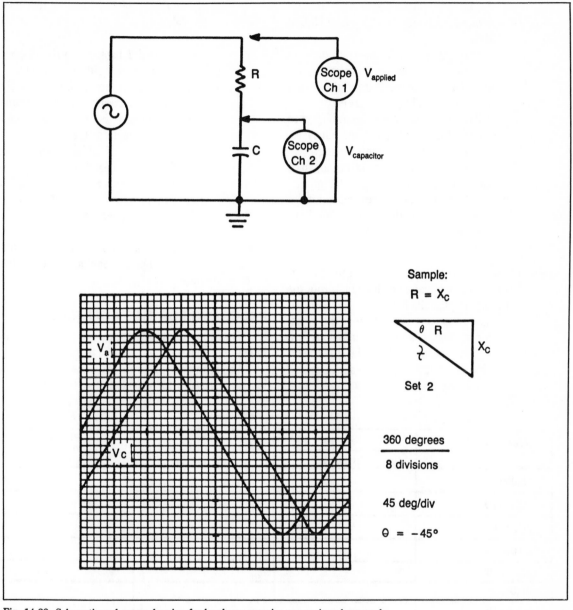

Fig. 14-29. Schematic and scope drawing for hands-on exercise measuring phase angle.

a. How does the relationship between resistance and reactance change?

b. How does the relationship of the voltage drops change?

c. How does theta change?

d. How does the shape of the triangles change?

Step 4. Connect the oscilloscope as shown in Fig. 14-29; channel 1 on the applied voltage and channel 2 across the capacitor.

a. Make certain that all ground wires are connected to the same point, on one side of the capacitor.

b. Set the applied voltage (from the signal

generator) to 10 volts peak to peak.

c. Adjust the signal generator to the desired frequency (starting with 15,000 Hz).

d. Adjust the oscilloscope volts/division control on each channel to make the two sine waves approximately the same size, almost filling the screen.

e. Adjust the oscilloscope time/division to allow a display of at least one full cycle, as shown in the sample drawing.

f. Oscilloscope trigger must be adjusted for channel 1, the applied voltage.

g. Adjust the ground reference line for the exact center of the screen, for both channels.

Step 5. For this step only, use the ground reference switch to remove channel 2 from the display (a straight line).

a. The remaining sine wave is the resistor voltage. Count the number of divisions in one complete cycle. It is always best to count the divisions at the ground reference line.

b. Divide this number into 360 and the result is the "deg/div." Record this value in Table 14-2.

Step 6. Switch channel 2 back on to the display. (Two sine waves should be present.)

a. At the ground reference line, count the number of divisions (to one decimal place) between the two sine waves. Record this value in the table.

b. Multiply the # of divisions times the deg/div and the result is the phase angle, theta, θ. Note: the phase angle is negative because the capacitor voltage "lags" the applied voltage.

Step 7. Use the above steps, as necessary to complete the table of results, for each frequency.

PROGRAMS FOR THIS CHAPTER

There are 2 programs for this chapter: reactance and phase angle.

The reactance program provides practice in using the formulas for calculating X_L and X_C. Note:

Table 14-2. Measured Values.

Frequency	Degrees ------------ Division	# of Divisions	Phase Angle θ
15,000 Hz			
20,000 Hz			
25,000 Hz			
30,000 Hz			
35,000 Hz			
40,000 Hz			
45,000 Hz			
50,000 Hz ••••••••••••••••••• 10,000 Hz	••••••••••••••••••••••	••••••••••••••••••••••	••••••••••••••••
7,500 Hz			
5,000 Hz			
2,500 Hz			

the program uses all capital letters, therefore milli-henry is MH, microfarads is UF, nanofarad is NF. Figure 14-30 is the reactance program sample.

The phase angle program asks two questions for each oscilloscope screen. The first question is to state if the two waveforms are in or out of phase. The second question is to determine how many degrees the two waveforms are apart. Figure 14-31 is the phase angle program sample. The help hints contain a review of how to perform the calculations.

AC CIRCUITS COMPETENCY TEST

Part A. Definitions.
Define the Following Terms

1. reactance
2. impedance
3. real power
4. reactive power
5. apparent power

Part B. Inductive Reactance. Calculate X_L

6. Given: f = 1000 Hz, L = 100 mH
   Find: X_L
7. Given: L = 250 mH, f = 800 Hz
   Find: X_L
8. Given: f = 25 kHz, L = 30 μH
   Find: X_L
9. Given: L = 3 H, f = 100 Hz
   Find: X_L
10. Given: L = 50 μH, f = 3 MHz
    Find: X_L

Part C. Capacitive Reactance. Calculate X_C

11. Given: f = 2500 Hz, C = .001 μF
    Find: X_C
12. Given: C = 1 pF, f = 1 GHz
    Find: X_C
13. Given: C = 180 pF, f = 12 kHz
    Find: X_C

```
                    REACTANCE
              SAMPLE  PROGRAM:


     NOTE:  UNITS  ARE  GIVEN,  JUST  GIVE
     THE  NUMERIC  VALUE.


     GIVEN:

              INDUCTOR  =  3  MH

              FREQUENCY  =  600  HZ

              REACTANCE  =  ?  OHMS


  1 .FIND  THE  UNKNOWN  ?    11.3


              ▓█▌▒▒▐█▌
     SPACE  BAR  =  NEXT,  E  =  EXIT
```

Fig. 14-30. Reactance program sample.

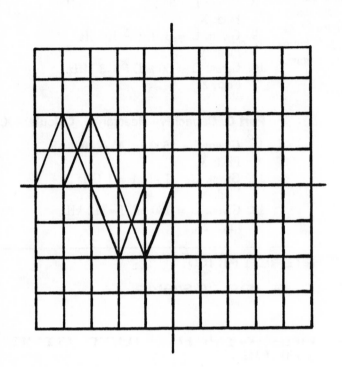

```
        PHASE ANGLE
      PROGRAM SAMPLE:
```

```
CH1 & CH2 VOLT/DIV = 5V TIME/DIV = 50US
   1. ARE THESE WAVES IN PHASE Y/N ? N

              CORRECT!

     SPACE BAR = NEXT, E = EXIT
```

Fig. 14-31. Phase angle sample program.

14. Given: C = .47 μF, f = 100 Hz
    Find: X_C
15. Given: f = 2.5 MHz, C = .022 μF
    Find: X_C

Part D. Series Inductive Reactance

Units must be included with answer.

Given: R = 300 ohms, X_L = 400 ohms, V = 100 volts.

Find:

16. impedance, Z
17. total current, I
18. voltage across the resistor, V_R
19. voltage across the inductor, V_L

238

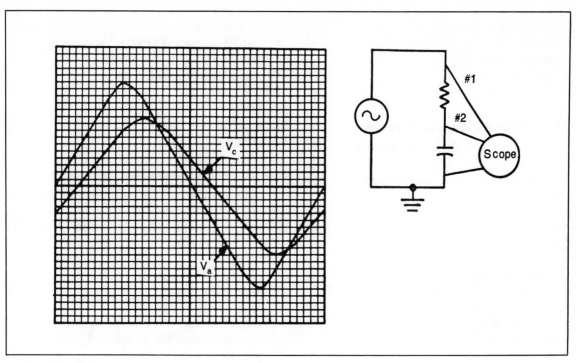

Fig. 14-32. Problem 49.

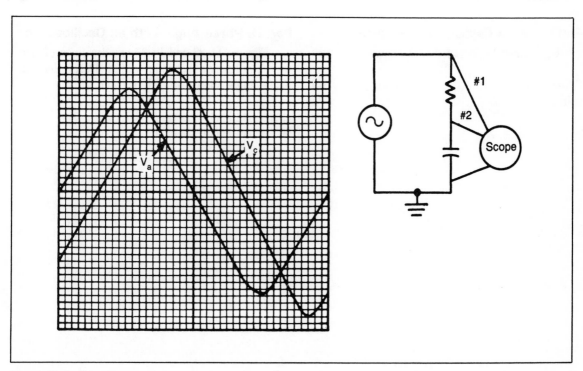

Fig. 14-33. Problem 50.

239

20. phase angle, theta, θ
21. real power, P_R
22. reactive power, P_X
23. apparent power, P_A
24. power factor, PF

Part E. Parallel Inductive Reactance

Units must be included with answer.

Given: R = 750 ohms, X_L = 500 ohms, V = 100 volts.
Find:

25. impedance, Z
26. total current, I_T
27. current through the resistor, I_R
28. current through the inductor, I_L
29. phase angle, theta, θ
30. real power, P_R
31. reactive power, P_X
32. apparent power, P_A
33. power factor, PF

Part F. Series Capacitive Reactance

Units must be included with answer.

Given: R = 120 ohms, X_C = 120 ohms, V = 100 volts.
Find:
34. impedance, Z

35. total current, I
36. voltage across the resistor, V_R
37. voltage across the capacitor, V_C
38. phase angle, theta, θ
39. real power, P_R
40. reactive power, P_X
41. apparent power, P_A
42. power factor, PF

Part G. Parallel Capacitive Reactance

Units must be included with answer.

Given: R = 150 ohms, X_C = 200 ohms, V = 100 volts.
Find:

43. impedance, Z
44. total current, I_T
45. current through the resistor, I_R
46. current through the capacitor, I_C
47. phase angle, theta, θ
48. power factor, PF

Part H. Phase Angle With an Oscilloscope

Figures 14-32 and 14-33 are drawings of sine waves on the oscilloscope screen. Determine the phase angle shown in each drawing.

49. phase angle, theta, θ
50. phase angle, theta, θ

Chapter 15

Resonance

Chapter Objectives: To determine the net reactance of circuits containing inductive and capacitive reactance. To examine the effects of resonance on current and voltage when inductive reactance equals capacitive reactance.

Chapter Outline:

INTRODUCTION

A circuit can contain a combination of resistance, inductance and capacitance. There are uses for the various combinations. This chapter will primarily deal with a circuit characteristic called "resonance," which occurs when the inductive reactance equals the capacitive reactance.

NET REACTANCE

Inductive and capacitive reactance have opposite characteristics and if they are used in the same circuit there will be some cancellation of their effects. Net reactance is the amount of reactance that "appears" to be in the circuit, after considering the cancellation.

Series Circuits

Figure 15-1 shows a series L-C with its associated vectors. In a series circuit, the vectors are reactance and voltage. In this sample circuit, resistance is ignored to better demonstrate the cancellation effect of the vectors.

Starting with the original circuit in Fig. 15-1A, notice that $X_L = 60$ ohms and $X_C = 40$ ohms. The vector for X_L is plotted up and the vector for X_C is plotted down. The two vectors are subtracted since they are opposite—leaving a net reactance of 20 ohms. The net reactance is inductive because X_L is larger than X_C. This circuit is classified as an "inductive" circuit.

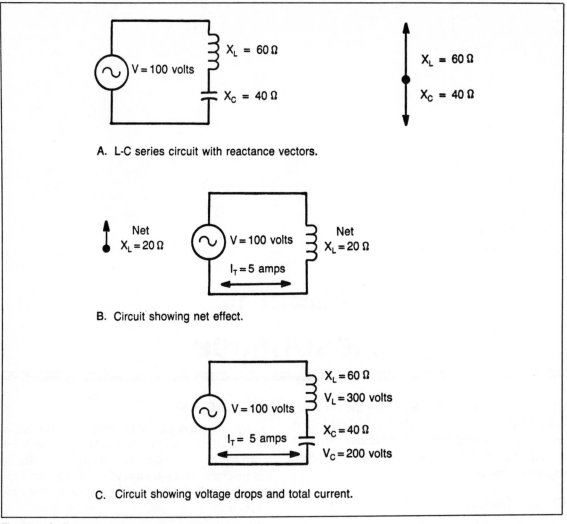

A. L-C series circuit with reactance vectors.

B. Circuit showing net effect.

C. Circuit showing voltage drops and total current.

Fig. 15-1. Series net reactance sample problem 15-1.

Total current is calculated based on the net reactance, using Ohm's law. If resistance were also included in this circuit, an impedance triangle would be drawn and impedance calculated. The circuit with the single inductor (Fig. 15-1B) is the net reactance, including the total current and applied voltage.

Voltage across each component is calculated based upon the total current and Ohm's law. Notice (in Fig. 15-1C) how the voltage across the components is considerably higher than the applied voltage. This can only occur in a circuit that has both inductance and capacitance, and is a result of the charging and energy storage capabilities of the individual components.

Sample Problem: Series Net Reactance
SP#15-1. Refer to Fig. 15-1.

Given: Figure 15-1A, X_L = 60 ohms, X_C = 40 ohms
           V = 100 volts

Find: a) net reactance
           b) state if net is L or C

c) total current, I_T
d) inductive voltage drop, V_L
e) capacitive voltage drop, V_C

a) Find net reactance by subtracting X_L and X_C.
Net = 20 ohms, shown in Fig. 15-1B.

b) The larger of X_L or X_C determines the net effect.
Net is L, shown in Fig. 15-1B.

c) Total current is found using Ohm's law with the applied voltage and net reactance.
I_T = 5 amps, shown in Fig. 15-1B.

d) Inductive voltage drop is found by using Ohm's law with the total current and inductive reactance.
V_L = 300 volts, shown in Fig. 15-1C.

e) Capacitive voltage drop is found by using Ohm's law with the total current and capacitive reactance.
V_C = 200 volts, shown in Fig. 15-1C.

Parallel Circuits

In a parallel circuit, it is current that has a phase shift. Therefore, it is the individual branch currents that will cancel.

Figure 15-2 shows a circuit with an inductor in parallel with a capacitor. The reactance values of the two components have been selected so that they are the same as the values of the series circuit in Fig. 15-1—the previous sample problem (X_L = 60 ohms, X_C = 40 ohms).

Voltage is the same throughout the parallel circuit, so the individual branch currents are calculated using the applied voltage (120 volts) with Ohm's law.

Notice that the branch current for the inductor is smaller than the branch current for the capacitor because the inductor has a larger value of reactance. The vectors are drawn for each branch current and the resultant current is the total current.

The total current is smaller than the branch currents. Between the inductor and capacitor there is a certain amount of "circulation current" flowing. The circulation current is a result of the charge and discharge of the inductor and capacitor.

This circuit (Fig. 15-2) is classified as "capacitive" because the capacitor has the largest current.

Sample Problem: Parallel Net Reactance

SP#15-2. Refer to Fig. 15-2.
Given: Figure 15-2A, X_L = 60 ohms, X_C = 40 ohms
         V = 120 volts

Find: a) inductive current, I_L
        b) capacitive current, I_C
        c) net current (total current), I_T
        d) net reactance
        e) state if net is L or C

a) Inductive current is calculated using Ohm's law with the applied voltage and inductive reactance.
I_L = 2 amps, shown in Fig. 15.2A.

b) Capacitive current is found using the same method as inductive current.
I_C = 3 amps, shown in Fig. 15-2A.

c) Net current is also called total current because it is the current from the power supply. Subtract the branch currents.
I_T = 1 amp, shown in Fig. 15-2B.

d) Net reactance is the reactance that would allow the total current to flow. Use Ohm's law with the applied voltage and net reactance.
Net = 120 ohms, shown in Fig. 15-2B.

e) The circuit is determined if it is L or C by which has the largest current.
Circuit is net C.

Practice Problems: Net Reactance

Part A. Series Circuits. With each of the following series circuits, find:

  a. net reactance
  b. state if net is L or C
  c. total current, I_T
  d. inductive voltage drop, V_L
  e. capacitive voltage drop, V_C

(1) X_L = 150 ohms, X_C = 275 ohms, V = 10 volts
(2) X_L = 50 ohms, X_C = 75 ohms, V = 15 volts
(3) X_L = 250 ohms, X_C = 175 ohms, V = 20 volts
(4) X_L = 750 ohms, X_C = 550 ohms, V = 25 volts

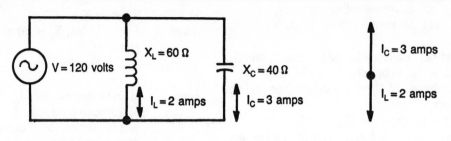

A. L-C parallel circuit with current vectors.

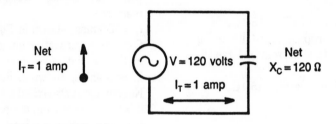

B. Circuit showing net effect.

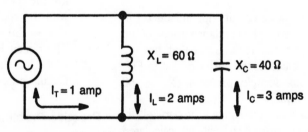

C. Circuit showing reactance and branch currents.

Fig. 15-2. Parallel net reactance sample problem 15-2.

(5) X_L = 450 ohms, X_C = 500 ohms, V = 30 volts
(6) X_L = 150 ohms, X_C = 125 ohms, V = 10 volts
(7) X_L = 15 ohms, X_C = 25 ohms, V = 10 volts
(8) X_L = 350 ohms, X_C = 375 ohms, V = 15 volts
(9) X_L = 300 ohms, X_C = 375 ohms, V = 20 volts
(10) X_L = 150 ohms, X_C = 200 ohms, V = 10 volts

a. inductive current, I_L
b. capacitive current, I_C
c. net current (total current, I_T)
d. net reactance
e. state if net is L or C

Part B. Parallel Circuits. With each of the following parallel circuits, find:

(11) X_L = 30 ohms, X_C = 40 ohms, V = 10 volts
(12) X_L = 35 ohms, X_C = 50 ohms, V = 15 volts
(13) X_L = 50 ohms, X_C = 40 ohms, V = 20 volts

(14) X_L = 300 ohms, X_C = 350 ohms, V = 25 volts
(15) X_L = 150 ohms, X_C = 100 ohms, V = 10 volts
(16) X_L = 20 ohms, X_C = 25 ohms, V = 15 volts
(17) X_L = 250 ohms, X_C = 240 ohms, V = 15 volts
(18) X_L = 60 ohms, X_C = 40 ohms, V = 30 volts
(19) X_L = 40 ohms, X_C = 45 ohms, V = 15 volts
(20) X_L = 80 ohms, X_C = 60 ohms, V = 40 volts

THE RESONANT EFFECT

Resonance occurs when $X_L = X_C$. The effect of this is significant because one reactance can cancel the effects of the other reactance. In a series circuit, there appears to be no reactance, only resistance. In a parallel circuit, there appears to be an open circuit.

Both parallel and series resonant circuits are used, with their application depending on which characteristic is required.

Calculating the Resonant Frequency

The formula to calculate the resonant frequency is shown below as formula #48. The formula is found by using the definition of resonance ($X_L = X_C$) and their respective formulas as follows:

$$X_L = 2 \, (\pi) \, f \, L$$

and

$$X_C = \frac{1}{2 \, (\pi) \, f \, C}$$

if

$$X_L = X_C$$

then:

$$2 \, (\pi) \, f \, L = \frac{1}{2 \, (\pi) \, f \, C}$$

Therefore, solving for f:

Formula #48. Frequency of Resonance

$$f_r = \frac{1}{2 \, (\pi) \, \sqrt{L \, C}}$$

When solving for the resonant frequency, it is possible to have a wide range of component values of L (inductance) and C (capacitance). To demonstrate this concept, Table 15-1 shows five different combinations of L and C that will produce the resonant frequency of 1 MHz. Notice that the table also includes the value of reactance for each combination.

The different combinations of X_L and X_C are selected based on their reactances and the particular application.

Sample Problems: Resonant Frequency

SP#15-3. Calculate the value of resonant frequency.

Given: L = 239 μH, C = 106 pF
Find: f_r

Formula: $f_r = \dfrac{1}{2(\pi) \, \sqrt{LC}}$

Substituting: $f_r = \dfrac{1}{6.28 \times \sqrt{239 \, \mu H \times 106 \, pF}}$

Solving: f_r = 1 MHz

Note: to solve this, first perform the multiplication inside the square root sign. Second, take the square root. Third, multiply by 6.28. Last, take the reciprocal.

Table 15-1. L-C Combinations Resonant at 1 MHz.

L (μH)	C (pF)	$X_L = X_C$ Reactance (Ohms)
23.9	1060	150
120	212	750
239	106	1500
478	53	3000
2390	10.6	15,000

Practice Problems: Resonant Frequency

Use the information given to find the resonant frequency.

(1)   Given: L = 10 mH, C = 25 μF
      Find: f

(2)   Given: L = 35 mH, C = 200 μF
      Find: f

(3)   Given: L = 75 mH, C = .005 μF
      Find: f

(4)   Given: L = .3 H, C = 25 pF
      Find: f

(5)   Given: L = 15 μH, C = .68 μF
      Find: f

(6)   Given: L = 35 μH, C = 6.5 pF
      Find: f

(7)   Given: L = .55 H, C = .33 μF
      Find: f

(8)   Given: L = 250 mH, C = 7 μF
      Find: f

(9)   Given: L = 17.3 μH, C = 3.7 μF
      Find: f

(10) Given: L = 1.5 H, C = 3.5 μF
      Find: f

SERIES RESONANCE

In any series circuit, current must flow through all series components. In a series resonant circuit, where $X_L = X_C$, the reactance is canceled, resulting in near-zero impedance.

Normally, a series resonant circuit is used where it is desired to pass only the resonant frequency, and filter out any other. An example is an antenna.

Minimum Impedance at Resonance

In an actual working circuit, the inductor, since it is made from a coil of wire, has a certain amount of resistance. That amount of resistance is a characteristic of the inductor and will be present in the circuit at any frequency, whether or not it is at resonance. Because of the built-in circuit resistances, when X_L and X_C cancel each other there still remains a small amount of impedance.

Table 15-2. Reactance at Frequencies Near 1 MHz.

Freq. (Hz)	L = .239 H, C = .106 μF			
	XL (Ohms)	Xc (Ohms)	Net (Ohms)	L/C
600	900	2500	1600	C
800	1200	1875	675	C
1000	1500	1500	0	
1200	1800	1250	550	L
1400	2100	1070	1030	L

Refer to Table 15-2 for a summary of the values of reactance at frequencies above and below the resonant frequency of 1000 Hz. The net is the difference between X_L and X_C, with the L/C column showing which had the higher reactance.

Maximum Current at Resonance

A series resonant circuit has a characteristic minimum impedance at resonance. Therefore, there must be a maximum of current flow at resonance. The only resistance in the circuit at resonance is the resistance of the coil.

Refer to Fig. 15-3. A series resonant circuit is drawn showing the inductor, capacitor and the resistance of the inductor's coil—labeled r_s. The resonant frequency is 1000 Hz, as calculated in Table 15-2. Accompanying the schematic diagram in Fig. 15-3 is the "bell curve" of current versus frequency.

The bell curve shows the resonant frequency at the center peak. At the resonant frequency, the current is at a maximum value. On either side of the "center" (resonant) frequency, the current drops off very quickly. See Table 15-2. Notice the net reactance increases above and below center frequency.

Effect Above and Below Resonant Frequency

As evidenced by the bell curve, one of the effects when above and below resonant frequency is that the current will decrease. The results on Ta-

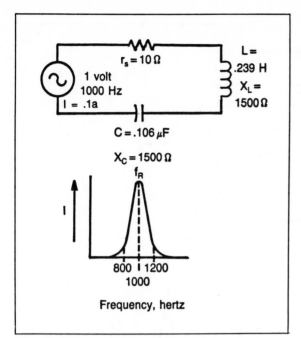

Fig. 15-3. Series resonant circuit and the bell curve of current vs. frequency.

ble 15-2 show the net reactance to be either capacitive or inductive.

Notice in Table 15-2, when below the resonant frequency, the net reactance is capacitive and when above the resonant frequency, the net reactance is inductive. The characteristics of a series circuit are determined, not by the reactance, but by the voltage drops. The voltage drop will be largest across the largest value of reactance.

A capacitive circuit has a lagging (negative) phase angle. An inductive circuit has a leading (positive) phase angle.

☐ A series resonant circuit is capacitive below resonance and inductive above resonance.

PARALLEL RESONANCE

A parallel circuit has voltage that is common throughout the circuit—with current dividing to the individual branches.

In a parallel resonant circuit, where X_L and X_C cancel, the inductor and capacitor produce a current that circulates only in the two components. The cir-

culating current is called the "flywheel" effect, where the inductor charges the capacitor and the capacitor charges the inductor. The circulating current does not flow in the rest of the circuit.

The circulating current in a parallel resonant circuit reaches a maximum at resonance. Any signal that has a frequency equal to resonance will support the circulating current, but cannot pass by the parallel circuit, therefore, the resonant frequency has the effect of being stopped. Any other frequency will pass by the parallel circuit, being ignored.

An application for the parallel resonant circuit is in the tuning of a radio, where each amplifier section is transformer coupled to the next stage. A transformer will pass the most voltage when the current in the primary is the largest—at resonant frequency. The transformer primary is the inductor in the parallel resonant circuit.

Maximum Impedance at Resonance

The term maximum impedance means that the signal cannot pass through the circuit, such as it does in an open circuit. Figure 15-4 shows the schematic diagram of a parallel resonant circuit, and the current and impedance curves. The impedance curve shows a maximum impedance at resonance, where at other frequencies there is less impedance. This means that at the resonant frequency, the power supply "sees" the parallel resonant circuit as an open circuit.

Minimum Current at Resonance

In Fig. 15-4, the current curve shows that the current drops to near zero at the resonant frequency. The current represented in this figure is the current from the power supply. At non-resonant frequencies, the current increases, as the reactance of either branch decreases.

Effect Above and Below Resonant Frequency

Refer to Table 15-2. Below resonant frequency, X_L is decreasing and X_C is increasing. Therefore, below resonance, there will be more inductive current and the circuit will have inductive characteristics.

247

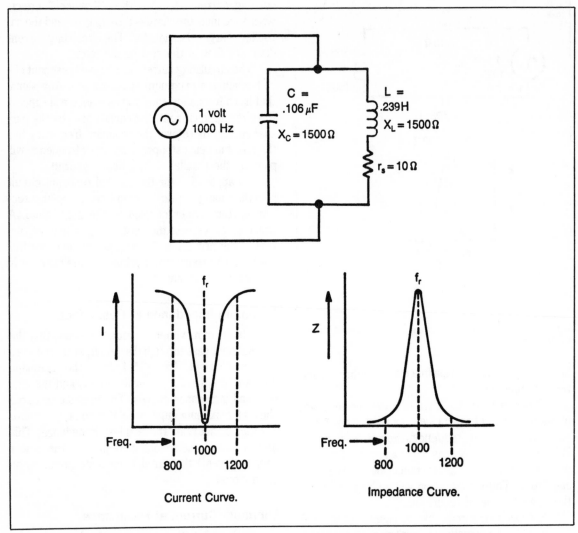

Fig. 15-4. Parallel resonant circuit and the bell curves of current vs. frequency and impedance vs. frequency.

Above resonant frequency, X_C is decreasing and X_L is increasing. Therefore, above resonance, there will be more capacitive current and the circuit will have capacitive characteristics.

☐ A parallel resonant circuit is inductive below resonance and capacitive above.

BANDWIDTH

The bandwidth of a circuit is the width of the bell curve. It essentially describes how the resonant circuit responds to frequencies that are above and below the resonant frequency.

70.7%, −3dB, Half-Power

The terms 70.7%, −3dB and half-power all refer to bandwidth and are exactly the same point on the bell curve. Each of the terms is explained below:

70.7% is a percentage of the maximum value of the response curve (bell curve). The response curve can be plotted in voltage or current. Therefore, it is 70.7% of the maximum voltage or current.

−3dB. Refers to a point that is down (−) 3dB (decibels) from the maximum value. Decibels is a unit of measure, usually associated with power. −3dB is the half-power point.

Half-Power. Refers to the point where the output power is ½ of the input power. Since response curves are plotted in voltage or current, it is necessary to exercise Ohm's law and the power formulas to demonstrate that ½ power = 70.7%.

Bandwidth

Bandwidth is defined as the range of frequencies on the response curve that have a response of at least 70.7%. The bandwidth describes how well the resonant circuit acts as a filter, and how it responds to frequencies near the resonant frequency. Refer to Fig. 15-5.

Bandwidth is also described as the "selectivity" of the resonant circuit. A smaller, narrower, bandwidth is more selective of which frequencies it will accept. A larger, wider, bandwidth is less selective and will accept a larger range of frequencies.

Q of a Resonant Circuit

The Q is a measure of the "quality" or "figure of merit" of the resonant circuit. A larger value of Q results in a narrower bandwidth. A smaller value of Q results in a wider bandwidth.

Refer to Fig. 15-6. There are three bell curves, each with a different Q. The curve with a Q of 80 has a bandwidth of 10kHz, the Q of 40 has a bandwidth of 20kHz and the Q of 10 has a bandwidth of 80kHz. Depending on the application, each of these curves could be the desired effect.

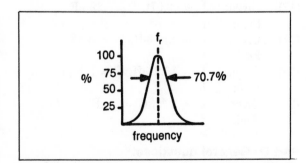

Fig. 15-5. Bell curve showing the 70.7% response point.

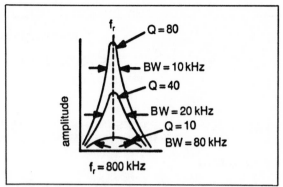

Fig. 15-6. Three bell curves, each with the same resonant frequency, with different Q.

PROGRAMS FOR THIS CHAPTER

There is one program for this chapter. Figure 15-7 is the program sample for the resonance program.

Included in the program are questions on calculations with the resonant frequency formula, and calculations with net reactance. Keep in mind that with net reactance problems, if there is no resistance in the circuit, then the reactances are simply subtracted and current and voltage calculations are made with Ohm's law, and do not require the use of vectors and Pythagorean's theorem.

RESONANCE COMPETENCY TEST
Part A. Net Reactance; Series Circuits

With each of the following series circuits, find: a. net reactance. b. state if net is L or C. c. total current, I_T. d. inductive voltage drop, V_L. e. capacitive voltage drop, V_C.

(1) X_L = 100 ohms, X_C = 250 ohms, V = 10 volts
(2) X_L = 75 ohms, X_C = 50 ohms, V = 25 volts
(3) X_L = 35 ohms, X_C = 50 ohms, V = 50 volts
(4) X_L = 200 ohms, X_C = 100 ohms, V = 25 volts
(5) X_L = 150 ohms, X_C = 140 ohms, V = 100 volts

Part B. Net Reactance; Parallel Circuits

With each of the following parallel circuits, find: a. inductive current, I_L b. capacitive current, I_C c.

```
          RESONANCE

       PROGRAM SAMPLE:


NOTE:  UNITS ARE GIVEN JUST GIVEN
       THE NUMERIC VALUE.
GIVEN:

       SERIES CIRCUIT

       XL = 100 OHMS

       XC = 250 OHMS

       V APPLIED = 10 VOLTS



1. FIND TOTAL CURRENT IN AMPS ? .066


          CORRECT!

     SPACE BAR = NEXT, E= EXIT
```

Fig. 15-7. Resonance program sample.

net current (total current), I_T d. net reactance e. state if net is L or C.

(6) X_L = 40 ohms, X_C = 30 ohms, V = 10 volts
(7) X_L = 35 ohms, X_C = 50 ohms, V = 10 volts
(8) X_L = 25 ohms, X_C = 30 ohms, V = 15 volts
(9) X_L = 50 ohms, X_C = 75 ohms, V = 20 volts
(10) X_L = 100 ohms, X_C = 75 ohms, V = 50 volts

Part C. Resonant Frequency

(11) Given: L = 25 mH, C = 10 μF
      Find: f
(12) Given: L = 200 mH, C = 35.2 μF
      Find: f
(13) Given: L = 50 mH, C = .001 μF
      Find: f

(14) Given: L = .1 H, C = 15 pF
      Find: f
(15) Given: L = 10 μH, C = .47 μF
      Find: f
(16) Given: L = 45 μH, C = 5.6 pF
      Find: f
(17) Given: L = .33 H, C = .22 μF
      Find: f
(18) Given: L = 150 mH, C = 5 μF
      Find: f
(19) Given: L = 16.2 μH, C = 2.5 μF
      Find: f
(20) Given: L = 2 H, C = 3 μF
      Find: f

Part D. General questions.

For questions 21-24; answer MAXIMUM or MINIMUM.

(21) In a series resonant circuit, the current is . . .

(22) In a parallel resonant circuit, the current is . . .

(23) In a series resonant circuit, the impedance is . . .

(24) In a parallel resonant circuit, the impedance is . . .

(25) Which type of resonant circuit (series or parallel) has the characteristic of capacitive above and inductive below resonant frequency?

Final Exam: dc and ac Building Blocks

☐ Engineering notation
☐ Ohm's law
☐ Power formulas
☐ dc circuits
☐ Sine wave analysis
☐ Transformers
☐ Inductors and capacitors
☐ Time constants
☐ Reactance, impedance and ac power
☐ Resonance

ENGINEERING NOTATION

Convert the given numbers to the units shown.

(1)	.005 A	_____	mA
(2)	65.7 mV	_____	V
(3)	5,600 kW	_____	W
(4)	87 MHz	_____	kHz
(5)	1500 pF	_____	μF

OHM'S LAW

Use Ohm's law to find the unknown value. The proper unit must be included with each answer.

(6)	R = 200 ohms	I = .5 amps	Find: V
(7)	V = 15 volts	R = 60 ohms	Find: I
(8)	I = 20 mA	V = 30 volts	Find: R
(9)	R = 2.2 kilohms	V = 6 volts	Find: I
(10)	I = 15 mA	R = 3 kilohms	Find: V

POWER FORMULAS

Use the power formulas to find the unknown value. The proper unit must be included with each answer.

(11)	V = 25 volts	I = .02 amps	Find: P
(12)	I = 3 amps	R = 40 ohms	Find: P
(13)	R = 50 ohms	V = 10 volts	Find: P
(14)	P = 60 watts	V = 120 volts	Find: I
(15)	I = .5 amps	P = 2 watts	Find: V

DC CIRCUITS

Refer to the schematic diagram for each problem.

252

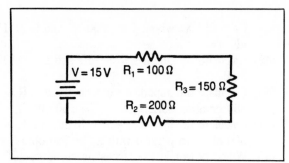

Fig. Ex2-1. Problem 16.

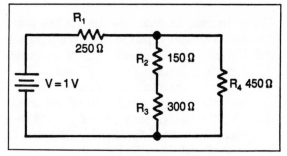

Fig. Ex2-5. Problem 20.

SINE WAVE ANALYSIS

Convert the information given to the unknown.

(21)   Given: 15 volts peak   Find: rms
(22)   Given: 33 volts rms   Find: peak to peak
(23)   Given: 60 volts peak   Find: average
(24)   Given: frequency   Find: period
        = 1500 Hz
(25)   Given: period   Find: frequency
        = 16.7 ms

TRANSFORMERS

Use the information given to find the unknown.
Note: turns ratios are stated as Pri:Sec.

(26)   Given: turns ratio = 8:1
                primary voltage = 40 volts
       Find: secondary volts
(27)   Given: turns ratio = 1:6
                primary voltage = 10 volts
       Find: secondary volts
(28)   Given: turns ratio = 12:1
                secondary voltage = 10 volts
       Find: primary voltage
(29)   Given: turns ratio = 1:5
                secondary voltage = 100 volts
       Find: primary voltage
(30)   Given: secondary power = 6 watts
                primary power = 8 watts
       Find: efficiency (percentage)

INDUCTORS AND CAPACITORS

All answers must have proper units.

(31) Determine the total inductance of two induc-
     tors connected in series; .5 H and 1 H.

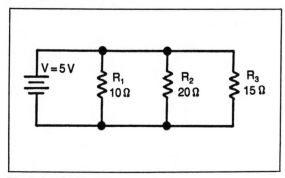

Fig. Ex2-2. Problem 17.

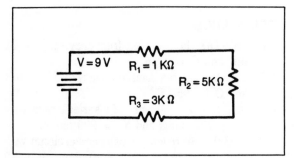

Fig. Ex2-3. Problem 18.

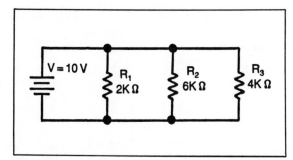

Fig. Ex2-4. Problem 19.

(32) Determine the total inductance of two inductors connected in parallel; 25 mH and 30 mH.

(33) Determine the total capacitance of two capacitors connected in series; 2 μF and 4 μF.

(34) Determine the total capacitance of two capacitors connected in parallel; 10 pF and 15 pF.

(35) Find the voltage across C_1 of the following capacitive voltage divider: V = 10 volts, C1 = 2 μF and C2 = 5 μF.

TIME CONSTANTS

(36) Determine the value of 1 time constant when; C = 2 μF and R = 3 kilohms.

(37) Determine the value of 1 time constant when; L = 25 mH and R = 50 ohms.

(38) Calculate the time for full charge; C = 50 μF and R = 200 ohms.

(39) Calculate the time for full charge; L = .5 mH and R = 2 kilohms.

(40) What percentage of full charge will be reached in 1 time constant?

REACTANCE, IMPEDANCE AND AC POWER

All answers must have correct units.

(41) Calculate X_C when; f = 2500 Hz and C = 4 μF.

(42) Calculate X_L when; f = 600 Hz and L = 150 mH.

(43) Calculate the impedance of a circuit with R = 250 ohms in series with X_L = 150 ohms.

(44) Calculate the impedance of a circuit with R = 500 ohms in parallel with X_C = 750 ohms.

(45) Which power is the largest in an ac circuit? (watts, VARs, VA)

RESONANCE

(46) Calculate the resonant frequency of; L = 24 mH and C = 4 μF.

(47) Calculate the resonant frequency of; L = 6 mH and C = .05 μF

(48) Find the net reactance of a series circuit with X_L = 175 ohms and X_C = 200 ohms.

(49) Find the net reactance of a parallel circuit with X_L = 50 ohms and X_C = 40 ohms, V = 10 volts.

(50) A series resonant circuit below resonance is net (L or C).

Appendix A:

Glossary

Alternating Current (ac). Current or voltage that periodically changes direction.

Ampere (A). Unit of measure of current, also know as amp.

Amplitude. The height of a waveform. It can be measured in; peak or peak to peak.

Analog. Constantly moving. When used in reference to meters, it is the type with a needle.

Apparent power. The total power of an ac circuit, unit of measure is VA.

Average. A measurement along a sine wave at 63.6% of the maximum amplitude.

Bandwidth. The group or band of frequencies with a response of 70.7% or better along the bell curve.

Bell curve. A curve showing the response of a filter circuit to various frequencies.

Capacitance (C). An electrical component with the ability to store a charge of electrons.

Competency. The ability to perform a task satisfactorily.

Conductor. Any substance that allows the flow of electricity.

Continuity. Continuously connected. When used in reference to an electric circuit, it is a complete current path.

Current (I). The flow of electricity, unit of measure is ampere.

Cycle. When a waveform repeats itself, unit of measure is hertz.

Dielectric. An insulator between the two plates of a capacitor.

Digital. Operates in a pulsating manner, either on or off. When used in reference to meters, it is the type that has a numerical display.

Direct current (dc). Current or voltage that stays always positive or always negative.

Electrolytic. A type of capacitor whose capacitance is formed only when the proper polarity is applied to the terminals.

Eddy current. An undesirable current flowing in the core of a transformer.

Electromagnetic. A magnet that is produced by electricity flowing through a coil of wire.

Electromotive force (EMF). Another name for voltage.

Electrons. The part of the atom that actually moves to produce electricity.

Engineering notation. A modification to scientific notation by replacing the powers of 10 with multiplier names.

Exponential notation. A modification to scientific notation by replacing the powers of 10 with the letter E.

Farad (F). Unit of measure of capacitance.

Flux. Another term used for a magnetic field.

Frequency. Cycles per second, CPS. Unit of measure is hertz.

Fuse. A device used to break a circuit when there is an excessive amount of current flow.

Giga. (G). A prefix used as a multiplier name in engineering notation to represent 10^9.

Ground. A point of zero volts.

Henry (H). Unit of measure of inductance.

Hertz (Hz). Unit of measure of frequency.

Hysteresis. The energy required to produce a magnetic field.

Impedance (Z). AC resistance, unit of measure is Ohms.

Inductance (L). An electrical component with the ability to produce a magnetic field.

Instantaneous. At a particular instant in time.

Insulator. Any substance that will not allow the flow of electricity.

Kilo- (k). A prefix used as a multiplier name in engineering notation to represent 10^3.

Mega- (M). A prefix used as a multiplier name in engineering notation to represent 10^6.

Micro- (μ). A prefix used as a multiplier name in engineering notation to represent 10^{-6}.

Milli- (m). A prefix used as a multiplier name in engineering notation to represent 10^{-3}.

Nano- (n). A prefix used as a multiplier name in engineering notation to represent 10^{-9}.

Nominal. A desired value of a component.

Ohm (Ω). Unit of measure of resistance.

Open circuit. A circuit that does not have a complete electrical path due to a break in the conductor.

Parallel circuit. A circuit connected in such a manner to allow the same voltage to be applied to all circuit components.

Parameter. The values of a circuit; resistance, current, voltage, power.

Peak. The maximum amplitude of a waveform in either the positive or negative direction.

Peak to Peak. The amplitude of a waveform measured from positive peak to negative peak.

Period. A measurement of the time of a wave to complete one cycle.

Phase angle (θ). The relationship between the reactive voltage (or current) and the circuit voltage (or current).

Phasor. A line drawn to represent the size and direction of an ac voltage or current.

Pico- (p). A prefix used as a multiplier name in engineering notation to represent 10^{-12}.

Potentiometer. A variable resistor.

Power (P). Work performed by electricity, unit of measure is watt.

Primary. The input to a transformer.

Reactance (X). The ac resistance of a capacitor (X_c) or inductor (X_L), unit of measure is ohm.

Reactive power. The ac power of a circuit associated with reactive component, unit of measure is VAR.

Relay. An electro-magnetic device used to operate a switch.

Resistance (R). The opposition to the flow of electricity, unit of measure is ohm.

Resonance. An electrical characteristic when $X_L = X_C$.

Rheostat. A variable resistor.

Rms. A measure along a waveform equal to 70.7% of the peak value.

Scientific notation. Writing of numbers using powers of 10.

Secondary. The output of a transformer.

Series circuit. A circuit connected in such a manner so the current must flow through each component equally.

Short. An electrical condition where the normal electrical path is shortened to allow the electricity to bypass the load, causing excessive current flow.

Solenoid. An electro-magnetic device used to move a metal bar.

Tera- (T). A prefix used as a multiplier name

in engineering notation to represent 10^{12}.

Time constant. The time required for a capacitor or inductor to charge to 63% of full charge.

True power. The ac power of a pure resistive component, unit of measure is watts.

Transformer. An electrical device that magnetically couples two coils of wire to allow electricity to pass from one coil to the other.

VA. Volt-ampere, unit of measure of the total power of an ac circuit.

VAR. Volt-ampere-reactive, unit of measure of the ac power of a reactive component.

Voltage (V or E). The force that causes electrical current flow, unit of measure is volt.

Wattage (W). Unit of measure of power, also called watts.

Appendix B:
Formulas

#1. Ohms's law to solve for voltage.

$$V = I \times R$$

#2. Ohm's law to solve for current.

$$I = \frac{V}{R}$$

#3. Ohm's law to solve for resistance.

$$R = \frac{V}{I}$$

#4. Power formula using the $V \times I$ relationship.

$$P = V \times I$$

#5. Power formula using I and R.

$$P = I^2 \times R$$

#6. Power formula using V and R.

$$P = \frac{V^2}{R}$$

#7. Total resistance in a series circuit.

$$R_T = R_1 + R_2 + R_3 + \ldots$$

#8. Voltage drops in a series circuit.

$$V_T = V_1 + V_2 + V_3 + \ldots$$

#9. IR drops in a series circuit.

$$V_T = IR_1 + IR_2 + IR_3 + \ldots$$

#10. Total power for all dc circuits.

$$P_T = P_{R1} + P_{R2} + P_{R3} + \ldots$$

#11. Total current in a parallel circuit.

$$I_T = I_1 + I_2 + I_3 + \ldots$$

#12. Total resistance in a parallel circuit, using total current (Ohm's law).

$$R_T = \frac{V}{I_T}$$

#13. Total resistance in a parallel circuit, reciprocal formula.

$$\frac{1}{R_T} = \frac{1}{R_1} + \frac{1}{R_2} + \frac{1}{R_3} + \ldots$$

#14. Short cut formula for total resistance with two resistors in parallel.

$$R_T = \frac{R_1 \times R_2}{R_1 + R_2}$$

#15. Short cut formula for total resistance with equal values of resistors in parallel.

$$R_T = \frac{R}{n} \quad \frac{\text{(resistance value)}}{\text{(number of resistors)}}$$

#16. Series inductors, no mutual inductance.

$$L_T = L_1 + L_2 + L_3 + \ldots$$

#17. Series inductors, aiding mutual inductance.

$$L_T = L_1 + L_2 + 2L_M$$

#18. Series inductors, opposing mutual inductance.

$$L_T = L_1 + L_2 - 2L_M$$

#19. Series inductors with aiding OR opposing mutual inductance.

$$L_T = L_1 + L_2 +/- 2L_M$$

#20. Inductors in parallel, reciprocal formula.

$$\frac{1}{L_T} = \frac{1}{L_1} + \frac{1}{L_2} + \frac{1}{L_3} + \ldots$$

#21. Instantaneous voltage of a sine wave.

$$V = V_{max} \times \sin \theta$$

#22. Peak to peak from peak.

$$\text{peak to peak} = 2 \times \text{peak}$$

#23. Rms from peak.

$$\text{Rms} = .707 \times \text{peak}$$

#24. Average from peak.

$$\text{Average} = .636 \times \text{peak}$$

#25. Frequency as the reciprocal of time.

$$f = \frac{1}{t}$$

#26. Transformer turns ratio.

$$Np : Ns \text{ (or)} \frac{Np}{Ns}$$

#27. Transformer voltage ratio.

$$\frac{Np}{Ns} = \frac{Vp}{Vs}$$

#28. Transformer current ratio.

$$\frac{Np}{Ns} = \frac{Is}{Ip}$$

#29. Transformer impedance ratio.

$$\frac{Zp}{Zs} = \frac{Np}{Ns}^2$$

#30. Efficiency.

$$\% \text{ eff} = \frac{P \text{ out}}{P \text{ in}} \times 100\%$$

#31. Capacitors in parallel.

$$C_T = C_1 + C_2 + C_3 + \ldots$$

#32. Capacitors in series.

$$\frac{1}{C_T} = \frac{1}{C_1} + \frac{1}{C_2} + \frac{1}{C_3} + \ldots$$

#33. Capacitive voltage divider.

$$V_{C1} = \frac{C_2}{(C_1 + C_2)} \times V$$

$$V_{C2} = \frac{C_1}{(C_1 + C_2)} \times V$$

#34. Instantaneous charging voltage.

$$\% \text{ of full charge} = (1 - e^{-T}) \times 100\%$$

#35. Instantaneous discharge voltage.

$$\% \text{ of full charge} = e^{-T} \times 100\%$$

#36. L/R time constant.

$$T = \frac{L}{R}$$

#37. RC time constant.

$$T = R \times C$$

#38. Inductive reactance, X_L.

$$X_L = 2 \, (\pi) \, f \, L$$

#39. Capacitive reactance, X_C.

$$X_C = \frac{1}{2 \, (\pi) \, f \, C}$$

#40. Hypotenuse of a right triangle.

a. Impedance triangle.

$$Z = \sqrt{R^2 + X^2}$$

b. Voltage triangle.

$$V_T = \sqrt{V_R^2 + V_X^2}$$

c. Current triangle.

$$I_T = \sqrt{I_R^2 + I_X^2}$$

#41. Phase angle, theta, θ.

$$\tan \theta = \frac{\text{opposite}}{\text{adjacent}}$$

a. Impedance triangle

$$\theta = \tan^{-1} \frac{X}{R}$$

b. Voltage triangle.

$$\theta = \tan^{-1} \frac{V_X}{V_R}$$

c. Current triangle.

$$\theta = \tan^{-1} \frac{I_X}{I_R}$$

#42. True power, watts.

$$P_R = I_R \times V_R$$

#43. Reactive power, VARs.

$$P_X = I_X \times V_X$$

#44. Apparent power, VA.

$$P_A = I_T \times V_T$$

#45. Power factor, PF.

$$PF = \cos \theta$$

#46. Degrees per division, from an oscilloscope.

$$\frac{\text{deg}}{\text{div}} = \frac{360 \text{ degrees}}{\# \text{ divisions}}$$

#47. Phase angle, from an oscilloscope.

$$0 = \# \text{ div} \times \frac{\text{deg}}{\text{div}}$$

#48. Frequency of resonance.

$$fr = \frac{1}{2 \, (\pi) \, \sqrt{L \, C}}$$

Appendix C:

Schematic Symbols

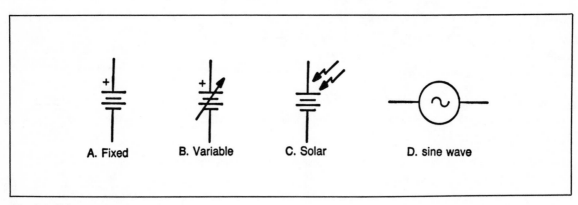

Fig. C-1. Voltage sources.

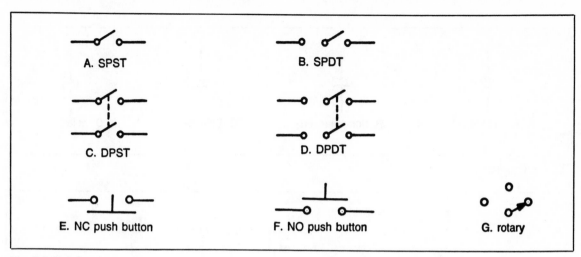

Fig. C-2. Switches.

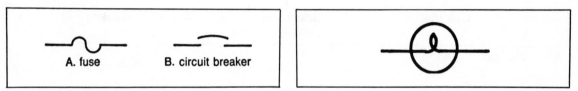

Fig. C-3. Current overload protection. Fig. C-4. Lamp.

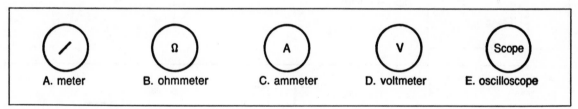

Fig. C-5. Test meters.

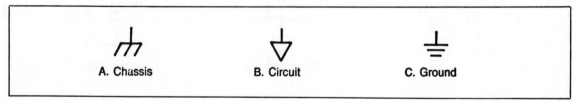

Fig. C-6. Circuit commons.

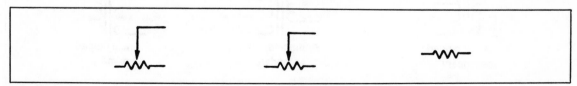

Fig. C-7. Resistors.

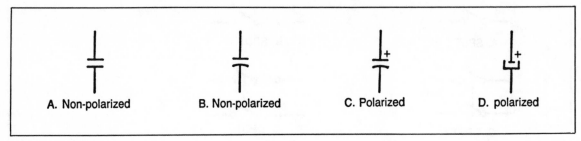

Fig. C-8. Capacitors.

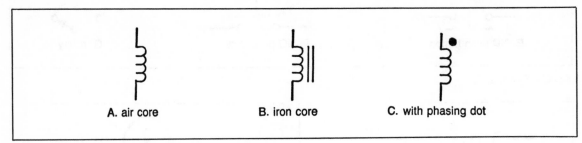

Fig. C-9. Inductors.

Fig. C-10. Relay.

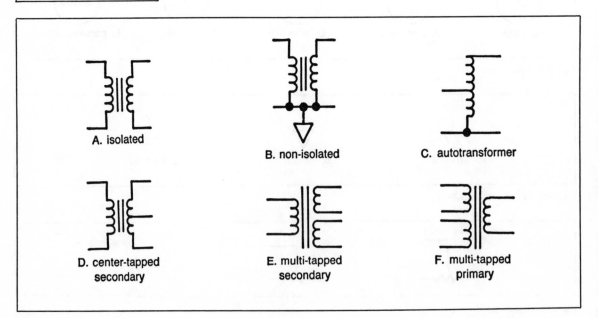

Fig. C-11. Transformers.

Appendix D:
Answers to Exams

CHAPTER 1. SAFETY TEST

(1)	a	(2)	b	(3)	b
(4)	b	(5)	d		
(6)	a	(7)	b	(8)	a
(9)	c	(10)	c		
(11)	c	(12)	a	(13)	b
(14)	a	(15)	c		
(16)	d	(17)	a	(18)	a
(19)	b	(20)	c		

CHAPTER 3. SHOP MATH PRETEST

(1) $\dfrac{2}{5}$ $\dfrac{3}{10}$ $\dfrac{1}{4}$ $\dfrac{1}{8}$

(2) $\dfrac{7}{8}$ $\dfrac{3}{4}$ $\dfrac{9}{16}$ $\dfrac{17}{32}$

(3) $1\dfrac{2}{2}$ (4) $15\dfrac{11}{15}$

(5) $23\dfrac{11}{18}$ (6) $\dfrac{3}{4}$

(7) $1\dfrac{1}{2}$ (8) $12\dfrac{1}{12}$

(9) 15 (10) 1
(11) increase (12) decrease
(13) 59.861 (14) 97.6
(15) 14.6102 (16) 7
(17) 32.15 (18) 643.875
(19) 113.06 (20) .7
(21) .0026 (22) 108.981
(23) .6 (24) 145.833
(25) 109.4 (26) .4
(27) .875 (28) 3.857
(29) 5.8 (30) 1.5
(31) 3.5

(32) $\dfrac{1}{3}$ (33) $\dfrac{3}{5}$

(34) $\dfrac{5}{8}$ (35) $\dfrac{3}{10}$

(36) $\dfrac{1}{4}$ (37) $\dfrac{2}{5}$

(38) $4\dfrac{3}{100}$ (39) $7\dfrac{3}{4}$

(40) -2 (41) 6
(42) 3   (43) -12
(44) -7 (45) -15
(46) $-.2$ (47) -18
(48) 2.1   (49) -4

(50) $-1\dfrac{3}{8}$ (51) -2

(52) $\dfrac{4}{15}$ (53) -1

(54) -11 (55) $\dfrac{1}{3}$

(56) 4   (57) 9
(58) -8 (59) 27
(60) 5   (61) 9
(62) 2.8   (63) .2
(64) .25 & 25%

(65) $\dfrac{1}{2}$ & 50%

(66) $\dfrac{1}{3}$ & .333

(67) $\dfrac{1}{8}$ & 12.5%

(68) .375 & 37.5%

(69) $\dfrac{1}{1000}$ & .001

(70) $\dfrac{2}{5}$ & 40%

(71) 105/95
(72) 283.5/256.5
(73) 363/297
(74) 564/376
(75) 1010/990
(76) 2310/2090
(77) 3850/3150
(78) 5635/4165

(79) 8874/8526
(80) 11000/9000
(81) $x = 5$ (82) $y = -10$
(83) $a = 5$ (84) $a = 2$
(85) $y = 2$ (86) $y = 20$
(87) $x = -8$ (88) $x = -2$
(89) $x = 0$ (90) $x = 2$
(91) $A = 75$ (92) $F = 68$
(93) $C = 4.44$ (94) $d = 125$
(95) $h = 16$ (96) $L = 60$
(97) $R = 60$ (98) $x = 1.33$
(99) $R_T = 18.5$
(100) $X_L = 31.4$

CHAPTER 3. PRACTICE FRACTIONS PROBLEMS:

(1) $\dfrac{11}{3}$ (2) $\dfrac{94}{7}$

(3) $\dfrac{81}{20}$ (4) $\dfrac{5}{3}$

(5) $\dfrac{35}{6}$ (6) $\dfrac{31}{8}$

(7) $\dfrac{13}{8}$ (8) $\dfrac{43}{10}$

(9) $\dfrac{68}{9}$ (10) $\dfrac{11}{4}$

(11) $4\dfrac{3}{4}$ (12) $6\dfrac{1}{6}$

(13) $9\dfrac{1}{3}$ (14) $4\dfrac{5}{8}$

(15) 4   (16) $1\dfrac{9}{25}$

(17) $5\dfrac{2}{9}$ (18) $2\dfrac{3}{4}$

(19) 9   (20) 4

(21) $\dfrac{7}{16}$ $\dfrac{1}{2}$ $\dfrac{5}{8}$ $\dfrac{3}{4}$

(22) $\dfrac{5}{64}$ $\dfrac{3}{32}$ $\dfrac{1}{8}$ $\dfrac{3}{16}$

(23) $\dfrac{4}{10}$ $\dfrac{12}{25}$ $\dfrac{1}{2}$ $\dfrac{51}{100}$

(24) $\dfrac{15}{16}$ 1 $1\dfrac{1}{64}$ $1\dfrac{1}{32}$

(25) $5\dfrac{3}{64}$ $5\dfrac{1}{4}$ $5\dfrac{1}{3}$ $5\dfrac{4}{9}$

CHAPTER 3. PRACTICE PROBLEMS: ARITHMETIC WITH FRACTIONS

(1) $\dfrac{1}{8}$ (2) 2

(3) $\dfrac{3}{4}$ (4) $\dfrac{1}{4}$

(5) $\dfrac{2}{5}$ (6) $2\ \dfrac{5}{8}$

(7) $1\dfrac{7}{30}$ (8) $\dfrac{11}{21}$

(9) 4   (10) $\dfrac{2}{7}$

(11) $2\dfrac{2}{3}$ (12) $1\dfrac{3}{4}$

(13) $9\dfrac{2}{7}$ (14) $\dfrac{1}{3}$

(15) $5\dfrac{13}{30}$ (16) $5\dfrac{6}{7}$

(17) $\dfrac{27}{35}$ (18) $\dfrac{5}{16}$

(19) $1\dfrac{3}{8}$ (20) $\dfrac{2}{3}$

CHAPTER 3. PRACTICE PROBLEMS: DECIMALS

(1) 14.99   (2) .3

(3) 1.2   (4) 3.21
(5) 10.37   (6) .09
(7) .0215   (8) 6.2
(9) 55.712   (10) 4.43
(11) .006   (12) .52
(13) 39.962   (14) 91.091
(15) 2040   (16) .000000606
(17) .796   (18) 31,847
(19) 318.47   (20) 10.6
(21) .375   (22) .4
(23) .1875   (24) 2.333
(25) 5.125

(26) $1\dfrac{3}{10}$ (27) $\dfrac{2}{3}$

(28) $\dfrac{9}{1000}$ (29) $\dfrac{4}{10}$

(30) $\dfrac{5}{16}$

CHAPTER 3. PRACTICE PROBLEMS: PERCENT TOLERANCE

(1) 105/95   (2) 517/423
(3) 1032/688   (4) 1100/900
(5) 1725/1275   (6) 2222/2178
(7) 3366/3234   (8) 4935/4465
(9) 7480/6120   (10) 11,000/9,000

CHAPTER 3. PRACTICE PROBLEMS: POSITIVE AND NEGATIVE NUMBERS

(1) 27   (2) −7
(3) −2   (4) −12
(5) 1   (6) −6
(7) −8   (8) −9
(9) 9   (10) 20
(11) −3   (12) 4
(13) 8   (14) −10
(15) −42   (16) 40
(17) 0   (18) −9
(19) −4   (20) 2
(21) +   (22) +
(23) +   (24) +
(25) −   (26) −

(27) − (28) −
(29) + (30 −

CHAPTER 3. PRACTICE PROBLEMS: SOLVING EQUATIONS

(1) x = 5 (2) x = 4
(3) y = −10 (4) y = −4
(5) a = 5 (6) a = 1
(7) a = 2

(8) $x = \dfrac{1}{4}$

(9) y = 2 (10) x = 9
(11) y = 20 (12) y = 1
(13) x = 25 (14) x = 2
(15) y = 1

CHAPTER 3. PRACTICE PROBLEMS: FORMULAS

(1) I = 4 (2) R = 5
(3) P = 500 (4) W = 2500
(5) R = 40 (6) I = 5
(7) $R_T = 35$ (8) $R_1 = 250$
(9) $R_T = 7.1$ (10) $R_2 = 30$
(11) $R_T = 20$ (12) $R_1 = 200$
(13) $X_L = 125.6$ (14) f = 60
(15) $X_C = 1000$

CHAPTER 3. SHOP MATH COMPETENCY TEST

(1) $\dfrac{11}{20}$ $\dfrac{3}{5}$ $\dfrac{7}{10}$ $\dfrac{12}{15}$

(2) $\dfrac{2}{3}$ $\dfrac{5}{6}$ $\dfrac{11}{12}$ $\dfrac{23}{24}$

(3) $3\dfrac{1}{6}$ (4) $7\dfrac{3}{8}$

(5) $\dfrac{31}{32}$ (6) $\dfrac{1}{2}$

(7) $37\dfrac{1}{3}$ (8) $2\dfrac{1}{8}$
(9) 70 (10) $\dfrac{10}{21}$
(11) decrease (12) increase
(13) 50.141 (14) 119.7
(15) 15.9103 (16) 8
(17) 41.23 (18) 75.625
(19) 555.555 (20) .9
(21) .0029 (22) 18.981
(23) .8 (24) 18.62
(25) 84.7875 (26) .6
(27) .625 (28) 3.7
(29) 4.167 (30) 1.33
(31) 2.33

(32) $\dfrac{2}{3}$ (33) $\dfrac{3}{10}$

(34) $\dfrac{5}{3}$ (35) $\dfrac{3}{10}$

(36) $6\dfrac{3}{4}$ (37) $6\dfrac{1}{2}$

(38) $4\dfrac{1}{20}$ (39) $5\dfrac{1}{4}$

(40) −4 (41) 20
(42) 4 (43) −18
(44) −7 (45) −42
(46) .2 (47) −72
(48) 2.2 (49) −5

(50) $1\dfrac{1}{2}$ (51) $-\dfrac{1}{2}$

(52) $\dfrac{1}{3}$ (53) $\dfrac{1}{4}$

(54) −11 (55) 126

(56) $-\dfrac{1}{6}$

(57) 0 (58) −1
(59) 80 (60) .75 & 75%

(61) $\dfrac{1}{4}$ & 25%

(62) $\dfrac{2}{3}$ & .666

(63) $\dfrac{1}{8}$ & 12.5%

(64) .375 & 37.5%

(65) $\dfrac{1}{1000}$ & .001

(66) $\dfrac{3}{5}$ & 60%

(67) $\dfrac{1}{200}$ & .005

(68) $\dfrac{2}{10}$ & 20%

(69) $\dfrac{1}{8}$ & .075

(70) $\dfrac{21}{200}$ & .105

(71) 101/99
(72) 275.4/264.6
(73) 346.5/313.5
(74) 517/423
(75) 816/544
(76) 1100/900
(77) 6325/4675
(78) 8619/7790
(79) 11500/8500
(80) 10.1/9.9

(81) $x = 4$	(82) $y = -17$
(83) $a = 8$	(84) $a = 8$
(85) $x = 3$	(86) $x = -4$
(87) $y = 10$	(88) $a = -25$
(89) $x = -8$	(90) $x = -2$
(91) $A = 72$	(92) $F = -40$
(93) $C = 0$	(94) $d = 110$
(95) $h = 16$	(96) $L = 30$
(97) $R_T = 7.5$	(98) $R_T = 4.167$
(99) $X_C = .637$	(100) $X_L = 62.8$

CHAPTER 4. PRACTICE PROBLEMS: ROUNDING NUMBERS

(1) 6410	(2) 4720
(3) 5350	(4) 9880
(5) 103,000	(6) 340,000
(7) 120,000	(8) 209,000
(9) 327	(10) 452
(11) 1000	(12) 224
(13) 56.3	(14) 69.5
(15) 10.6	(16) 25.9
(17) 1.06	(18) 3.53
(19) 5.99	(20) 8.91
(21) .0036	(22) .00268
(23) .00556	(24) .00667
(25) .00333	(26) .01
(27) .9	(28) .87
(29) .505	(30) .96

CHAPTER 4. PRACTICE PROBLEMS: WRITING IN SCIENTIFIC NOTATION

(1) $8.76 \times 10^5 = 8.76E5$
(2) $1.03 \times 10^9 = 1.03E9$
(3) $4.3 \times 10^4 = 4.3E4$
(4) $2.5 \times 10^1 = 2.5E1$
(5) $6.9 \times 10^0 = 6.9E0$
(6) $3 \times 10^{-3} = 3E-3$
(7) $3.2 \times 10^{-6} = 3.2E-6$
(8) $4.5 \times 10^{-5} = 4.5E-5$
(9) $1.59 \times 10^{-9} = 1.59E-9$
(10) $5 \times 10^{-1} = 5E-1$
(11) $1.2 \times 10^9 = 1.2E9$
(12) $5.32 \times 10^6 = 5.32E6$
(13) $3.5 \times 10^{-2} = 3.5E-2$
(14) $4.5 \times 10^{-2} = 4.5E-2$
(15) $6.7 \times 10^1 = 6.7E1$
(16) $2.5 \times 10^1 = 2.5E1$
(17) $3.5 \times 10^{-5} = 3.5E-5$
(18) $2 \times 10^{-7} = 2E-7$
(19) $5.6 \times 10^{-8} = 5.6E-8$
(20) $9.5 \times 10^0 = 9.5E0$

(21) 480,000	(22) 850,000
(23) 3,000	(24) .00025
(25) 250	(26) .01
(27) .055	(28) 68,000,000
(29) .000000000025	(30) 10

CHAPTER 4. PRACTICE PROBLEMS: CONVERTING ENGINEERING NOTATION

(1) 5,600 kΩ & 5.6 MΩ

(2) 273 kHz & .273 MHz

(3) 2,900,000 mW & 2.9 kW

(4) 15,000 mA & .015 kA

(5) 3.5 mV & 3500 μV

(6) 125 mH & 125,000 μH

(7) .05 μF & 50 nF

(8) 8.7 μs & .0087 ms

(9) .25 W & .00025 kW

(10) .0015 kV & 1.5 V

(11) 55 μA & .000055 A

(12) .000000001 s & .001 μs

(13) 630,000 Hz & .630 MHz

(14) 250 mW & 250,000,000 W

(15) .75 A & 750 mA

(16) 5,000 mV & 5 V

(17) .025 mV & 25,000 nV

(18) 750 nA & .00000075 A

(19) .05 μF & 50,000 pF

(20) .00000000005 s & .00005 μs

(21) .150 nF & .000150 μF

(22) 75,000 kΩ & .075 GΩ

(23) 3,000 Hz & 3 kHz

(24) 1,200,000 MW & 1,200,000,000,000 W

(25) 5,000 MHz & 5 GHz

(5) 640

(6) 231

(7) .714

(8) .0909

(9) .667

(10) .333

(11) 8.76×10^5

(12) 3.2×10^3

(13) 9.8×10^8

(14) 1.2×10^6

(15) 3.5×10^{-7}

(16) 1.89×10^{-4}

(17) 2×10^{-4}

(18) 1.8×10^0

(19) 2.5×10^6

(20) 3.6×10^{-8}

(21) 2.5E5

(22) 1.8E3

(23) 6.8E7

(24) 5.6E2

(25) 2.5E-10

(26) 3.57E-6

(27) 1.3E-3

(28) 9.8E-4

(29) 5.6E3

(30) 4.7E-3

(31) 25 kV

(32) 1250 mA

(33) .0255 W

(34) 3500 Hz

(35) 15 μH

(36) .680 mH

(37) 1,500,000,000 pF

(38) 37 Megohms

(39) 82 μV

(40) .96 mA

(41) 13.8 kilohms

(42) 740 ohms

(43) 26.5 MW

(44) 125 μV

(45) 500 V

(46) 15 V

(47) 2.5 W

(48) 8 mA

(49) 5 kilohms

(50) 3 kV

CHAPTER 4. PRACTICE PROBLEMS: ARITHMETIC OPERATIONS

(1) 5.5 kilohms

(2) 1100 ohms

(3) 48.1 MW

(4) 100 V

(5) 1.75 A

(6) 3.3 mW

(7) .45 mH

(8) .011 μF

(9) 10 kV

(10 5 μF

(11) 150 V

(12) 7.5 V

(13) 60 V

(14) .75 W

(15) 500 μW

(16) 4 mA

(17) 2.5 kilohms

(18) .5A

(19) 100 kV

(20) 10 W

CHAPTER 4. ENGINEERING NOTATION COMPETENCY TEST

(1) 104,000

(2) 556,000

(3) 321

(4) 598

CHAPTER 5. PRACTICE PROBLEMS: RESISTOR COLOR CODE

(All answers in ohms).

(1) 100

(2) 270

(3) 1.5 k

(4) 2.2 k

(5) 3.9 k

(6) 5.6 k

(7) 10 k

(8) 15 k

(9) 47 k

(10) 82 k

(11) 120 k

(12) 680 k

(13) 3.3 M

(14) 10

(15) 1

(16) brown-red-brown

(17) orange-orange-brown

(18) orange-white-brown

(19) brown-black-red
(20) brown-grey-red
(21) red-violet-red
(22) yellow-violet-red
(23) blue-grey-red
(24) grey-red-red
(25) brown-black-orange
(26) brown-red-orange
(27) brown-black-green
(28) brown-grey-blue
(29) brown-black-black
(30) yellow-black-silver-gold
(31) 150+/−10% & 165/135
(32) 220+/−5% & 231/209
(33) 470+/−20% & 564/376
(34) 560+/−10% & 616/504
(35) 3.3 k+/−5% & 3465/3135
(36) 6.8 k+/−20% & 8160/5440
(37) 12 k+/−10% & 13200/10800
(38) 18 k+/−5% & 18900/17100
(39) 1.2 M+/−20% & 1.44 M/.96M
(40) 39 M+/−10% & 42.9 M/35.1M
(41) brown-grey-black-gold
(42) brown-grey-brown-silver
(43) red-violet-brown-no color
(44) blue-grey-brown-gold
(45) orange-white-red-silver
(46) grey-red-red-silver
(47) red-red-orange-silver
(48) orange-orange-orange-gold
(49) red-violet-green-gold
(50) brown-green-blue-no color

CHAPTER 5. DC CIRCUIT COMPONENTS COMPETENCY TEST

(1) 1.5 volts
(2) (See Fig. D-1.)
(3) (See Fig. D-1.)
(4) low
(5) high
(6) 18 AWG
(7) 14 AWG
(8) 0
(9) short
(10) infinite
(11) open

(12) closed
(13) (See Fig. D-1.)
(14) (See Fig. D-1.)
(15) (See Fig. D-1.)
(16) (See Fig. D-1.)
(17) (See Fig. D-1.)
(18) (See Fig. D-1.)
(19) fuse
(20) (See Fig. D-1.)
(21) (See Fig. D-1.)
(22) (See Fig. D-1.)
(23) .47 kilohms
(24) 33,000 ohms
(25) .15 megohms
(26) 8600 ohms
(27) 4700 ohms
(28) 1200 kilohms
(29) 18,000,000 ohms
(30) .22 megohms
(31) 100 ohms
(32) 2.2 kilohms
(33) 56 kilohms
(34) 680 kilohms
(35) 3.9 megohms
(36) 150+/−10% & 165/135
(37) 4.7 k+/−5% & 4935/4465
(38) 33 k+/−20% & 39.6 k/26.4 k
(39) 100 k+/−10% & 110 k/90 k
(40) 82 M+/−10%& 90.2 M/73.8 M
(41) brown-black-black-silver
(42) red-violet-brown-gold
(43) orange-orange-brown-no color
(44) brown-black-red-silver
(45) brown-grey-red-gold
(46) yellow-violet-red-silver
(47) blue-grey-red-no color
(48) brown-black-orange-gold
(49) brown-black-green-silver
(50) (See Fig. D-1.)

CHAPTER 6. OHMMETER WRITTEN COMPETENCY TEST

(1) A. infinity   B. 20 ohms
     C. 9 ohms   D. 4 ohms
     E. 0 ohms
(2) A. 100 ohms   B. 40 ohms

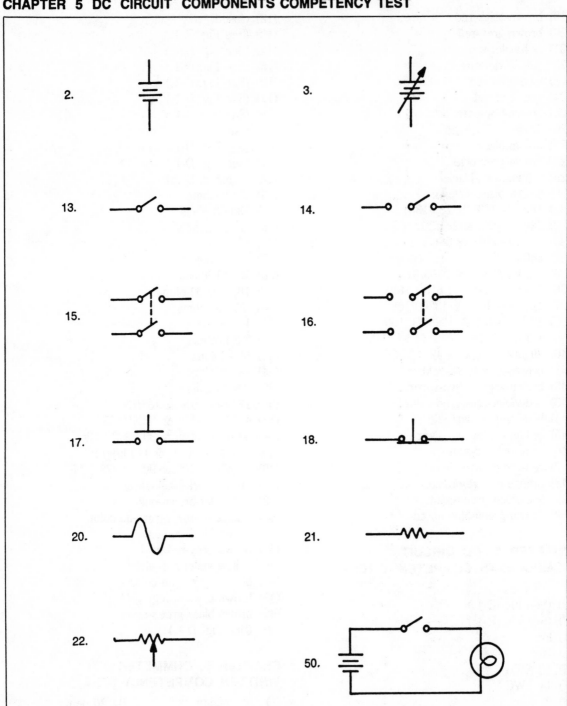

C. 15 ohms D. 7.5 ohms
E. .5 ohms
(3) A. 7000 ohms B. 2500 ohms
C. 1000 ohms D. 560 ohms
E. 100 ohms
(4) A. infinity B. 600 kohms
C. 180 kohms D. 71 kohms
E. 25 kohms
(5) A. 5000 ohms B. 3000 ohms
C. 1700 ohms D. 800 ohms
E. 350 ohms
(6) bad (open) (7) good
(8) 0 ohms (9) infinity
(10) 150 ohms
(11) 495 kohms or
infinity
(12) 70 kohms (13) 1 kohms
(14) 0
(15) Short the leads together and adjust for zero.
(16) no (120+/−5%, min 114)
(17) yes (3900+/−10%, max 4290)
(18) no (47,000+/−10%, min 42,300)
(19) no (10+/−5%, min 9.5)
(20) no (220+/−10%, max 242)
(21) 1200 kilohms
(22) 33,000 ohms
(23) 1.5 volts
(24) 500 milliwatts
(25) 250 microamps
(26) (See Fig. D-2.)
(27) (See Fig. D-2.)
(28) (See Fig. D-2.)
(29) (See Fig. D-2.)
(30) (See Fig. D-2.)

CHAPTER 7. PRACTICE PROBLEMS: OHM'S LAW

(1) 20 V (2) 125 V
(3) 30 V (4) 22 V
(5) 4 A (6) .10 A
(7) .3 A (8) 2 mA
(9) 20 Ω (10) 200 Ω
(11) 5 kΩ (12) 200 Ω
(13) 50 V (14) 45 V
(15) .3 mA

CHAPTER 6 OHMMETER WRITTEN COMPETENCY TEST

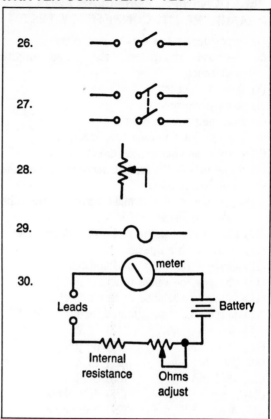

CHAPTER 7. PRACTICE PROBLEMS: OHM'S LAW AND POWER FORMULAS

(1) V = 30 V and P = 450 W
(2) V = 2.5 V and R = 1.25 Ω
(3) R = 10 kΩ and P = 1 W
(4) I = 50 A and P = 12.5 kW
(5) I = 6.67 mA and R = 2250 Ω
(6) V = 3.16 V and I = 3.16 mA
(7) V = 250 V and P = 6.25 W
(8) V = 12.5 V and R = 6250 Ω
(9) R = 10 kΩ and P = .25 W
(10) I = 2 mA and 10 mW
(11) I = 6 mA and P = 36 mW
(12) R = 4 ohms and I = 3 amps
(13) P = 12 W and R = 3 ohms
(14) R = 240 ohms and I = .5 A
(15) I = .0638 mA and P = .19 mW

CHAPTER 7. DC CIRCUITS: RELATIONSHIPS, FORMULAS AND MEASUREMENTS COMPETENCY TEST

(1) opposition to the flow of electricity
(2) electrical driving force also called potential difference
(3) flow of electricity
(4) work performed
(5) from negative to positive
(6) current flows in only one direction
(7) current flow alternates direction
(8) if one side of the formula increases, the other side increases
(9) if one side of the formula increases, the other side decreases
(10) the positive and negative of a dc voltage
(11) meter with a needle
(12) changes the range of a voltmeter
(13) changes the range of an ammeter
(14) internal resistance of an ohmmeter
(15) percent accuracy, stated for full scale

(16) 600 V	(17) .1 W
(18) 600 ohms	(19) 60 μW
(20) 20 mA	(21) 14.4 W
(22) .365 mA	(23) 3.16 V
(24) 2 V	(25) 400 ohms
(26) 4 A	(27) 150 ohms
(28) 50 μW	(29) 120 V
(30) 20 μA	
(31) (See Fig. D-3.)	(32) (See Fig. D-3.)
(33) (See Fig. D-3.)	(34) (See Fig. D-3.)
(35) (See Fig. D-3.)	(36) 4.4 V
(37) 6 V	(38) 8 V
(39) .14 mA	(40) .3 mA
(41) .5 mA	(42) 1.75 V
(43) 2.25 V	(44) 2.5 V
(45) 0 mA	(46) 100 mA
(47) 300 mA	(48) 4000 ohms
(49) 2000 ohms	(50) 1000 ohms

CHAPTER 9. PRACTICE PROBLEMS: SERIES CIRCUITS

(1) I_T = .2 A, R_T = 250 ohms, V_{R1} = 20 V, V_{R2} = 30 V, P_{R1} = 4 W, P_{R2} – 6 W
(2) IT = 50 mA, R_T – 300 ohms, V_{R1} = V_{R2} =

V_{R3} = 5 V, P_{R1} = P_{R2} = P_{R3} .25 W
(3) I_T = 50 mA, R_T = 280 ohms
(4) I_T = 3 A, V = 150 V
(5) I_T = 1.5 A, R_T = 80 ohms, V = 120 V
(6) R_T = 2.5 kΩ, R_1 = 1.5 kΩ
(7) R_T = 800 ohms, R_3 = 100 ohms, V = 80 V
(8) I_T = 25 mA, R_2 = 320 ohms, V_{R1} = 4 V
(9) I_T = 400 mA, V = 32 V
(10) I_T = 2 A, R_2 = 20 ohms, V = 120 V

CHAPTER 9. PRACTICE PROBLEMS: PARALLEL CIRCUITS

(1) R_T = 13.6 ohms, I_T = 1.83 A, I_A = 1 A, I_B = .5 A, I_C = .33 A
(2) R_T = 513 ohms, I_T = 29 mA
(3) R_T = 40 ohms
(4) R_T = 125 ohms
(5) R_3 = 1500 ohms
(6) R_4 = 33.3 ohms
(7) R_T = 200 ohms, I_T = 100 mA, R_3 = 1000 ohms
(8) R_T = 60 ohms, I_A = .333 A, I_B = .2 A, I_C = .133 A
(9) R_T = 200 ohms, I_A = 50 mA, I_B = 16.7 mA, I_C = I_D = 33.3 mA
(10) R_T = 9.1 ohms, I_A = 1 A, I_B = .364 A, I_C = .637 A, I_D = .228 A, I_E = .409 A, I_F = .228 A, I_G = .182 A

CHAPTER 9. PRACTICE PROBLEMS: COMPLEX CIRCUITS

(1) R_T = 2.2 kΩ, I_T = 20 mA, V_{R1} = 20 V, V_{R2} = 24 V, V_{R3} = 24 V, I_{R2} = 12 mA, I_{R3} = 8 mA
(2) R_T = 4 kΩ, I_T = 5 mA, V_{R1} = 5 V, V_{R2} = 1.5 V, V_{R3} = 1.5 V, V_{R4} = 13.5 V, I_{R2} = 2.21 mA, I_{R3} = 2.68 mA
(3) R_T = 50 ohms, I_T = 100 mA, V_{R1} = 1 V, V_{R2} = V_{R3} = .5 V, V_{R4} = 1 V, V_{R5} = V_{R6} = .5 V, V_{R7} = V_{R8} 1 V, I_{R2} = I_{R5} = 50 mA
(4) R_T = 315 ohms, I_T = 31.8 mA, I_{R1} = 31.8 mA, I_{R2} = 21.2 mA, I_{R3} 10.6 mA, I_{R4} = 31.8 mA, I_{R5} = 20 mA, I_{R6} = 8 mA, I_{R7} = 4 mA, V_{R1} = 3.18 V, V_{R2} = V_{R3} = 5.72 V, V_{R4} = .7 V, V_{R5} = V_{R6} = V_{R7} = .4 V
(5) R_T = 133 ohms, I_T = 75 mA, I_{R2} = 50 mA, I_{R3}

31.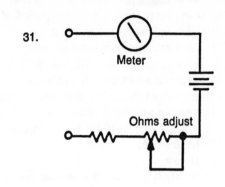

32.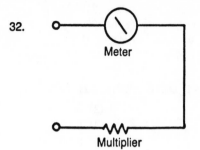

33.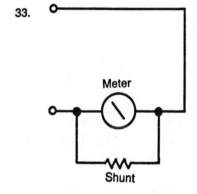

34.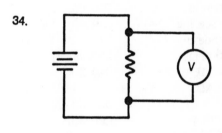

35.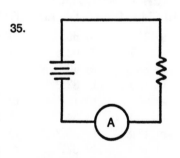

= 25 mA, V_{R1} = 7.5 V, V_{R2} = 2.5 V, V_{R3} = 2.5 V

(6) R_T = 16.9 ohms

(7) R_T = 100 ohms

(8) R_T = 1 kΩ

(9) R_T = 275 ohms, I_T = 200 mA

(10) R_T = 2520 ohms, I_T = 39.7 mA

CHAPTER 9. DC CIRCUIT ANALYSIS COMPETENCY TEST

(1) b   (2) b   (3) a   (4) a

(5) b   (6) a   (7) a   (8) d

(9) b   (10) a   (11) 50 ohms

(12) .2 A

(13) 8 V   (14) 2 V

(15) .2 A   (16) 32.4 ohms

(17) .525 A   (18) .142 A

(19) .17 A   (20) .213 A

(21) 40 ohms   (22) .25 A

(23) 5 V   (24) 5 V

(25) 3.125 V

EXAM #1. DC BUILDING BLOCKS

(1) d   (2) b

(3) b   (4) b

(5) c   (6) 5,600 kHz

(7) 15,000 mA   (8) 3.5 mV

(9) .250 W   (10) .025 mV

(11) 10 ohms   (12) 270 ohms

(13) 5,600 ohms   (14) 47 kΩ

(15) 680 kΩ (16) (See Fig. D-4)

(17) (See Fig. D-4)   (18) (See Fig. D-4)

(19) (See Fig. D-4)   (20) (See Fig. D-4)

(21) 0 ohms   (22) infinity

(23) 4 kΩ (24) 2 kΩ

(25) 1 kΩ (26) 20 V

(27) 4 A   (28) 20 ohms

(29) 125 V   (30) 2 mA

(31) 2 W   (32) 450 W

(33) 2.5 V   (34) 6.67 mA

(35) 1.25 ohms   (36) (See Fig. D-4)

(37) (See Fig. D-4)   (38) (See Fig. D-4)

(39) 3.5 divisions   (40) 1.75 V

(41) 2.25 V   (42) 2.5 V

(43) 0 mA   (44) 100 mA

(45) 300 mA   (46) current

(47) voltage   (48) 1000 ohms

(49) 2 A   (50) 4 kΩ

CHAPTER 10. PRACTICE PROBLEMS: INDUCTANCE

(1) 1200 μH   (2) 90 mH

(3) 470 mH   (4) 3.75 mH

(5) 66.7 mH   (6) 200 mH

(7) 220 mH   (8) 180 mH

(9) 220 mH   (10) 180 mH

CHAPTER 10. MAGNETISM AND INDUCTANCE COMPETENCY TEST

(1) The lines of force from north to south.

(2) Invisible field surrounding a magnet.

(3) Left-over magnetism.

(4) Holds magnetism for a short period of time.

(5) Holds magnetism for a long period of time.

(6) Opposes magnetic lines of force.

(7) Electricity through a coil of wire.

(8) To concentrate the magnetic field.

(9) Electro-magnet that moves a bar.

(10) Electro-magnet that operates a switch.

(11) Voltage produced within its own coil.

(12) Voltage produced by a magnetic field.

(13) Inductance.

(14) Henry.

(15) Ability to produce a magnetic field with electricity.

(16) Separate magnetic fields interact.

(17) Schematic symbol showing polarity of magnetic field.

(18) $L_T = L_1 + L_2 + L_3 + \ldots$

(19) $\dfrac{1}{L_T} = \dfrac{1}{L_1} + \dfrac{1}{L_2} + \dfrac{1}{L_3} + \ldots$

(20) Unit of inductance.

(21) 130 mH   (22) 800 mH

(23) 13 H   (24) 42.8 mH

(25) 50 mH

CHAPTER 11. PRACTICE PROBLEMS: UNITS OF AMPLITUDE

(1)   a) 21.2   b) 60   c) 19.1

(2)   a) 200   b) 63.6   c) 70.7

(3)   a) 28.3   b) 40   c) 25.4

(4)   a) 130   b) 82.7   c) 91.9

(5)   a) 99   b) 198   c) 63

(6)   a) 10.8   b) 34   c) 17

(7)   a) 17.8   b) 25.2   c) 50.3

(8)   a) 189   b) 377   c) 133

(9)   a) 120   b) 240   c) 76.5

(10)   a) 140   b) 44.5   c) 49.5

(11) p-to-p = 40, peak = 20, rms = 14.1, Avg = 12.7

(12) peak = 35, p-to-p = 70, rms = 24.7, Avg = 22.3

(13) p-to-p = 400, peak = 200, rms = 141, Avg = 127

16.

17.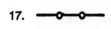

18.

19.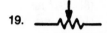

20.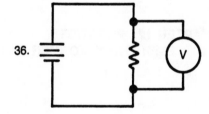

36.

37.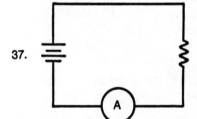

38.

(14) peak = 60, p-to = 120, rms = 42.4, Avg = 38.2

(15) p-to-p = 80, peak = 40, rms = 28.3, Avg = 25.4

CHAPTER 11. PRACTICE PROBLEMS: UNITS OF TIME

(1) .1 s	(2) .02 s
(3) .0167	(4) .01 s
(5) 2 ms	(6) 1.43 ms
(7) 1 ms	(8) .667 ms
(9) .133 ms	(10) .1 ms
(11) 83.3 μs	(12) 66.6 μs
(13) 50 μs	(14) 20 μs
(15) 13.3 μs	(16) 10 μs
(17) 2 μs	(18) 1 μs
(19) .667 μs	(20) .01 μs
(21) .2 Hz	(22) .1 Hz
(23) 10 Hz	(24) 2 Hz
(25) 100 Hz	(26) 50 Hz
(27) 20 Hz	(28) 1000 Hz
(29) 333 Hz	(30) 200 Hz
(31) 66.7 Hz	(32) 60 Hz
(33) 50 Hz	(34) 16.7 Hz
(35) 10 Hz	(36) 10 kHz
(37) 100 kHz	(38) 50 kHz
(39) 200 kHz	(40) 1 MHz

CHAPTER 11. SINE WAVE ANALYSIS COMPETENCY TEST

(1) Waveform periodically changes direction.
(2) All positive or all negative.
(3) 120 volts/60 Hz.
(4) At an instant in time.
(5) Height of the waveform.
(6) Maximum in one direction.
(7) Maximum swing in both directions.
(8) peak × .707
(9) peak × .636
(10) From 0 to 360
(11) When the wave repeats itself.
(12) Time of one cycle.
(13) Number of cycles in one second.
(14) Cycles per second.
(15) Distance one cycle travels in air.
(16) a) 17.7   b) 50

(17) a) 9.54	b) 10.6
(18) a) 20	b) 14.4
(19) a) 84.8	b) 76.3
(20) a) 170	b) 340
(21) a) 63.6	b) 40.5
(22) a) 23.6	b) 16.7
(23) a) 283	b) 142
(24) a) 70.7	b) 63.6
(25) a) 56.6	b) 50.9
(26) 16.7 ms	
(27) 20 Hz	
(28) 5 ms	
(29) 1 kHz	
(30) .5 MHz	
(31) a) .6 V	b) 250 Hz
(32) a) .07 V	b) 8.3 MHz
(33) a) .2 V	b) 1 MHz
(34) a) 2.5 V	b) 36.3 KHz
(35) a) 5 V	b) 1.67 MHz
(36) a) .06 V	b) 50 kHz
(37) a) .05 V	b) 5 kHz
(38) a) 1 V	b) 12.5 kHz
(39) a) 20 V	b) 125 Hz
(40) a) .15 V	b) 12.5 kHz

CHAPTER 12. PRACTICE PROBLEMS: TRANSFORMER RATIOS

(1) 12 V, 1 A, down
(2) 120 V, .1 A, down
(3) 150 V, 1 A, up
(4) 119 V, .0043 A, up
(5) 1:4, 4 A, up
(6) 3:1, 81 V, down
(7) 2:1, .6A, down
(8) 1:5, 225 V, up
(9) 6:1, 6 A, down
(10) 1:20, 20 A, up

CHAPTER 12. PRACTICE PROBLEMS: POWER AND EFFICIENCY

(1) 4.25 W	(2) 4.8 mW
(3) 11.1 W	(4) 107 mW
(5) 90%	(6) 60%
(7) 66.7%	(8) 3.2 A
(9) 75%	(10) 80%

CHAPTER 12.
TRANSFORMERS COMPETENCY TEST

(1) Uses magnetism to pass voltage from input to output.
(2) Input.
(3) Output.
(4) Concentrates the magnetic field.
(5) Wire coupled through magnetism.
(6) Hysteresis or eddy currents.
(7) Turns of the primary as compared to turns of the secondary.
(8) Secondary has more turns than the primary.
(9) Secondary has fewer turns than the primary.
(10) How well it passes voltage.

(11) 10 V	(12) 108 V
(13) 60 V	(14) 20 V
(15) 5 A	(16) 2 mA
(17) .2 A	(18) 8 A
(19) 10:1	(20) 1:9
(21) 5.1 W	(22) 12.5 W
(23) 66.7%	(24) 90%
(25) 75%	

CHAPTER 13. PRACTICE
PROBLEMS: CAPACITANCE

(1) 4 μF
(2) 1015 pF
(3) .23 μF
(4) 141 μF
(5) 1500 μF
(6) C_T = .667 μF, V_{C1} = 6.7 V, V_{C2} = 3.3 V
(7) C_T = 3.33 pF, V_{C1} = 6.7 V, V_{C2} = 3.3 V
(8) C_T = .009 μF, V_{C1} = 4.5 V, V_{C2} = .5 V
(9) C_T = 5 μF, V_{C1} = 7.5 V, V_{C2} = 7.5 V
(10) C_T = .0667 μF, V_{C1} = 13.2 V, V_{C2} = 6.8 V

CHAPTER 13. PRACTICE
PROBLEMS: TIME CONSTANTS

(1)	a) 20 ms	b) 100 ms	c) .15 A
	d) 20 ms	e) 100 ms	f) 15 V
(2)	a) 2 ms	b) 10 ms	c) 15 mA
	d) .2 s	e) 1 s	f) .15 V
(3)	a) .2 s	b) 1 s	c) 1.5 A
	d) .2 ms	e) 1 ms	f) 15 kV
(4)	a) 5 μs	b) 25 μs	c) .75 mA
	d) 5 μs	e) 25 μs	f) 15 V

(5)	a) 30 ms	b) 150 ms	c) .12 A
	d) 6.67 μs	e) 33.3 μs	f) 54 kV
(6)	a) 5 ms	b) 25 ms	c) 12 V
	d) 5 ms	e) 25 ms	f) .12 A
(7)	a) 10 ms	b) 50 ms	c) 12 V
	d) 25 ms	e) 125 ms	f) 48 mA
(8)	a) .375 s	b) 1.8 s	c) 15 V
	d) .15 s	e) .75 s	f) 15 mA
(9)	a) 10 ms	b) 50 ms	c) 15 V
	d) 20 μs	e) 100 μs	f) .75 A
(10)	a) 1.25 s	b) 6.25 s	c) 1.5 V
	d) .5 ms	e) 2.5 ms	f) 1.5 A

CHAPTER 13. CAPACITORS AND
TIME CONSTANTS COMPETENCY TEST

(1) farad
(2) the insulator between the two plates of a capacitor
(3) 63% of full charge
(4) 5 time constants
(5) shows the charge and discharge for any circuit

(6) $\dfrac{1}{C_T} = \dfrac{1}{C_1} + \dfrac{1}{C_2} + \ldots$

(7) $C_T = C_1 + C_2 + \ldots$

(8) $V_{C1} = \dfrac{C_2}{C_1 + C_2} \times V$

(9) $V_{C2} = \dfrac{C_1}{C_1 + C_2} \times V$

(10) $T = \dfrac{L}{R}$

(11) $T = R \times C$

(12) $t = \dfrac{1}{f}$

(13) $f = \dfrac{1}{t}$

(14) $\frac{1}{2}$ × period

(15) $\frac{1}{2}$ × period

(16) Two conductors separated by an insulator.
(17) increase
(18) Electrons gather on one plate and vacate the other during charge and equalize themselves during discharge.
(19) voltage
(20) current

(21) 7 μF		(22) 90 μF	
(23) .08 μF		(24) 135 pF	
(25) 1.22 μF		(26) 1.43 μF	
(27) 10 μF		(28) 5880 pF	
(29) 6.67 pF		(30) .18 μF	

(31) $V_{C1} = 6$ V, $V_{C2} = 4$ V
(32) $V_{C1} = 10$ V, $V_{C2} = 5$ V
(33) $V_{C1} = 11.4$ V, $V_{C2} = 8.57$ V
(34) $V_{C1} = 15$ V, $V_{C2} = 10$ V
(35) $V_{C1} = 20$ V, $V_{C2} = 10$ V

(36) 4.16 ms	(37) 20.8 ms
(38) .167 A	(39) 12.5 μs
(40) 33,400 V	(41) .101 s
(42) .505 s	(43) 15 V
(44) 10 ms	(45) .75 A

(46) a) .1 ms b) .1 ms
(47) a) 20 μs b) 100 μs
(48) medium
(49) refer to Fig. 13-17
(50) refer to Fig. 13-17

CHAPTER 14. PRACTICE PROBLEMS: REACTANCE

(1)	628 Ω	(2)	15.9 mH
(3)	3.2 mH	(4)	1990 Hz
(5)	5970 Hz	(6)	62.8 kΩ
(7)	6.4 mH	(8)	9950 Hz
(9)	942 Ω	(10)	0 Ω
(11)	159 kΩ	(12)	.1 μF
(13)	10 kHz	(14)	.01 μF
(15)	1 kHz	(16)	.106 Ω
(17)	infinity	(18)	0 Ω (approx.)
(19)	159 Ω	(20)	infinity

CHAPTER 14. PRACTICE PROBLEMS: REACTANCE, IMPEDANCE, AC POWER

(1) $Z = 750$ Ω
$I = 66.7$ mA
$V_R = 30$ V
$V_L = 40$ V
$\theta = 53.1^0$
$P_R = 2$ watts
$P_X = 2.67$ VARs
$P_A = 3.33$ VA
$PF = .600$

(2) $Z = 992$ Ω
$I = 50.4$ mA
$V_R = 41.2$ V
$V_L = 27.7$ V
$\theta = 33.7^0$
$P_R = 2.08$ watts
$P_X = 1.40$ VARs
$P_A = 2.5$ VA
$PF = .832$

(3) $Z = 391$ Ω
$I = 128$ mA
$V_R = 32$ V
$V_L = 38.4$ V
$\theta = 50.2^0$
$P_R = 4.09$ watts
$P_X = 4.91$ VARs
$P_A = 6.39$ VA
$PF = .640$

(4) $Z = 530$ Ω
$I = 94.3$ mA
$V_R = 35.4$ V
$V_L = 35.4$ V
$\theta = 45^0$
$P_R = 3.34$ watts
$P_X = 3.34$ VARs
$P_A = 4.72$ VA
$PF = .707$

(5) $Z = 750$ Ω
$I = 66.7$ mA
$V_R = 40$ V
$V_L = 30$ V
$\theta = 36.9^0$
$P_R = 2.67$ watts
$P_X = 2$ VARs

P_A = 3.33 VA
PF = .800

(6) I_R = .3 A
I_L = .25 A
I_T = .391 A
Z = 192 Ω
θ = −39.8⁰
P_R = 22.5 watts
P_X = 18.8 VARs
P_A = 29.3 VA
PF = .768

(7) I_R = .167 A
I_L = .25 A
I_T = .301 A
Z = 249 Ω
θ = −56.3⁰
P_R = 12.5 watts
P_X = 18.8 VARs
P_A = 22.6 VA
PF = .555

(8) I_R = .6 A
I_L = .273 A
I_T = .659 A
Z = 114 Ω
θ = −24.5⁰
P_R = 45 watts
P_X = 20.5 VARs
P_A = 49.4 VA
PF = .910

(9) I_R = .1 A
I_L = .15 A
I_T = .18 A
Z = 417 Ω
θ = −56.3⁰
P_R = 7.5 watts
P_X = 11.3 VARs
P_A = 13.5 VA
PF = .555

(10) I_R = .167 A
I_L = .167 A
I_T = .236 A
Z = 318 Ω
θ = −45⁰
P_R = 12.5 watts
P_X = 12.5 VARs
P_A = 17.7 VA

PF = .707

(11) Z = 442 Ω
I = 22.6 mA
V_R = 6.79 V
V_L = 7.35 V
θ = −47.3⁰
P_R = .154 watts
P_X = .166 VARs
P_A = .226 VA
PF = .678

(12) Z = 515 Ω
I = 19.4 mA
V_R = 4.85 V
V_L = 8.74 V
θ = −60.9⁰
P_R = .0942 watts
P_X = .170 VARs
P_A = .194 VA

(13) PF = .486
Z = 583 Ω
I = 17.2 mA
V_R = 8.58 V
V_L = 5.15 V
θ = −31.0⁰
P_R = .147 watts
P_X = .0883 VARs
P_A = .172 VA

(14) PF = .857
Z = 1097 Ω
I = 9.12 mA
V_R = 6.84 V
V_L = 7.29 V
θ = −46.8⁰
P_R = .0624 watts
P_X = .0665 VARs

(15) P_A = .0912 VA
PF = .685
Z = 354 Ω
I = 28.2 mA
V_R = 7.06 V
V_L = 7.06 V
θ = −45⁰
P_R = .199 watts
P_X = .199 VARs
P_A = .282 VA
PF = .707

(16) I_R = 71.4 mA
I_L = 76.9 mA
I_T = 105 mA
Z = 238 Ω
θ = 47.1^0
P_R = 1.79 watts
P_X = 1.92 VARs
P_A = 2.63 VA

(17) PF = .681
I_R = 125 mA
I_L = 76.9 mA
I_T = 147 mA
Z = 170 Ω
θ = 31.6^0
P_R = 3.13 watts
P_X = 1.92 VARs
P_A = 3.68 VA

(18) PF = .852
I_R = 50 mA
I_L = 58 mA
I_T = 77.2 mA
Z = 324 Ω
θ = 49.2^0
P_R = 1.25 watts
P_X = 1.45 VARs
P_A = 1.93 VA

(19) PF = .653
I_R = 32.3 mA
I_L = 27.8 mA
I_T = 42.6 mA
Z = 587 Ω
θ = 40.7^0
P_R = .808 watts
P_X = .695 VARs

(20) P_A = 1.07 VA
PF = .758
I_R = 250 mA
I_L = 76.9 mA
I_T = 262 mA
Z = 95.4 Ω
θ = 17.1^0
P_R = 6.25 watts
P_X = 1.92 VARs
P_A = 6.55 VA
PF = .956

CHAPTER 14. PRACTICE PROBLEMS: PHASE ANGLE

(Note: due to the difficulty in reading drawings, student answers may vary.)

(1)	a) 8	b) 45	c) 1	d) 45
(2)	a) 8	b) 45	c) 1.2	d) 54
(3)	a) 6	b) 60	c) 1	d) 60
(4)	a) 6	b) 60	c) .5	d) 30
(5)	a) 5	b) 72	c) .4	d) 28.8
(6)	a) 5	b) 72	c) .8	d) 57.6
(7)	a) 8	b) 45	c) .8	d) 36
(8)	a) 4	b) 90	c) .5	d) 45
(9)	a) 6	b) 60	c) .5	d) 30
(10)	a) 5	b) 72	c) .6	d) 43.2

CHAPTER 14. REACTANCE, IMPEDANCE, AC POWER AND PHASE ANGLES COMPETENCY TEST

(1) AC resistance of a capacitor or inductor.
(2) Total ac resistance.
(3) Power of a resistor, measured in watts.
(4) Power of a reactive component, measured in VARs.
(5) Total circuit power, measured in VA.

(6)	628 Ω	(7)	1256 Ω
(8)	4.71 Ω	(9)	1884 Ω
(10)	942 Ω	(11)	63.7 kΩ
(12)	159 Ω	(13)	73.7 kΩ
(14)	3390 Ω	(15)	2.9 Ω
(16)	500 Ω	(17)	.2 A
(18)	60 V	(19)	80 V
(20)	53^0	(21)	12 watts
(22)	10 VARs	(23)	20 VA
(24)	.6	(25)	416 Ω
(26)	.24 A	(27)	.133 A
(28)	.2 A	(29)	-56.3^0
(30)	13.3 watts	(31)	20 VARs
(32)	24 VA	(33)	.559
(34)	170	(35)	.588 A
(36)	70.6 V	(37)	70.6 V
(38)	-45^0	(39)	41.5 watts
(40)	41.5 VARs	(41)	58.8 VA
(42)	.707	(43)	120 Ω

(44) .833 A   (45) .667 A
(46) .5 A   (47) 36.8⁰
(48) .8   (49) 27⁰
(50) 63⁰

CHAPTER 15. PRACTICE PROBLEMS: NET REACTANCE

(1)   a) 25 Ω   b) C   c) .4 A
     d) 60 V   e) 110 V

(2)   a) 25Ω   b) C   c) .6 A
     d) 30 V   e) 45 V

(3)   a) 25 Ω   b) C   c) .8 A
     d) 200 V   e) 140 V

(4)   a) 50Ω   b) L   c) .5 A
     d) 375 V   e) 275 V

(5)   a) 50 Ω   b) C   c) .6 A
     d) 270 V   e) 300 V

(6)   a) 25 Ω   b) L   c) .4 A
     d) 60 V   e) 50 V

(7)   a) 10 Ω   b) C   c) 1 A
     d) 15 V   e) 25 V

(8)   a) 25 Ω   b) C   c) .6 A
     d) 210 V   e) 225 V

(9)   a) 75 Ω   b) C   c) .267 A
     d) 80 V   e) 100 V

(10) a) 50 Ω   b) C   c) .2 A
     d) 30 V   e) 40 V

(11) a) .373 A   b) .25 A   c) .083 A
     d) 120 Ω   e) L

(12) a) .429 A   b) .3 A   c) .129 A
     d) 116 Ω   e) L

(13) a) .4 A   b) .5 A   c) .1 A
     d) 200 Ω   e) C

(14) a) .0833 A   b) .0714 A   c) .0119 A
     d) 2100 Ω   e) L

(15) a) .0667 A   b) .1 A   c) .0333 A
     d) 200 Ω   e) C

(16) a) .75 A   b) .6 A   c) .15 A
     d) 100 Ω   e) L

(17) a) .06 A   b) .0625 A   c) .0025 A
     d) 6000 Ω   e) C

(18) a) .5 A   b) .75 A   c) .25 A
     d) 120 Ω   e) C

(19) a) .375 A   b) .333 A   c) .0417 A
     d) 360 Ω   e) L

(20) a) .5 A   b) .667 A   c) .167 A
     d) 240 Ω   e) C

CHAPTER 15. PRACTICE PROBLEMS: RESONANT FREQUENCY

(1)   318 Hz   (2)   60.2 Hz
(3)   8.22 kHz   (4)   58.1 kHz
(5)   49.9 kHz   (6)   10.6 MHz
(7)   374 Hz   (8)   120 Hz
(9)   19.9 kHz   (10) 69.5 Hz

CHAPTER 15. RESONANCE COMPETENCY TEST

(1)   a) 150 Ω   b) C   c) 66.7 mA
     d) 6.67 V   e) 16.7 V

(2)   a) 25 Ω   b) L   c) 1 A
     d) 75 V   e) 50 V

(3)   a) 15 Ω   b) C   c) 3.33 A
     d) 117 V   e) 167 V

(4)   a) 100 Ω   b) L   c) .25 A
     d) 50 V   e) 25 V

(5)   a) 10 Ω   b) L   c) 10 A
     d) 1500 V   e) 1400 V

(6)   a) .25 A   b) .333 A   c) .083 A
     d) 120 Ω   e) C

(7)   a) .286 A   b) .2 A   c) .086 A
     d) 116 Ω   e) L

(8)   a) .6 A   b) .5 A   c) .1 A
     d) 150 Ω   e) L

(9)   a) .4 A   b) .267 A   c) .133 A
     d) 150Ω   e) L

(10) a) .5 A   b) .667 A   c) .167 A
     d) 299 Ω   e) C

(11) 318 Hz   (12) 60 Hz
(13) 22.5 kHz   (14) 130 kHz
(15) 73.4 kHz   (16) 10 MHz
(17) 591 Hz   (18) 184 Hz
(19) 25 kHz   (20) 65 Hz
(21) max   (22) min
(23) min   (24) max
(25) parallel

DC AND AC BUILDING BLOCKS FINAL EXAM

(1)   5 mA   (2)   .0657 V
(3)   5,600,000 W   (4)   87,000 kHz

(5) .0015 μF
(7) .25 A
(9) 2.72 mA
(11) .5 W
(13) 2 W
(15) 4 volts
(17) 1 mA
(19) 1.09 kΩ
(21) 10.6 V
(23) 38.2 V
(25) 599 Hz
(27) 60 V

(6) 100 V
(8) 1500 Ω
(10) 45 V
(12) 360 W
(14) .5 A
(16) 5 volts
(18) .25 A
(20) 450 Ω
(22) 93.4 V
(24) .667 ms
(26) 5 V
(28) 120 V

(29) 20 V
(31) 1.5 H
(33) 1.33 μF
(35) 7.14 V
(37) .5 ms
(39) 1.25 μs
(41) 15.9 Ω
(43) 292 Ω
(45) VA
(47) 9190 Hz
(49) 200 Ω

(30) 75%
(32) 13.6 mH
(34) 25 pF
(36) 6 ms
(38) 50 ms
(40) 63%
(42) 565 Ω
(44) 416 Ω
(46) 514 Hz
(48) 25 Ω
(50) C

Appendix E:
Computer Programs

```
CATALOG

/TAB

 NAME             TYPE   BLOCKS  MODIFIED        CREATED          ENDFILE SUBTYPE

*STARTUP          BAS      4    <NO DATE>       <NO DATE>           1536
*PRODOS           SYS     31    <NO DATE>       <NO DATE>          15360
*BASIC.SYSTEM     SYS     21    <NO DATE>       <NO DATE>          10240
*SHOPMATH         BAS     12    <NO DATE>       <NO DATE>           5545
*ENG.NOTE         BAS     10    <NO DATE>       <NO DATE>           4519
*COLORCODE        BAS      8    <NO DATE>       <NO DATE>           3330
*INTRODUCTION     BAS      4    <NO DATE>       <NO DATE>           1255
*OHMMETER         BAS      8    <NO DATE>       <NO DATE>           3510
*VAMETER          BAS      6    <NO DATE>       <NO DATE>           2385
*OHMLAW           BAS     10    <NO DATE>       <NO DATE>           4372
*SCOPEDC          BAS      8    <NO DATE>       <NO DATE>           3200
*DCANALYSIS       BAS      9    <NO DATE>       <NO DATE>           3624
*SCOPEAC          BAS     11    <NO DATE>       <NO DATE>           4854
*PHASE            BAS     10    <NO DATE>       <NO DATE>           4237
*TIMEC            BAS     13    <NO DATE>       <NO DATE>           5897
*TRANS            BAS     11    <NO DATE>       <NO DATE>           4726
*REACT            BAS      9    <NO DATE>       <NO DATE>           4042
*RESON            BAS     11    <NO DATE>       <NO DATE>           4871
*MAGNET           BAS      6    <NO DATE>       <NO DATE>           2559

BLOCKS FREE:   71     BLOCKS USED:   209    TOTAL BLOCKS:   280
```

Fig. E-1. Main menu program.

```
5    HOME : PRINT : PRINT : PRINT
     : PRINT : PRINT
10   PRINT "   COMPETENCY IN ELECT
     RONICS TECHNOLOGY"
12   PRINT : PRINT "       DC AND
     AC BUILDING BLOCKS"
13   PRINT "_____
     _____"
16   PRINT : PRINT  TAB( 12)"BY:
     R. JESSE PHAGAN"
17   PRINT : PRINT  TAB( 8)"CIA B
     Y: BILL SPAULDING"
18   INVERSE : VTAB 18: HTAB 10: PRINT
     "SPACE BAR FOR MENU";: NORMAL

19   GET F$: IF F$ <  >  CHR$ (32
     ) THEN  GOTO 19
20   HOME : VTAB 8: INVERSE
25   FOR R = 1 TO 16
30   READ A$
32   IF R = 9 THEN  VTAB 8
33   IF R = 9 OR R > 9 THEN  GOTO
     35
34   IF R < 9 THEN  GOTO 40
35   HTAB 20: PRINT  CHR$ (64 + R
     ); CHR$ (41); CHR$ (32);A$: GOTO
     41
40   PRINT  CHR$ (64 + R); CHR$ (
     41); CHR$ (32);A$
41   PRINT
45   NEXT R
46   NORMAL : PRINT : PRINT : PRINT
     "CHOOSE BY LETTER ?";
50   GET S$: IF S$ <  CHR$ (65) OR
     S$ >  CHR$ (80) THEN  GOTO 5
     0
55   C =  ASC (S$) - 64
56   IF C = 1 THEN  PRINT  CHR$ (
     4);"-INTRODUCTION"
57   IF C = 2 THEN  PRINT  CHR$ (
     4);"-SHOPMATH"
58   IF C = 3 THEN  PRINT  CHR$ (
     4);"-ENG.NOTE"
59   IF C = 4 THEN  PRINT  CHR$ (
     4);"-COLORCODE"
60   IF C = 5 THEN  PRINT  CHR$ (
     4);"-OHMMETER"
61   IF C = 6 THEN  PRINT  CHR$ (
     4);"-VAMETER"
62   IF C = 7 THEN  PRINT  CHR$ (
     4);"-OHMLAW"
63   IF C = 8 THEN  PRINT  CHR$ (
     4);"-SCOPEDC"
64   IF C = 9 THEN  PRINT  CHR$ (
     4);"-DCANALYSIS"
65   IF C = 10 THEN  PRINT  CHR$
     (4);"-SCOPEAC"
66   IF C = 11 THEN  PRINT  CHR$
     (4);"-PHASE"
67   IF C = 12 THEN  PRINT  CHR$
     (4);"-TIMEC"
68   IF C = 13 THEN  PRINT  CHR$
     (4);"-TRANS"
69   IF C = 14 THEN  PRINT  CHR$
     (4);"-REACT"
70   IF C = 15 THEN  PRINT  CHR$
     (4);"-RESON"
71   IF C = 16 THEN  PRINT  CHR$
     (4);"-MAGNET"
301  DATA INTRODUCTION,SHOP MATH
     ,ENG. NOTATION,COLOR CODE
302  DATA OHM METER,V&A METER,OH
     M'S LAW,OSCILLOSCOPE DC
303  DATA DC ANALYSIS,OSCILLOSCO
     PE AC,PHASE ANGLE
304  DATA TIME CONSTANTS,TRANSFO
     RMERS,REACTANCE,RESONANCE
305  DATA  MAGNETISM
```

Fig. E-2. Introduction program.

```
20   REM   INTRODUCTION
40   HOME
60   PRINT "     HOW TO USE THESE
     PROGRAMS"
80   PRINT
100  PRINT "     THESE PROGRAMS A
     RE INTENDED"
120  PRINT "     TO SUPPLEMENT TH
     E BOOK"
140  PRINT "     "; CHR$ (34);"CO
     MPETENCY IN ELECTRONICS"
160  PRINT "     TECHNOLOGY"; CHR$
     (34);" BY R. JESSE PHAGAN."
180  PRINT
200  PRINT "     A GOOD WAY TO US
     E THESE WOULD"
220  PRINT "     BE AS A STUDY GU
     IDE."
240  PRINT "     RUN THROUGH THE
     PROGRAM DEALING"
260  PRINT "     WITH THE CHAPTER
     YOU ARE ABOUT"
280  PRINT "     TO STUDY, AND WR
     ITE DOWN YOUR"
300  PRINT "     SCORE."
320  PRINT
340  PRINT "     WHEN YOU BELIEVE
     YOU ARE READY"
360  PRINT "     FOR THE CHAPTER
     TEST, RUN THROUGH"
380  PRINT "     THE PROGRAM AGAI
     N TO CHECK YOUR"
400  PRINT "     PROGRESS.": PRINT
     : PRINT
420  INVERSE : HTAB 12: PRINT "S
     PACE BAR FOR MORE": NORMAL
440  GET A$: IF A$ <  > CHR$ (3
     2) THEN  GOTO 440
460  HOME
480  PRINT
500  PRINT "     THEY ARE GOOD FO
     R FUTURE"
520  PRINT "     REFERENCE AS WEL
     L, THE HELP"
540  PRINT "     HINTS IN EACH PR
     OGRAM CONTAIN"
560  PRINT "     FORMULAS AND INF
     ORMATION THAT"
580  PRINT "     WE SOMETIMES HAV
     E TO GO BACK"
600  PRINT "     AND LEARN AGAIN
     BECAUSE WE"
620  PRINT "     CAN'T POSSIBLY R
     EMEMBER IT ALL,"
640  PRINT "     SO WE REMEMBER W
     HAT WE USE DAILY"
660  PRINT "     AND KEEP REFEREN
     CE CLOSE BY"
680  PRINT "     FOR THOSE THAT W
     E DON'T."
700  PRINT : PRINT : PRINT
720  PRINT "     OH AND WELCOME T
     O THE WORLD"
740  PRINT "     OF ELECTRONICS!"

760  PRINT : PRINT
780  INVERSE : HTAB 12: PRINT "S
     PACE BAR FOR MENU": NORMAL
800  GET S$: IF S$ <  > CHR$ (3
     2) THEN  GOTO 800
820  PRINT  CHR$ (4);"-STARTUP"
```

Fig. E-3. Shop math program.

```
1   REM   SHOPMATH
2   HOME : REM   ****** INTRODUCT
    ION ******
3   VTAB 2
4   PRINT  TAB( 4)"THIS PROGRAM W
    ILL ALLOW THE USER TO"
5   PRINT  TAB( 4)"PRACTICE SOME
    OF THE MATH SKILLS"
6   PRINT  TAB( 4)"USED IN THE EL
    ECTRONICS FIELD.": PRINT
7   PRINT  TAB( 4)"IT OFFERS PRAC
    TICE PROBLEMS FOR THE"
8   PRINT  TAB( 4)"WORK COVERED I
    N CHAPTER 3.": PRINT : PRINT

9   PRINT  TAB( 15)"NOTES:": PRINT

10  PRINT  TAB( 4)"1. OMIT INSIG
    NIFICANT O'S IN ANSWERS.": PRINT

11  PRINT  TAB( 4)"2. THERE MUST
    BE A SPACE BETWEEN"
12  PRINT  TAB( 4)"   WHOLE #'S,
    AND FRACTION (2 2/3).": PRINT

13  PRINT  TAB( 4)"3. ALL ANSWER
    S MUST BE FOLLOWED BY"
14  PRINT  TAB( 4)"   RETURN KEY
    ."
260 INVERSE : VTAB 22: HTAB 8: PRINT
    "SPACE BAR TO CONTINUE": NORMAL

280 GET RT$: IF RT$ < > CHR$
    (32) THEN  GOTO 280
300 HOME
301 REM  ** MENU **
302 S = 0:V = 0:X = 0:S = 0:K =
    0: CLEAR : RESTORE
310 PRINT "1 FRACTION TO DECIMA
    L": PRINT
311 PRINT "2 DECIMAL TO FRACTIO
    N": PRINT
312 PRINT "3 MIXED TO IMPROPER"
    : PRINT
313 PRINT "4 IMPROPER TO PROPER
    ": PRINT
314 PRINT "5 EVALUATION": PRINT

315 PRINT "6 OPERATIONS": PRINT

316 PRINT "7 PERCENT": PRINT
317 PRINT "8 + AND - NUMBERS": PRINT

318 PRINT "9 RETURN TO MAIN MEN
    U": PRINT
340 PRINT "ENTER THE NUMBER OF
    YOUR SELECTION ";
341 INPUT V: IF V < 1 OR V > 9 THEN
    GOTO 341
342 IF V = 1 THEN  GOTO 357
```

```
343 IF V = 2 THEN X = 22: GOTO
    352
344 IF V = 3 THEN X = 44: GOTO
    352
345 IF V = 4 THEN X = 66: GOTO
    352
346 IF V = 5 THEN X = 88: GOTO
    352
347 IF V = 6 THEN X = 110: GOTO
    352
348 IF V = 7 THEN X = 152: GOTO
    352
349 IF V = 8 THEN X = 174: GOTO
    352
350 IF V = 9 THEN  GOTO 1200
352 FOR W = 1 TO X: READ W$: NEXT
    W
357 READ Q,Q$
358 FOR K = 1 TO Q:AA = 0
359 HOME
360 READ Q2$,A$
520 PRINT : PRINT
540 PRINT K;".";Q$: PRINT : PRINT
    TAB( 15)Q2$;" = ";
560 INPUT AA$
620 IF AA$ = A$ OR AA$ = A$ THEN
    GOSUB 700: REM   CORRECT
640 IF AA$ < A$ OR AA$ > A$ THEN
    GOSUB 840: REM   *** WRONG
    *
660 IF K = Q THEN  GOTO 1020
680 NEXT K
700 REM  **** CORRECT ****
719 INVERSE
720 PRINT : PRINT : PRINT : HTAB
    14: PRINT "CORRECT!":S = S +
    1
740 PRINT : HTAB 5: PRINT "SPAC
    E BAR = NEXT, E = EXIT"
741 NORMAL
760 GET RR$: IF RR$ < > CHR$
    (32) AND RR$ < > CHR$ (69)
    THEN  GOTO 760
780 IF RR$ = CHR$ (32) AND K =
    Q THEN  GOTO 1020: REM   **S
    CORE **
800 IF RR$ = CHR$ (32) THEN  RETURN

820 IF RR$ = CHR$ (69) THEN  GOTO
    1020: REM  SCORE
840 REM  **** WRONG *****
859 INVERSE
860 PRINT : PRINT : PRINT : HTAB
    12: PRINT "WRONG ";A$
880 PRINT : HTAB 4: PRINT "SPAC
    E BAR = NEXT, H=HELP HINTS"
900 HTAB 4: PRINT "E = EXIT"
901 NORMAL
920 GET WW$: IF WW$ < > CHR$
    (32) AND WW$ < > CHR$ (69)
```

```
     AND WW$ <  > CHR$ (72) THEN
     GOTO 920
940  IF WW$ = CHR$ (32) AND K =
     Q THEN  GOTO 1020
960  IF WW$ = CHR$ (32) THEN  RETURN

1000 IF WW$ = CHR$ (72) AND V <
     7 THEN  GOSUB 1280: RETURN :
     REM  ** HELP **
1001 IF WW$ = CHR$ (72) AND V =
     7 THEN  GOSUB 1323: RETURN :
     REM  HELP II
1002 IF WW$ = CHR$ (72) AND V =
     8 THEN  GOSUB 1337: RETURN :
     REM  HELP III
1004 IF WW$ = CHR$ (69) THEN  GOTO
     1020
1008 END
1020 REM  *** SCORE ****
1060 HOME : VTAB 8
1080 E = (S / K) * 100
1100 PRINT  TAB( 8)"YOUR SCORE
     IS ";E;"%": PRINT
1120 PRINT  TAB( 8)"FOR ";K;" Q
     UESTIONS ASKED": PRINT : PRINT
     : PRINT
1160 PRINT  TAB( 8)"SPACE BAR F
     OR MAIN MENU."
1180 GET MM$: IF MM$ <  > CHR$
     (32) THEN 1180
1181 GOTO 300
1200 PRINT  CHR$ (4);"-STARTUP"
1280 REM  ** HELPHINTS **
1300 HOME : VTAB 3
1301 PRINT  TAB( 4)"WAS THE ANS
     WER ENTERED CORRECTLY ?"
1302 PRINT  TAB( 3)"(SPACE BETW
     EEN WHOLE #'S AND FRACTION)"
     : PRINT
1303 PRINT  TAB( 4)"DID YOU CHA
     NGE THE VALUE OF THE"
1304 PRINT  TAB( 4)"PROBLEM ?":
     PRINT
1305 PRINT  TAB( 4)"IS THE ANSW
     ER IN IT'S SIMPLEST FORM"
1306 PRINT  TAB( 4)"FOR THE TYP
     E OF ANSWER ?"
1307 VTAB 20: HTAB 8: INVERSE :
     PRINT "SPACE BAR FOR MORE";
     : NORMAL : HTAB 1
1308 GET CT$: IF CT$ <  > CHR$
     (32) THEN 1308
1309 HOME
1310 VTAB 2: HTAB 16: INVERSE :
     PRINT "SAMPLES:": NORMAL : HTAB
     1: PRINT
1311 PRINT  TAB( 4)"FRAC-DEC
            1/2 = .5": PRINT
1312 PRINT  TAB( 4)"DEC-FRAC
            .25 = 1/4": PRINT
1313 PRINT  TAB( 4)"MIX-IMPROP
```

```
            1 1/4 = 5/4": PRINT
1314 PRINT  TAB( 4)"IMPROP-MIX
            17/16 = 1 1/16": PRINT
1315 PRINT  TAB( 4)"EVALUATION
     1/2 OR 1/4 = 1/2": PRINT
1316 PRINT  TAB( 4)"ADD
     1/8 + 1/4 = 3/8": PRINT
1317 PRINT  TAB( 4)"SUBTRACT
     1/4 - 1/8 = 1/8": PRINT
1318 PRINT  TAB( 4)"MULT
     1/2 X 1/2 = 1/4": PRINT
1319 PRINT  TAB( 4)"DIV.  1/2 (
     DIV.BY) 3/4 = 2/3": PRINT
1320 HTAB 8: INVERSE : PRINT "S
     PACE BAR TO CONTINUE": NORMAL
     : HTAB 1
1321 GET AM$: IF AM$ <  > CHR$
     (32) THEN 1321
1322 RETURN
1323 REM  PERCENT HELP
1324 HOME
1325 VTAB 2
1326 PRINT  TAB( 4)"TO REMOVE T
     HE PERCENT SIGN, MOVE"
1327 PRINT  TAB( 4)"THE DECIMAL
     TWO PLACES TO THE LEFT.": PRINT

1328 PRINT  TAB( 16)"EXAMPLE:":
     PRINT
1329 PRINT  TAB( 10)"10% OF 100
     = ?": PRINT : PRINT
1330 PRINT  TAB( 7)"100": PRINT
1331 PRINT  TAB( 5)"X .10 (DECI
     MAL FORM OF 10%)"
1332 PRINT  TAB( 5)"_____"
1333 PRINT  TAB( 8)"10 (ANSWER)
     ": PRINT
1334 INVERSE : HTAB 8: PRINT "S
     PACE BAR TO CONTINUE": NORMAL
     : HTAB 1
1335 GET RS$: IF RS$ <  > CHR$
     (32) THEN 1335
1336 RETURN
1337 REM  POS & NEG
1338 HOME
1339 PRINT  TAB( 4)"MULTIPLICAT
     ION AND DIVISION:": PRINT
1340 PRINT  TAB( 2)"SIGNS THE S
     AME: ANSWER IS POSITIVE.": PRINT

1341 PRINT  TAB( 2)"SIGNS OPPOS
     ITE: ANSWER IS NEGATIVE.": PRINT
     : PRINT : PRINT
1342 PRINT  TAB( 4)"ADDITION:":
     PRINT
1343 PRINT  TAB( 2)"THE ANSWER
     WILL HAVE THE SIGN OF"
1344 PRINT  TAB( 2)"THE LARGER
     NUMBER.": PRINT
1345 PRINT  TAB( 4)"SUBTRACTION
```

```
        :": PRINT
1346  PRINT  TAB( 2)"CHANGE THE
      SIGN OF THE NUMBER TO BE"
1347  PRINT  TAB( 2)"SUBTRACTED,
      THEN ADD.": PRINT : PRINT
1348  INVERSE : HTAB 8: PRINT "S
      PACE BAR TO CONTINUE";: NORMAL
      : HTAB 1
1349  GET RF$: IF RF$ < > CHR$
      (32) THEN 1349
1350  RETURN
4999  REM  ** FRAC-DEC **
5000  DATA 10,WHAT IS THE DECIMA
      L EQUIVALENT OF       THIS F
      RACTION ?
5001  DATA 1/2,.5,1/4,.25,1/8,.1
      25,2 1/4,2.25,1 1/2,1.5,3/4,
      .75,2/5,.4,7/8,.875
5002  DATA 1 3/4,1.75,1/10,.1
5003  DATA 10,WHAT IS THE FRACTI
      ON EQUIVALENT OF       THIS D
      ECIMAL NUMBER ?
5004  DATA 0.333,1/3,0.0625,1/16
      ,.75,3/4,0.125,1/8,2.25,2 1/
      4,0.5,1/2
5005  DATA 0.25,1/4,0.875,7/8,.4
      ,2/5,0.375,3/8
5006  DATA 10,CHANGE TO IMPROPER
      FORM.
5007  DATA 2 1/2,5/2,3 2/3,11/3,
      1 5/8,13/8,1 1/10,11/10,4 2/
      5,22/5,8 3/4,35/4
5008  DATA 2 1/6,13/6,1 5/7,12/7
      ,3 1/4,13/4,1 2/5,7/5
5009  REM  ** IMPROP-MIX **
5010  DATA 10,CHANGE THIS IMPROP
      ER FRACTION TO         PROPER
      FORM.
5011  DATA 22/11,2,9/4,2 1/4,5/3
      ,1 2/3,3/3,1,5/4,1 1/4,7/5,1
      2/5
5012  DATA 12/10,1 1/5,24/8,3,7/
      3,2 1/3,9/5,1 4/5
5013  REM  ** EVALUATE **
5014  DATA 10,WHICH FRACTION HAS
      THE GREATER          VALUE
      ?
5015  DATA 1/2 OR 1/8,1/2,1/4 OR
      1/2,1/2,1/16 OR 1/8,1/8,1/4
```

```
      OR 3/16,1/4
5016  DATA 5/6 OR 6/7,6/7,2/3 OR
      3/4,3/4,1/2 OR 2/3,2/3,3/8
      OR 1/4,3/8
5017  DATA 4/5 OR 3/4,4/5,1/10 O
      R 1/20,1/10
5018  REM  OPERATIONS
5019  DATA  20,PERFORM THE FOLLO
      WING OPERATIONS.
5020  DATA 1/2 X 1/8,1/16,1/4 X
      1/8,1/32,1 1/2 X 1/4,3/8
5021  DATA 2/3 X 1/6,1/9,11/4 X
      2/5,1 1/10
5022  DATA 1/2 (DIV. BY) 8,1/16,
      8 (DIV. BY) 1/2,16,1/4 (DIV.
      BY) 1/2,1/2
5023  DATA 1/8 (DIV. BY) 1/4,1/2
      ,1/8 (DIV. BY) 1/2,1/4
5024  DATA 1/4 + 1/2,3/4,2 1/8 +
      1 1/8,3 1/4,3/8 + 2/16,1/2
5025  DATA 1/16 + 3/8,7/16,2 2/6
      + 3/9,2 2/3
5026  DATA 1/2 - 1/4,1/4,1/4 - 3
      /16,1/16,4/5 - 2/10,3/5,3/32
      - 1/32,1/16,3/4 - 1/2,1/4
5027  REM  PERCENT
5028  DATA 10,SOLVE THE FOLLOWIN
      G.
5029  DATA 10% OF 100,10,2% OF 1
      0,.2,5% OF 50,2.5,50% OF 20,
      10
5030  DATA 100% OF 60,60,5% OF 2
      0,1,45% OF 8,3.6,20% OF 150,
      30
5031  DATA 15% OF 200,30,30% OF
      15,4.5
5032  REM  +/- NUMBERS
5033  DATA 20,SOLVE THE FOLLOWIN
      G.
5034  DATA -1 X 5,-5,-2 X -2,4,8
      X -2,-16,4 X 2,8,-3 X 3,-9
5035  DATA 8 / -2,-4,2 / 2,1,-9
      / -3,3,6 / -2,-3,15 / -3,-5
5036  DATA -5 + 3,-2,6 + -4,2,12
      + -12,0,-14 + -7,-21,10 + -
      5,5
5037  DATA 5 - 2,3,-5 - 2,-7,-8
      - -4,-4,16 - -4,20,-9 - 7,-1
      6
```

Fig. E-4. Engineering notation program.

```
1    REM   ENG NOTATION
2    HOME : VTAB 3: REM   *** INTRO
     DUCTION ***
3    PRINT   TAB( 4)"THIS PROGRAM O
     FFERS PRACTICE"
4    PRINT   TAB( 4)"PROBLEMS FOR T
     HE WORK COVERED IN"
5    PRINT   TAB( 4)"CHAPTER 4.": PRINT
     : PRINT : PRINT
6    PRINT   TAB( 16)"NOTES:"
7    PRINT : PRINT   TAB( 2)"1. OMI
     T COMMAS IN ANSWERS.": PRINT
8    PRINT   TAB( 2)"2. ANSWERS MUS
     T BE FOLLOWED BY ";: INVERSE
     : PRINT "RETURN";: NORMAL : PRINT
     "."
260  INVERSE : VTAB 20: HTAB 8: PRINT
     "SPACE BAR TO CONTINUE": NORMAL

280  GET RT$: IF RT$ <  > CHR$
     (32) THEN   GOTO 280
300  HOME
301  CLEAR : RESTORE : REM   ***
     MENU ***
302  VTAB 2:S = 0:V = 0:K = 0
303  PRINT   TAB( 4)"1. SIGNIFICA
     NT FIGURES": PRINT
304  PRINT   TAB( 4)"2. ROUNDING"
     : PRINT
305  PRINT   TAB( 4)"3. SCIENTIFI
     C NOTATION": PRINT
306  PRINT   TAB( 4)"4. REMOVING
     POWERS OF TEN": PRINT
307  PRINT   TAB( 4)"5. ENGINEERI
     NG NOTATION": PRINT
308  PRINT   TAB( 4)"6. REMOVING
     ENG. NOTATION": PRINT
309  PRINT   TAB( 4)"7. RETURN TO
     MAIN MENU"
310  VTAB 18
340  PRINT "ENTER THE NUMBER OF
     YOUR SELECTION ";:V = 0
341  INPUT V: IF V < 1 OR V > 7 THEN
     GOTO 300
342  IF V = 1 THEN   GOTO 357
343  IF V = 2 THEN X = 22: GOTO
     352
344  IF V = 3 THEN X = 44: GOTO
     352
345  IF V = 4 THEN X = 66: GOTO
     352
346  IF V = 5 THEN X = 88: GOTO
     352
347  IF V = 6 THEN X = 110: GOTO
     352
348  IF V = 7 THEN   GOTO 1200
352  FOR W = 1 TO X: READ W$: NEXT
     W
356  REM   *** QUESTION LOOP ***
357  READ Q, Q$
358  FOR K = 1 TO Q:AA = 0
359  HOME
360  READ Q2$,A$
520  PRINT : PRINT
540  PRINT K;".";Q$: PRINT : PRINT
     TAB( 15)Q2$;" = ";
560  INPUT AA$
620  IF AA$ = A$ THEN   GOSUB 700
     : REM **CORRECT
640  IF AA$ < A$ OR AA$ > A$ THEN
     GOSUB 840: REM   *** WRONG
     ***
660  IF K = Q THEN   GOTO 1020
680  NEXT K
700  REM **** CORRECT ****
719  INVERSE
720  PRINT : PRINT : PRINT : HTAB
     14: PRINT "CORRECT!":S = S +
     1
740  PRINT : HTAB 5: PRINT "SPAC
     E BAR = NEXT, E = EXIT"
741  NORMAL
760  GET RR$: IF RR$ <  > CHR$
     (32) AND RR$ <  > CHR$ (69)
     THEN   GOTO 760
780  IF RR$ = CHR$ (32) AND K =
     Q THEN   GOTO 1020: REM **S
     CORE **
800  IF RR$ = CHR$ (32) THEN   RETURN
820  IF RR$ = CHR$ (69) THEN   GOTO
     1020: REM   SCORE
840  REM   **** WRONG *****
859  INVERSE
860  PRINT : PRINT : PRINT : HTAB
     12: PRINT "WRONG ";A$
880  PRINT : HTAB 4: PRINT "SPAC
     E BAR = NEXT, H=HELP HINTS"
900  HTAB 4: PRINT "E = EXIT"
901  NORMAL
920  GET WW$: IF WW$ <  > CHR$
     (32) AND WW$ <  > CHR$ (69)
     AND WW$ <  > CHR$ (72) THEN
     GOTO 920
940  IF WW$ = CHR$ (32) AND K =
     Q THEN   GOTO 1020
960  IF WW$ = CHR$ (32) THEN   RETURN
980  IF WW$ = CHR$ (72) THEN   GOSUB
     1210: RETURN : REM   *** HELP
     HINTS
1000 IF WW$ = CHR$ (69) THEN   GOTO
     1020
1020 REM   *** SCORE ****
1060 HOME : VTAB 8
1080 E = (S / K) * 100
1100 PRINT   TAB( 8)"YOUR SCORE
     IS ";E;"%": PRINT
1120 PRINT   TAB( 8)"FOR ";K;" Q
     UESTIONS ASKED": PRINT : PRINT
     : PRINT
```

```
1160   PRINT  TAB( 8)"SPACE BAR F
       OR MAIN MENU."
1180   GET MM$: IF MM$ <  > CHR$
       (32) THEN 1180
1181   GOTO 300
1200   PRINT  CHR$ (4);"-STARTUP"

1210   REM  ** HELP ***
1211   HTAB 0
1220   HOME
1221   ON V GOSUB 1226,1230,1238,
       1243,1249,1261
1222   INVERSE : VTAB 20: HTAB 8
1223   PRINT "SPACE BAR TO CONTIN
       UE";: NORMAL
1224   GET RR$: IF RR$ <  > CHR$
       (32) THEN 1224
1225   RETURN
1226   REM  ** SIG DIGITS **
1227   VTAB 4: PRINT "1. DID YOU
       INCLUDE PLACE HOLDING ZEROS
       ?"
1228   PRINT : PRINT "2. DID YOU
       ENTER THE NUMBER CORRECTLY ?
       "
1229   RETURN
1230   REM  ** ROUNDING **
1231   VTAB 4: PRINT " 1. DID YOU
       ROUND TO THREE SIGNIFICANT"

1232   PRINT "     DIGITS ?"
1233   PRINT : PRINT " 2. DID YOU
       ADD 1 TO A DIGIT THAT"
1234   PRINT "     SHOULD HAVE REM
       AINED THE SAME ?": PRINT
1235   PRINT " 3. DID YOU FORGET
       TO ADD 1 TO A DIGIT"
1236   PRINT "     THAT YOU SHOULD
       HAVE ?"
1237   RETURN
1238   REM  ** SCI NOTE **
1239   VTAB 4: PRINT " 1. DID YOU
       USE (E) NOTATION (1.1E5) ?"
       : PRINT
1240   PRINT " 2. DID YOU CHANGE
       THE VALUE ?": PRINT
1241   PRINT " 3. DID YOU USE THE
       CORRECT EXPONENT ?"
1242   RETURN
1243   REM  **REMOVE POWERS **
1244   VTAB 4: PRINT " 1. DID YOU
       MOVE THE DECIMAL POINT THE"

1245   PRINT "     CORRECT NUMBER
       OF DIGITS ?": PRINT
1246   PRINT " 2. DID YOU CHANGE
       THE VALUE ?": PRINT
1247   PRINT " 3. DID YOU ENTER T
       HE VALUE CORRECTLY ?"
1248   RETURN
1249   REM  ** ENG NOTE **
1250   PRINT
1251   PRINT "GIGA MEG KILO     M
       ILLI MICRO NANO PICO"
1252   PRINT ": :   : :   : :
       : :   : :   : :   : :"
1253   PRINT "000  000  000 000.
       000   000  000   000"
1254   PRINT : PRINT : PRINT
1255   PRINT " 1. HAVE YOU USED E
       NG NOTATION TO IT'S"
1256   PRINT "     BEST ABILITY ?"
       : PRINT
1257   PRINT " 2. DID YOU CHANGE
       THE VALUE ?": PRINT
1258   PRINT " 3. HAVE YOU USED T
       HE CORRECT NAME"
1259   PRINT "     FOR THE POWER Y
       OU WANTED ?"
1260   RETURN
1261   REM  ** REMOVE ENG **
1262   PRINT
1263   PRINT "GIGA MEG KILO     M
       ILLI MICRO NANO PICO"
1264   PRINT ": :   : :   : :
       : :   : :   : :"
1265   PRINT "000  000  000 000.
       000   000  000   000"
1266   PRINT : PRINT : PRINT
1267   PRINT " 1. DID YOU MOVE TH
       E DECIMAL POINT"
1268   PRINT "     THE CORRECT NUM
       BER OF SPACES FOR"
1269   PRINT "     THE NAME OF THE
       POWER OF TEN ?": PRINT
1270   PRINT " 2. DID YOU CHANGE
       THE VALUE ?": PRINT
1271   RETURN
5000   DATA 10,HOW MANY SIGNIFIC
       ANT DIGITS DOES       THIS
       NUMBER HAVE ?
5001   DATA 106,3,100,3,1.00,1,1.
       50,2,.003,1,2.45,3,0.100,1,2
       .300,2,5.05,3,10.00,2
5002   DATA 10,ROUND TO THREE SIG
       NIFICANT FIGURES.
5003   DATA 1606,1610,67.52,67.5,
       123.5,124,2.563,2.56
5004   DATA 3025,3030,.33333,.333
       ,.4520,.452,5685,5690,3797,3
       800,9995,10000
5005   DATA 10,CHANGE THE FOLLOW
       ING TO SCIENTIFIC      NOTAT
       ION (USE "E" NOTATION).
5006   DATA 100,1E2,10000,1E4,250
       0,2.5E3,10.0,1E1,25.5,2.55E1
       ,.125,1.25E-1
5007   DATA .001,1E-3,.75,7.5E-1,
       .0001,1E-4,.500,5E-1
5008   DATA 10,REMOVE THE POWER O
```

Fig. E-4. Engineering notation program. (Continued from page 292).

```
F TEN FROM THE          FOLLOW
ING NUMBERS.
5009   DATA 1E5,100000,2.5E3,2500
,3.3E6,3300000,2.5E1,25,5.5E
3,5500,5.25E-2,.0525
5010   DATA 1E-4,.0001,1.25E-1,.1
25,5E-6,.000005,6E-3,.006
5011   DATA 10,WRITE THE FOLLOWIN
G USING                 ENGINE
ERING NOTATION.
5012   DATA 20000,20KILO,94000000
,94MEG,2000000000,2GIGA,2500
0,25KILO,20,20
```

```
5013   DATA .025,25MILLI,.0001,10
OMICRO,.3,300MILLI,.00000000
0180,180PICO
5014   DATA .000010,10MICRO
5015   DATA 10,REMOVE ENGINEERING
NOTATION.
5016   DATA 2K,2000,4.5K,4500,56
K,56000,2M,2000000,500MILLI,
.5,20MICRO,.00002
5017   DATA 180PICO,.00000000018,
320M,320000000,10K,10000,20M
,20000000
```

Fig. E-5. Color code program.

```
1    REM   COLOR CODE
2    REM   **** INTRODUCTION ****
3    HOME
4    PRINT : PRINT : PRINT
5    PRINT  TAB( 4)"THIS PROGRAM W
     ILL ALLOW THE USER TO"
6    PRINT  TAB( 4)"PRACTICE READI
     NG THE RESISTOR"
7    PRINT  TAB( 4)"COLOR CODE."
8    PRINT
9    PRINT  TAB( 4)"IT WILL DISPLA
     Y A RESISTOR, AND ASK"
10   PRINT  TAB( 4)"THE USER TO D
     ETERMINE THE"
11   PRINT  TAB( 4)"VALUE BY READ
     ING THE COLOR CODE."
12   INVERSE
13   VTAB 20: HTAB 10: PRINT "SPA
     CE BAR TO CONTINUE"
14   NORMAL
15   GET SB$: IF SB$ <  > CHR$ (
     32) THEN  GOTO 15
16   HOME
17   PRINT  TAB( 16)"NOTES:"
18   PRINT : PRINT
19   PRINT  TAB( 2)"1.OMIT COMMAS
     WHEN ENTERING NUMBERS."
20   PRINT  TAB( 4)"EXAMPLE:1.5K
     OR 1500 NOT 1,500"
21   PRINT  TAB( 2)"2.ALL ENTERIE
     S MUST BE FOLLOWED BY"
22   PRINT  TAB( 4)"RETURN KEY."
23   INVERSE
24   VTAB 20: HTAB 10: PRINT "SPA
     CE BAR TO CONTINUE"
25   NORMAL
26   GET G$: IF G$ <  > CHR$ (32
     ) THEN  GOTO 26
27   HOME
30   B1$ = " BRN":B2$ = " BLU":B3$
     = " ORG"
31   B1 = 8:B2 = 6:B3 = 9
32   GOSUB 2000
33   PRINT  TAB( 6)"BAND COLORS =
     ";B1$;B2$;B3$
34   INVERSE
35   HTAB 8: PRINT "ADJUST TINT A
     S NEEDED"
36   HTAB 8: PRINT "SPACE BAR TO
     CONTINUE"
37   NORMAL
280  GET RT$: IF RT$ <  > CHR$
     (32) THEN  GOTO 280
300  HOME
320  REM   QUESTION LOOP ********
     ***
340  FOR K = 1 TO 20:AA = 0
341  HOME
350  READ B1$,B2$,B3$
360  READ B1,B2,B3,A1$,A2$
361  GOSUB 2000
380  PRINT "BAND COLORS = ";B1$;
     " ";B2$;" ";B3$
381  PRINT
540  PRINT K;".";"WHAT IS THE VA
     LUE OF THIS RESISTOR"
541  INPUT AA$
542  IF AA$ = A1$ OR AA$ = A2$ THEN
     GOSUB 700
543  IF AA$ <  > A1$ AND AA$ <  >
     A2$ THEN  GOSUB 840
680  NEXT K
700  REM   **** CORRECT ****
719  INVERSE
720  PRINT : PRINT : PRINT : HTAB
     14: PRINT "CORRECT!":S = S +
     1
740  HTAB 5: PRINT "SPACE BAR =
     NEXT, E = EXIT"
741  NORMAL
760  GET RR$: IF RR$ <  > CHR$
     (32) AND RR$ <  > CHR$ (69)
     THEN  GOTO 760
780  IF RR$ = CHR$ (32) AND K =
     20 THEN  GOTO 1020: REM  **
     SCORE **
800  IF RR$ = CHR$ (32) THEN  RETURN
820  IF RR$ = CHR$ (69) THEN  GOTO
     1020: REM  SCORE
840  REM   **** WRONG *****
859  INVERSE
860  PRINT : PRINT : PRINT : HTAB
     15: PRINT "WRONG ";A1$
880  HTAB 5: PRINT "SPACE BAR =
     NEXT, H = HELP HINTS"
900  HTAB 5: PRINT "E = EXIT"
901  NORMAL
920  GET WW$: IF WW$ <  > CHR$
     (32) AND WW$ <  > CHR$ (69)
     AND WW$ <  > CHR$ (72) THEN
     GOTO 920
940  IF WW$ = CHR$ (32) AND K =
     20 THEN  GOTO 1020
960  IF WW$ = CHR$ (32) THEN  RETURN
980  IF WW$ = CHR$ (72) THEN  GOSUB
     1280: RETURN : REM *** HELP
     HINTS
1000 IF WW$ = CHR$ (69) THEN  GOTO
     1020
1020 REM  *** SCORE ****
1021 TEXT
1060 HOME : VTAB 8
1080 E = (S / K) * 100
1100 PRINT  TAB( 8)"YOUR SCORE
     IS ";E;"%": PRINT
1120 PRINT  TAB( 8)"FOR ";K;" Q
     UESTIONS ASKED": PRINT : PRINT
     : PRINT
```

Fig. E-5. Color code program. (Continued from page 294)

```
1160  PRINT  TAB( 8)"SPACE BAR F
      OR MAIN MENU."
1180  GET MM$: IF MM$ < > CHR$
      (32) THEN 1180
1200  PRINT  CHR$ (4);"-STARTUP"

1280  REM  **** HELP ****
1285  TEXT : HOME
1290  PRINT  TAB( 4)"THE BAND CL
      OSER TO ONE END THEN"
1295  PRINT  TAB( 4)"THE OTHERS
      REPRESENTS THE FIRST"
1300  PRINT  TAB( 4)"DIGIT OF TH
      E VALUE, THE NEXT BAND"
1301  PRINT  TAB( 4)"IN REPRESEN
      TS THE SECOND DIGIT,"
1302  PRINT  TAB( 4)"THE THIRD B
      AND IS THE MULTIPLIER,"
1303  PRINT  TAB( 4)"THE FOURTH
      BAND IF ANY IS THE"
1304  PRINT  TAB( 4)"TOLERANCE R
      ATING (IF NONE TOLERANCE"
1305  PRINT  TAB( 4)"IS 20%)."
1306  INVERSE
1307  VTAB 20: HTAB 8: PRINT "SP
      ACE BAR FOR MORE"
1308  NORMAL
1309  GET HH$: IF HH$ < > CHR$
      (32) THEN GOTO 1309
1310  B1 = 12:B2 = 6:B3 = 9
1311  HOME : GOSUB 2000
1315  PRINT "THEREFORE THIS RESI
      STOR READS:"
1320  PRINT "GRN (5) BLU (6) ORG
      (3)"
1325  PRINT "SO THE VALUE IS 560
      00 OR 56K."
1330  INVERSE
1335  HTAB 8: PRINT "SPACE BAR T
      O CONTINUE";
1340  NORMAL
1345  GET RT$: IF RT$ < > CHR$
      (32) THEN GOTO 1345
1350  RETURN
2000  GR
2001  COLOR= 15
2002  HLIN 7,30 AT 6
2003  HLIN 7,30 AT 12
2004  VLIN 6,12 AT 7
2005  VLIN 6,12 AT 30
2006  HLIN 5,7 AT 9
2007  HLIN 30,32 AT 9
2008  HLIN 7,30 AT 5
2009  HLIN 7,30 AT 13
2010  COLOR= B1: FOR D = 6 TO 12
      : HLIN 10,12 AT D: NEXT D
2020  COLOR= B2: FOR D = 6 TO 12
      : HLIN 15,17 AT D: NEXT D
2030  COLOR= B3: FOR D = 6 TO 12
      : HLIN 20,22 AT D: NEXT D
2090  RETURN
5000  DATA BRN,BLK,BLK,8,0,0,10,
      10
5001  DATA RED,RED,BLK,1,1,0,22,
      22
5002  DATA  ORG,ORG,RED,9,9,1,3
      .3K,3300
5003  DATA BRN,GRY,ORG,8,5,9,18K
      ,18000
5004  DATA YEL,VIO,RED,13,3,1,4.
      7K,4700
5005  DATA GRN,BLU,BLK,12,6,0,56
      ,56
5006  DATA BRN,BLK,BRN,8,0,8,100
      ,100
5007  DATA GRY,RED,RED,5,1,1,8.2
      K,8200
5008  DATA YEL,VIO,BLK,13,3,0,47
      ,47
5009  DATA ORG,ORG,YEL,9,9,13,33
      0K,330000
5010  DATA GRN,BLU,ORG,12,6,9,56
      K,56000
5011  DATA BRN,GRY,BRN,8,5,8,180
      ,180
5012  DATA RED,RED,GRN,1,1,12,2.
      2M,2200000
5013  DATA ORG,WHT,RED,9,15,1,3.
      9K,3900
5014  DATA BLU,GRY,BRN,6,5,8,680
      ,680
5015  DATA ORG,ORG,ORG,9,9,9,33K
      ,33000
5016  DATA RED,VIO,RED,1,3,1,2.7
      K,2700
5017  DATA BRN,GRN,YEL,8,12,13,1
      50K,150000
5018  DATA BRN,RED,BLU,8,1,6,12M
      ,12000000
5019  DATA GRY,RED,BLK,5,1,0,82,
      82
```

Fig. E-6. Ohmmeter program.

```
1    REM   OHM METER
2    REM   *** INTRODUCTION ***
3    HOME
4    PRINT   TAB( 4)"THIS PROGRAM A
     LLOWS THE USER TO"
5    PRINT   TAB( 4)"PRACTICE READI
     NG A DIGITAL OHM METER."
6    PRINT : PRINT   TAB( 4)"IT WIL
     L DISPLAY A DIGITAL TYPE OHM
     "
7    PRINT   TAB( 4)"METER WITH THE
      RANGE SETTING, AND A"
8    PRINT   TAB( 4)"READING ON IT'
     S DISPLAY."
9    PRINT   TAB( 4)"THE USER WILL
     BE ASKED TO DETERMINE"
10   PRINT   TAB( 4)"THE RESISTANC
     E BEING MEASURED."
11   PRINT
12   PRINT   TAB( 4)"THE PROGRAM E
     XPECTS THE ANSWERS TO"
13   PRINT   TAB( 4)"BE WITHIN 5%
     OF THE COMPUTER'S"
14   PRINT   TAB( 4)"ANSWERS.": PRINT

15   PRINT   TAB( 4)"USER SHOULD N
     OT USE ENG. NOTATION,"
16   PRINT   TAB( 4)"OR SCIENTIFIC
      NOTATION."
260  INVERSE : VTAB 20: HTAB 8: PRINT
     "SPACE BAR TO CONTINUE": NORMAL

280  GET RT$: IF RT$ < > CHR$
     (32) THEN   GOTO 280
300  HOME
320  REM   QUESTION LOOP ********
     ***
340  FOR K = 1 TO 20:AA = 0
341  HOME
360  READ CT,G1$,A
362  GOSUB 3000
520  PRINT : PRINT
540  PRINT K;".";"WHAT IS THE RE
     SISTANCE BEING"
541  AA = 0
560  INPUT "  MEASURED IN OHMS ?
     ";AA$:AA =  VAL (AA$)
561  LU = A - (A * .05):HU = A +
     (A * .05)
580  IF A < 0 THEN LU =  = A + (
     A * .05):HU = A - (A * .05)
600  IF AA > LU AND AA < HU THEN
     GOSUB 700: REM  **** CORREC
     T *****
620  IF AA = LU OR AA = HU THEN
     GOSUB 700: REM   CORRECT
640  IF AA < LU OR AA > HU THEN
     GOSUB 840: REM  *** WRONG *
     **
660  IF K = 20 THEN   GOTO 1020
```

```
680  NEXT K
700  REM   **** CORRECT ****
719  INVERSE
720  PRINT : HTAB 14: PRINT "COR
     RECT!":S = S + 1
740  PRINT : HTAB 5: PRINT "SPAC
     E BAR = NEXT, E = EXIT"
741  NORMAL
760  GET RR$: IF RR$ < > CHR$
     (32) AND RR$ < > CHR$ (69)
      THEN   GOTO 760
780  IF RR$ = CHR$ (32) AND K =
     20 THEN   GOTO 1020: REM  **
     SCORE **
800  IF RR$ = CHR$ (32) THEN   RETURN
820  IF RR$ = CHR$ (69) THEN   GOTO
     1020: REM  SCORE
840  REM   **** WRONG *****
859  INVERSE
860  PRINT : HTAB 12: PRINT "WRO
     NG ";A
880  PRINT : HTAB 4: PRINT "SPAC
     E BAR = NEXT, H=HELP HINTS"
900  HTAB 4: PRINT "E = EXIT"
901  NORMAL
920  GET WW$: IF WW$ < > CHR$
     (32) AND WW$ < > CHR$ (69)
     AND WW$.< > CHR$ (72) THEN
     GOTO 920
940  IF WW$ = CHR$ (32) AND K =
     20 THEN   GOTO 1020
960  IF WW$ = CHR$ (32) THEN   RETURN
980  IF WW$ = CHR$ (72) THEN   GOSUB
     1280: RETURN : REM *** HELP
     HINTS
1000 IF WW$ = CHR$ (69) THEN   GOTO
     1020
1020 REM   *** SCORE ****
1060 HOME : VTAB 8
1080 E = (S / K) * 100
1100 PRINT   TAB( 8)"YOUR SCORE
     IS ";E;"%": PRINT
1120 PRINT   TAB( 8)"FOR ";K;" Q
     UESTIONS ASKED": PRINT : PRINT
     : PRINT
1160 PRINT   TAB( 8)"SPACE BAR F
     OR MAIN MENU."
1180 GET MM$: IF MM$ < > CHR$
     (32) THEN 1180
1200 PRINT   CHR$ (4);"-STARTUP"

1280 REM  ** HELP HINTS **
1290 HOME
1300 CT = 4:G1$ = "32.50"
1310 GOSUB 3000
1320 PRINT
1330 PRINT   TAB( 4)"THE RANGE I
     S SET FOR 200K,THIS"
```

```
1340   PRINT   TAB( 4)"MEANS THE M
       AXIMUM RESISTANCE THIS"
1350   PRINT   TAB( 4)"SETTING CAN
       MEASURE IS 200K OHMS."
1360   PRINT   TAB( 4)"TO INTERPET
       THE DISPLAY, USE"
1370   PRINT   TAB( 4)"ENGINEERING
       NOTATION, THE VALUE"
1380   PRINT   TAB( 4)"DISPLAYED S
       HOULD BE MULTIPLIED BY"
1390   PRINT   TAB( 4)"1000 IF IT
       IS A K RANGE, OR 1000000"
1400   PRINT   TAB( 4)"IF IT IS A
       M RANGE."
1410   HTAB 8: INVERSE : PRINT "S
       PACE BAR FOR MORE";: NORMAL

1420   GET HT$: IF HT$ <  > CHR$
       (32) THEN  GOTO 1420
1430   VTAB 15: HTAB 1
1440   FOR KK = 1 TO 9
1450   PRINT "
                        "
1460   NEXT KK
1470   VTAB 16
1480   PRINT   TAB( 4)"THEREFORE T
       HIS METER IS MEASURING A"
1490   PRINT   TAB( 4)"32500 OHM R
       ESISTOR."
1500   PRINT   TAB( 4)"32.50 X 100
       0 (K) = 32500."
1510   PRINT   TAB( 4)"YOUR ANSWER
       SHOULD BE IN THIS"
1520   PRINT   TAB( 4)"FORM 32500.
       "
1530   VTAB 24: HTAB 26
1800   GET RT$: IF RT$ <  > CHR$
       (32) THEN  GOTO 1800
1810   RETURN
3000   HOME
3003   PRINT " ******************
       ***********"
3004   PRINT " *
                        *"
3005   PRINT " *
                        *"
3006   PRINT " * *********  2 2 2
       2 2 2      *"
3007   PRINT " * *           *    O O
       O M O    *"
3008   PRINT " * *           *    O K
       O  M   *"
3009   PRINT " * *           *
       K       *"
3010   PRINT " * *********
                *"
3011   PRINT " *               * * *
       * * *     *"
3012   PRINT " *
                *"
3013   PRINT " *
                *"
3014   PRINT " *                   OH
       MS        *"
3015   PRINT " *
                *"
3016   PRINT " ******************
       ***********"
3020   VTAB 6: HTAB 6: PRINT G1$
3025   IF CT = 2 THEN L = 17
3026   IF CT = 3 THEN L = 19
3027   IF CT = 4 THEN L = 21
3028   IF CT = 5 THEN L = 23
3029   IF CT = 6 THEN L = 25
3030   INVERSE : VTAB 9: HTAB (L)
       : PRINT "*": NORMAL : VTAB 1
       5
3031   RETURN
5000   DATA  3,1.500,1500
5001   DATA  2,15.00,15.00
5002   DATA  3,6.000,6000
5003   DATA  4,15.00,15000
5004   DATA  5,1.500,1500000
5005   DATA  6,8.300,8300000
5006   DATA  5,1.999,1999000
5007   DATA  2,8.500,8.500
5008   DATA  3,18.00,18000
5009   DATA  4,150.0,150000
5010   DATA  5,1.800,1800000
5011   DATA  6,12.50,12500000
5012   DATA  2,50.00,50
5013   DATA  2,89.00,89
5014   DATA  3,1.200,1200
5015   DATA  4,56.00,56000
5016   DATA  5,1.200,1200000
5017   DATA  6,6.800,6800000
5018   DATA  3,.7500,750
5019   DATA  4,12.10,12100
```

Fig. E-7. Ohm's law program.

```
1    REM  OHM'S LAW
2    HOME : REM  ****** INTRODUCT
     ION ******
3    PRINT  TAB( 4)"THIS PROGRAM W
     ILL ALLOW THE USER TO"
4    PRINT  TAB( 4)"PRACTICE OHM'S
      LAW, AND POWER"
5    PRINT  TAB( 4)"FORMULAS.": PRINT

6    PRINT  TAB( 4)"IT WILL DISPLA
     Y A DC CIRCUIT, AND"
7    PRINT  TAB( 4)"GIVE TWO OF TH
     E THREE VARIABLES"
8    PRINT  TAB( 4)"NEEDED FOR THE
      FORMULA (V = I X R).": PRINT

9    PRINT  TAB( 4)"EACH QUESTION
     HAS TWO PARTS."
10   PRINT : PRINT  TAB( 6)"A. SO
     LVE FOR THE UNKNOWN.": PRINT

11   PRINT  TAB( 6)"B. FIND THE P
     OWER DISSIPATED."
12   PRINT : PRINT  TAB( 4)"ANSWE
     RS ARE EXPECTED TO BE WITHIN
     "
13   PRINT  TAB( 4)"5% OF THE COM
     PUTER'S ANSWER."
14   INVERSE : VTAB 20: HTAB 8: PRINT
     "SPACE BAR TO CONTINUE": NORMAL

15   GET OK$: IF OK$ <  >  CHR$ (
     32) THEN  GOTO 15
16   HOME
17   VTAB 4: HTAB 1
18   PRINT  TAB( 4)"THE METERS IN
     THE DISPLAY ARE TO"
19   PRINT  TAB( 4)"DEMONSTRATE T
     HE CORRECT WAY TO"
20   PRINT  TAB( 4)"CONNECT THEM
     TO A CIRCUIT ONLY,"
21   PRINT  TAB( 4)"THEY ARE NOT
     MEANT TO SUPPLY"
22   PRINT  TAB( 4)"INFORMATION F
     OR CALCULATIONS."
260  INVERSE : VTAB 20: HTAB 8: PRINT
     "SPACE BAR TO CONTINUE": NORMAL

280  GET RT$: IF RT$ <  >  CHR$
     (32) THEN  GOTO 280
300  HOME
320  REM  QUESTION LOOP ********
     ***
340  FOR K = 1 TO 20:AA = 0
341  HOME
342  KP = 1
360  READ CT,V$,I$,R$,A,PA
361  GOSUB 3000
365  VTAB 21
368  PRINT "V = ";V$;" VOLTS ";"
```

```
     I = ";I$;" AMPS": PRINT "R
     = ";R$;" OHMS": INVERSE
369  PRINT " NUMBERS ONLY, DO NO
     T INCLUDE UNITS.": NORMAL
370  PRINT K;".FIND THE MISSING
     VALUE.";: PRINT " ";
541  AA = 0
560  INPUT AA$:AA =  VAL (AA$)
561  LU = A - (A * .05):HU = A +
     (A * .05)
580  IF A < 0 THEN LU =  = A + (
     A * .05):HU = A - (A * .05)
600  IF AA > LU AND AA < HU THEN
     GOSUB 700: REM  **** CORREC
     T *****
620  IF AA = LU OR AA = HU THEN
     GOSUB 700: REM  CORRECT
640  IF AA < LU OR AA > HU THEN
     GOSUB 840: REM  *** WRONG *
     **
641  HOME : GOSUB 3000:KP = 2: VTAB
     21
642  IF V$ =  CHR$ (63) THEN  PRINT
     "V = ";A;" VOLTS";" I = ";I$
     ;" AMPS": PRINT "R = ";R$;"
     OHMS": INVERSE
643  IF I$ =  CHR$ (63) THEN  PRINT
     "V = ";V$;" VOLTS";" I = ";A
     ;" AMPS": PRINT "R = ";R$;"
     OHMS": INVERSE
644  IF R$ =  CHR$ (63) THEN  PRINT
     "V = ";V$;" VOLTS";" I = ";I
     $;" AMPS": PRINT "R = ";A;"
     OHMS": INVERSE
652  PRINT " NUMBERS ONLY, DO NO
     T INCLUDE UNITS.": NORMAL
653  PRINT "FIND POWER DISSIPATE
     D IN WATTS ";
654  PR$ = "0":PR = 0: INPUT PR$:
     PR =  VAL (PR$)
655  LP = PA - (PA * .05):HP = PA
     + (PA * .05)
656  IF PR > LP AND PR < HP THEN
     GOSUB 700: REM   CORRECT
657  IF PR = LP OR PR = HP THEN
     GOSUB 700
658  IF PR < LP OR PR > HP THEN
     GOSUB 840: REM   WRONG
659  KP = 1
660  IF K = 20 THEN  GOTO 1020
680  NEXT K
700  REM  **** CORRECT ****
719  INVERSE
720  HTAB 14: PRINT "CORRECT!":S
     = S + .5
740  PRINT : HTAB 5: PRINT "SPAC
     E BAR = NEXT, E = EXIT"
741  NORMAL
760  GET RR$: IF RR$ <  >  CHR$
     (32) AND RR$ <  >  CHR$ (69)
```

Fig. E-7. Ohm's law program. (Continued from page 298)

```
        THEN  GOTO 760
800   IF RR$ =  CHR$ (32) THEN  RETURN

820   IF RR$ =  CHR$ (69) THEN  GOTO
      1020: REM  SCORE
840   REM  **** WRONG *****
859   INVERSE
860   IF KP = 1 THEN  HTAB 12: PRINT
      "WRONG ";A
861   IF KP = 2 THEN  HTAB 12: PRINT
      "WRONG ";PA
880   HTAB 4: PRINT "SPACE BAR =
      NEXT, H=HELP HINTS"
900   HTAB 4: PRINT "E = EXIT"
901   NORMAL
920   GET WW$: IF WW$ <  > CHR$
      (32) AND WW$ <  > CHR$ (69)
      AND WW$ <  > CHR$ (72) THEN
      GOTO 920
960   IF WW$ =  CHR$ (32) THEN  RETURN

980   IF WW$ =  CHR$ (72) THEN  GOSUB
      1280: RETURN : REM *** HELP
      HINTS
1000  IF WW$ =  CHR$ (69) THEN  GOTO
      1020
1020  REM  *** SCORE ****
1021  TEXT
1060  HOME : VTAB 8
1080  E = (S / K) * 100
1100  PRINT  TAB( 8)"YOUR SCORE
      IS ";E;"%": PRINT
1120  PRINT  TAB( 8)"FOR ";K;" Q
      UESTIONS ASKED": PRINT : PRINT
      : PRINT
1160  PRINT  TAB( 8)"SPACE BAR F
      OR MAIN MENU."
1180  GET MM$: IF MM$ <  > CHR$
      (32) PRINT 1180
1200  PRINT  CHR$ (4);"-STARTUP"

1280  REM  ** HELP ***
1300  TEXT : HOME
1310  VTAB 2
1320  PRINT  TAB( 4)"WITH WHAT I
      S GIVEN ONE OF THESE"
1330  PRINT  TAB( 4)"FORMULAS SH
      OULD APPLY.": PRINT
1340  PRINT  TAB( 4)"OHM'S LAW
            POWER FORMULAS"
1350  PRINT : PRINT  TAB( 4)"V=
      I X R          P= I X V"
1360  PRINT : PRINT  TAB( 4)"R=
      V/I            P= I X I X R
      "
1370  PRINT : PRINT  TAB( 4)"I=
      V/R            P= (E X E)/
      R"
1380  VTAB 20: HTAB 8: INVERSE
1390  PRINT "SPACE BAR TO CONTIN
```

```
      UE.": NORMAL : HTAB 1
1400   GET DO$: IF DO$ <  > CHR$
       (32) THEN 1400
1410   RETURN
3000   REM  ** CIRCUIT **
3010   HGR
3011   HCOLOR= 3
3012   REM  BOX
3015   HPLOT 20,60 TO 20,120
3020   HPLOT 20,60 TO 40,60
3025   HPLOT 85,60 TO 200,60
3030   HPLOT 200,60 TO 200,120
3035   HPLOT 20,120 TO 80,120
3038   REM  3040-3048 RESISTOR
3040   HPLOT 105,120 TO 200,120
3041   HPLOT 40,60 TO 45,55
3042   HPLOT 45,55 TO 50,65
3043   HPLOT 50,65 TO 55,55
3044   HPLOT 55,55 TO 60,65
3045   HPLOT 60,65 TO 65,55
3046   HPLOT 65,55 TO 70,65
3047   HPLOT 70,65 TO 75,55
3048   HPLOT 75,55 TO 80,65
3049   HPLOT 80,65 TO 85,60
3050   REM  BATT
3051   HPLOT 80,110 TO 80,130
3052   HPLOT 85,115 TO 85,125
3053   HPLOT 90,110 TO 90,130
3054   HPLOT 95,115 TO 95,125
3055   HPLOT 100,110 TO 100,130
3056   HPLOT 105,115 TO 105,125
3057   IF CT = 2 THEN  GOTO 3110
3060   REM  METER
3061   HPLOT 130,50 TO 130,70
3062   HPLOT 130,70 TO 150,80
3063   HPLOT 150,80 TO 170,70
3064   HPLOT 170,70 TO 170,50
3065   HPLOT 130,50 TO 150,40
3066   HPLOT 150,40 TO 170,50
3067   HCOLOR= 0: HPLOT 130,60 TO
       170,60
3068   HCOLOR= 3
3069   HPLOT 150,50 TO 150,65
3070   HPLOT 150,50 TO 145,55
3071   HPLOT 150,50 TO 155,55
3072   HPLOT 140,58 TO 136,68
3073   HPLOT 140,58 TO 144,68
3074   HPLOT 143,65 TO 137,65
3100   RETURN
3110   REM  METER II
3120   HPLOT 45,20 TO 45,40
3130   HPLOT 45,40 TO 65,50
3140   HPLOT 65,50 TO 85,40
3150   HPLOT 85,40 TO 85,20
3160   HPLOT 45,20 TO 65,10
3170   HPLOT 85,20 TO 65,10
3190   HCOLOR= 3: REM  NEEDLE
3200   HPLOT 65,20 TO 65,35
3210   HPLOT 65,20 TO 70,25
3220   HPLOT 65,20 TO 60,25
```

Fig. E-7. Ohm's law program. (Continued from page 299)

```
3230    HPLOT 55,38 TO 51,28          5007    DATA 2,15,?,500,.03,.45
3240    HPLOT 55,38 TO 59,28          5008    DATA 1,100,?,25,4,400
3241    HPLOT 40,30 TO 45,30          5009    DATA 2,12,.3,?,40,3.6
3242    HPLOT 40,30 TO 40,60          5010    DATA 2,20,.2,?,100,4
3243    HPLOT 85,30 TO 90,30          5011    DATA 1,?,.16,500,80,12.8
3244    HPLOT 90,30 TO 90,60          5012    DATA 1,?,2,15,30,60
3260    RETURN                        5013    DATA 1,24,2,?,12,48
5000    DATA 1,?,.25,20,5,1.25        5014    DATA 1,48,.024,?,2000,1.15
5001    DATA 2,10,?,20,.5,5           2
5002    DATA 1,10,.25,?,40,2.5        5015    DATA 1,36,.02,?,1800,.72
5003    DATA 2,20,.2,?,100,4          5016    DATA 1,?,.15,500,75,11.25
5004    DATA 1,?,.04,1250,50,2        5017    DATA 1,40,?,200,.2,8
5005    DATA 1,40,.02,?,2000,.8       5018    DATA 1,18,.2,?,90,3.6
5006    DATA 2,5,?,1000,.005,.025     5019    DATA 1,?,.25,120,30,7.5
```

Fig. E-8. V&A meter program.

```
2    HOME : REM  ****** INTRODUCT
     ION ******
3    PRINT  TAB( 4)"THIS PRORGAM W
     ILL ALLOW THE USER"
4    PRINT  TAB( 4)"TO PRACTICE ME
     TER READING."
5    PRINT
6    PRINT  TAB( 4)"IT WILL DISPLA
     Y A METER SCALE"
7    PRINT  TAB( 4)"THE METER NEED
     LE, AND THE SCALE'S     VA
     LUE."
8    PRINT : PRINT  TAB( 4)"THE US
     ER WILL BE ASKED TO DETERMIN
     E"
9    PRINT  TAB( 4)"THE VOLTAGE OR
     CURRENT THAT THE "
10   PRINT  TAB( 4)"METER IS MEAS
     URING."
11   PRINT
12   PRINT  TAB( 4)"THE USER IS E
     XPECTED TO BE WITH IN"
13   PRINT  TAB( 4)"THE FOLLOWING
     TOLERANCES:"
14   PRINT : PRINT  TAB( 4)"30 SC
     ALE +/- .5"
15   PRINT  TAB( 4)"300 SCALE +/-
     5"
16   PRINT  TAB( 4)"3000 SCALE +/
     - 50"
260  INVERSE : VTAB 20: HTAB 8: PRINT
     "SPACE BAR TO CONTINUE": NORMAL

280  GET RT$: IF RT$ <  > CHR$
     (32) THEN  GOTO 280
300  HOME
320  REM   QUESTION LOOP ********
     ***
340  FOR K = 1 TO 20:AA = 0
341  HOME
360  READ MN,MS$,MT$,A
400  GOSUB 3000
410  PRINT : PRINT : INVERSE
420  HTAB 4: PRINT "PRESENT SCAL
     E IS ";MS$;" ";MT$: NORMAL
430  PRINT : PRINT
440  PRINT K;". WHAT IS THE VALU
     E IN ";MT$;" ";
541  AA = 0
560  INPUT AA$:AA =  VAL (AA$)
561  E =  VAL (MS$)
562  IF E = 30 THEN LU = A - .5:
     HU = A + .5
563  IF E = 300 THEN LU = A - 5:
     HU = A + 5
564  IF E = 3000 THEN LU = A - 5
     0:HU = A + 50
600  IF AA > LU AND AA < HU THEN
     GOSUB 700: REM  **** CORREC
     T *****
```

```
620  IF AA = LU OR AA = HU THEN
     GOSUB 700: REM  CORRECT
640  IF AA < LU OR AA > HU THEN
     GOSUB 840: REM  *** WRONG *
     **
660  IF K = 20 THEN  GOTO 1020
680  NEXT K
700  REM  **** CORRECT ****
719  INVERSE
720  PRINT : PRINT : PRINT : HTAB
     14: PRINT "CORRECT!":S = S +
     1
740  PRINT : HTAB 5: PRINT "SPAC
     E BAR = NEXT, E = EXIT."
741  NORMAL
760  GET RR$: IF RR$ <  > CHR$
     (32) AND RR$ <  > CHR$ (69)
     THEN  GOTO 760
780  IF RR$ =  CHR$ (32) AND K =
     20 THEN  GOTO 1020: REM  **
     SCORE **
800  IF RR$ =  CHR$ (32) THEN  RETURN
820  IF RR$ =  CHR$ (69) THEN  GOTO
     1020: REM  SCORE
840  REM  **** WRONG *****
859  INVERSE
860  PRINT : PRINT : PRINT : HTAB
     12: PRINT "WRONG ";A
880  PRINT : HTAB 4: PRINT "SPAC
     E BAR = NEXT, E = EXIT."
901  NORMAL
920  GET WW$: IF WW$ <  > CHR$
     (32) AND WW$ <  > CHR$ (69)
     AND WW$ <  > CHR$ (72) THEN
     GOTO 920
940  IF WW$ =  CHR$ (32) AND K =
     20 THEN  GOTO 1020
960  IF WW$ =  CHR$ (32) THEN  RETURN

1000 IF WW$ =  CHR$ (69) THEN  GOTO
     1020
1020 REM  *** SCORE ****
1060 HOME : VTAB 8
1080 E = (S / K) * 100
1100 PRINT  TAB( 8)"YOUR SCORE
     IS ";E;"%": PRINT
1120 PRINT  TAB( 8)"FOR ";K;" Q
     UESTIONS ASKED": PRINT : PRINT
     : PRINT
1160 PRINT  TAB( 8)"SPACE BAR F
     OR MAIN MENU."
1180 GET MM$: IF MM$ <  > CHR$
     (32) THEN 1180
1200 PRINT  CHR$ (4);"-STARTUP"

3000 REM  ** SCALE **
3001 HOME
3003 PRINT  TAB( 4)"0    5    1
     0   15   20   25   30": PRINT
```

301

Fig. E-8. V&A meter program. (Continued from page 301)

```
3004  PRINT  TAB( 4)"¦      ¦    ¦
      ¦    ¦    ¦       ¦ "
3005  PRINT  TAB( 4)"¦¦¦¦¦¦¦¦¦¦¦
   ¦¦¦¦¦¦¦¦¦¦¦¦¦¦¦¦¦¦¦¦¦ "
3006  PRINT  TAB( 4)"_____
   _____ "

3007  VTAB 4
3008  HTAB MN: PRINT "¦"
3009  HTAB MN: PRINT "¦"
3010  HTAB MN: PRINT "¦"
3011  HTAB 1
3012  RETURN
5000  DATA  14,30,VOLTS,10
5001  DATA 17,300,MILLIAMPS,130
5002  DATA 15,3000,VOLTS,1100
5003  DATA 29,3000,MILLIAMPS,250
```

```
                          0
5004  DATA 34,30,MILLIAMPS,30
5005  DATA 19,30,VOLTS,15
5006  DATA 9,30,VOLTS,5
5007  DATA 13,300,VOLTS,90
5008  DATA 27,300,MILLIAMPS,230
5009  DATA 24,300,MILLIAMPS,200
5010  DATA 29,3000,VOLTS,2500
5011  DATA 19,30,VOLTS,15
5012  DATA 25,30,MILLIAMPS,21
5013  DATA 16,30,VOLTS,12
5014  DATA 7,30,MILLIAMPS,3
5015  DATA 13,30,VOLTS,9
5016  DATA 32,300,MILLIAMPS,280
5017  DATA 16,300,MILLIAMPS,120
5018  DATA 22,30,VOLTS,18
5019  DATA 28,300,VOLTS,240
```

Fig. E-9. Oscilloscope dc program.

```
1    REM   SCOPE DC
2    REM   *** INTRODUCTION ***
3    HOME
5    PRINT  TAB( 4)"THIS PROGRAM A
     LLOWS THE USER TO"
6    PRINT  TAB( 4)"PRACTICE READI
     NG DC VOLTAGES ON"
7    PRINT  TAB( 4)"THE OSCILLOSCO
     PE.": PRINT
8    PRINT  TAB( 4)"THE OSCILLOSCO
     PE SCREEN WILL BE"
9    PRINT  TAB( 4)"DISPLAYED WITH
      A TRACE REPRESENTING"
10   PRINT  TAB( 4)"A DC VOLTAGE,
     THE USER WILL BE ASKED"
11   PRINT  TAB( 4)"TO DETERMINE
     THE VOLTAGE USING THE"
12   PRINT  TAB( 4)"SCREEN AND TH
     E VOLT/DIV SETTING FOR"
13   PRINT  TAB( 4)"CHANNEL 1 (TH
     IS IS THE ONLY CHANNEL"
14   PRINT  TAB( 4)"USED IN THIS
     EXERCISE).": PRINT
15   PRINT  TAB( 4)"GROUND REFERE
     NCE IS SET TO BE THE"
16   PRINT  TAB( 4)"CENTER LINE."
     : PRINT
17   PRINT  TAB( 4)"THE USER IS E
     XPECTED TO BE WITHIN 5%"
18   PRINT  TAB( 4)"OF THE ACTUAL
      READING."
260  INVERSE : VTAB 20: HTAB 8: PRINT
     "SPACE BAR TO CONTINUE": NORMAL

280  GET RT$: IF RT$ < > CHR$
     (32) THEN  GOTO 280
300  HOME
320  REM   QUESTION LOOP ********
     ***
340  FOR K = 1 TO 20:AA = 0
341  HOME
520  READ T$,V$,DL,A
530  GOSUB 3000
535  VTAB 21
536  PRINT "VOLT/DIV = ";V$;"  T
     IME/DIV = ";T$: PRINT
540  PRINT K;". WHAT IS THE VOLT
     AGE ";
541  AA = 0
560  INPUT AA$:AA =  VAL (AA$)
561  LU = A - (A * .05):HU = A +
     (A * .05)
580  IF A < 0 THEN LU = A + (A *
     .05):HU = A - (A * .05)
600  IF AA > LU AND AA < HU THEN
     GOSUB 700: REM  **** CORREC
     T *****
620  IF AA = LU OR AA = HU THEN
     GOSUB 700: REM  CORRECT
640  IF AA < LU OR AA > HU THEN

     GOSUB 840: REM  *** WRONG *
     **
660  IF K = 20 THEN  GOTO 1020
680  NEXT K
700  REM  **** CORRECT ****
719  INVERSE
720  HTAB 14: PRINT "CORRECT!":S
     = S + 1
740  HTAB 5: PRINT "SPACE BAR =
     NEXT, E = EXIT"
741  NORMAL : PRINT
760  GET RR$: IF RR$ < > CHR$
     (32) AND RR$ < > CHR$ (69)
     THEN  GOTO 760
780  IF RR$ = CHR$ (32) AND K =
     20 THEN  GOTO 1020: REM  **
     SCORE **
800  IF RR$ = CHR$ (32) THEN  RETURN
820  IF RR$ = CHR$ (69) THEN  GOTO
     1020: REM  SCORE
840  REM  **** WRONG *****
859  INVERSE
860  HTAB 12: PRINT "WRONG ";A
880  HTAB 4: PRINT "SPACE BAR =
     NEXT, H=HELP HINTS"
900  HTAB 4: PRINT "E = EXIT"
901  NORMAL
920  GET WW$: IF WW$ < > CHR$
     (32) AND WW$ < > CHR$ (69)
     AND WW$ < > CHR$ (72) THEN
     GOTO 920
940  IF WW$ = CHR$ (32) AND K =
     20 THEN  GOTO 1020
960  IF WW$ = CHR$ (32) THEN  RETURN
980  IF WW$ = CHR$ (72) THEN  GOSUB
     1280: RETURN : REM *** HELP
     HINTS
1000 IF WW$ = CHR$ (69) THEN  GOTO
     1020
1020 REM  *** SCORE ****
1021 TEXT
1060 HOME : VTAB 8
1080 E = (S / K) * 100
1100 PRINT  TAB( 8)"YOUR SCORE
     IS ";E;"%": PRINT
1120 PRINT  TAB( 8)"FOR ";K;" Q
     UESTIONS ASKED": PRINT : PRINT
     : PRINT
1160 PRINT  TAB( 8)"SPACE BAR F
     OR MAIN MENU."
1180 GET MM$: IF MM$ < > CHR$
     (32) THEN 1180
1200 PRINT  CHR$ (4);"-STARTUP"

1280 REM  *** HELP ***
1281 TEXT : HOME
1285 PRINT  TAB( 4)"THIS EXERCI
     SE IS CONCERNED WITH"
```

Fig. E-9. Oscilloscope dc program. (Continued from page 303)

```
1286  PRINT   TAB( 4)"DC VOLTAGE
      READING ONLY.": PRINT
1287  PRINT   TAB( 4)"FOR THAT RE
      ASON THE ONLY DIVISIONS"
1288  PRINT   TAB( 4)"WE NEED TO
      READ ARE THE ONES"
1289  PRINT   TAB( 4)"GOING FROM
      TOP TO BOTTOM."
1290  PRINT   TAB( 4)"THE CENTER
      LINE IS SET TO BE GROUND"
1291  PRINT   TAB( 4)"REFERENCE,
      SO ANY TRACE ABOVE THE"
1292  PRINT   TAB( 4)"CENTER LINE
      WOULD BE A POSITIVE"
1293  PRINT   TAB( 4)"VOLTAGE, AN
      D ANY TRACE BELOW THE"
1294  PRINT   TAB( 4)"CENTER LINE
      WOULD BE A NEGATIVE"
1295  PRINT   TAB( 4)"VOLTAGE."
1296  INVERSE
1297  VTAB 20: HTAB 8: PRINT "SP
      ACE BAR FOR MORE"
1298  NORMAL
1299  GET HH$: IF HH$ <  > CHR$
      (32) THEN  GOTO 1299
1300 T$ = "50US ":V$ = "5V":DL =
      35
1301  GOSUB 3000
1302  VTAB 21: PRINT "VOLTS/DIV
      = ";V$;"  TIME/DIV = ";T$;: INVERSE
      : PRINT "EXAMPLE": NORMAL
1303  PRINT "THIS TRACE IS 2 DIV
      ISIONS UP FROM"
1304  PRINT "REFERENCE, SO: 2 X
      5V PER DIV.= +10V."
1305  INVERSE
1306  HTAB 8: PRINT "SPACE BAR T
      O CONTINUE";: NORMAL
1320  GET BK$: IF BK$ <  > CHR$
```

```
     (32) THEN   GOTO 1320
1321  RETURN
3000  REM  *** SCREEN & TRACE **
      *
3005  HOME : HGR
3010  HCOLOR= 6
3020  FOR I = 5 TO 125 STEP 15
3030  HPLOT 10,I TO 170,I
3040  NEXT I
3050  FOR H = 10 TO 170 STEP 16
3060  HPLOT H,5 TO H,125
3070  NEXT H
3071  HPLOT 5,65 TO 175,65
3072  HPLOT 90,1 TO 90,130
3080  HCOLOR= 7
3090  HPLOT 25,DL TO 155,DL
3091  HPLOT 25,(DL + 1) TO 155,(
      DL + 1)
3100  RETURN
5000  DATA   50US,5V,35,10
5001  DATA 50US,2V,20,6
5002  DATA 50US,1V,35,2
5003  DATA 50US,5V,20,15
5004  DATA 50US,2V,80,-2
5005  DATA 50US,100V,35,200
5006  DATA 50US,10V,95,-20
5007  DATA 50US,50V,110,-150
5008  DATA 50US,20V,35,40
5009  DATA 50US,5V,35,10
5010  DATA 50US,10V,95,-20
5011  DATA 50US,5V,110,-15
5012  DATA 50US,20V,35,40
5013  DATA 50US,50V,35,100
5014  DATA 50US,1V,20,3
5015  DATA 50US,10V,35,20
5016  DATA 50US,20V,20,60
5017  DATA 50US,10V,110,-30
5018  DATA 50US,20V,95,-40
5019  DATA 50US,5V,20,15
```

Fig. E-10. dc analysis program.

```
1    REM   DC ANALYSIS
2    HOME : REM   ****** INTRODUCT
     ION ******
3    PRINT  TAB( 4)"THIS PROGRAM A
     LLOWS THE USER TO"
4    PRINT  TAB( 4)"PRACTICE THE F
     ORMULAS USED IN"
5    PRINT  TAB( 4)"CALCULATING RE
     SISTOR NETWORKS."
6    PRINT : PRINT  TAB( 4)"IT WIL
     L DISPLAY A CIRCUIT, GIVE"
7    PRINT  TAB( 4)"THE VALUE OF T
     HE RESISTORS USED"
8    PRINT  TAB( 4)"IN THE CIRCUIT
     , AND ASK THE USER"
9    PRINT  TAB( 4)"TO CALCULATE T
     HE TOTAL RESISTANCE"
10   PRINT  TAB( 4)"OF THE CIRCUI
     T.": PRINT
11   PRINT  TAB( 4)"THE PROGRAM E
     XPECTS THE ANSWERS"
12   PRINT  TAB( 4)"TO BE WITHIN
     5% OF THE COMPUTERS"
13   PRINT  TAB( 4)"ANSWERS.": PRINT

14   PRINT  TAB( 4)"USER SHOULD N
     OT USE ENG. NOTATION,"
15   PRINT  TAB( 4)"OR SCIENTIFIC
     NOTATION IN ANSWERS."
16   INVERSE : PRINT
17   PRINT  TAB( 4)"(DO NOT USE C
     OMAS IN ANSWERS).   ": NORMAL

260  INVERSE : VTAB 20: HTAB 8: PRINT
     "SPACE BAR TO CONTINUE": NORMAL

280  GET RT$: IF RT$ <  > CHR$
     (32) THEN  GOTO 280
300  HOME
320  REM   QUESTION LOOP ********
     ***
340  FOR K = 1 TO 20:AA = 0
341  HOME
360  READ SU1,HZ$,VT$,A
361  GOSUB 3000
365  VTAB 21
367  INVERSE
368  IF SU1 = 3 THEN  PRINT "VER
     T RES. =";VT$;" OHMS.": GOTO
     370
369  PRINT "HORZ RES. =";HZ$;"
     VERT RES. =";VT$;" OHMS."
370  PRINT "NUMBERS ONLY, DO NOT
     INCLUDE UNITS."
371  PRINT K;") FIND RESISTANCE
     TOTAL (RT) IN OHMS": NORMAL

541  AA = 0
560  INPUT AA$:AA =  VAL (AA$)
561  LU = A - (A * .05):HU = A +
```

```
     (A * .05)
580  IF A < 0 THEN LU =  = A + (
     A * .05):HU = A - (A * .05)
600  IF AA > LU AND AA < HU THEN
     GOSUB 700: REM  **** CORREC
     T *****
620  IF AA = LU OR AA = HU THEN
     GOSUB 700: REM   CORRECT
640  IF AA < LU OR AA > HU THEN
     GOSUB 840: REM  *** WRONG *
     **
660  REM  K = 20 THEN  GOTO 1020

680  NEXT K
681  GOTO 1020
700  REM  **** CORRECT ****
719  INVERSE
720  PRINT : PRINT : PRINT : HTAB
     14: PRINT "CORRECT!":S2 = S2
     + 1
740  PRINT : HTAB 5: PRINT "SPAC
     E BAR = NEXT, E = EXIT.": HTAB
     1
741  NORMAL
760  GET RR$: IF RR$ <  > CHR$
     (32) AND RR$ <  > CHR$ (69)
     THEN  GOTO 760
780  IF RR$ =  CHR$ (32) AND K =
     20 THEN  GOTO 1020: REM  **
     SCORE **
800  IF RR$ =  CHR$ (32) THEN  RETURN
820  IF RR$ =  CHR$ (69) THEN  GOTO
     1020: REM  SCORE
840  REM  **** WRONG *****
859  INVERSE
860  PRINT : PRINT : PRINT : HTAB
     12: PRINT "WRONG ";A
880  HTAB 4: PRINT "SPACE BAR =
     NEXT, H=HELP HINTS"
900  HTAB 4: PRINT "E = FOR EXIT
     "
901  NORMAL
920  GET WW$: IF WW$ <  > CHR$
     (32) AND WW$ <  > CHR$ (69)
     AND WW$ <  > CHR$ (72) THEN
     GOTO 920
940  IF WW$ =  CHR$ (32) AND K =
     20 THEN  GOTO 1020
960  IF WW$ =  CHR$ (32) THEN  RETURN

980  IF WW$ =  CHR$ (72) THEN  GOSUB
     1280: RETURN : REM *** HELP
     HINTS
1000 IF WW$ =  CHR$ (69) THEN  GOTO
     1020
1020 REM  *** SCORE ****
1060 HOME : TEXT : VTAB 8
1080 E = (S2 / K) * 100
1100 PRINT  TAB( 8)"YOUR SCORE
```

Fig. E-10. dc analysis program. (Continued from page 305)

```
        IS ";E;"%": PRINT
1120  PRINT  TAB( 8)"FOR ";K;" Q
      UESTIONS ASKED": PRINT : PRINT
      : PRINT
1160  PRINT  TAB( 8)"SPACE BAR F
      OR MAIN MENU."
1180  GET MM$: IF MM$ <  > CHR$
      (32) THEN 1180
1200  PRINT  CHR$ (4);"-STARTUP"

1280  REM  ** HELP **
1300  TEXT : HOME
1310  VTAB 3
1320  PRINT  TAB( 4)"WITH WHAT I
      S GIVEN ONE OR"
1330  PRINT  TAB( 4)"BOTH OF THE
      FORMULAS SHOULD"
1340  PRINT  TAB( 4)"APPLY."
1350  PRINT : PRINT  TAB( 8)"SER
      IES:": PRINT
1360  PRINT  TAB( 6)"RT = R1 + R
      2 + R3 ETC.": PRINT
1370  PRINT  TAB( 8)"PARALLEL:":
      PRINT
1380  PRINT  TAB( 6)"1/RT = 1/R1
      + 1/R2 + 1/R3 ETC."
1381  PRINT : PRINT : PRINT  TAB(
      31)"¦"
1382  PRINT  TAB( 6)"HORIZONTAL
      ___  VERTICAL ¦"
1390  VTAB 20: HTAB 8
1400  INVERSE : PRINT "SPACE BAR
      TO CONTINUE": NORMAL : HTAB
      1
1410  GET DO$: IF DO$ <  > CHR$
      (32) THEN  GOTO 1410
1420  RETURN
3000  REM  ** CIRCUIT **
3001  Z =  - 10
3010  HGR
3011  HCOLOR= 3
3038  REM  3040-3048 RESISTOR
3039  IF SU1 = 3 GOTO 3058
3040  FOR X =  - 20 TO 160 STEP
      60: REM  ** HORZ RES **
3041  HPLOT 42 + X,40 + Y TO 45 +
      X,35 + Y
3042  HPLOT 45 + X,35 + Y TO 50 +
      X,45 + Y
3043  HPLOT 50 + X,45 + Y TO 55 +
      X,35 + Y
3044  HPLOT 55 + X,35 + Y TO 60 +
      X,45 + Y
3045  HPLOT 60 + X,45 + Y TO 65 +
      X,35 + Y
3046  HPLOT 65 + X,35 + Y TO 70 +
      X,45 + Y
3047  HPLOT 70 + X,45 + Y TO 73 +
      X,40 + Y
3048  NEXT X
```

```
3058  GOSUB 3500: REM  ** SETUP
      **
3059  FOR S =  - 5 TO 220 STEP T
      : IF S = 85 OR S = 130 THEN
      NEXT S
3060  HPLOT 20 + S,62 + Z TO 25 +
      S,65 + Z
3061  HPLOT 25 + S,65 + Z TO 15 +
      S,70 + Z
3062  HPLOT 15 + S,70 + Z TO 25 +
      S,75 + Z
3063  HPLOT 25 + S,75 + Z TO 15 +
      S,80 + Z
3064  HPLOT 15 + S,80 + Z TO 25 +
      S,85 + Z
3065  HPLOT 25 + S,85 + Z TO 15 +
      S,90 + Z
3066  HPLOT 15 + S,90 + Z TO 20 +
      S,93 + Z
3067  HPLOT 20 + S,52 TO 20 + S,
      40
3068  HPLOT 20 + S,83 TO 20 + S,
      92
3069  IF M = 2 THEN  GOTO 3075
3070  IF M = 1 THEN  HPLOT 15,93
      TO 110,93: HPLOT 150,93 TO
      240,93
3071  HPLOT 15,40 TO 22,40: HPLOT
      53,40 TO 82,40
3072  HPLOT 113,40 TO 142,40: HPLOT
      173,40 TO 202,40
3073  HPLOT 233,40 TO 240,40
3074  NEXT S: RETURN
3075  HPLOT 15,40 TO 255.40
3076  HPLOT 15,93 TO 255,93
3077  HPLOT 255,40 TO 255,50: HPLOT
      255,93 TO 255,83
3080  NEXT S
3100  RETURN
3500  REM  ** SETUP **
3505  IF SU1 = 1 THEN T = 45:M =
      1
3515  IF SU1 = 3 THEN T = 45:M =
      2
3520  IF SU1 = 4 THEN T = 225:M =
      1
3525  RETURN
5000  DATA 4,1K,200,4400
5001  DATA  3,0,2.2K,550
5002  DATA 4,470,1K,3880
5003  DATA  3,0,10K,2500
5004  DATA 1,330,150,888
5005  DATA  3,0,1M,250000
5006  DATA  3,0,6.8K,1700
5007  DATA 4,220K,22K,924000
5008  DATA 1,100,150,387
5009  DATA 4,470,10K,21880
5010  DATA 1,330,330,1100
5011  DATA  3,0,22K,5500
5012  DATA 4,15K,10K,80000
```

Fig. E-10. dc analysis program. (Continued from page 306)

```
5013    DATA 4,1.8K,1.8K,10800       5017    DATA 1,10,100,38
5014    DATA  3,0,470,117            5018    DATA  3,0,33K,8250
5015    DATA 1,27K,3.3K,59951        5019    DATA 1,270,1K,1658 ·
5016    DATA 4,1M,100K,4200000
```

Fig. E-11. Oscilloscope ac program.

```
1    REM    SCOPE AC
2    REM    *** INTRODUCTION ***
3    HOME
4    PRINT    TAB( 4)"THIS PROGRAM A
     LLOWS THE USER TO"
5    PRINT    TAB( 4)"PRACTICE READI
     NG AC VOLTAGES ON"
6    PRINT    TAB( 4)"THE OSCILLOSCO
     PE.": PRINT
7    PRINT    TAB( 4)"THE OSCILLOSCO
     PE SCREEN WILL BE"
8    PRINT    TAB( 4)"DISPLAYED WITH
     A TRACE REPRESENTING"
9    PRINT    TAB( 4)"AN AC VOLTAGE,
     THE USER WILL BE ASKED"
10   VTAB 8: PRINT    TAB( 4)"TO DE
     TERMINE THE VOLTAGE USING"
11   PRINT    TAB( 4)"THE SCREEN, T
     HE TIME/DIVISION,"
12   PRINT    TAB( 4)"AND THE VOLTS
     /DIVISION SETTING"
13   PRINT    TAB( 4)"FOR CHANNEL 1
     (THIS IS THE ONLY"
14   PRINT    TAB( 4)"CHANNEL USED
     IN THIS EXERCISE)."
15   PRINT
16   PRINT    TAB( 4)"GROUND REFERE
     NCE IS SET TO BE"
17   PRINT    TAB( 4)"THE CENTER LI
     NE."
18   PRINT
19   PRINT    TAB( 4)"THE USER IS E
     XPECTED TO BE WITHIN 5%"
20   PRINT    TAB( 4)"OF THE ACTUAL
     READING."
21   PRINT
22   PRINT    TAB( 4)"NOTE: UNITS A
     RE EXPECTED AS PART OF"
23   PRINT    TAB( 4)"THE ANSWER."
260  INVERSE : VTAB 24: HTAB 8: PRINT
     "SPACE BAR TO CONTINUE";: NORMAL

280  GET RT$: IF RT$ <  > CHR$
     (32) THEN  GOTO 280
300  HOME
320  REM   QUESTION LOOP ********
     ***
340  FOR K = 1 TO 20:AA = 0
341  HOME
520  READ T$,V$,CT,Q$,A$,SU$
521 A =  VAL (A$)
530  GOSUB 3000
531  INVERSE
535  VTAB 21
536  PRINT "VOLT/DIV=";V$;" TIME
     /DIV=";T$: HTAB 12: PRINT "I
     NCLUDE UNITS"
537  NORMAL
540  PRINT K;". ";Q$;
541 AA = 0
560  INPUT AA$:CO =  LEN (A$):CU
     =  LEN (SU$)
561 AB$ =  LEFT$ (AA$,CO):AC$ =
     RIGHT$ (AA$,CU)
562 AA =  VAL (AB$)
579 LU = A - (A * .20):HU = A +
     (A * .20)
580  IF A < 0 THEN LU = A + (A *
     .20):HU = A - (A * .20)
600  IF AA > LU AND AA < HU AND
     AC$ = SU$ THEN  GOSUB 700: REM
     ** CORRECT **
620  IF AA = LU OR AA = HU AND A
     C$ = SU$ THEN  GOSUB 700: REM
     ** CORRECT **
640  IF AA < LU OR AA > HU OR AC
     $ <  > SU$ THEN  GOSUB 840: REM
     WRONG
660  IF K = 20 THEN  GOTO 1020
680  NEXT K
700  REM   **** CORRECT ****
719  INVERSE
720  HTAB 14: PRINT "CORRECT!":S
     = S + 1
740  HTAB 5: PRINT "SPACE BAR =
     NEXT, E = EXIT"
741  NORMAL : PRINT
760  GET RR$: IF RR$ <  > CHR$
     (32) AND RR$ <  > CHR$ (69)
     THEN  GOTO 760
780  IF RR$ =  CHR$ (32) AND K =
     20 THEN  GOTO 1020: REM  **
     SCORE **
800  IF RR$ =  CHR$ (32) THEN  RETURN
820  IF RR$ =  CHR$ (69) THEN  GOTO
     1020: REM   SCORE
840  REM   **** WRONG *****
859  INVERSE
860  HTAB 12: PRINT "WRONG ";A$;
     " ";SU$
880  HTAB 4: PRINT "SPACE BAR =
     NEXT, H=HELP HINTS"
900  HTAB 4: PRINT "E = EXIT"
901  NORMAL
920  GET WW$: IF WW$ <  > CHR$
     (32) AND WW$ <  > CHR$ (69)
     AND WW$ <  > CHR$ (72) THEN
     GOTO 920
940  IF WW$ =  CHR$ (32) AND K =
     20 THEN  GOTO 1020
960  IF WW$ =  CHR$ (32) THEN  RETURN
980  IF WW$ =  CHR$ (72) THEN  GOSUB
     1280: RETURN : REM *** HELP
     HINTS
1000 IF WW$ =  CHR$ (69) THEN  GOTO
     1020
1020 REM   *** SCORE ****
1021 TEXT
```

```
1060   HOME : VTAB 8
1080   E = (S / K) * 100
1100   PRINT  TAB( 8)"YOUR SCORE
       IS ";E;"%": PRINT
1120   PRINT  TAB( 8)"FOR ";K;" Q
       UESTIONS ASKED": PRINT : PRINT
       : PRINT
1160   PRINT  TAB( 8)"SPACE BAR F
       OR MAIN MENU."
1180   GET MM$: IF MM$ <  >  CHR$
       (32) THEN 1180
1200   PRINT  CHR$ (4);"-STARTUP"

1280   REM  *** HELP ***
1290   TEXT : HOME
1300   PRINT  TAB( 4)"THIS EXERCI
       SE IS CONCERNED WITH AC"
1310   PRINT  TAB( 4)"VOLTAGE REA
       DING.": PRINT
1320   PRINT  TAB( 4)"WE NEED TO
       TAKE BOTH VERTICAL (VOLTS)"
1321   VTAB 5
1330   PRINT  TAB( 4)"AND HORIZON
       TAL (TIME) DIVISIONS INTO"
1340   PRINT  TAB( 4)"CONSIDERATI
       ON.": PRINT
1350   PRINT  TAB( 4)"THE CENTER
       LINE IS SET TO BE GROUND"
1360   PRINT  TAB( 4)"REFERENCE,
       SO ANY TRACE ABOVE THE"
1370   PRINT  TAB( 4)"CENTER LINE
       WOULD REPRESENT A"
1380   PRINT  TAB( 4)"POSITIVE PE
       AK, AND ANY TRACE BELOW"
1390   PRINT  TAB( 4)"THE CENTER
       LINE WOULD BE A NEGATIVE"
1391   PRINT  TAB( 4)"PEAK.": PRINT

1400   INVERSE : VTAB 20: HTAB 8
1410   PRINT "SPACE BAR FOR MORE"
       : NORMAL : HTAB 1
1420   GET GO$: IF GO$ <  >  CHR$
       (32) THEN  GOTO 1420
1430   HOME
1440   CT = 1: GOSUB 3000
1441   VTAB 21
1442   INVERSE
1450   PRINT "VOLT/DIV=5V TIME/DI
       V=50US (EXAMPLE)"
1451   NORMAL
1452   PRINT "THIS TRACE IS 4 DIV
       ISIONS LONG (TIME),"
1453   PRINT "AND 6 DIVISIONS FRO
       M TOP TO BOTTOM."
1454   INVERSE
1455   HTAB 6: PRINT "SPACE BAR F
       OR CALCULATIONS";
1456   NORMAL
1460   GET HH$: IF HH$ <  >  CHR$
       (32) THEN 1460
1470   TEXT : HOME
1471   PRINT  TAB( 4)"TIME (PERIO
       D)= 6(DIV) X 50US": PRINT
1472   PRINT  TAB( 4)"TIME (PERIO
       D)= 200US": PRINT
1473   PRINT  TAB( 4)"VOLTAGE PP
       = 6(DIV) X 5V": PRINT
1474   PRINT  TAB( 4)"VOLTAGE PP
       = 30V": PRINT
1475   PRINT  TAB( 4)"FREQUENCY =
       1/(PERIOD)": PRINT
1476   PRINT  TAB( 4)"FREQUENCY =
       5KHZ": PRINT
1477   PRINT  TAB( 4)"UNITS ARE E
       XPECTED AS PART OF THE"
1478   PRINT  TAB( 4)"ANSWER."
1479   INVERSE : VTAB 20: HTAB 8
1480   PRINT "SPACE BAR TO CONTIN
       UE";: NORMAL : HTAB 1
1481   GET RT$: IF RT$ <  >  CHR$
       (32) THEN 1481
1482   RETURN
3000   REM  *** SCREEN & TRACE **
       *
3005   HOME : HGR
3010   HCOLOR= 6
3020   FOR I = 5 TO 125 STEP 15
3030   HPLOT 10,I TO 170,I
3040   NEXT I
3050   FOR H = 10 TO 170 STEP 16
3060   HPLOT H,5 TO H,125
3070   NEXT H
3071   HPLOT 5,65 TO 175,65
3072   HPLOT 90,1 TO 90,130
3080   HCOLOR= 7
3100   REM  *** SINE ***
3110   HCOLOR= 7
3111   IF CT = 2 THEN  GOTO 3300
3112   IF CT = 3 THEN  GOTO 3400
3120   HPLOT 59,65 TO 64,40
3130   HPLOT 64,40 TO 68,28
3140   HPLOT 68,28 TO 74,20
3150   HPLOT 74,20 TO 80,28
3160   HPLOT 80,28 TO 84,40
3170   HPLOT 84,40 TO 90,65
3180   HPLOT 90,65 TO 96,90
3190   HPLOT 96,90 TO 100,102
3200   HPLOT 100,102 TO 106,110
3210   HPLOT 106,110 TO 112,102
3220   HPLOT 112,102 TO 116,90
3230   HPLOT 116,90 TO 122,65
3240   RETURN
3300   REM  *** SQR WAVE ***
3310   HPLOT 58,65 TO 58,20
3311   HPLOT 59,65 TO 59,20
3320   HPLOT 58,20 TO 90,20
3330   HPLOT 90,20 TO 90,110
3331   HPLOT 91,20 TO 91,110
3340   HPLOT 90,110 TO 122,110
3350   HPLOT 122,110 TO 122,65
```

Fig. E-11. Oscilloscope ac program. (Continued from page 309)

```
3351   HPLOT 123,110 TO 123,65
3360   RETURN
3400   REM  *** SAW TOOTH ***
3410   HPLOT 58,65 TO 90,20
3420   HPLOT 90,20 TO 90,65
3421   HPLOT 91,20 TO 91,65
3430   HPLOT 90,65 TO 122,20
3440   HPLOT 123,20 TO 123,65
3450   RETURN
5000   DATA   50US,5V,1,WHAT IS T
       HE VOLTAGE PP,30,V
5001   DATA    20US,2V,1,THE PER
       IOD OF THE WAVE IS,80,US
5002   DATA     50US,5V,2,WHAT IS
       THE VOLTAGE PP,30,V
5003   DATA    50US,2V,2,THE PERIO
       D OF THE WAVE IS,200,US
5004   DATA   10US,20V,3,WHAT IS T
       HE VOLTAGE PP,60,V
5005   DATA    50MS,10V,3,THE PERI
       OD OF THE WAVE IS,100,MS
5006   DATA  10US,2V,1,THE PERIOD
       OF THE WAVE IS,40,US
5007   DATA 20US,20V,1,WHAT IS TH
       E VOLTAGE PP,120,V
5008   DATA 2US,10V,2,THE PERIOD
       OF THE WAVE IS,8,US
5009   DATA 10US,5V,3,THE FREQUEN
       CY OF THE WAVE IS,50,KHZ
5010   DATA 2US,10V,1,THE FREQUEN
       CY OF THE WAVE IS,125,KHZ
5011   DATA 2MS,20V,2,THE FREQUEN
       CY OF THE WAVE IS,125,HZ
5012   DATA 10US,1V,3,WHAT IS THE
       VOLTAGE PP,3,V
5013   DATA 50US,100V,1,WHAT IS T
       HE VOLTAGE PP,600,V
5014   DATA 20US,10V,2,WHAT IS TH
       E VOLTAGE PP,60,V
5015   DATA 50US,2V,1,THE PERIOD
       OF THE WAVE IS,200,US
5016   DATA 5MS,10V,1,THE FREQUEN
       CY OF THE WAVE IS,50,HZ
5017   DATA 50US,10V,2,WHAT IS TH
       E VOLTAGE PP,60,V
5018   DATA 50US,20V,1,CALCULATE
       THE RMS VOLTAGE,42,V
5019   DATA 50US,50V,1,CALCULATE
       THE RMS VOLTAGE,106,V
```

Fig. E-12. Phase angle program.

```
1    REM   PHASE ANGLE
2    REM   *** INTRODUCTION ***
3    HOME
4    PRINT  TAB( 4)"THIS PROGRAM A
     LLOWS THE USER TO"
5    PRINT  TAB( 4)"PRACTICE READI
     NG PHASE DIFFERENCES"
6    PRINT  TAB( 4)"ON THE OSCILLO
     SCOPE."
7    PRINT
8    PRINT  TAB( 4)"THE OSCILLOSCO
     PE SCREEN WILL BE"
9    PRINT  TAB( 4)"DISPLAYED WITH
     TWO TRACES."
10   PRINT  TAB( 4)"THE USER WILL
     BE ASKED TO DETERMINE"
11   PRINT  TAB( 4)"THE PHASE DIF
     FERENCE USING THE"
12   PRINT  TAB( 4)"SCREEN, AND T
     HE TIME/DIVISION"
13   PRINT  TAB( 4)"SETTING."
14   PRINT  TAB( 4)"THE TRACE TO
     THE LEFT IS CHANNEL 1."
15   PRINT
16   PRINT  TAB( 4)"THE USER IS E
     XPECTED TO BE WITHIN"
17   PRINT  TAB( 4)"20% OF THE CO
     MPUTER'S ANSWERS."
260   INVERSE : VTAB 24: HTAB 8: PRINT
     "SPACE BAR TO CONTINUE";: NORMAL

280  GET RT$: IF RT$ < > CHR$
     (32) THEN  GOTO 280
300  HOME
320   REM  QUESTION LOOP ********
     ***
340   FOR K = 1 TO 20:AA = 0
341  HOME
520   READ D,Q$,A$
521  A =  VAL (A$)
530   GOSUB 3000
531   INVERSE
535  VTAB 21
536   PRINT "CH1 & CH2 VOLT/DIV =
     5V  TIME/DIV =50US": PRINT
537  NORMAL
540   PRINT K;". ";Q$;
541  AA = 0
560  INPUT AA$
561   IF A$ =  CHR$ (78) AND AA$ =
     CHR$ (78) THEN  GOSUB 700: GOTO
     660
562   IF A$ =  CHR$ (78) AND AA$ <
     > CHR$ (78) THEN  GOSUB 84
     0: GOTO 660
570  AA =  VAL (AA$)
579  LU = A - (A * .20):HU = A +
     (A * .20)
580   IF A < 0 THEN LU = A + (A *
     .20):HU = A - (A * .20)
600   IF AA > LU AND AA < HU THEN
     GOSUB 700: REM  ** CORRECT
     **
620   IF AA = LU OR AA = HU THEN
     GOSUB 700: REM   ** CORRECT
     **
640   IF AA < LU OR AA > HU THEN
     GOSUB 840: REM WRONG
660   IF K = 20 THEN  GOTO 1020
680   NEXT K
700   REM  **** CORRECT ****
719   INVERSE
720   HTAB 14: PRINT "CORRECT!":S
     = S + 1
740   HTAB 5: PRINT "SPACE BAR =
     NEXT, E = EXIT"
741   NORMAL : PRINT
760   GET RR$: IF RR$ < > CHR$
     (32) AND RR$ < > CHR$ (69)
     THEN  GOTO 760
780   IF RR$ =  CHR$ (32) AND K =
     20 THEN  GOTO 1020: REM  **
     SCORE **
800   IF RR$ =  CHR$ (32) THEN  RETURN

820   IF RR$ =  CHR$ (69) THEN  GOTO
     1020: REM  SCORE
840   REM  **** WRONG *****
859   INVERSE
860   HTAB 12: PRINT "WRONG ";A$;
     " ";SU$
880   HTAB 4: PRINT "SPACE BAR =
     NEXT, H=HELP HINTS"
900   HTAB 4: PRINT "E = EXIT"
901   NORMAL
920   GET WW$: IF WW$ < > CHR$
     (32) AND WW$ < > CHR$ (69)
     AND WW$ < > CHR$ (72) THEN
     GOTO 920
940   IF WW$ =  CHR$ (32) AND K =
     20 THEN  GOTO 1020
960   IF WW$ =  CHR$ (32) THEN  RETURN
980   IF WW$ =  CHR$ (72) THEN  GOSUB
     1280: RETURN : REM *** HELP
     HINTS
1000  IF WW$ =  CHR$ (69) THEN  GOTO
     1020
1020  REM  *** SCORE ****
1021  TEXT
1060  HOME : VTAB 8
1080  E = (S / K) * 100
1100  PRINT  TAB( 8)"YOUR SCORE
     IS ";E;"%": PRINT
1120  PRINT  TAB( 8)"FOR ";K;" Q
     UESTIONS ASKED": PRINT : PRINT
     : PRINT
1160  PRINT  TAB( 8)"SPACE BAR F
     OR MAIN MENU."
1180  GET MM$: IF MM$ < >  CHR$
```

311

```
          (32) THEN 1180
1200   PRINT   CHR$ (4);"-STARTUP"

1280   REM  *** HELP ***
1281   TEXT : HOME
1285   PRINT   TAB( 4)"THIS EXERCI
       SE IS CONCERNED WITH"
1286   PRINT   TAB( 4)"PHASE RELAT
       IONSHIPS."
1287   PRINT   TAB( 4)"WE NEED TO
       TAKE HORIZONTAL (TIME)"
1288   PRINT   TAB( 4)"DIVISIONS I
       NTO CONSIDERATION."
1289   PRINT : PRINT   TAB( 4)"CHA
       NNEL 1 (THE LEFT MOST TRACE)
       ,"
1290   PRINT   TAB( 4)"REPRESENTS
       THE REFERENCE WAVE.": PRINT

1291   PRINT   TAB( 4)"NOTE: COUNT
        TIME DIVISIONS AT"
1292   PRINT   TAB( 4)"THE HORIZON
       TAL CENTER LINE."
1293   PRINT
1294   PRINT   TAB( 1)"1. COUNT TH
       E NUMBER OF DIVISIONS FOR"
1295   PRINT   TAB( 4)"ONE CYCLE O
       F WAVE 1."
1296   PRINT   TAB( 1)"2. DIVIDE 3
       60 BY THE NUMBER OF"
1297   PRINT   TAB( 4)"DIVISIONS (
       = DEGREES PER DIVISIONS)."
1298   PRINT   TAB( 1)"3. COUNT TH
       E NUMBER OF DIVISIONS"
1299   PRINT   TAB( 4)"BETWEEN THE
        START OF THE TWO WAVES."
1300   PRINT   TAB( 1)"4. MULTIPLY
        THE NUMBER OF DIVISIONS"
1301   PRINT   TAB( 4)"FROM STEP 3
       , BY THE (DEGREES PER"
1302   PRINT   TAB( 4)"DIVISION) F
       ROM STEP 2 (= DEGREES"
1303   PRINT   TAB( 4)"OUT OF PHAS
       E)."
1305   INVERSE : VTAB 23
1306   HTAB 8: PRINT "SPACE BAR T
       O CONTINUE";: NORMAL
1320   GET BK$: IF BK$ <  > CHR$
       (32) THEN  GOTO 1320
1321   HOME
1330   D = 16: GOSUB 3000
1331   INVERSE : VTAB 21
1350   HTAB 13: PRINT "EXAMPLE": NORMAL
       : HTAB 1
1360   PRINT "DEGREES PER DIVISIO
       N = 360/4 = 90"
1370   PRINT "DEGREES OUT OF PHAS
       E = 1 X 90 = 90"
1380   INVERSE : HTAB 8: PRINT "S
       PACE BAR TO CONTINUE";: NORMAL
       : HTAB 1
1390   GET RT$: IF RT$ <  > CHR$
       (32) THEN 1390
1400   RETURN
3000   REM  *** SCREEN & TRACE **
       *
3005   HOME : HGR
3010   HCOLOR= 6
3020   FOR I = 5 TO 125 STEP 15
3030   HPLOT 10,I TO 170,I
3040   NEXT I
3050   FOR H = 10 TO 170 STEP 16
3060   HPLOT H,5 TO H,125
3070   NEXT H
3071   HPLOT 5,65 TO 175,65
3072   HPLOT 90,1 TO 90,130
3080   HCOLOR= 7
3100   REM  *** SINE ***
3110   HCOLOR= 7
3120   HPLOT 11,65 TO 16,40
3130   HPLOT 16,40 TO 20,28
3140   HPLOT 20,28 TO 26,20
3150   HPLOT 26,20 TO 32,28
3160   HPLOT 32,28 TO 36,40
3170   HPLOT 36,40 TO 42,65
3180   HPLOT 42,65 TO 48,90
3190   HPLOT 48,90 TO 52,102
3200   HPLOT 52,102 TO 58,110
3210   HPLOT 58,110 TO 64,102
3220   HPLOT 64,102 TO 68,90
3230   HPLOT 68,90 TO 74,65
3300   HPLOT 11 + D,65 TO 16 + D,
       40
3310   HPLOT 16 + D,40 TO 20 + D,
       28
3320   HPLOT 20 + D,28 TO 26 + D,
       20
3330   HPLOT 26 + D,20 TO 32 + D,
       28
3340   HPLOT 32 + D,28 TO 36 + D,
       40
3350   HPLOT 36 + D,40 TO 42 + D,
       65
3360   HPLOT 42 + D,65 TO 48 + D,
       90
3370   HPLOT 48 + D,90 TO 52 + D,
       102
3380   HPLOT 52 + D,102 TO 58 + D
       ,110
3390   HPLOT 58 + D,110 TO 64 + D
       ,102
3400   HPLOT 64 + D,102 TO 68 + D
       ,90
3410   HPLOT 68 + D,90 TO 74 + D,
       65
3420   RETURN
5000   DATA 8,ARE THESE WAVES IN
       PHASE Y/N,N
5001   DATA 8,HOW MANY DEGREES AP
       ART,45
```

Fig. E-12. Phase angle program. (Continued from page 312)

5002 DATA 16,ARE THESE WAVE IN
      PHASE Y/N,N
5003 DATA 16,HOW MANY DEGREES A
      PART,90
5004 DATA 24,ARE THESE WAVES IN
      PHASE Y/N,N
5005 DATA 24,HOW MANY DEGREES A
      PART,135
5006 DATA 32,ARE THESE WAVES IN
      PHASE Y/N,N
5007 DATA 32,HOW MANY DEGREES A
      PART,180
5008 DATA 36,ARE THESE WAVES IN
      PHASE Y/N,N
5009 DATA 36,HOW MANY DEGREES A
      PART,200
5010 DATA 40,ARE THESE WAVES IN
      PHASE Y/N,N

5011 DATA 40,HOW MANY DEGREES A
      PART,225
5012 DATA 11,ARE THESE WAVES IN
      PHASE Y/N,N
5013 DATA 11,HOW MANY DEGREES A
      PART,60
5014 DATA 21,ARE THESE WAVES IN
      PHASE Y/N,N
5015 DATA 21,HOW MANY DEGREES A
      PART,120
5016 DATA 27,ARE THESE WAVES IN
      PHASE Y/N,N
5017 DATA 27,HOW MANY DEGREES A
      PART,150
5018 DATA 57,ARE THESE WAVES IN
      PHASE Y/N,N
5019 DATA 57,HOW MANY DEGREES A
      PART,320

Fig. E-13. Time constants program.

```
20   HOME
40   PRINT   TAB( 4)"THIS PROGRAM
     IS AN EXERCISE"
60   PRINT   TAB( 4)"IN CALCULATIN
     G TIME CONSTANTS,"
80   PRINT   TAB( 4)"THE FORMULAS
     LEARNED IN"
100  PRINT   TAB( 4)"CHAPTER 13."
110  PRINT
120  PRINT   TAB( 4)"THE USER WIL
     L BE GIVEN TWO"
130  PRINT   TAB( 4)"KNOWNS, AND
     BE ASKED TO SOLVE"
140  PRINT   TAB( 4)"FOR THE UNKN
     OWN."
150  PRINT : PRINT   TAB( 4)"NOTE
     : POWER ON, AND POWER OFF"
160  PRINT   TAB( 4)"TIMES, ARE S
     TATED FROM"
170  PRINT   TAB( 4)"TOTAL DISCHA
     RGE, OR CHARGE,"
180  PRINT   TAB( 4)"RESPECTFULLY
     .": PRINT
190  PRINT   TAB( 4)"YOUR ANSWERS
     ARE EXPECTED TO BE"
200  PRINT   TAB( 4)"WITH IN 5% O
     F THE COMPUTER'S"
210  PRINT   TAB( 4)"ANSWERS."
260  INVERSE : VTAB 20: HTAB 8: PRINT
     "SPACE BAR TO CONTINUE": NORMAL
280  GET RT$: IF RT$ <  > CHR$
     (32) THEN  GOTO 280
300  HOME
320  REM  QUESTION LOOP ********
     ***
340  FOR K = 1 TO 20:AA = 0
341  HOME
360  READ L$,F$,X$,Q$,A
400  PRINT "    NOTE: UNITS ARE
     GIVEN JUST GIVE"
401  PRINT "          THE NUMERI
     C VALUE."
420  PRINT : PRINT "    GIVEN:":
     PRINT
460  HTAB 10: PRINT L$: PRINT
480  HTAB 10: PRINT F$: PRINT
500  HTAB 10: PRINT X$: PRINT
520  PRINT : PRINT
540  PRINT K;".";Q$;
541  AA = 0
560  INPUT AA$:AA = VAL (AA$)
561  LU = A - (A * .05):HU = A +
     (A * .05)
580  IF A < 0 THEN LU = = A + (
     A * .05):HU = A - (A * .05)
600  IF AA > LU AND AA < HU THEN
     GOSUB 700: REM  **** CORREC
     T *****
620  IF AA = LU OR AA = HU THEN
     GOSUB 700: REM   CORRECT
640  IF AA < LU OR AA > HU THEN
     GOSUB 840: REM  *** WRONG *
     **
660  IF K = 20 THEN  GOTO 1020
680  NEXT K
700  REM  **** CORRECT ****
719  INVERSE
720  PRINT : PRINT : PRINT : HTAB
     14: PRINT "CORRECT!":S = S +
     1
740  PRINT : HTAB 5: PRINT "SPAC
     E BAR = NEXT, N = NEW SELECT
     ION."
741  NORMAL
760  GET RR$: IF RR$ <  > CHR$
     (32) AND RR$ <  > CHR$ (69)
     THEN  GOTO 760
780  IF RR$ =  CHR$ (32) AND K =
     20 THEN  GOTO 1020: REM  **
     SCORE **
800  IF RR$ =  CHR$ (32) THEN  RETURN
820  IF RR$ =  CHR$ (69) THEN  GOTO
     1020: REM  SCORE
840  REM  **** WRONG *****
859  INVERSE
860  PRINT : PRINT : PRINT : HTAB
     12: PRINT "WRONG ";A
880  PRINT : HTAB 4: PRINT "SPAC
     E BAR = NEXT, H=HELP HINTS"
900  HTAB 4: PRINT "E = FOR EXIT
     "
901  NORMAL
920  GET WW$: IF WW$ <  > CHR$
     (32) AND WW$ <  > CHR$ (69)
     AND WW$ <  > CHR$ (72) THEN
     GOTO 920
940  IF WW$ =  CHR$ (32) AND K =
     20 THEN  GOTO 1020
960  IF WW$ =  CHR$ (32) THEN  RETURN
980  IF WW$ =  CHR$ (72) THEN  GOSUB
     1400: RETURN : REM  ** HELP
     HINTS
1000 IF WW$ =  CHR$ (69) THEN  GOTO
     1020
1020 REM  *** SCORE ****
1060 HOME : VTAB 8
1080 E = (S / K) * 100
1100 PRINT   TAB( 8)"YOUR SCORE
     IS ";E;"%": PRINT
1120 PRINT   TAB( 8)"FOR ";K;" Q
     UESTIONS ASKED": PRINT : PRINT
     : PRINT
1160 PRINT   TAB( 8)"SPACE BAR F
     OR MAIN MENU."
1180 GET MM$: IF MM$ <  > CHR$
```

```
     (32) THEN 1180
1200   PRINT  CHR$ (4);"-STARTUP"

1400   REM  *** HELP HINTS ****
1420   HOME
1440   PRINT : PRINT  TAB( 4)"THI
  S EXERCISE NOT ONLY"
1460   PRINT  TAB( 4)"GIVES YOU P
  RACTICE AT THE"
1480   PRINT  TAB( 4)"FORMULAS, I
  T DOUBLES AS A"
1500   PRINT  TAB( 4)"PRACTICE IN
   TRANSPOSING."
1520   PRINT : PRINT  TAB( 4)"NOT
  E: POWER ON, AND POWER OFF"
1540   PRINT  TAB( 4)"TIMES, ARE
  STATED FROM"
1560   PRINT  TAB( 4)"TOTAL DISCH
  ARGE, OR CHARGE"
1580   PRINT  TAB( 4)"RESPECTFULL
  Y."
1600   PRINT
1620   PRINT  TAB( 4)"THE LIST OF
   FORMULAS ON THE NEXT"
1640   PRINT  TAB( 4)"PAGE SHOULD
   HELP."
1660   INVERSE
1661   VTAB 20: HTAB 8: PRINT "SP
  ACE BAR FOR LIST"
1662   NORMAL
1680   GET ZC$: IF ZC$ <  > CHR$
   (32) THEN  GOTO 1680
1700   HOME
1720   VTAB 3: PRINT  TAB( 6)"IND
  UCTOR", "CAPACITOR"
1721   PRINT
1740   PRINT  TAB( 6)"T=L/R","T=R
   X C": PRINT
1760   PRINT  TAB( 6)"L=T/R","C=
  T/R": PRINT
1780   PRINT  TAB( 6)"R= L X T","
  R= T/C": PRINT
1800   PRINT  TAB( 4)"WHERE T IS
  THE TIME CONSTANT."
1820   PRINT
1839   INVERSE
1840   VTAB 20: HTAB 10: PRINT "S
  PACE BAR TO CONTINUE"
1841   NORMAL
1860   GET MC$: IF MC$ <  > CHR$
   (32) THEN  GOTO 1860
1880   HOME
1900   PRINT  TAB( 4)"USE UNIVERS
  AL TIME CONSTANT CURVE"
1920   PRINT  TAB( 4)"FOUND IN CH
  APTER 13 FOR % OF CHARGE"
1921   PRINT  TAB( 4)"QUESTIONS."
  : PRINT
1940   PRINT  TAB( 4)"TO FIND THE
   TIME (ON OR OFF)"
1960   PRINT  TAB( 4)"WHEN GIVEN
  THE TIME CONSTANT,"
1980   PRINT  TAB( 4)"AND % OF CH
  ARGE: FIND THE %"
2000   PRINT  TAB( 4)"OF CHARGE O
  N THE CURVE AND LOOK"
2020   PRINT  TAB( 4)"STRAIGHT DO
  WN FROM THAT POINT"
2040   PRINT  TAB( 4)"TO THE NUMB
  ER OF TIME CONSTANTS"
2060   PRINT  TAB( 4)"THEN MULTIP
  LY THE NUMBER OF"
2080   PRINT  TAB( 4)"TIME CONSTA
  NTS BY THE TIME OF"
2100   PRINT  TAB( 4)"ONE TIME CO
  NSTANT TO GET THE"
2120   PRINT  TAB( 4)"TIME (ON OR
   OFF) USE CHARGING"
2140   PRINT  TAB( 4)"CURVE, OR D
  ISCHARGING CURVE"
2160   PRINT  TAB( 4)"RESPECTFULL
  Y."
2169   INVERSE
2170   VTAB 20: HTAB 9: PRINT "SP
  ACE BAR TO CONTINUE"
2171   NORMAL
2200   GET LC$: IF LC$ <  > CHR$
   (32) THEN  GOTO 2200
2220   HOME
2240   PRINT  TAB( 4)"TO FIND THE
   TIME CONSTANT WHEN"
2260   PRINT  TAB( 4)"GIVEN TIME
  (ON OR OFF), AND THE"
2280   PRINT  TAB( 4)"% OF CHARGE
  : FIND THE NUMBER"
2300   PRINT  TAB( 4)"OF TIME CON
  STANTS AS BEFORE,"
2320   PRINT  TAB( 4)"ONLY DIVIDE
   THE TIME (ON OR OFF)"
2340   PRINT  TAB( 4)"BY THE NUMB
  ER OF TIME CONSTANTS"
2360   PRINT  TAB( 4)"TO GET THE
  TIME OF ONE TIME"
2380   PRINT  TAB( 4)"CONSTANT."
2400   PRINT
2420   PRINT  TAB( 4)"TO FIND THE
   % OF CHARGE WHEN"
2440   PRINT  TAB( 4)"GIVEN THE T
  IME CONSTNAT AND"
2460   PRINT  TAB( 4)"THE TIME (O
  N OR OFF): DIVIDE"
2480   PRINT  TAB( 4)"THE TIME (O
  N OR OFF) BY ONE"
2500   PRINT  TAB( 4)"TIME CONSTA
  NT, TO GET THE"
2520   PRINT  TAB( 4)"NUMBER OF T
  IME CONSTANTS, THEN"
2540   PRINT  TAB( 4)"GOTO THE CU
  RVE AND LOCATE"
2560   PRINT  TAB( 4)"THE NUMBER
```

Fig. E-13. Time constants program. (Continued from page 315)

```
     OF TIME CONSTANTS"
2580 PRINT  TAB( 4)"WHERE IT IN
     TERSECTS WITH THE CURVE"
2600 PRINT  TAB( 4)"AND THAT PO
     INT ON THE CURVE"
2620 PRINT  TAB( 4)"REPRESENTS
     THE % OF CHARGE."
2639 INVERSE
2640 VTAB 22: HTAB 9: PRINT "SP
     ACE BAR TO CONTINUE"
2641 NORMAL
2660 GET RC$: IF RC$ <  >  CHR$
     (32) THEN  GOTO 2660
2680 RETURN
2700 DATA TIME CONSTANT = ? US,
     INDUCTOR = 2 MH
2720 DATA RESISTANCE = 1 KOHM,C
     ALCULATE THE UNKNOWN,2
2740 DATA TIME CONSTANT = ? MS,
     CAPACITOR = 2 UF
2760 DATA RESISTANCE = 1 KOHM,C
     ALCULATE THE UNKNOWN,2
2780 DATA TIME CONSTANT = 166 U
     S,INDUCTOR = ? MH
2800 DATA RESISTANCE = 300 OHMS
     ,CALCULATE THE UNKNOWN,50
2820 DATA TIME CONSTANT = 50 MS
     ,CAPACITOR = ? UF
2840 DATA RESISTANCE = 500 OHMS
     ,CALCULATE THE UNKNOWN,100
2860 DATA TIME CONSTANT = 2.5 M
     S,INDUCTOR = 5 H
2880 DATA RESISTANCE = ? KOHMS,
     CALCULATE THE UNKNOWN,2
2900 DATA TIME CONSTANT = 14 MS
     ,CAPACITOR = 47 UF
2920 DATA RESISTANCE = ? OHMS,C
     ALCULATE THE UNKNOWN,300
2940 DATA TIME CONSTANT = 100 U
     S,CAPACITOR = ? UF
2960 DATA RESISTANCE = 10 OHMS,
     CALCULATE THE UNKNOWN,10
2980 DATA TIME CONSTANT = ? US,
     INDUCTOR = 25 MH
3000 DATA RESISTANCE = 100 OHMS
     ,CALCULATE THE UNKNOWN,250
3020 DATA TIME CONSTANT = ? US,
     INDUCTOR = 90 MH
3040 DATA RESISTANCE = 10 KOHMS
     ,CALCULATE THE UNKNOWN,9
3060 DATA TIME CONSTANT = 16.5
     MS,CAPACITOR = ? UF
3080 DATA RESISTANCE = 500 OHMS
     ,CALCULATE THE UNKNOWN,33
3100 DATA TIME CONSTANT = 2 US,
     TIME POWER ON = 2 US
3120 DATA PERCENT OF CHARGE = ?
     %,FIND THE UNKNOWN,63
3140 DATA TIME CONSTANT = ? MS,
     TIME POWER OFF = 100 MS
3160 DATA PERCENT OF CHARGE = 1
     4 %,FIND THE UNKNOWN,50
3180 DATA TIME CONSTANT = 100 U
     S,TIME POWER ON = ? US
3200 DATA PERCENT OF CHARGE = 9
     5%,FIND THE UNKNOWN,300
3220 DATA TIME CONSTANT = 2.5 M
     S,TIME POWER ON = 3.75 MS
3240 DATA PERCENT OF CHARGE = ?
     %,FIND THE UNKNOWN,76
3260 DATA TIME CONSTANT = 9 US,
     TIME POWER OFF = 36 US
3280 DATA PERCENT OF CHARGE = ?
     %, FIND THE UNKNOWN,2
3300 DATA TIME CONSTANT = 125 U
     S,TIME POWER OFF = ? US
3320 DATA PERCENT OF CHARGE = 1
     %,FIND THE UNKNOWN,625
3340 DATA TIME CONSTANT = ? US,
     TIME POWER OFF = 100 US
3360 DATA PERCENT OF CHARGE = 1
     4 %,FIND THE UNKNOWN,50
3380 DATA TIME CONSTANT = 25 US
     ,POWER ON = 50 US
3400 DATA PERCENT OF CHARGE = ?
     %,FIND THE UNKNOWN,86
3420 DATA TIME CONSTANT = 10 US
     ,TIME POWER ON = 50 US
3440 DATA PERCENT OF CHARGE = ?
     %,FIND THE UNKNOWN,99
3460 DATA TIME CONSTANT = ? MS,
     TIME POWER ON = 5 MS
3480 DATA PERCENT OF CHARGE = 4
     2%,FIND THE UNKNOWN,10
```

316

```
1    REM   TRANSFORMERS
2    HOME : REM  ******* INTRODUCT
     ION ******
10   PRINT : PRINT : PRINT : PRINT

20   PRINT  TAB( 4)"THIS PROGRAM
     IS A MULTIPLE"
30   PRINT  TAB( 4)"CHOICE QUIZ O
     N MAGNETISM."
40   PRINT
50   PRINT  TAB( 4)"THE USER WILL
     BE ASKED TO CHOOSE"
60   PRINT  TAB( 4)"THE BEST ANSW
     ER FOR THE QUESTION"
70   PRINT  TAB( 4)"ASKED."
80   PRINT
260  INVERSE : VTAB 20: HTAB 8: PRINT
     "SPACE BAR TO CONTINUE": NORMAL

280  GET RT$: IF RT$ <  > CHR$
     (32) THEN  GOTO 280
300  HOME
320  REM  QUESTION LOOP ********
     ***
340  FOR K = 1 TO 10:AA = 0
341  HOME
360  READ L$,F$,X$,CT$,Q$,A$
400  PRINT "    CHOOSE THE MOST
     CORRECT ANSWER."
401  PRINT : PRINT : PRINT
460  HTAB 10: PRINT "A) ";L$: PRINT

480  HTAB 10: PRINT "B) ";F$: PRINT

500  HTAB 10: PRINT "C) ";X$: PRINT

501  HTAB 10: PRINT "D) ";CT$: PRINT

520  PRINT : PRINT
540  PRINT K;".";Q$: PRINT
560  INPUT "    THE LETTER OF YO
     UR CHOICE IS ?";AA$
580  IF AA$ = A$ THEN  GOSUB 700

600  IF AA$ <  > A$ THEN  GOSUB
     840
660  IF K = 10 THEN  GOTO 1020
680  NEXT K
700  REM  **** CORRECT ****
719  INVERSE
720  PRINT : HTAB 14: PRINT "COR
     RECT!":S = S + 1
721  PRINT
740  HTAB 4: PRINT "SPACE BAR FO
     R NEXT, E = EXIT."
741  NORMAL
760  GET RR$: IF RR$ <  > CHR$
     (32) AND RR$ <  > CHR$ (69)
     THEN  GOTO 760
780  IF RR$ =  CHR$ (32) AND K =

20   THEN  GOTO 1020: REM  **
     SCORE **
800  IF RR$ =  CHR$ (32) THEN  RETURN

820  IF RR$ =  CHR$ (69) THEN  GOTO
     1020: REM  SCORE
840  REM  **** WRONG *****
859  INVERSE
860  PRINT : HTAB 12: PRINT "WRO
     NG ";A$
880  PRINT : HTAB 4: PRINT "SPAC
     E BAR FOR NEXT";
900  HTAB 22: PRINT ", E = EXIT"

901  NORMAL
920  GET WW$: IF WW$ <  > CHR$
     (32) AND WW$ <  > CHR$ (69)
     THEN  GOTO 920
940  IF WW$ =  CHR$ (32) AND K =
     20 THEN  GOTO 1020
960  IF WW$ =  CHR$ (32) THEN  RETURN

1000 IF WW$ =  CHR$ (69) THEN  GOTO
     1020
1020 REM  *** SCORE ****
1060 HOME : VTAB 8
1080 E = (S / K) * 100
1100 PRINT  TAB( 8)"YOUR SCORE
     IS ";E;"%": PRINT
1120 PRINT  TAB( 8)"FOR ";K;" Q
     UESTIONS ASKED": PRINT : PRINT
     : PRINT
1160 PRINT  TAB( 8)"SPACE BAR F
     OR MAIN MENU."
1180 GET MM$: IF MM$ <  > CHR$
     (32) THEN 1180
1200 PRINT  CHR$ (4);"-STARTUP"

1220 DATA REPEL,ATTRACT,MELT,DE
     STROY THE MAGNETS
1240 DATA MAGNETS DO THIS WHEN
     LIKE POLES ARE     PLACED CL
     OSE TOGETHER.,A
1260 DATA PERMANENT MAGNETS,NOR
     THS,MAGNETIC FLUX,COILS
1280 DATA THE LINES OF FORCE AR
     OUND A MAGNET     ARE ALSO
     CALLED?,C
1300 DATA PERMANENT,MAGNETIC,NU
     CLEAR,PHASOR
1320 DATA WHEN CURRENT FLOWS TH
     ROUGH A WIRE     IT CREATE
     S A -------- FIELD.,B
1340 DATA VOLTAGE,CURRENT,AIR,N
     ONE OF THE ABOVE
1360 DATA INDUCTORS RESIST A CH
     ANGE IN --------.,B
1380 DATA CHARGING,VOLTAGE,INDU
     CTANCE,NONE OF THE ABOVE
1400 DATA AN INDUCTORS ABILITY
```

317

Fig. E-14. Magnetism program. (Continued from page 317)

```
      TO RESIST A          CHANGE IN
      CURRENT IS CALLED ?,C
1420  DATA MAGNETIC,FORCE,AIR,NU
      CLEAR
1440  DATA WHEN CURRENT DECREASE
      S IN AN INDUCTOR    THIS FIEL
      D COLAPSES.,A
1460  DATA WATER,VOLTAGE,AIR,NON
      E OF THE ABOVE
1480  DATA A CHANGING MAGNETIC F
      IELD INDUCES        WHAT IN T
      HE INDUCTOR ?,B
1500  DATA A RESISTOR,A CAPACITO
      R,THE INDUCED VOLTAGE,NONE O
      F THE ABOVE
1520  DATA WHAT CAUSES AN INDUCT
      OR TO RESIST        A CHANGE
```

```
      IN CURRENT ?,C
1540  DATA CONCENTRATE THE FLUX,
      INCREASE THE INDUCTANCE,BOTH
      A AND B
1550  DATA NONE OF THE ABOVE
1560  DATA A MAGNETIC CORE IS PL
      ACED INSIDE AN       INDUCTOR
      TO DO WHAT ?,C
1580  DATA THE NUMBER OF TURNS O
      F WIRE,THE SPACE BETWEEN THE
      TURNS
1600  DATA THE AREA OF THE TURNS
      ,ALL OF THE ABOVE
1620  DATA WHICH OF THE FOLLOWIN
      G WILL AFFECT        THE INDUC
      TANCE OF A COIL ?,D
```

Fig. E-15. Transformers program.

```
1    REM   TRANSFORMERS
2    HOME
3    REM  **** INTRODUCTION ****
40   PRINT : PRINT : PRINT : PRINT
     TAB( 4)"THIS IS A PRACTICE"

60   PRINT  TAB( 4)"EXERCISE FOR
     THE TRANSFORMER"
80   PRINT  TAB( 4)"FORMULAS LEAR
     NED IN CHAPTER 12."
100  PRINT
120  PRINT  TAB( 4)"IT WILL GIVE
     TWO KNOWNS, AND"
140  PRINT  TAB( 4)"ASK THE USER
     TO SOLVE FOR"
160  PRINT  TAB( 4)"THE UNKNOWN.
     "
180  PRINT
200  PRINT  TAB( 4)"THE ANSWERS
     ARE EXPECTED TO"
220  PRINT  TAB( 4)"BE WITH IN 5
     % OF THE COMPUTER'S"
240  PRINT  TAB( 4)"ANSWERS."
260  INVERSE : VTAB 20: HTAB 8: PRINT
     "SPACE BAR TO CONTINUE": NORMAL

280  GET RT$: IF RT$ <  > CHR$
     (32) THEN  GOTO 280
300  HOME
320  REM   QUESTION LOOP ********
     ***
340  FOR K = 1 TO 20:AA = 0
341  HOME
360  READ L$,F$,X$,Q$,A
400  PRINT "    NOTE: UNITS ARE
     GIVEN JUST GIVE"
401  PRINT "          THE NUMERI
     C VALUE."
420  PRINT : PRINT "    GIVEN:":
     PRINT
460  HTAB 10: PRINT L$: PRINT
480  HTAB 10: PRINT F$: PRINT
500  HTAB 10: PRINT X$: PRINT
520  PRINT : PRINT
540  PRINT K;".";Q$;
541  AA = 0
560  INPUT AA$:AA =  VAL (AA$)
561  LU = A - (A * .05):HU = A +
     (A * .05)
580  IF A < 0 THEN LU =  = A + (
     A * .05):HU = A - (A * .05)
600  IF AA > LU AND AA < HU THEN
     GOSUB 700: REM  **** CORREC
     T *****
620  IF AA = LU OR AA = HU THEN
     GOSUB 700: REM  CORRECT
640  IF AA < LU OR AA > HU THEN
     GOSUB 840: REM  *** WRONG *
     **
660  IF K = 20 THEN  GOTO 1020

680  NEXT K
700  REM  **** CORRECT ****
719  INVERSE
720  PRINT : PRINT : PRINT : HTAB
     14: PRINT "CORRECT!":S = S +
     1
740  PRINT : HTAB 5: PRINT "SPAC
     E BAR = NEXT, E = EXIT."
741  NORMAL
760  GET RR$: IF RR$ <  > CHR$
     (32) AND RR$ <  > CHR$ (69)
     THEN  GOTO 760
780  IF RR$ =  CHR$ (32) AND K =
     20 THEN  GOTO 1020: REM **
     SCORE **
800  IF RR$ =  CHR$ (32) THEN  RETURN

820  IF RR$ =  CHR$ (69) THEN  GOTO
     1020: REM  SCORE
840  REM  **** WRONG *****
859  INVERSE
860  PRINT : PRINT : PRINT : HTAB
     12: PRINT "WRONG ";A
880  PRINT : HTAB 4: PRINT "SPAC
     E BAR = NEXT, H=HELP HINTS"
900  HTAB 4: PRINT "E = FOR EXIT
     "
901  NORMAL
920  GET WW$: IF WW$ <  > CHR$
     (32) AND WW$ <  > CHR$ (69)
     AND WW$ <  > CHR$ (72) THEN
     GOTO 920
940  IF WW$ =  CHR$ (32) AND K =
     20 THEN  GOTO 1020
960  IF WW$ =  CHR$ (32) THEN  RETURN
980  IF WW$ =  CHR$ (72) THEN  GOSUB
     1280: RETURN : REM *** HELP
     HINTS
1000 IF WW$ =  CHR$ (69) THEN  GOTO
     1020
1020 REM  *** SCORE ****
1060 HOME : VTAB 8
1080 E = (S / K) * 100
1100 PRINT  TAB( 8)"YOUR SCORE
     IS ";E;"%": PRINT
1120 PRINT  TAB( 8)"FOR ";K;" Q
     UESTIONS ASKED": PRINT : PRINT
     : PRINT
1160 PRINT  TAB( 8)"SPACE BAR F
     OR MAIN MENU."
1180 GET MM$: IF MM$ <  > CHR$
     (32) THEN 1180
1200 PRINT  CHR$ (4);"-STARTUP"

1280 REM  *** HELP HINTS ***
1300 HOME
1320 PRINT  TAB( 4)"THIS THREE
     PART LIST SHOULD"
1321 PRINT  TAB( 4)"HELP YOU.":
```

Fig. E-15. Transformers program. (Continued from page 319)

```
     PRINT : PRINT
1340  PRINT  TAB( 4)"TURNS RATIO
      :": PRINT
1360  PRINT  TAB( 4)"VOLTAGE SEC
         TURNS SEC"
1380  PRINT  TAB( 4)"------------
      = -----------"
1400  PRINT  TAB( 4)"VOLTAGE PRI
         TURNS PRI"
1420  PRINT : PRINT : PRINT : PRINT
      TAB( 4)"EFFICIENCY:": PRINT

1440  PRINT : PRINT  TAB( 20)"PO
      WER OUT"
1460  PRINT  TAB( 4)"% EFFICIENC
      Y = ---------- X 100"
1480  PRINT  TAB( 20)"POWER IN"
1500  INVERSE
1501  PRINT : PRINT : HTAB 8: PRINT
      "SPACE BAR FOR MORE": NORMAL

1520  GET RC$: IF RC$ <  > CHR$
      (32) THEN  GOTO 1520
1540  HOME
1541  VTAB 4: PRINT  TAB( 4)"TUR
      NS RATIO VOLTAGE:": PRINT
1560  PRINT  TAB( 4)"VS/VP = NS/
      NP": PRINT
1580  PRINT  TAB( 4)"VS = (NS/NP
      ) X VP": PRINT
1600  PRINT  TAB( 4)"VP = (NP/NS
      ) X VS": PRINT
1620  PRINT  TAB( 4)"NS = (VS/VP
      ) X NP": PRINT
1640  PRINT  TAB( 4)"NP = (VP/VS
      ) X NS": PRINT
1659  INVERSE
1660  VTAB 19: HTAB 8: PRINT "SP
      ACE BAR FOR MORE"
1661  NORMAL
1680  GET ZC$: IF ZC$ <  > CHR$
      (32) THEN  GOTO 1680
1700  HOME
1720  VTAB 2: PRINT  TAB( 4)"TUR
      NS RATIO CURRENT:": PRINT
1740  PRINT  TAB( 4)"IP/IS = NS/
      NP": PRINT
1760  PRINT  TAB( 4)"IP = (NS/NP
      ) X IS": PRINT
1780  PRINT  TAB( 4)"IS = (NP/NS
      ) X IP": PRINT
1800  PRINT  TAB( 4)"NS = (IP/IS
      ) X NP": PRINT
1820  PRINT  TAB( 4)"NP = (IS/IP
      ) X NS": PRINT
1840  PRINT : PRINT  TAB( 4)"EFF
      ICIENCY FORMULAS:": PRINT
1860  PRINT  TAB( 4)"% EFFICIENC
      Y = (P OUT/ P IN) X 100": PRINT

1880  PRINT  TAB( 4)"P OUT = (%
      EFF/100) X P IN": PRINT
1900  PRINT  TAB( 4)"P IN = P OU
      T / (% EFF/100)": PRINT : PRINT

1919  INVERSE
1920  HTAB 8: PRINT "SPACE BAR T
      O CONTINUE"
1921  NORMAL
1940  GET YC$: IF YC$ <  > CHR$
      (32) THEN  GOTO 1940
1960  IF YC$ =  CHR$ (32) THEN  RETURN
1980  DATA TURNS RATIO = 10 TO 1
      ,PRIMARY VOLTAGE = 120 V
2000  DATA SECONDARY VOLTAGE = ?
      V,FIND THE UNKNOWN,12
2020  DATA TURNS RATIO = ? TO 10
      ,PRIMARY VOLTAGE = 100 V
2040  DATA SECONDARY VOLTAGE = 1
      000 V,FIND THE UNKNOWN,1
2060  DATA TURNS RATIO = 6 TO 1,
      PRIMARY VOLTAGE = ? V
2080  DATA SECONDARY VOLTAGE = 1
      8 V,FIND THE UNKNOWN,108
2100  DATA TURNS RATIO = 1 TO 5,
      PRIMARY VOLTAGE = 12 V
2120  DATA SECONDARY VOLTAGE = ?
      V,FIND THE UNKNOWN,60
2140  DATA TURNS RATIO = 8 TO ?,
      PRIMARY VOLTAGE = 160 V
2160  DATA SECONDARY VOLTAGE = 2
      O V,FIND THE UNKNOWN,1
2180  DATA TURNS RATIO = 1 TO 1,
      PRIMARY VOLTAGE = 100 V
2200  DATA SECONDARY VOLTAGE = ?
      V,FIND THE UNKNOWN,100
2220  DATA TURNS RATIO = 1 TO 5,
      PRIMARY VOLTAGE = 60 V
2240  DATA SECONDARY VOLTAGE = ?
      V,FIND THE UNKNOWN,300
2260  DATA TURNS RATIO = 8 TO 1,
      PRIMARY VOLTAGE = ? V
2280  DATA SECONDARY VOLTAGE = 2
      4 V,FIND THE UNKNOWN,192
2300  DATA TURNS RATIO = 3 TO 1,
      PRIMARY CURRENT = 2 AMPS
2320  DATA SECONDARY CURRENT = ?
      AMPS,FIND THE UNKNOWN,6
2340  DATA TURNS RATIO = ? TO 1,
      PRIMARY CURRENT = .3 AMPS
2360  DATA SECONDARY CURRENT = 3
      AMPS,FIND THE UNKNOWN,10
2380  DATA EFFICIENCY = 85%,PRIM
      ARY POWER = 6 WATTS
2400  DATA SECONDARY POWER = ? W
      ATTS,FIND THE UNKNOWN,5.1
2420  DATA EFFICIENCY = ?%,PRIMA
      RY POWER = 3 WATTS
2440  DATA SECONDARY POWER = 2.8
      WATTS,FIND THE UNKNOWN,93
2460  DATA EFFICIENCY = 70%,PRIM
      ARY POWER = 20 WATTS
```

Fig. E-15. Transformers program. (Continued from page 320)

2480 DATA SECONDARY POWER = ? W
      ATTS,FIND THE UNKNOWN,14
2500 DATA EFFICIENCY = 75%,PRIM
      ARY POWER = ? WATTS
2520 DATA SECONDARY POWER = 7.5
      WATTS,FIND THE UNKNOWN,10
2540 DATA EFFICIENCY = 95%,PRIM
      ARY POWER = 8 WATTS
2560 DATA SECONDARY POWER = ? W
      ATTS,FIND THE UNKNOWN,7.6
2580 DATA EFFICIENCY = ?%,PRIMA
      RY POWER = 6 WATTS
2600 DATA SECONDARY POWER = 4.8
      WATTS,FIND THE UNKNOWN,80
2620 DATA EFFICIENCY = ?%,PRIMA
      RY POWER = 10 WATTS

2640 DATA SECONDARY POWER = 9 W
      ATTS,FIND THE UNKNOWN,90
2660 DATA EFFICIENCY = 90%,PRIM
      ARY POWER = 7 WATTS
2680 DATA SECONDARY POWER = ? W
      ATTS,FIND THE UNKNOWN,6.3
2700 DATA EFFICIENCY = 95%,PRIM
      ARY POWER = ? WATTS
2720 DATA SECONDARY POWER = 10
      WATTS,FIND THE UNKNOWN,10.53

2740 DATA EFFICIENCY = 75%,PRIM
      ARY POWER = ? WATTS
2760 DATA SECONDARY POWER = 5 W
      ATTS,FIND THE UNKNOWN,6.6

Fig. E-16. Reactance program.

```
2    HOME : REM   ****** INTRODUCT
     ION ******
22   VTAB 3: PRINT  TAB( 4)"THIS
     PROGRAM IS A PRACTICE"
42   PRINT  TAB( 4)"EXERCISE FOR
     THE REACTANCE"
62   PRINT  TAB( 4)"FORMULAS LEAR
     NED IN CHAPTER 14."
82   PRINT
102  PRINT  TAB( 4)"IT WILL GIVE
     TWO KNOWNS, AND"
122  PRINT  TAB( 4)"ASK THE USER
     TO SOLVE FOR"
142  PRINT  TAB( 4)"THE UNKNOWN.
     "
162  PRINT
182  PRINT  TAB( 4)"THE ANSWERS
     ARE EXPECTED TO"
202  PRINT  TAB( 4)"BE WITH IN 5
     % OF THE COMPUTER'S"
222  PRINT  TAB( 4)"ANSWERS."
240  VTAB 20: INVERSE
242  HTAB 8: PRINT "SPACE BAR TO
     CONTINUE"
243  NORMAL
280  GET RT$: IF RT$ <  > CHR$
     (32) THEN  GOTO 280
300  HOME
320  REM   QUESTION LOOP ********
     ***
340  FOR K = 1 TO 20:AA = 0
341  HOME
360  READ L$,F$,X$,Q$,A
400  PRINT "    NOTE: UNITS ARE
     GIVEN JUST GIVE"
401  PRINT "           THE NUMERI
     C VALUE."
420  PRINT : PRINT "    GIVEN:":
     PRINT
460  HTAB 10: PRINT L$: PRINT
480  HTAB 10: PRINT F$: PRINT
500  HTAB 10: PRINT X$: PRINT
520  PRINT : PRINT
540  PRINT K;".";Q$;
541  AA = 0
560  INPUT AA$:AA =  VAL (AA$)
561  LU = A - (A * .05):HU = A +
     (A * .05)
580  IF A < O THEN LU =  = A + (
     A * .05):HU = A - (A * .05)
600  IF AA > LU AND AA < HU THEN
     GOSUB 700: REM  **** CORREC
     T *****
620  IF AA = LU OR AA = HU THEN
     GOSUB 700: REM  CORRECT
640  IF AA < LU OR AA > HU THEN
     GOSUB 840: REM  *** WRONG *
     **
660  IF K = 20 THEN  GOTO 1020
680  NEXT K
```

```
700  REM   **** CORRECT ****
719  INVERSE
720  PRINT : PRINT : PRINT : HTAB
     14: PRINT "CORRECT!":S = S +
     1
740  PRINT : HTAB 5: PRINT "SPAC
     E BAR = NEXT, E = EXIT"
741  NORMAL
760  GET RR$: IF RR$ <  > CHR$
     (32) AND RR$ <  > CHR$ (69)
     THEN  GOTO 760
780  IF RR$ =  CHR$ (32) AND K =
     20 THEN  GOTO 1020: REM  **
     SCORE **
800  IF RR$ =  CHR$ (32) THEN  RETURN
820  IF RR$ =  CHR$ (69) THEN  GOTO
     1020: REM  SCORE
840  REM   **** WRONG *****
859  INVERSE
860  PRINT : PRINT : PRINT : HTAB
     12: PRINT "WRONG ";A
880  PRINT : HTAB 4: PRINT "SPAC
     E BAR = NEXT, H=HELP HINTS"
900  HTAB 4: PRINT "E = EXIT"
901  NORMAL
920  GET WW$: IF WW$ <  > CHR$
     (32) AND WW$ <  > CHR$ (69)
     AND WW$ <  > CHR$ (72) THEN
     GOTO 920
940  IF WW$ =  CHR$ (32) AND K =
     20 THEN  GOTO 1020
960  IF WW$ =  CHR$ (32) THEN  RETURN
980  IF WW$ =  CHR$ (72) THEN  GOSUB
     1280: RETURN : REM  *** HELP
     HINTS
1000 IF WW$ =  CHR$ (69) THEN  GOTO
     1020
1020 REM   *** SCORE ****
1060 HOME : VTAB 8
1080 E = (S / K) * 100
1100 PRINT  TAB( 8)"YOUR SCORE
     IS ";E;"%": PRINT
1120 PRINT  TAB( 8)"FOR ";K;" Q
     UESTIONS ASKED": PRINT : PRINT
     : PRINT
1160 PRINT  TAB( 8)"SPACE BAR F
     OR MAIN MENU."
1180 GET MM$: IF MM$ <  > CHR$
     (32) THEN 1180
1200 PRINT  CHR$ (4);"-STARTUP"

1280 REM   *** HELP HINTS ***
1282 HOME : VTAB 4
1322 PRINT  TAB( 4)"MOST PEOPLE
     GET CONFUSED WHEN"
1342 PRINT  TAB( 4)"FIRST TRANS
     POSING THESE"
1362 PRINT  TAB( 4)"FORMULAS.":
```

```
          PRINT
1402   PRINT   TAB( 4)"THIS LIST S
       HOULD HELP TILL YOU"
1422   PRINT   TAB( 4)"MEMORIZE TH
       EM."
1440   INVERSE
1442   PRINT : PRINT : PRINT : HTAB
       8: PRINT "SPACE BAR FOR LIST
       "
1443   NORMAL
1462   GET ZC$: IF ZC$ <  > CHR$
       (32) THEN   GOTO 1462
1482   HOME
1502   PRINT   TAB( 4)"INDUCTOR:":
        PRINT
1522   PRINT   TAB( 4)"XL = 2 (PI)
       F L": PRINT
1542   PRINT   TAB( 4)"L = XL/(2 (
       PI) F)": PRINT
1562   PRINT   TAB( 4)"F = XL/(2 (
       PI) L)": PRINT
1582   PRINT   TAB( 4)"CAPACITOR:"
       : PRINT
1602   PRINT   TAB( 4)"XC = 1/(2 (
       PI) F C)": PRINT
1622   PRINT   TAB( 4)"C = 1/(2 (P
       I) F XC)": PRINT
1642   PRINT   TAB( 4)"F = 1/(2 (P
       I) XC C)": PRINT
1662   PRINT   TAB( 4)"NOTE: (2 (P
       I)) CAN BE REPLACED"
1682   PRINT   TAB( 4)"BY 6.28 IN
       THE FORMULAS.": PRINT
1700   INVERSE
1701   HTAB 8: PRINT "SPACE BAR T
       O CONTINUE"
1702   NORMAL
1722   GET RC$: IF RC$ <  > CHR$
       (32) THEN   GOTO 1722
1742   IF RC$ =  CHR$ (32) THEN   RETURN
1762   DATA INDUCTOR = 3 MH,FREQU
       ENCY = 600 HZ
1782   DATA REACTANCE = ? OHMS,FI
       ND THE UNKNOWN,11.3
1802   DATA INDUCTOR = 3 MH,FREQU
       ENCY = 10 KHZ
1822   DATA REACTANCE = ? OHMS,FI
       ND THE UNKNOWN,188
1842   DATA CAPACITOR = 2 UF,FREQ
       UENCY = 600 HZ
1862   DATA REACTANCE = ? OHMS,FI
       ND THE UNKNOWN,132
1882   DATA CAPACITOR = 2 UF,FREQ
       UENCY = 10 KHZ
1902   DATA REACTANCE = ? OHMS,FI
       ND THE UNKNOWN,7.9
1922   DATA CAPACITOR = 1.5 UF,FR
       EQUENCY = ? HZ
1942   DATA REACTANCE = 1769 OHMS
       ,FIND THE UNKNOWN,60
1962   DATA INDUCTOR = 300 MH,FRE
       QUENCY = ? HZ
1982   DATA REACTANCE = 37.6 OHMS
       ,FIND THE UNKNOWN,20
2002   DATA INDUCTOR = ? H,FREQUE
       NCY = 60 HZ
2022   DATA REACTANCE = 753 OHMS,
       FIND THE UNKNOWN,2
2042   DATA CAPACITOR = ? UF,FREQ
       UENCY = 60 HZ
2062   DATA REACTANCE = 26.5 OHMS
       ,FIND THE UNKNOWN,100
2082   DATA INDUCTOR = 50 MH,FREQ
       UENCY = 1 KHZ
2102   DATA REACTANCE = ? OHMS,FI
       ND THE UNKNOWN,314
2122   DATA CAPACITOR = 50 NF,FRE
       QUENCY = 50 KHZ
2142   DATA REACTANCE = ? OHMS,FI
       ND THE UNKNOWN,63
2162   DATA CAPACITOR = 50 NF,FRE
       QUENCY = 4 KHZ
2182   DATA REACTANCE = ? OHMS,FI
       ND THE UNKNOWN,796
2202   DATA INDUCTOR = 10 H,FREQU
       ENCY = ? HZ
2222   DATA REACTANCE = 628 OHMS,
       FIND THE UNKNOWN,10
2242   DATA INDUCTOR = ? MH,FREQU
       ENCY = 100 HZ
2262   DATA REACTANCE = 125.6 OHM
       S,FIND THE UNKNOWN,200
2282   DATA CAPACITOR = ? PF,FREQ
       UENCY = 1 MHZ
2302   DATA REACTANCE 13269 OHMS,
       FIND THE UNKNOWN,12
2322   DATA CAPACITOR = 10 UF,FRE
       QUENCY = ? HZ
2342   DATA REACTANCE = 530 OHMS,
       FIND THE UNKNOWN,30
2362   DATA INDUCTOR = 25 MH,FREQ
       UENCY = ? HZ
2382   DATA REACTANCE = 12.5 OHMS
       ,FIND THE UNKNOWN,80
2402   DATA INDUCTOR = 100 MH,FRE
       QUENCY = 100 HZ
2422   DATA REACTANCE = ? OHMS,FI
       ND THE UNKNOWN,62.8
2442   DATA CAPACITOR = 47 UF,FRE
       QUENCY = ? HZ
2462   DATA REACTANCE = 1.6 OHMS,
       FIND THE UNKNOWN,2117
2482   DATA CAPACITOR = ? UF,FREQ
       UENCY = 40 HZ
2502   DATA REACTANCE = 120 OHMS,
       FIND THE UNKNOWN,33
2522   DATA INDUCTOR = 1 MH,FREQU
       ENCY = ? HZ
2542   DATA REACTANCE = 37.7 OHMS
       ,FIND THE UNKNOWN,6000
```

Fig. E-17. Resonance program.

```
1    REM   RESONANCE
2    HOME : REM   **** INTRODUCTION
     ***
40   VTAB 3: PRINT  TAB( 4)"THIS
     PROGRAM IS A PRACTICE"
60   PRINT   TAB( 4)"EXERCISE FOR
     THE RESONANCE"
80   PRINT   TAB( 4)"FORMULAS LEAR
     NED IN CHAPTER 15."
100  PRINT
120  PRINT   TAB( 4)"IT WILL GIVE
     THE INFORMATION NEEDED,"
140  PRINT   TAB( 4)"AND ASK THE
     USER TO SOLVE FOR"
160  PRINT   TAB( 4)"A PARTICULAR
     UNKNOWN."
180  PRINT
200  PRINT   TAB( 4)"THE ANSWERS
     ARE EXPECTED TO"
220  PRINT   TAB( 4)"BE WITH IN 5
     % OF THE COMPUTER'S"
240  PRINT   TAB( 4)"ANSWERS."
260  INVERSE : VTAB 20: HTAB 8: PRINT
     "SPACE BAR TO CONTINUE": NORMAL

280  GET RT$: IF RT$ <  >  CHR$
     (32) THEN  GOTO 280
300  HOME
320  REM   QUESTION LOOP ********
     ***
340  FOR K = 1 TO 20:AA = 0
341  HOME
360  READ L$,F$,X$,Q$,A,CT$
400  PRINT "     NOTE: UNITS ARE
     GIVEN JUST GIVE"
401  PRINT "          THE NUMERI
     C VALUE."
420  PRINT : PRINT "     GIVEN:":
     PRINT
430  HTAB 10: PRINT CT$: PRINT
460  HTAB 10: PRINT L$: PRINT
480  HTAB 10: PRINT F$: PRINT
500  HTAB 10: PRINT X$: PRINT
520  PRINT : PRINT
540  PRINT K;".";Q$;
541  AA = 0
560  INPUT AA$:AA =  VAL (AA$)
561  LU = A - (A * .05):HU = A +
     (A * .05)
580  IF A < 0 THEN LU =  = A + (
     A * .05):HU = A - (A * .05)
600  IF AA > LU AND AA < HU THEN
     GOSUB 700: REM   **** CORREC
     T *****
620  IF AA = LU OR AA = HU THEN
     GOSUB 700: REM   CORRECT
640  IF AA < LU OR AA > HU THEN
     GOSUB 840: REM   *** WRONG *
     **
660  IF K = 20 THEN  GOTO 1020
680  NEXT K
700  REM   **** CORRECT ****
719  INVERSE
720  PRINT : PRINT : PRINT : HTAB
     14: PRINT "CORRECT!":S = S +
     1
740  PRINT : HTAB 5: PRINT "SPAC
     E BAR = NEXT, E = EXIT"
741  NORMAL
760  GET RR$: IF RR$ <  >  CHR$
     (32) AND RR$ <  >  CHR$ (69)
     THEN  GOTO 760
780  IF RR$ =  CHR$ (32) AND K =
     20 THEN  GOTO 1020: REM  **
     SCORE **
800  IF RR$ =  CHR$ (32) THEN  RETURN
820  IF RR$ =  CHR$ (69) THEN  GOTO
     1020: REM  SCORE
840  REM   **** WRONG *****
859  INVERSE
860  PRINT : PRINT : PRINT : HTAB
     12: PRINT "WRONG ";A
880  PRINT : HTAB 4: PRINT "SPAC
     E BAR = NEXT, H=HELP HINTS"
900  HTAB 4: PRINT "E = EXIT"
901  NORMAL
920  GET WW$: IF WW$ <  >  CHR$
     (32) AND WW$ <  >  CHR$ (69)
     AND WW$ <  >  CHR$ (72) THEN
     GOTO 920
940  IF WW$ =  CHR$ (32) AND K =
     20 THEN  GOTO 1020
960  IF WW$ =  CHR$ (32) THEN  RETURN
980  IF WW$ =  CHR$ (72) THEN  GOSUB
     1280: RETURN : REM *** HELP
     HINTS
1000 IF WW$ =  CHR$ (69) THEN  GOTO
     1020
1020 REM  *** SCORE ****
1060 HOME : VTAB 8
1080 E = (S / K) * 100
1100 PRINT  TAB( 8)"YOUR SCORE
     IS ";E;"%": PRINT
1120 PRINT  TAB( 8)"FOR ";K;" Q
     UESTIONS ASKED": PRINT : PRINT
     : PRINT
1160 PRINT  TAB( 8)"SPACE BAR F
     OR MAIN MENU."
1180 GET MM$: IF MM$ <  >  CHR$
     (32) THEN 1180
1200 PRINT  CHR$ (4);"-STARTUP"

1280 REM  *** HELP HINTS ***
1360 HOME
1380 VTAB 2: PRINT  TAB( 4)"SER
     IES NET REACTANCE:"
1400 PRINT : PRINT  TAB( 4)"(GR
     EATER X) - (LESSER X)= (NET
```

```
      X)"
1420  PRINT : PRINT  TAB( 4)"(NE
      T X) WILL BE THE TYPE OF X T
      HAT"
1460  PRINT  TAB( 4)"HAS THE GRE
      ATER VALUE."
1480  PRINT : PRINT  TAB( 4)"PAR
      ALLEL NET REACTANCE:"
1500  PRINT : PRINT  TAB( 4)"(GR
      EATER I) - (LESSER I) = (NET
      I)"
1520  PRINT : PRINT  TAB( 4)"(NE
      T X) = (V APPLIED) / (NET I)
      "
1540  PRINT : PRINT  TAB( 4)"(NE
      T X) WILL BE THE TYPE OF X T
      HAT"
1560  PRINT  TAB( 4)"HAD THE GRE
      ATER VALUE OF CURRENT."
1561  INVERSE
1562  VTAB 20: HTAB 8: PRINT "SP
      ACE BAR FOR MORE"
1563  NORMAL
1564  GET ZC$: IF ZC$ <  > CHR$
      (32) THEN  GOTO 1564
1600  HOME
1620  PRINT  TAB( 4)"SERIES CURR
      ENT:": PRINT
1640  PRINT  TAB( 4)"I = V APPLI
      ED / NET X": PRINT
1660  PRINT  TAB( 4)"PARALLEL NE
      T CURRENT:": PRINT
1680  PRINT  TAB( 4)"(NET I) = (
      GREATER IX) - (LESSER IX)": PRINT

1700  PRINT  TAB( 4)"SERIES VLOT
      AGE DROPS:": PRINT
1720  PRINT  TAB( 4)"VD = (NET I
      ) X (REACTANCE)": PRINT
1740  PRINT  TAB( 4)"PARALLEL BR
      ANCH CURRENT:": PRINT
1760  PRINT  TAB( 4)"BC = V APPL
      IED / REACTANCE": PRINT
1761  INVERSE
1762  VTAB 20: HTAB 8: PRINT "SP
      ACE BAR FOR MORE"
1763  NORMAL
1764  GET TC$: IF TC$ <  > CHR$
      (32) THEN  GOTO 1764
1820  HOME
1840  PRINT  TAB( 4)"RESONANT FR
      EQUENCY (FR)": PRINT : PRINT
      : PRINT
1860  PRINT  TAB( 22)"1"
1880  PRINT  TAB( 4)"FR = ------
      --------------------"
1900  PRINT  TAB( 11)"2 (PI) X (
      SQR (L X C))"
1920  PRINT : PRINT : PRINT : PRINT
      TAB( 4)"SQR = SQUARE ROOT"
1921  INVERSE
1922  VTAB 20: HTAB 8: PRINT "SP
      ACE BAR TO CONTINUE"
1923  NORMAL
1924  GET RC$: IF RC$ <  > CHR$
      (32) THEN  GOTO 1924
1925  IF RC$ = CHR$ (32) THEN  RETURN
2000  REM  *** SERIES ***
2020  DATA XL = 100 OHMS,XC = 25
      0 OHMS,V APPLIED = 10 VOLTS
2040  DATA FIND TOTAL CURRENT IN
      AMPS,.066,SERIES CIRCUIT
2060  DATA XL = 75 OHMS,XC = 50
      OHMS,V APPLIED = 25 VOLTS
2080  DATA FIND NET REACTANCE IN
      OHMS,25,SERIES CIRCUIT
2100  DATA XL = 35 OHMS,XC = 50
      OHMS,V APPLIED = 50 VOLTS
2120  DATA FIND NET REACTANCE IN
      OHMS,15,SERIES CIRCUIT
2140  DATA XL = 200 OHMS,XC = 17
      5 OHMS,V APPLIED = 25 VOLTS
2160  DATA FIND VL IN VOLTS,200,
      SERIES CIRCUIT
2180  DATA XL = 150 OHMS,XC = 14
      0 OHMS,V APPLIED = 100 VOLTS

2200  DATA FIND VC IN VOLTS,1400
      ,SERIES CIRCUIT
2220  REM  *** PARLLEL ****
2240  DATA XL = 40 OHMS,XC = 30
      OHMS,V APPLIED = 10 VOLTS
2260  DATA FIND IL IN AMPS,.25,P
      ARALLEL CIRCUIT
2280  DATA XL = 35 OHMS,XC = 50
      OHMS,V APPLIED = 10 VOLTS
2300  DATA FIND IC IN AMPS,.2,PA
      RALLEL CIRCUIT
2320  DATA XL = 25 OHMS,XC = 30
      OHMS,V APPLIED = 15 VOLTS
2340  DATA FIND NET CURRENT IN A
      MPS,.1,PARALLEL CIRCUIT
2360  DATA XL = 25 OHMS,XC = 30
      OHMS,V APPLIED = 15 VOLTS
2380  DATA FIND NET REACTANCE IN
      OHMS,150,PARALLEL CIRCUIT
2400  DATA XL = 50 OHMS,XC = 75
      OHMS,V APPLIED = 20 VOLTS
2420  DATA FIND NET REACTANCE IN
      OHMS,142,PARALLEL CIRCUIT
2440  REM  *** RESONANT FREQUENC
      Y ***
2460  DATA INDUCTOR = 25 MH,CAPA
      CITOR = 10 UF,REASONANT FREQ
      UENCY = ?
2480  DATA RESONANT FREQUENCY IN
      HZ = ,318,
2500  DATA INDUCTOR = 200 MH,CAP
      ACITOR = 1 UF,RESONANT FREQU
      ENCY = ?
```

Fig. E-17. Resonance program. (Continued from page 325)

```
2520   DATA RESONANT FREQUENCY IN
   HZ = ,356,
2540   DATA INDUCTOR = 10 MH,CAPA
   CITOR = 30 PF,RESONANT FREQU
   ENCY = ?
2560   DATA RESONANT FREQUENCY IN
   HZ = ,290723,
2580   DATA INDUCTOR = 10 UH,CAPA
   CITOR = .47 UF,RESONANT FREQ
   UENCY = ?
2600   DATA RESONANT FREQUENCY IN
   HZ = ,73449,
2620   DATA INDUCTOR = 10 MH,CAPA
   CITOR = 5 UF,RESONANT FREQUE
   NCY = ?
2640   DATA RESONANT FREQUENCY IN
   HZ = ,712,
2660   DATA INDUCTOR = 2 H,CAPACI
   TOR = 3 UF,RESONANT FREQUENC
   Y = ?
2680   DATA RESONANT FREQUENCY IN
   HZ = ,65,

2700   DATA INDUCTOR = 3 MH,CAPAC
   ITOR = 10 UF,RESONANT FREQUE
   NCY = ?
2720   DATA RESONANT FREQUENCY IN
   HZ = ,919,
2740   DATA INDUCTOR = 150 MH,CAP
   ACITOR = 5 UF,RESONANT FREQU
   ENCY = ?
2760   DATA RESONANT FREQUENCY IN
   HZ = ,184,
2780   DATA INDUCTOR = 33 MH,CAPA
   CITOR = 220 NF,RESONANT FREQ
   UENCY = ?
2800   DATA RESONANT FREQUENCY IN
   HZ = ,1868,
2820   DATA INDUCTOR = 10 H,CAPAC
   ITOR = 100 UF,RESONANT FREQU
   ENCY = ?
2840   DATA RESONANT FREQUENCY IN
   HZ = ,5,
```

Index

Learning Electronics:
Theory and Experiments,
with Computer-Aided
Instruction for the Apple

If you are intrigued with the possibilities of the programs included in *Learning Electronics: Theory and Experiments with Computer-Aided Instruction for the Apple* (TAB Book No. 2982), you should definitely consider having the ready-to-run disk containing the software applications. This software is guaranteed free of manufacturer's defects. (If you have any problems, return the disk within 30 days, and we'll send you a new one.) Not only will you save the time and effort of typing the programs, but disk also eliminates the possibility of errors that can prevent the programs from functioning. Interested?

Available on disk for Apple II/II+/IIe/IIc/IIGS at $24.95 for each disk plus $1.50 shipping and handling.